WORLD WAR TWO
BEHIND CLOSED DOORS

To Ian Kershaw

WORLD WAR TWO

BEHIND
CLOSED DOORS

STALIN, THE NAZIS AND THE WEST

LAURENCE REES

BBC
BOOKS

This book is published to accompany the television series entitled
World War Two: Behind Closed Doors, first broadcast on BBC2 in 2008.

10 9 8 7 6 5 4 3 2 1

Published in 2008 by BBC Books, an imprint of Ebury Publishing,
A Random House Group Company.

The Random House Group Limited Reg. No. 954009

Addresses for companies within the Random House Group can be found
at www.randomhouse.co.uk

A CIP catalogue record for this book is available from the British Library.

ISBN 978 0 563 49335 8 (hardback)
ISBN 978 1 846 07606 0 (paperback)

The Random House Group Limited supports The Forest Stewardship
Council (FSC), the leading international forest certification organisation.
All our titles that are printed on Greenpeace approved FSC certified paper
carry the FSC logo. Our paper procurement policy can be found at
www.rbooks.co.uk/environment

Commissioning editor: Martin Redfern
Project editor: Eleanor Maxfield
Copy-editor: Esther Jagger
Designer: Jonathan Baker
Picture researcher: Sarah Hopper
Production controller: Antony Heller

Printed and bound in Great Britain by Clays Ltd, St Ives PLC

CONTENTS

INTRODUCTION

When do you think the Second World War ended? In August 1945 after the surrender of the Japanese?

Well, it depends how you look at it. If you believe that the end of the war was supposed to have brought 'freedom' to the countries that had suffered under Nazi occupation, then for millions of people the war did not really end until the fall of Communism less than twenty years ago. In the summer of 1945 the people of Poland, of the Baltic states and a number of other countries in eastern Europe simply swapped the rule of one tyrant for that of another. It was in order to demonstrate this unpleasant reality that the presidents of both Estonia and Lithuania refused to visit Moscow in 2005 to participate in 'celebrations' marking the sixtieth anniversary of the 'end of the war' in Europe.

How did this injustice happen? That is one of the crucial questions this book attempts to answer. And it is a history that it has only been possible to tell since the fall of Communism. Not just because the hundred or so eye witnesses I met in the former Soviet Union and eastern Europe would never have been able to speak frankly under Communist rule, but also because key archival material that successive Soviet governments did all they could to hide has been made available only recently. The existence of these documents has allowed a true 'behind-the-scenes' history of the West's dealings with Stalin to be attempted. All of which means, I hope, that this book contains much that is new.

I have been lucky that the collapse of the Eastern Bloc has permitted this work. It was certainly something I could never have predicted would happen when I was taught the history of the Second World War at school back in the early 1970s. Then my history teacher got round the moral and political complexities of the Soviet Union's[1] participation in the war by the simple expedient of largely ignoring it. At the time, in the depths of the Cold War, that was how most people dealt with the awkward legacy of the West's relationship with Stalin. The focus was on the heroism of the Western Allies – on Dunkirk, the Battle of Britain and D-Day. None of which, of course, must be forgotten. But it is not the whole story.

Before the fall of Communism the role of the Soviet Union in the Second World War was, to a large extent, denied a proper place in our culture because it was easier than facing up to a variety of unpalatable truths. Did we, for example, really contribute to the terrible fate that in 1945 befell Poland, the very country we went to war to protect? Especially when we were taught that this was a war about confronting tyranny? And if, as we should, we do start asking ourselves these difficult questions, then we also have to pose some of the most uncomfortable of all. Was anyone in the West to blame in any way for what happened at the end of the war? What about the great heroes of British and American history, Winston Churchill and Franklin Roosevelt?

Paradoxically, the best way to attempt an answer to all this is by focusing on someone else entirely – Joseph Stalin. Whilst this is a book that is fundamentally about relationships, it is Stalin who dominates the work. And a real insight into the Soviet leader's attitude to the war is gained by examining his behaviour immediately before his alliance with the West. This period, of the Nazi–Soviet pact between 1939 and 1941, has been largely ignored in the popular consciousness. It was certainly ignored in the post-war Soviet Union. I remember asking one Russian after the fall of the Berlin Wall: 'How was the Nazi–Soviet pact taught when you were in school during the Soviet era? Wasn't it a tricky piece of history to explain away?' He smiled in response. 'Oh, no,' he said, 'not tricky at all. You see, I didn't learn there had ever been a Nazi–Soviet pact until after 1990 and the collapse of the Soviet Union.'

Stalin's relationship with the Nazis is a vital insight into the kind of person he was; because, at least in the early days of the relationship, he got on perfectly well with them. The Soviet Communists and the German Nazis had a lot in common – not ideologically, of course, but in practical terms. Each of them respected the importance of raw power. And each of them despised the values that a man like Franklin Roosevelt held most dear, such as freedom of speech and the rule of law. As a consequence, we see Stalin at his most relaxed in one of the first encounters in the book, carving up Europe with Joachim von Ribbentrop, the Nazi Foreign Minister. The Soviet leader was never to attain such a moment of mutual interest and understanding at any point in his relationship with Churchill and Roosevelt.

It is also important to understand the way in which the Soviets ran their occupation of eastern Poland between 1939 and 1941. That is because many of the injustices that were to occur in parts of occupied eastern Europe at the end of the war were broadly similar to those the Soviets had previously committed in eastern Poland – the torture, the arbitrary arrests, the deportations, the sham elections and the murders. What the earlier Soviet occupation of eastern Poland demonstrates is that the fundamental nature of Stalinism was obvious from the start.

So it isn't that Churchill and Roosevelt were unaware in the beginning of the kind of regime they were dealing with. Neither of them was initially enthusiastic about the forced alliance with Stalin following the German invasion of the Soviet Union in June 1941. Churchill considered it akin to a pact with 'the Devil', and Roosevelt, even though the United States was still officially neutral in the summer of 1941, was careful in his first statement after the Nazi invasion to condemn the Soviets for their previous abuses.

How the British and Americans moved from that moment of justified scepticism about Stalin to the point immediately after the Yalta Conference in February 1945 when they stated, with apparent sincerity, that Stalin 'meant well to the world' and was 'reasonable and sensible', is the meat of this book. And the answer to why Churchill and Roosevelt publicly altered their position about Stalin and the Soviet Union doesn't lie just in understanding the massive geo-political issues that were at stake in the war – and crucially the effect on the West of the successful Soviet fight-back against the Nazis – but also takes us into the realm of personal emotions. Both Churchill and Roosevelt had gigantic egos and both of them liked to dominate the room. And both of them liked the sound of their own voices. Stalin wasn't like that at all. He was a watcher – an aggressive listener.

It was no accident that it took two highly intelligent functionaries on the British side – Sir Alexander Cadogan, Permanent Under Secretary at the Foreign Office, and Lord Alanbrooke, Chief of the Imperial General Staff – to spot Stalin's gifts most accurately. They saw him not as a politician playing to the crowd and awash with his own rhetoric, but more like a bureaucrat – a practical man who got things done. As Cadogan confided in his diary at Yalta: 'I must say I think Uncle Joe [Stalin] much the most impressive of the three men. He is very quiet and restrained.... The President flapped about and the PM boomed, but Joe just sat taking it all in and being rather amused. When he did chip in, he never used a superfluous word and spoke very much to the point.'[2]

Field Marshal Lord Alanbrooke 'formed a very high idea of his [Stalin's] ability, force of character and shrewdness'.[3] In particular, Alanbrooke was impressed that Stalin 'displayed an astounding knowledge of technical railway details'.[4] No one would ever accuse Churchill or Roosevelt – those biggest of 'big picture' men – of having 'an astounding knowledge of technical railway details'. And it was Alanbrooke who spotted early on what was to be the crux of the final problem between Stalin and Churchill: 'Stalin is a realist if ever there was one,' he wrote in his diary, 'facts only count with him...[Churchill] appealed to sentiments in Stalin which I do not think exist there.'[5]

As one historian has put it, the Western leaders at the end of the war 'were not dealing with a normal, everyday, run-of-the-mill, statesmanlike head of government. They confronted instead a psychologically disturbed but fully functional and highly intelligent dictator who had projected his own personality not only onto those around him but onto an entire nation and had thereby with catastrophic results, remade it in his image.'[6]

One of the problems was that Stalin in person was very different from the image of Stalin the tyrant. Anthony Eden, one of the first Western politicians to spend time with Stalin in Moscow during the war, remarked on his return that he had tried hard to imagine the Soviet leader 'dripping with the blood of his opponents and rivals, but somehow the picture wouldn't fit'.[7]

But Roosevelt and Churchill were sophisticated politicians and it is wrong to suppose that they were simply duped by Stalin. No, something altogether more interesting – and more complicated – takes place in this history. Roosevelt and Churchill wanted to win the war at the least possible cost to their own respective countries – in both human and financial terms. Keeping Stalin 'on side', particularly during the years before D-Day when the Soviets believed they were fighting the war almost on their own, was a difficult business and required, as Roosevelt would have put it, 'careful handling'. As a result, behind closed doors the Western leaders felt it necessary to make hard political compromises. One of them was to promote propaganda that painted a rosy picture of the Soviet leader; another was deliberately to suppress material that told the truth about both Stalin and the nature of the Soviet regime. In the process the Western leaders might easily, for the sake of convenience, have felt they had to 'distort the normal and healthy operation' of their 'intellectual and moral judgements' as one senior British diplomat was memorably to put it during the war.[8]

However, this isn't just a 'top-down' history, examining the mentality and beliefs of the elite. I felt from the first that it was also important to show in human terms the impact of the decisions taken by Stalin and the Western Allies behind closed doors. And so in the course of writing this book I travelled across the former Soviet Union and Soviet-dominated eastern Europe and asked people who had lived through this testing time to tell their stories.

Uncovering this history was a strange and sometimes emotional experience. And – at least to me – it all seemed surprisingly fresh and relevant. I felt this most strongly standing in the leafy square by the opera house in Lviv. This elegant city had started the twentieth century in the Austro-Hungarian Empire, become part of Poland after the First World War, then part of the Soviet Union between 1939 and 1941, then part of the Nazi Empire until 1944, then part of the Soviet Union again, until finally in 1991 it became part of an independent Ukraine. At various times in the last hundred years the city has been called Lemberg, Lvov, Lwów and Lviv. There was not one group of citizens I met there who had not at one time or another suffered because of who they were. Catholic or Jew, Ukrainian, Russian or Pole, they had all faced persecution in the end. It was the Nazis, of course, who operated the most infamous and murderous policy of persecution against the Jews of the city, but we are apt to forget that such was the change and turmoil in this part of central Europe that ultimately few non-Jews escaped suffering of one kind or another either.

I was fortunate to have a chance to meet these witnesses to history – all the more so since in the near future there will be no one left alive who personally experienced the war. And after having spent so much time with these veterans from the former Soviet Union and Eastern Bloc I am left with an overwhelming sense of the importance of recovering their history as part of our own. Our nations were all in the war together. And we owe it to them, and to ourselves, to face up to the consequences of that truth.

Laurence Rees
London, May 2008

1
AN ALLIANCE IN ALL BUT NAME

A SURPRISING FRIENDSHIP

Just before four o'clock on the afternoon of Wednesday, 23 August 1939, Stalin's personal car drove across Red Square. Inside was an unlikely guest of the Soviet leader. In one of the most remarkable turnarounds in the history of diplomacy, Joachim von Ribbentrop, Foreign Minister of Nazi Germany, the sworn enemy of the Soviet Union, was about to be welcomed into the Kremlin. As the car pulled past the domes of St Basil's cathedral and neared the Kremlin's Spasskaya gate, Ribbentrop was apprehensive. He had arrived in the Soviet Union only a few hours before and his unease had immediately been noted by the German General Ernst Köstring. 'I tried to calm him,' recorded the general. '[But] Ribbentrop remained nervous and agitated.'[1]

The car was waved past the NKVD guards – the secret police – at the Kremlin gate and pulled up in front of the Senate building. There Ribbentrop, the German ambassador, Count Schulenburg, and Councillor Hilger from the German embassy (who was to act as interpreter) were escorted down a corridor to a shabby ante-room outside the office of Vyacheslav Molotov, the Soviet Foreign Minister. After a few minutes they were ushered into a rectangular room that contained a conference table along one wall and a desk at the end. Like all the offices of the Communist elite in the Kremlin, this one resembled, as one British visitor was later to remark, 'a second class railway waiting room'.[2]

Standing waiting to greet them was Molotov. But next to him was someone Ribbentrop was surprised to see – a shortish, sixty-year-old man[3] with pockmarked skin and discoloured teeth who coolly appraised Ribbentrop with eyes that seemed to have a tinge of yellow about them. It was the supreme leader of the Soviet Union – Joseph Stalin. He rarely met foreigners, and so his presence in the room was a sign of great significance. 'It was a move,' recorded Hilger, 'that was calculated to put the [Nazi] foreign minister off balance.'[4]

The contrast between the two most important people in that room could scarcely have been greater. Ribbentrop stood several inches taller than Stalin and was dressed – as he always was – immaculately. His perfectly cut, expensive suit contrasted sharply with Stalin's baggy tunic and trousers.

Ribbentrop was immensely pompous – ever conscious of the need to preserve his own dignity. Unlike the core of die-hard believers who formed National Socialism, Ribbentrop had joined the Nazi Party late, in 1932, only when it was clear that Hitler was a figure of real importance. In the 1920s, during the Weimar Republic, he had been a wealthy champagne importer. Many of the other leading Nazis had little respect for him. Joseph Goebbels, for example, the Nazi Propaganda Minister, alleged that 'he bought his name, he married his money and he swindled his way into office'.[5] Hermann Göring, the commander of the Luftwaffe, told Hitler that Ribbentrop had been 'an ass' in his dealings with the British when he had been German ambassador in London. Hitler had replied, 'But he knows quite a lot of important people in England.' Göring responded: '*Mein Führer*, that may be right, but the bad thing is, they know him.'[6] Even some of the Nazis' own allies didn't think much of Ribbentrop. Count Ciano, the Italian Foreign Minister, remarked with contempt that: 'The Duce [Benito Mussolini] says that you only have to look at his head to see that he has a small brain.'[7]

Ribbentrop may have elicited little respect from his colleagues, but Stalin was accustomed to creating another emotion entirely in those who encountered him – fear. 'All of us around Stalin were temporary people,' said Nikita Khrushchev, later himself leader of the Soviet Union. 'As long as he trusted us to a certain degree, we were allowed to go on living and working. But the moment

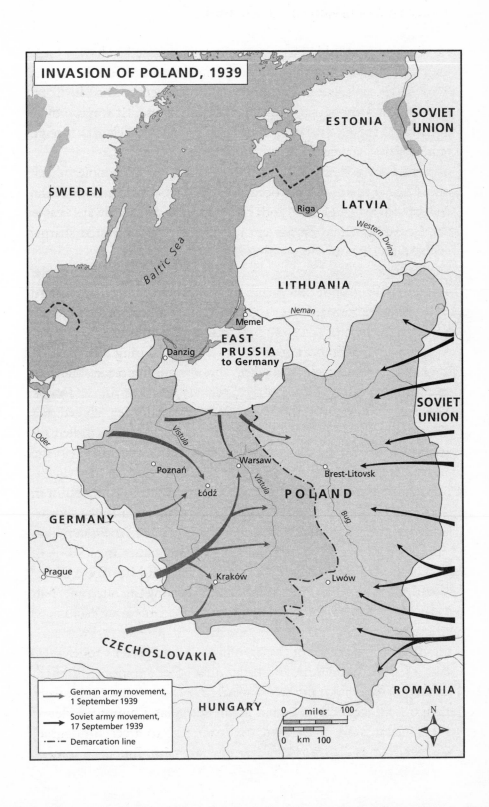

INVASION OF POLAND, 1939

SWEDEN

ESTONIA

SOVIET UNION

LATVIA

Riga

Western Dvina

Baltic Sea

LITHUANIA

Neman

Memel

EAST PRUSSIA
to Germany

Danzig

Oder

Vistula

Poznań

Warsaw

SOVIET UNION

Brest-Litovsk

Łódź

Vistula

POLAND

GERMANY

Bug

Prague

Kraków

Lwów

CZECHOSLOVAKIA

ROMANIA

HUNGARY

→ German army movement,
1 September 1939

→ Soviet army movement,
17 September 1939

-·-·- Demarcation line

0   miles   100

0   km   100

N

he stopped trusting you, the cup of his distrust overflowed.'[8] Stepan Mikoyan,[9] son of the Politburo member Anastas Mikoyan, grew up in the Kremlin compound in the 1930s and confirms Khrushchev's judgement. '[Stalin] watched people's eyes when he was speaking,' said Stepan Mikoyan, 'and if you didn't look him straight in the eye, he might well suspect that you were deceiving him. And then he'd be capable of taking the most unpleasant steps.... He was very suspicious. That was his main character trait.... He was a very unprincipled man.... He could betray and deceive if he thought it was necessary. And that's why he expected the same behaviour from others...anyone could turn out to be a traitor.' Stalin was, of course, first and foremost a revolutionary – he had been a Marxist terrorist before the Bolsheviks came to power, involved in bank robberies, kidnappings and other nefarious activities, and had served several periods in exile in Siberia as a result.

This contrast between the self-important Ribbentrop and the shrewd and cynical Stalin manifested itself immediately in Molotov's office that August afternoon when Ribbentrop began the meeting by portentously announcing that: 'The Führer has authorized me to propose a non-aggression agreement between our two countries that will last for a hundred years.'

'If we agree to a hundred years,' replied Stalin, 'people will laugh at us for not being serious. I propose the agreement should last ten years.'[10] So, with this none too subtle put-down, the negotiations between the Nazis and the Communists began.

These were discussions that would shock the world: a coming together of two ideological opposites; a meeting, as one Nazi put it, between 'fire and water';[11] a marriage at first sight that made little sense. Indeed, how was it possible that Ribbentrop was ever admitted into the heart of the Kremlin in the first place? The Nazis, after all, had never hidden their hatred for the Soviet Union. During a speech at the Nuremberg rally in 1937, Hitler had referred to the country's leaders as 'an uncivilized Jewish-Bolshevik international guild of criminals' and stated that the Soviet Union was 'the greatest danger for the culture and civilization of mankind which has ever threatened it since the collapse of the states of the ancient world'.[12]

In *Mein Kampf* [My Struggle] Hitler had explicitly written that he believed Germany should covet the agriculturally rich land of Russia and the rest of the Soviet Union: 'We are putting an end to the perpetual German march towards the south and west of Europe and turning our eye towards the east.... However, when we speak of new land in Europe today, we must principally bear in mind Russia and the border states subject to her [the Soviet Union]. Destiny itself seems to wish to point the way for us here.'[13]

But for the Nazis, by the summer of 1939 pragmatism had taken precedence over principle. Hitler wanted the German army to invade Poland within a matter of days. As he saw it, there were German territories to retrieve – the city of Danzig, West Prussia, and the former German lands around Posen – as well as the rest of Poland's valuable agricultural land to conquer. But he knew that any move into Poland risked war with Britain and France. In March 1939 the British had promised to try to protect Poland from foreign aggression after Neville Chamberlain, the British Prime Minister, had finally realized when Hitler invaded the Czech lands that the promises the German Führer had made in the Munich Agreement the year before were worthless. Moreover, from the Nazi point of view, a vast question – the answer apparently unknowable – hung over their plan to invade Poland; what would be the reaction of the Soviet Union, Poland's neighbour in the East? If the Soviet Union formed an alliance with the French and British, the Germans would be surrounded by enemies.

So in the summer of 1939, off the back of trade talks that were taking place in Berlin, the Germans began to sound out the Soviets about a possible treaty of convenience. To begin with, not surprisingly, the Soviets were sceptical. During one discussion earlier that summer the Soviet trade negotiator, Astakhov, remarked to Schnurre, his opposite number on the German side, that his colleagues in Moscow were not 'certain that the hinted changes in German policy are of a serious and non-conjunctural nature and are calculated for a long period'. Schnurre replied: 'Tell me what proof you want. We are ready to demonstrate the possibility of reaching agreement on any question – to give any guarantees.'[14] By 2 August the urgency of the Germans was palpable. Ribbentrop himself said to Astakhov that 'there was no problem from the Baltic to the Black Sea' that could not be resolved between them.[15] The economic treaty between Germany and the Soviet Union was signed on 19 August in Berlin. Ribbentrop then pressed the Soviets to allow him to come to Moscow to sign a non-aggression treaty. When the Soviets seemed to dither for a moment, Hitler himself stepped in and wrote a personal appeal to Stalin to allow Ribbentrop to come. The Soviets relented and Ribbentrop, with alacrity, arrived in Moscow on the 23rd.

The motivation of the Germans is thus not hard to read. Hitler's long-term policy – almost a messianic vision – remained clear. The Soviet Union was his ideological enemy – an enemy, in addition, that possessed rich farmland its people were not 'worthy' of owning. One day there would be a new German Empire on this land. But now was not the moment to pursue visions. Now was the moment to deal with the urgent and practical problem of neutralizing a potential aggressor. The Nazi regime was nothing if not dynamic. And the speed at which the Nazis moved to instigate and then close this deal astonished and impressed the Soviets. 'The fact that Mr Ribbentrop acted at a tempo of 650 kilometres an hour called forth the Soviet government's sincere admiration,' said Molotov in a speech in September 1939. 'His energy and his strength of will were a pledge to the firmness of the friendly relations that had been created with Germany.'[16]

Whilst it is relatively easy to see what the Germans were getting out of the deal, it is initially less simple to explain the attitude of the Soviets; because, unlike the Germans, the Soviets had a choice of partners. They could have rejected the Germans and decided to form an alliance with the British and the French. At a cursory glance, that would seem to have been the logical course of action; not least because in July 1932 the Soviets had signed a non-aggression treaty with Poland. In addition, neither the British nor the French were as vehemently opposed to the Soviet Union as the

Nazis, and the British had already made peaceful overtures towards Moscow. But Stalin knew that Britain in particular had previously preferred a policy of appeasement to the Germans, rather than alliance with the Soviets – a policy symbolized by the fact that the Soviet Union had not even been consulted about the Munich Agreement of September 1938 when Chamberlain signed away the ethnically German Sudetenland region of Czechoslovakia to the Nazis.

When Chamberlain returned from Munich he had quoted Shakespeare's *Henry IV Part 1*: '...out of this nettle danger, we pluck this flower, safety'. But in a scathing article in *Izvestiya*, the Soviets responded with a quote of their own from the same play: 'The purpose you undertake is dangerous; the friends who you have named uncertain; the time itself unsorted; and your whole plot too light for the counterpoise of so great an opposition.'[17]

And the fact that it had taken the Nazi invasion of the remainder of the Czech lands on 15 March 1939 to make the British suddenly realize the possible benefits of an arrangement with the Soviet Union did not impress Stalin, who five days earlier had made a bitter speech to the 18th Party Congress in Moscow. He talked of a 'war' that was being waged by 'aggressor states who in every way infringe upon the interests of the non-aggressive states, primarily Britain, France and the USA, while the latter draw back and retreat, making concession after concession to the aggressors. Thus we are witnessing an open redivision of the world and spheres of influence at the expense of the non-aggressive states, without the least attempt at resistance, and even with a certain connivance, on their part. Incredible, but true.'[18] It was partly this contempt for the passivity of the 'non-aggressive' states that led Stalin, in this same speech, famously to warn that the Soviet Union was not prepared to 'be drawn into conflict by warmongers who are accustomed to have others pull their chestnuts out of the fire for them'.

Nonetheless, Stalin and the Soviet leadership were still prepared to consider a possible treaty of mutual assistance with Britain and France. But there were problems from the very start.

In sharp contrast with the '650 kilometres an hour' attitude of the Nazis, the Western Allies were perceived as dawdling through the discussions. On 27 May the British and the French proposed a military and political alliance, but Molotov dismissed the plan. It was vague and lacked the necessary detail, especially when it came to explaining just how the Soviet Union would be expected to respond to a German attack on Poland.

As far as the Soviets were concerned, the British lack of commitment to a serious alliance was crystallized in their mission to Moscow that summer, led by the splendidly named Admiral the Hon. Sir Reginald Aylmer Ranfurly Plunkett-Ernle-Erle-Drax. The Soviet ambassador to London, Maisky, had previously asked whether the British Foreign Secretary, Lord Halifax, would come to Moscow that summer to discuss matters directly with Molotov. Instead the British despatched first the more minor head of the central department of the Foreign Office, and then this obscure quadruple-barrelled admiral. To make matters worse Drax and his team displayed no sense of urgency, leaving England on 5 August on a merchant ship that took four days to reach Leningrad.

Once the British delegation arrived in Moscow, the Soviets soon found evidence to confirm Maisky's intelligence report from London that 'the delegates will not be able to make any decisions on the spot.... This does not promise any particular speed in the conduct of the negotiations.'[19] In fact, before he left for Moscow Drax had been specifically told by the Prime Minister and Foreign Secretary that in case of any difficulties with the Soviets he should try and string the negotiations out until October, when winter conditions in Poland would make a Nazi invasion difficult.[20] The British hoped that the mere threat of an alliance with the Soviet Union might act as a deterrent to the Germans.

It is not hard to see what caused the British to take this lack-adaisical approach in their discussions with the Soviets. In the first place, British foreign policy had been predicated for years on the basis that a friendly relationship with Germany was of more value than an accommodation with the Soviet Union. Not only did many British loathe Stalin's Communist regime for ideological

reasons, but there was also little respect for the power and usefulness of the Soviet armed forces. Moreover, there was a further,
intensely practical reason why the British found it hard to reach a
comprehensive agreement with the Soviet Union that summer: the
question of Poland. Difficulties of policy over this one country,
which will haunt this entire history, were evident even before the
war began. The British knew that in order for any military treaty
to have meaning, the Soviets would have to be given permission to
cross the Polish border to fight the Germans if, as looked likely,
the Nazis decided to invade. But the Poles were against any such
idea. In the face of this impasse the British delegation adopted the
understandable – but ultimately self-defeating – tactic of simply
ignoring the subject whenever the question of Poland and its territorial integrity came up in discussion. When the Soviet Marshal
Voroshilov asked directly on 14 August if the Red Army would be
permitted to enter Poland in order to engage the Nazis, the Allied
delegation made no reply.

However, we must not run away with the idea that Stalin and
the Soviet leadership were somehow driven into the hands of the
Nazis by British and French misjudgement. Ultimately the
Western Allies had very little to offer the Soviets at the bargaining
table. Why, Stalin must have been thinking, should the Red Army
be 'drawn into conflict' in order to help other, unsympathetic
regimes out of their self-created difficulties? Stalin was just as ideologically opposed to Britain and France as he was to Nazi
Germany. Each of these countries, according to Marxist theory,
was dominated by big business and oppressed the working people.
Only the Soviet Union, which proposed free education, free
healthcare, 'votes for all' and common ownership, was a 'proper'
state in Stalin's world view. And Lenin's own teachings called for
the Soviet state to stand back in such circumstances and let the
capitalists fight between themselves. So, dealing between these
equally unpalatable other countries, it remained far more sensible
from Stalin's perspective to consider an arrangement, albeit a potentially temporary one, with Nazi Germany. For as well as offering
the Soviet Union a seemingly secure way out of any forthcoming

war, the Nazis could offer something the Western Allies never could – the prospect of additional territory and material gain for the Soviet Union. So the meeting on the afternoon of 23 August 1939 between Ribbentrop and Schulenburg for the Germans, and Stalin and Molotov for the Soviets, was, whilst not a meeting of minds, certainly a meeting of common interests.

THE NEGOTIATIONS BEGIN

A sign of the intensely practical nature of the talks was the swiftness with which the discussion turned to what was euphemistically described as 'spheres of influence'. This deliberately innocuous phrase could mean as little or as much as each of the participants wished. Eventually, of course, after the Nazi invasion of Poland it was used to determine who should exercise control over various eastern European countries.

Ribbentrop announced: 'The Führer accepts that the eastern part of Poland and Bessarabia as well as Finland, Estonia and Latvia, up to the river Duena, will all fall within the Soviet sphere of influence.'[21] Stalin objected at once to the German proposals, insisting that the *entire* territory of Latvia fall within the 'Soviet sphere of influence'. Ribbentrop felt unable to agree to Stalin's request without contacting Hitler. So the meeting was adjourned until he had received instructions directly from the Führer.

Hitler was waiting for news of the negotiations at the Berghof, his retreat in the mountains of southern Bavaria. That morning there had already been a commanders' conference at which Hitler had notified senior army figures that Ribbentrop was on his way from Königsberg to Moscow in order to sign a non-aggression pact. 'The generals were upset, they were looking at each other' said Herbert Döring, the SS officer who administered the Berghof, who witnessed events that day. 'It took their breath away that such a thing could be possible. Stalin the Communist, Hitler the National Socialist, that these [two] would suddenly unite. What was behind it, nobody knew.'[22]

As the talks continued in Moscow, the atmosphere at the Berghof grew strained. 'It was a sultry, hot summer evening,' recalled Döring. 'Groups of ADCs, civilian staff, ministers and secretaries were standing around the switchboard and on the terrace, because the first call would come to the switchboard. And everybody was tense, and they waited and waited.' Suddenly the call from Moscow came through with news of Stalin's demand. 'Hitler was speechless during the phone call, everybody noticed,' said Döring. 'Stalin had put a pistol to his head.' And with this 'pistol to his head', Hitler agreed to grant Stalin the whole of Latvia as part of his 'sphere of influence'.

Once the main issues around the 'spheres of influence' were decided, and then enshrined in a secret protocol to the pact, the conversation in Moscow became more discursive. Stalin revealed his frank views on the nation that would, by the summer of 1941, be his ally: 'I dislike and distrust the British; they are skilful and stubborn opponents. But the British army is weak. If England is still ruling the world it is due to the stupidity of other countries which let themselves be cheated. It is ridiculous that only a few hundred British are still able to rule the vast Indian population.'[23] Stalin went on to assert that the British had tried to prevent Soviet– German understanding for many years, and that it was a 'good idea' to put an end to these 'shenanigans'.

But at the talks in Moscow there was no open discussion of the Nazis' immediate plan to invade Poland – nor, of course, of what the Soviet response to it was expected to be. The nearest Ribbentrop came to outlining Nazi intentions was when he said: 'The government of the German Reich no longer finds acceptable the persecution of the German population in Poland and the Führer is determined to resolve the German–Polish disputes without delay.' Stalin's response to this statement was the noncommittal 'I understand'.

A draft communiqué announcing the pact was shown to both Stalin and Ribbentrop. The Soviet leader seems to have found the flowery language of the first draft rather comic. 'Don't you think we have to pay a little more attention to public opinion in our countries?' he said. 'For many years now we have been pouring buckets of shit over each other's heads and our propaganda boys could never do enough in that direction; and all of a sudden are we to make believe that all is forgiven and forgotten? Things don't work so fast.'[24] And with that, Stalin began to tone down the words of the statement.

At midnight, a woman wearing a red headscarf brought in first tea and then sweets, caviar, sandwiches and copious amounts of vodka, Russian wines and finally Crimean champagne. 'The atmosphere,' recalled Andor Hencke, a German diplomat who acted as an additional translator, 'which had already been pleasant, became warmly convivial. Stalin and Molotov were the most welcoming hosts imaginable. The ruler of Russia filled his guests' glasses himself, offered them cigarettes and even to light them. The cordial and yet at the same time dignified manner in which Stalin, without losing face, attended to each one of us, left a strong impression on us all.... I translated what was probably the first toast that Stalin ever made to Adolf Hitler. He said: "Because I know how much the German people love their Führer, I want to drink to his health!"'[25]

The Non-Aggression Pact between the Soviet Union and Germany was finally signed in the early hours of 24 August 1939. German and Soviet photographers were allowed into the room to immortalize the unlikely friendship that had blossomed between the two countries. Stalin remarked that he had only one condition for any photographs: 'The empty bottles should be removed beforehand,' he said, 'because otherwise people might think that we got drunk first and then signed the treaty.'[26] Despite Stalin's – albeit jocular – concerns about hiding the evidence of alcohol in the room, one of the German photographers, Helmut Laux, took a picture of Stalin and Ribbentrop each with a champagne glass in his hand. Stalin remarked that publishing a photo of the two of them drinking together might give the 'wrong impression'. Laux started to remove the film from his camera in order to give it to Stalin – but the Soviet leader gestured to him not to bother, saying he trusted the word of a German that the photo in question would not be used.[27]

Heinrich Hoffmann, Hitler's personal photographer, was also present, and with his innate sense of German superiority recalled the 'antediluvian' camera equipment of the 'Russians'. He also approached Stalin directly: 'Your Excellency,' he said, 'I have the very great honour of conveying to you the hearty greetings and good wishes of my Führer and good friend, Adolf Hitler! Let me say how much he looks forward to one day meeting the great leader of the Russian people in person.' According to Hoffmann these words 'made a great impression on Stalin', who replied by saying that there 'should be a lasting friendship with Germany and her great Führer'.[28]

The party lasted into the small hours, and when the Germans finally took their leave Stalin was, according to Hoffmann, 'well and truly lit up'![29] The Soviet leader clearly understood the incongruity – almost the comic nature – of this pact with his former enemy. 'Let's drink to the new anti-Cominternist,' he said at one point, 'Stalin!'[30] But his last words to Ribbentrop were spoken with apparent sincerity: 'I assure you that the Soviet Union takes this pact very seriously. I guarantee on my word of honour that the Soviet Union will not betray its new partner.'[31]

Back at the Berghof, the atmosphere grew ever more anxious in the hours before news of the signing of the pact came through. Herbert Döring watched that evening as Hitler and his guests stared at a dramatic sky over the high mountain peaks. 'The entire sky was in turmoil,' he remembered. 'It was blood-red, green sulphur grey, black as the night, a jagged yellow. Everyone was looking horrified – it was intimidating…. Everyone was watching. Without good nerves one could easily have become frightened.' Döring observed one of Hitler's guests, a Hungarian woman, remark: 'My Führer, this augurs nothing good. It means blood, blood, blood and again blood.' 'Hitler was totally shocked,' said Döring. 'He was almost shaking. He said, "If it has to be, then let it be now." He was agitated, completely crazed. His hair was wild. His gaze was locked on the distance.' Then, when the good news that the pact had been signed finally arrived, Hitler 'said goodbye, went upstairs and the evening was over'.

The reaction of the British public to the rapprochement between Germany and the Soviet Union might have lacked the drama on the terrace at the Berghof, but it was certainly one of immense surprise. 'This is a new and incomprehensible chapter in German diplomacy,' declared one British newsreel. 'What has happened to the principles of *Mein Kampf*? Equally, what can Russia have in common with Germany?'[32]

All over the world individual Communist parties struggled to make sense of the news. In Britain, Brian Pearce,[33] then a devoted follower of Stalin, simply fell back on straightforward faith: 'We did have this idea that Stalin was a very clever man, a very shrewd fellow, and when the pact came I think the attitude of most Communists – those that were not absolutely shocked by it, even in some cases to the point of leaving the party – was, well, it's hard to understand but after all it is a complicated situation...maybe Comrade Stalin, with all that he must know through his intelligence sources, thinks that this is the best way to keep Russia out of a situation in which he [Stalin] would be just let down by the Western allies.'

In Germany, SS officer Hans Bernhard[34] heard the news of the signing of the pact as he waited with his unit to invade Poland. For him the signing of the pact 'was a surprise without doubt. We couldn't make sense of it...in German propaganda for years it had been made clear that the Bolsheviks were our main enemy.' As a result, he and his comrades saw this new arrangement as 'politically unnatural'.

But Lord Halifax, the British Foreign Secretary, was not so taken aback. Four months before, on 3 May, he had warned the British Cabinet of the possibility of a deal between Stalin and Hitler.[35] Both the British and French governments now realized that the agreement between the Soviet Union and Nazi Germany freed Hitler's hands for an invasion of Poland – and so it proved. On 1 September German troops crossed into Poland and two days later, Britain, in accordance with its treaty obligations with Poland, declared war on Germany. The Second World War had begun.

But as the Germans invaded Poland from the west, the Soviet Union made no move to invade from the east. Consequently,

Ribbentrop was concerned about Stalin's reaction to any German incursion into eastern Poland, the region that adjoined the Soviet Union and that it had just been agreed was within the Soviet sphere of influence. He cabled Schulenburg, the German ambassador in Moscow, on 3 September: 'We should naturally, however, for military reasons, have to continue to take action against such Polish military forces as are at that time located in the Polish territory belonging to the Russian sphere of influence. Please discuss this at once with Molotov and see if the Soviet Union does not consider it desirable for Russian forces to move at the proper time against Polish forces in the Russian sphere of influence and, for their part, to occupy this territory. In our estimation this would not only be a relief for us, but also, in the sense of the Moscow agreements, be in the Soviet interest as well.'[36]

The Soviet leadership did not respond immediately to the German suggestion. Stalin was never a man to act on impulse. And there were important issues to consider. What, for example, would be the likely British and French response to any Soviet incursion? The Western Allies had just declared war on Germany because they had agreed by treaty to protect Poland against aggression. If the Red Army moved into eastern Poland, would they now decide to fight the Soviet Union as well? In fact, was the pact of 'non-aggression' with the Nazis about to drag the Soviets into the very war it had been designed to exclude them from?

But there remained strong arguments in favour of military action. The Soviets didn't just recognize the obvious material benefits to be gained from annexing a large chunk of another country – they were motivated by powerful historical reasons as well. Not least because Stalin felt he had a score to settle with the Poles. He still remembered with bitterness the war the Bolsheviks had fought with the Poles between 1919 and 1920 (most often called the Polish–Soviet war, although the 'Soviet Union' was only agreed in principle in 1922 and was not formally recognised until 1924). Poland, which had vanished as an independent country in the eighteenth century, carved up between its more powerful neighbours, was reconstituted by the Versailles peace treaty at the end of the

First World War. And whilst the Polish leader, Józef Piłsudski, wanted to push the border as far east as possible, Lenin saw Poland as an obstruction on the road the Communists needed to take in order to spread the revolution into Europe, particularly into a post-war Germany that he believed was ripe for Marxist conquest.

Initially the Bolshevik army performed well, advancing by the summer of 1920 almost to Warsaw. But then the Poles counter-attacked and defeated them at the battle of the river Niemen. Subsequently, through the Treaty of Riga, which was signed in March 1921, the Poles gained western Ukraine and western Belarus and this new border was ratified at an Allied conference in 1923. (It was this tortuous history that lay behind Molotov's infamous remark that Poland was 'the monstrous bastard of the Peace of Versailles'.)[37] Significantly, this whole Polish affair was not just a general humiliation for the Bolsheviks but an individual humiliation for the Commissar of the Southwestern Front – a man called Joseph Stalin. When Marshal Tukhachevsky, the Bolshevik commander, called for reinforcements, Stalin had failed to send them. In 1925 Stalin even attempted to conceal this blot on his early career by removing the relevant documents from the Kiev archives.[38]

But although he felt a strong antipathy towards the Poles, in September 1939 Stalin wasn't about to let his emotions decide his next move. He also knew that the Soviets could attempt to legit-imize any incursion into Polish territory with propaganda, hiding behind a proposal that in 1919 Lord Curzon, then British Foreign Secretary, had put forward as the border between Poland and its eastern neighbours – the so-called 'Curzon Line'. This suggestion was rejected by the Bolsheviks at the time, but it was, as it happened, broadly similar to the border that Stalin and Molotov had just agreed with Ribbentrop would divide their 'spheres of influence' in Poland. Moreover, the Poles were not in a majority in these eastern territories. Whilst around 40 per cent of the popu-lation were of Polish origin, 34 per cent were Ukrainian and 9 per cent Belarusian. This, the Soviet propagandists realized, allowed any incursion to be couched as an act of 'liberation' – freeing the 'local' population from Polish domination.

A combination of all these factors meant that on 9 September, six days after Ribbentrop had sent his original cable, Molotov replied to say that the Red Army was about to move into the agreed Soviet 'sphere of influence' in Poland. At a meeting in Moscow the following day with the German ambassador, Molotov told Schulenburg that the pretext for the invasion would be that the Soviet Union was helping Ukrainians and Belarusians. 'This argument,' he said, 'was to make the intervention of the Soviet Union plausible and at the same time avoid giving the Soviet Union the appearance of an aggressor.'[39]

THE SOVIETS INVADE POLAND

On 17 September six hundred thousand Soviet troops crossed into eastern Poland, led by Marshal Kovalov in the north on the Belarusian front and Marshal Timoshenko in the south on the Ukrainian front. In a radio broadcast that same day, Molotov justi-fied the Soviet action by relying on the 'plausible' argument he had outlined to Schulenburg. He announced that this military action was necessary in order to save the 'blood brothers' of the Soviet people who lived in eastern Poland. Not to have taken action would, according to Molotov, have been an act of 'abandonment'.

'We officially extended the hand of friendship to our brother Russians and Ukrainians,' says Georgy Dragunov,[40] one of the Soviet soldiers who entered former Polish territory that September. 'Our military propaganda literature and our political officers tried to brainwash us into believing that the workers needed our help and that they were being exploited by the Polish bureaucracy.' The Red Army was initially welcomed in many places. Indeed, there was confusion as to whether this was actually an invasion at all. Perhaps, some thought, the Soviet troops had really come to 'help'. Maybe they would just motor through the flat countryside of eastern Poland and confront the Germans, who had already captured most of the west of the country.

Boguslava Gryniv[41] and her family lived near Lwów,[42] one of the major cities of southeast Poland. They were of Ukrainian descent, so felt they had little to fear from the Soviets. 'People welcomed them [the soldiers] by waving at them,' she says. 'People also sometimes welcomed them with flowers and also with the [Ukrainian] blue-yellow flag.... All they [the Red Army soldiers] did was open up the hatches on their tanks and smile at the population. That was how they arrived.... We didn't expect anything terrible to happen.... My father said so himself when my mother asked to leave. He said: "These are not the same Bolsheviks as in 1919. After twenty years there is already culture, there is already a state, there is already a justice system." In other words, he hoped that...well, that they would not be bandits.'

'When the Red Army arrived in 1939, people, me included, did not feel negatively towards them but nor was there any love,' says Zenon Vrublevsky,[43] who was a twelve-year-old schoolboy at the time. 'People really were very divided. You know, we lived on the same floor as a number of other families. Some of them were glad that [the Red Army] had come. And others said: "Just you wait, they will show you! Siberia is really big, they will take you away to Siberia!" And I didn't really feel either of those things. Neither love nor hate. I just accepted them as a new army, a new government, a new power.'

The Polish army was initially ordered by their government to pull back and not confront the Soviets – though some clashes did occur, notably at Grodno – but it quickly became clear to the Polish leadership that the Red Army had not come to 'help'. However, the Poles knew they had no hope of surviving against the combined aggression of the Germans and Soviets. They realized that, just as Poland had been swallowed up by its mighty neighbours at the end of the eighteenth century, it was about to be swallowed up once again.

But as the Red Army marched into eastern Poland that September, they did not resemble the mighty army of an immense power. In fact, they stank. 'The smell that came off them,' says Zenon Vrublevsky, 'to us it was like the smell of toilet disinfectant. The type we used in public toilets.' 'They smelt rather odd,' confirms Anna Levitska,[44] another inhabitant of Lwów. 'It was a kind of distinctive, sharp smell.' Many locals remarked on the contrast between the 'elegant' and 'well turned out' soldiers of the Polish army with their shiny leather and immaculate uniforms, and the malodorous, tattered rag-bag of a force that now entered their towns and villages. 'Many people used to laugh at them,' says Zenon Vrublevsky. 'Look at what they're wearing! Look at these beggars who have come!'

'As we moved ahead we saw that [Polish] people were much better off, both in military life and in everyday life,' says Georgy Dragunov, who was astonished to witness the disparity in wealth between the Communist Soviet Union and the capitalist Poland. 'We saw beautifully furnished houses – even peasant houses. [Even] their poorest people were better off than our people – their furniture was polished. Only later did we start to furnish our apartments with similar sorts of furniture. Each poor peasant [in eastern Poland] had no less than two horses and every household had three or four cows and a lot of poultry. This was so unexpected for us because of the propaganda – which was [now] wasted on us because we could see electricity in the peasants' houses whereas in Soviet Belarus we didn't have electricity.'

Wiesława Saternus, a Polish schoolgirl who lived with her family near the border with the Ukraine, was surprised at her first sight of a soldier of the Red Army: 'This Russian soldier was running through this empty field and he was shouting that we should give him something to eat. And he came into our house and he wasn't dressed well, in proper dress, and his weapon was hanging on a string. And my mother said that he would get some food.... [Then] this Russian soldier got a small clock which sat on the table and he put it in his pocket without even asking whether he could take this clock or not, and he was just [still] shouting, "Give me some food", and my mother gave him lots of food and he was [also] packing this food in his coat.'

In a cultured city like Lwów, which had once been a jewel – albeit a provincial one – in the Austro-Hungarian Empire, many of the new arrivals from the Soviet Union felt as if they had entered a kind of fairyland. Much was strange to them. Anna Levitska saw the wife of a Red Army officer wearing a nightgown she had found, calling it a 'pretty dress'; and on a visit to the market the same woman bought a chamber pot and announced that she had purchased a nice 'bowl'. Elsewhere there were reports of Red Army soldiers wearing bras as earmuffs.

Not surprisingly, many of the Soviets felt insecure in this bourgeois wonderland and took to vainglorious boasting about what they had left behind. 'They would say: "We have so much,"' remembers Zenon Vrublevsky. '"Jobs? We have so many jobs!" "Do you have such and such?" "Yes! We have so much of that!" But people guessed that these things were not true.'

Once, in the centre of Lwów, Vrublevsky watched as one of the locals teased two Red Army soldiers: 'He said: "Comrades, do you have typhus back home?" And the soldiers said: "Of course we do – we have loads of it. We'll be bringing you two trainloads of it soon!" Then the people burst out laughing, and the soldiers realized they had said something stupid and left.'

Anna Levitska witnessed a similar conversation between a Red Army officer and her mother. 'He said: "Everything here is for the bourgeois. Everything is for them and the simple people cannot obtain anything. But in our country, the Soviet Union, these things are available to anyone who works. We have a surfeit of everything, you know. Oranges which are made in a factory. You can get as many as you want. Caviar of the finest quality. From a factory. It is being sent out. It is all being sent out, so soon we will have it here too.... That's what it is like in our country. We manufacture oranges, tangerines, caviar – it's all made in the factories. So everyone can afford it." This really made us smile! How could these things possibly be made in factories?'

But a far darker side to the Soviet occupation quickly became apparent. It ranged from casual theft – there were cases of Soviet soldiers simply taking any jewellery they fancied from passers-by – to more serious crime. Anna Levitska knew of two schoolfriends who were raped by Red Army officers: 'Those two girls were shaking the entire time that they were telling me about what had happened. They were in tears. They simply did not understand how this could have happened. They were dreadfully affected by it, and, of course, I too was affected when they told me about it.'

And though theft and rape were officially crimes in the Red Army, there was a sense from the very beginning of the occupation that the Soviets were intent on despoiling eastern Poland – despoiling property, despoiling people, despoiling ideas. In pursuit of the Marxist ideal of 'equality', the Soviet authorities turned conventional values upside-down. To be rich was no longer pleasurable but dangerous. Whereas before it had been acceptable to stroll, smartly dressed, down the central promenade in Lwów past the ornate opera house, now it was evidence of 'bourgeois' behaviour and rendered you liable to arrest. It is often forgotten that just as the Nazi occupation of western Poland in 1939 was driven by ideological beliefs, so was the Soviet occupation of eastern Poland.

The shops of Lwów and the other towns and cities in eastern Poland soon emptied of goods because in the early days of the occupation the Soviet authorities instituted a novel way of robbery. They set an exchange rate of one Soviet rouble for one Polish zloty – whereas in reality the zloty was worth far more. This meant that Red Army soldiers could 'buy' whatever they wanted from the shops. The consequence, of course, was that the zloty became worthless. Boguslava Gryniv witnessed the catastrophic effect of this development on her neighbour, a teacher of Latin and Greek at a prestigious Lwów school: 'State employees were well paid and he had put all his money in a savings bank. At the first intimation of war he had withdrawn all his money from the bank. He had a suitcase full of money.... One day [his nephew] came round and said: "We are having a fire today. Uncle is burning his suitcase." He went and got the suitcase and then he emptied the banknotes on the fire, saying: "This is my thirty years of service – these are my savings." It was mere paper now.' A primitive barter economy soon replaced the sophisticated previous world of banks, paper money and cheques. People would 'give away their fur coats in exchange for three to five litres of petrol', or take a sweater to the green-grocer's to buy 'a bucket of potatoes'.

And the Soviets didn't just destroy previous certainties, such as the security of currency – they swept away the whole concept of ownership of personal property. Red Army soldiers, looking for somewhere to live, merely walked down a street until they saw a house they liked, and then banged on the door and announced they were moving in. The first that Anna Levitska and her family knew about the appropriation of their comfortable villa in the suburbs of Lwów was when two Red Army officers appeared on their doorstep and announced: 'We are going to be billeted with you.'

Each Red Army officer then took several rooms in the house and moved in with his wife. 'They took over the furniture and all the other things,' says Anna Levitska, 'which meant that every-thing was now theirs.... It was a small house which had five rooms – they occupied four of the rooms.... We no longer had any right to any of it.... Even the clothes: "This dress would really suit my wife," he [one of the officers] would say [as he took it]....'

Anna, her father and her mother had previously lived a happy family life in the house. Now they were all confined to one room: 'We were just astounded by it all, you know. It was simply incom-prehensible that these strangers who had no relationship with us whatsoever could just come and take over somebody else's prop-erty and furniture and things and consider this to be normal behaviour...that this was how things ought to be. It seemed utterly outrageous to us. We could not understand it and we suffered because of it. We suffered because we didn't know if tomorrow they might not say to us: "Get out of here! You have no business being here!" It was just terrifying.'

People like Anna Levitska's family – the so-called 'bourgeois' intelligentsia – were particularly at risk. As the Soviet troops moved into eastern Poland, they had distributed leaflets calling on the inhabitants to turn against their so-called 'real' enemies – the rich, the landlords and the leadership and officer class. This was an inva-sion designed to reorder and restructure Polish society. 'They ordered us to line up and they checked everybody's hands,' recalled one villager. 'And they ordered to step forward those whose hands were not worn out from physical labour and [then] beat them with rifle butts, and one policeman was shot with a revolver.'⁴⁵

Casual abuse of the 'class enemies' of the Communist system soon turned into systematic arrest. On 27 September – just ten days after Red Army troops had crossed into Poland – the Soviets came for Boguslava Gryniv's father. He was a prominent lawyer and head of the regional branch of UNDO – the Ukrainian National Democratic Party. Because UNDO was a legally constituted organization he felt he had nothing to fear from the Soviet authorities. He was wrong.

That day was a church holiday, so when there was a knock at their door the Gryniv family were surprised to see a member of the local Soviet authority. He said that Boguslava Gryniv's father was 'invited' to come and visit the temporary government. 'And my mother said: "It's a holiday – we're having a special dinner. Come back after dinner." I could tell by the expression on my father's face that he was a little bit nervous. He said to my mother, "As they are asking, I have to go." As soon as they took him away, my mother announced that every evening we would kneel down in front of the icon and pray for our father to be returned to us. I think that was the most we could do, turn to God and ask that such a good, kind person as my father not be punished.' Boguslava Gryniv's father was one of the first to suffer at the hands of the Soviets in eastern Poland. Over the next months there would be many more.

RIBBENTROP RETURNS

On the same day that Boguslava Gryniv's father was arrested in eastern Poland a very different human interaction was taking place in Moscow. In the light of the swift conquest of Poland, the Soviet government had asked their new friend Joachim von Ribbentrop to return to the Kremlin to finalize the exact borders that would now exist between them. The mood – on both sides – was jubilant. The Soviets had occupied their 'sphere of influence' without meeting any significant military opposition – they hadn't even formally declared war on Poland. And, despite the Germans having faced fierce Polish resistance, they had by now almost completely consolidated their hold on western Poland – indeed, Warsaw would fall the next day, 28 September.

The contrast between Ribbentrop's first, almost furtive visit four weeks before and this grandiose second one could scarcely have been greater. Ribbentrop now needed not one but two Condor planes to deliver himself and his entourage. The reception at Moscow airport was, according to General Köstring who accompanied him, 'a ceremony of huge dimensions'.[46] There was a guard of honour and a band played the 'International'. Above the airport fluttered a number of Nazi flags. The fact that the crosses of the swastikas were hung back to front was dismissed by the arriving Nazis 'smilingly' as 'a little mistake', since the 'intention was good'.

Ribbentrop landed in Moscow at six in the evening, and by ten o'clock he was ensconced with Stalin and Molotov at the scene of their previous encounter – Molotov's office in the Kremlin. Stalin expressed his 'satisfaction'[47] over the German success in Poland as well as the expectation that the collaboration between the Soviet Union and Germany would remain positive. Then, true to character, Ribbentrop began with a series of extravagant, vague statements about the immense value of the friendship between the two countries. He emphasized that the Germans wanted to 'cooperate' with the Soviet Union. But such was his pomposity and overblown eloquence that it wasn't completely clear what form he hoped this 'cooperation' would take. Stalin, who impressed foreign diplomats with his ability to cut through to the heart of any discussion, replied that 'the German foreign minister has hinted cautiously that by "cooperation" Germany did not imply any need for military assistance or an intention to drag the Soviet Union into a war. This was well and tactfully said.'

The Soviet leader then went on to make what, on the face of it, was an extraordinary statement (remarks, moreover, that remained secret until the 1990s when Gustav Hilger's detailed minutes of this meeting were discovered in Ambassador Schulenburg's papers).[48] 'The fact is that for the time being Germany does not need foreign help,' said Stalin, 'and it is possible that in the future they will not need foreign help either. However, if, against all expectations, Germany finds itself in a difficult situation, then she can be sure that the Soviet people will come to Germany's aid and will not allow Germany to be suppressed. A strong Germany is in the interests of the Soviet Union and she will not allow Germany to be thrown down to the ground.'

Was Stalin really laying open the possibility of the Red Army offering military assistance to Germany if the Nazis ever found themselves in a 'difficult' situation? For the Western Allies this would have been a terrifying prospect. Of course, in the event, nothing came of Stalin's words. The Germans never found themselves in sufficient 'difficulties' to pursue any potential military alliance. But Stalin's statement still shows how far he might have been prepared to go in pursuit of his alliance with Hitler, and it remains, given what was to happen later, an enormously embarrassing comment for him to have made.

Stalin then moved on to discuss practicalities, and revealed that he wanted to revisit the question of the borders drawn up at the 23 August meeting. He now wanted to exchange some of Soviet-held Poland – the territory of Lublin and the southern part of the Warsaw region – for a free hand in Lithuania. That way, the Soviet Union would keep the eastern territories of Poland which contained significant numbers of Russians and Ukrainians, and give up those areas that were overwhelmingly Polish in ethnic origin. The discussions continued in this intensely pragmatic way. Ribbentrop announced that Germany wanted the forest of Avgustova between East Prussia and Lithuania (apparently only because the area was supposed to offer good hunting), and Stalin revealed how the Soviets planned to put pressure on each of the Baltic states in turn to ensure that they complied with Soviet policy.

That night there was a lavish banquet in the Andreevsky Hall of the Kremlin. In contrast to the shabby utilitarianism of Molotov's office, the banqueting hall was 'decorated with flowers and covered with precious porcelain and gold-plated cutlery'.[49] Amidst this tsarist splendour, members of Ribbentrop's extensive entourage mingled freely with the Communist leadership. Stalin introduced Lavrenti Beria, chief of the NKVD, to Ribbentrop with the memorable words: 'Look, this is our Himmler – he isn't bad [at his work] either.'[50] The atmosphere was friendly, and much alcohol was consumed. 'In terms of presentation, generous hospitality and warmth of atmosphere,' recalled the German diplomat Andor Hencke, 'this dinner was one of the most remarkable events I have witnessed during my twenty-three-year-long diplomatic career.'[51] Stalin insisted on walking around the banqueting hall and toasting each member of the German delegation individually. Meanwhile, Molotov took every opportunity to drink to Stalin's health, celebrating him as 'the Soviet Union's great leader and the spearhead of German–Russian friendship'. Stalin reacted jokingly to Molotov's toadying: 'If Molotov wants to have a drink,' he said, 'I certainly don't mind. But he shouldn't always use me as an excuse.'[52]

At the banquet the German diplomat Gustav Hilger was placed next to Lavrenti Beria. The Soviet secret police chief – short, bald and cruel-hearted – was not the most congenial of dinner companions. Hilger later recalled how Beria kept trying to make him drink more than he wanted to. Stalin, sitting diagonally opposite, noticed the friendly dispute between the two and asked what was going on. When Hilger explained, Stalin replied: 'Well, if you don't want to drink, no one can force you.' 'Not even the chief of the NKVD himself?' asked Hilger as a joke. 'Here at this table,' said Stalin, 'even the chief of the NKVD has no more say than anyone else.'[53]

Molotov proposed a toast to Ribbentrop. 'A hearty welcome for our guest who brings with him such good fortune!' he declaimed. 'Hurrah to Germany, her Führer and her Foreign Minister!'

'Being immediate neighbours once more,' said Ribbentrop in reply, 'as Germany and Russia had been for so many centuries, represents a hopeful foundation for friendship between both countries. The Führer considers the further realisation of that friendship entirely possible in spite of the differences that exist between both of our systems. In that spirit I propose a toast to the health of comrades Stalin and Molotov who have given me such a sincere welcome.'[54]

After the banquet the German party left for the ballet, to watch the Bolshoi perform *Swan Lake*. Stalin and Molotov for their part immediately began the process of threatening the leaders of the Baltic states. Waiting for them elsewhere in the Kremlin was the Foreign Minister of Estonia, who was informed by Molotov that thirty-five thousand Red Army troops would be despatched to be garrisoned in his country. 'Come on, Molotov,' said Stalin, 'you're rather harsh on our friends.' The Soviet leader then suggested the troop numbers should be reduced to twenty-five thousand.[55]

In the early hours of the morning the German and Soviet delegations met up once again and, after Hitler had been consulted by phone, the details of the agreement were finalized. A map was brought in and Stalin signed it in huge letters, joking: 'Is my signature clear enough for you?'[56]

To a number of those present at the talks in the Kremlin, this was the beginning of a new world order. 'To me it seemed certain that the new German–Soviet friendship,' recorded Hilger, 'sealed by two solemn treaties, would be of advantage to both partners and that it would be of long duration.'[57] But it is unlikely that Stalin thought this was a deal to last – much more likely that he saw it as a way of standing back while the Nazis and the Western Allies slugged it out between them. He is alleged to have said at a Politburo meeting on 19 August that 'the Soviet Union had to do everything possible to prolong the war and exhaust the Western powers',[58] and the Non-Aggression Pact certainly fitted that self-serving purpose.

Nevertheless, further down the Soviet chain of command there was more belief that this was a sincere agreement. Just days after the border treaty had been signed, Tuleniev, one of the Soviet military commanders in occupied Poland, gave the captured Polish general Władysław Anders 'a long lecture' in which he declared that: 'The treaty of friendship with Germany would secure the mastery of the world to the Russians and Germans. Together the two peoples would defeat France, and Britain, the greatest enemy of the Soviet Union, who would be finished for ever.' According to Anders, Tuleniev then went on to say that 'They did not expect the entry of the United States into the war, as they would use the influence of their Communist organisation to prevent it.'[59]

But across the Atlantic, although there was no immediate prospect of the United States intervening militarily in the conflict, there was no question which side President Franklin Roosevelt supported. In the middle of August he had told Konstantin Oumansky, the Soviet ambassador to Washington, that in order to safeguard its future the Soviet Union should reach an agreement with Britain and France rather than with Nazi Germany. Furthermore, the ambassador was informed that he should 'tell Stalin that if his Government joined up with Hitler, it was as certain as night followed day that as soon as Hitler had conquered France, he would turn on Russia and that it would be the Soviets' turn next'.[60]

Roosevelt's considerable political gifts told him that Hitler was not to be trusted. But by the end of September 1939 the Soviet leadership must have thought the American President had been indulging in provocation with his dire prediction. For all seemed to be going well – perhaps even better than expected. Not least because the Soviets now basked in the certain knowledge that one of their greatest fears – that Britain or France would declare war on them in the wake of the Red Army's invasion of eastern Poland, and drag the Soviet Union into the conflict – had not been realized.

THE ALLIES FIGHT BACK – BUT ONLY WITH WORDS

On 20 September the British Prime Minister, Neville Chamberlain, spoke to the House of Commons about the Soviet invasion of eastern Poland: 'For the unhappy victim of this cynical attack, the result has been a tragedy of the grimmest character. The world which has watched the vain struggle of the Polish nation against overwhelming odds with profound pity and sympathy admires their valour, which even now refuses to admit defeat.... There is no sacrifice from which we will not shrink, there is no operation we will not undertake provided our responsible advisers, our Allies, and we ourselves are convinced that it will make an appropriate contribution to victory. But what we will not do is to rush into adventures that offer little prospect of success and are calculated to impair our resources and to postpone ultimate victory.'[61] So fine words – but no action.

British diplomats were even less enthusiastic about the prospect of conflict with the Soviet Union (or 'adventures that offer little prospect of success' as Chamberlain had just put it) than the politicians. 'I do not myself see what advantage war with the Soviet Union would be to us,' wrote the British ambassador to Moscow, Sir William Seeds, on 18 September in a secret telegram to the Foreign Office, 'though it would please me personally to declare it on M. Molotov.'[62] Seeds then went on, in the same telegram, to make a prediction that was to turn out to be woefully wrong: '...the Soviet invasion of Poland is not without advantages to us in the long run, for it will entail the keeping of a large army on a war footing outside Russia consuming food and petrol and wearing out material and transport, thus reducing German hopes of military or food supplies.'[63]

But after the signing of the German–Soviet border treaty late that month, Sir William was to make a prophecy of much greater accuracy – one, indeed, that is remarkable given that Britain had been at war for less than a month. 'It must be borne in mind,' he wrote in a telegram of 30 September, 'that if war continues any considerable time, the Soviet part of Poland will, at its close, have been purged of any non-Soviet population or classes whatever, and that it may well be consequently impossible, in practice, to separate it from the rest of Russia.' Seeds then went on to ask his superiors in London whether it might not be possible to intimate to the Kremlin that 'our war aims are not incompatible with reasonable settlement [in Poland] on ethnographic and cultural lines'.[64]

On the face of it, this was an incredible suggestion. The Soviet Union had just invaded, and was in the process of subjugating, the eastern part of a nation that the British had openly pledged to protect, yet here was a senior British official privately suggesting that this aggression should be immediately rewarded. But back in London another senior diplomat, Sir Ivone Kirkpatrick, endorsed Seeds's views in a report of 1 October: 'The intervention of Russia has of course made the reconstitution of Poland much more diffi-cult, if not wholly impossible. We should therefore be wise not to proclaim that we stand for the old boundaries of Poland. Such an attitude would render inevitable a conflict with Russia, which we do not wish to precipitate. There is much force in Sir W. Seeds's argument....'[65] Kirkpatrick appended a 'sketch map of Poland' to his report and pointed out significantly that the new Soviet-imposed border of Poland mostly followed the 'Curzon Line', the demarcation line that had been proposed by Lord Curzon, the British Foreign Secretary in 1919, and that had then been rejected by the Poles and Bolsheviks.

Meantime, some of the British population were bemused that their country had not been obliged to declare war on the Soviet Union. If the British treaty to protect Poland from aggression had resulted in war with the Germans, why hadn't it also resulted in war with the Soviet Union?

It was on this point that the British government found itself in a somewhat delicate position because the Nazi–Soviet pact was not the only treaty that had a secret protocol – the 1939 Anglo–Polish treaty had one as well. Whilst the section of that treaty that had been made public spoke of Britain's obligation to defend Poland from 'aggression' in general terms, there was another, private section that specifically limited that obligation to aggression from Germany. In order to explain the British inaction in the face of Soviet aggression, the Earl of Perth, a senior figure in the British Ministry of Information, wrote on 5 October to the Permanent Under Secretary at the Foreign Office, Sir Alexander Cadogan, urging 'that the time has now come to make known the existence of the secret protocol between Poland and ourselves'.[66]

Significantly, he also added that this action would have the additional benefit that 'knowledge of this protocol might have a considerable effect on the Russian government, who it seems to me are somewhat anxious that part of our war aims may be the return of the Polish State with the boundaries which it had previous to the outbreak of war'.

Cadogan, Eton- and Oxford-educated and often cool in his judgements to the point of freezing, did not reply to Perth's letter until 3 November, but when he did he revealed that, whilst the Polish government in exile had agreed that the secret protocol could be made public, 'we decided that it would be inadvisable to make any statement admitting the existence of a secret protocol, as this would only provoke curiosity about the existence of similar secret protocols attached to other treaties....'[67] By the time of Cadogan's letter, the British government's line on this potentially embarrassing subject had become clear. Although the secret protocol was not to be admitted openly, a statement was made in the House of Commons revealing that the Poles had 'understood' that 'the agreement should only cover the case of aggression by Germany'.[68]

So from the beginning, Soviet aggression was treated differently from German aggression. And it is not hard to see why. On a purely practical level it was scarcely to the advantage of Britain to declare war on a second totalitarian power. The British government had already shown that they could not defend Poland against one aggressor – let alone two. Poland was simply too far away for the British to protect. But more than that, these secret diplomatic exchanges demonstrate how from the earliest days of the war there was a reluctance in some quarters ever to guarantee to the Poles that Britain's aim was to recover all their territory. And this was not just another example of straightforward pragmatism, but also a demonstration of the fact that some mandarins in the Foreign Office considered the eastern boundary of Poland somewhat 'fluid'. We can also see in these diplomatic and governmental discussions a gap beginning to open between the grandiloquent words of the British government in public – 'a cynical attack...a tragedy of the grimmest character' – and the very different tone in private – 'the Soviet invasion of Poland is not without advantages to us in the long run'.

At one level, of course, this isn't a surprise. It comes as no shock to learn that politicians and diplomats are capable of dissembling. However, it is significant here because the Second World War took on the mantle of an entirely 'moral' war, almost a modern-day crusade against evil, and, as we shall see, later statements by the leaders of the Western Allies made this moral stance explicit. But from the first, behind the scenes there was a clear balance to be struck between 'morality' and traditional, old-fashioned, national self-interest.

REPRESSION

Secure in the knowledge that the Western Allies would do nothing in practical terms to prevent them benefiting from their aggression, the Soviet authorities moved quickly to consolidate their control over the population of eastern Poland. And a crucial part of the process of repression was a sham pretence of democracy, with the first 'elections' held as early as 22 October.

Only candidates approved of by the Soviets could stand for election – and in some cases that meant there was no choice at all. 'Yes,' comfirms Nikolai Dyukarev,[69] who was a member of the Soviet NKVD in occupied Poland, '[if] there was only one candidate, [then] we would elect him, all of us. So it's not like it is now.'

The Soviet authorities often deliberately selected potential candidates from ill-educated, often illiterate, peasants. 'We tried to elect poor people because we trusted them more,' admits Dyukarev. 'They would support the Soviet Union, whilst rich people had their own interests. After all, [a poor person] was somebody who had worked all their life, and they could be good people.' At one election meeting a Mr Kowalewski was brave enough to speak out and let the Soviets know that their ruse was obvious to all: 'You are on purpose selecting idiots for candidates,' he said, 'so that they will merely appear as names on a list.'[70] His subsequent fate is not recorded, but – given the ruthlessness with which the Soviets pushed through political change – he is likely to have been arrested by the NKVD.

Another crucial part of enforcing change was the systematic destruction of the old educational system. Those teachers who managed to keep their jobs in the new system were required to instruct their pupils in a variety of previously alien ideas – speaking out against the Catholic Church and in favour of Stalin and Communism. And behind this reversal of the previous belief system was the ever-present feeling of threat.

'When the Red Army arrived,' says Zenon Vrublevsky, then a schoolboy, 'they hung a portrait of Stalin in the classroom. We were used to the old regime and we did not know this one was different. So, you see, we did what we had always done and Stalin acquired a new kind of moustache! This very elderly teacher spotted it and ran to the school principal. The principal came running in. There was noise and commotion and he took down the portrait. And we were laughing. But later on we understood. The teacher said to us: "How can you not understand this, you idiots! Can't you understand that nothing would happen to you, but they would put us teachers and the principal in prison [for this]!" We were so shocked. Who would have imagined that just a little [extra] moustache could get our teachers put in jail?'

But the Soviet authorities didn't just rely on fear to transform the Polish educational system – they also used incentives. The Polish General Anders learnt of one technique that the Soviets used to make the children understand that their world had changed: 'A Bolshevik commission…visited a school for small children, most of whom were hungry owing to the shortage of food. "You are used to saying prayers," said the Russians. "Now pray to your God to give you some bread." The children were then made to pray. A long pause – "You see, you get nothing. Now ask the great Stalin for the same thing." Almost immediately tea, sandwiches and sweets were brought into the classroom. "Now you see who is the better and more powerful."'[71]

And hand in hand that autumn with this attempt to 're-educate' the population of eastern Poland went close cooperation with the Germans in the form of the practical work of the German–Soviet border committee. This group had been set up after the 27 September meeting between Ribbentrop and the Soviets, and charged with the task of formalizing the precise route of the boundary between the two states. At the end of October all the various sub-committees were gathered in German-occupied Warsaw to receive instructions. 'This [meeting] was hosted by the German embassy,' wrote Andor Hencke,[72] 'which, as leader of the German delegation, I had to represent. This was the first opportunity since the change of policy to return the hospitality the Russians had extended to us. On the Reich Foreign Minister's express orders, special emphasis was placed on making the two-day stay of the Soviet officials (and officers belonging to the central border committee and the sub-committees in the German sphere of control) as pleasant as was possible in the Polish capital.'

Hans Frank, recently appointed Nazi ruler of this part of German-occupied Poland, even hosted a luncheon party for the Soviet delegation. In his speech to the German–Soviet border committee, Frank expressed 'delight' that one of his first tasks as governor-general was to welcome the Soviets. He added that the 'committee shared the aim of restoring peaceable day-to-day life to the inhabitants of the [former] Polish territory, on whom the blind Polish government had inflicted incredible misery'.[73] The head of the Soviet delegation, Ministry Director Alexandrov, replied, saying that 'the spirit in which these negotiations had been conducted was one of cooperation for the benefit of the German and Soviet nations, the two greatest peoples in Europe'. This atmosphere of intense bonhomie was further consolidated as Frank offered Alexandrov a cigarette, saying, 'You and I are both smoking Polish cigarettes to symbolise the fact that we have thrown Poland to the winds.'[74] (Frank certainly knew what he was talking about – indeed, he would later be executed for the war crimes he committed in Poland.)

Meantime, in the portion of eastern Poland occupied by the Red Army, the process of Sovietization continued at the national level as the delegates who had been 'elected' immediately

requested that the captured territories of eastern Poland be 'incor-
porated' into the Soviet Union. The Supreme Soviet – not surprisingly – agreed to the request, and on 28 November 1939 all the
inhabitants of eastern Poland duly became Soviet citizens whether
they liked it or not.

And, of course, a crucial part of Soviet control – one that went
hand-in-hand with radical administrative change – was terror.
Altogether, during this first period of Soviet domination, between
September 1939 and June 1941, around 110,000 people were
arrested.[75] Indeed, as we have already seen in the case of Boguslava
Gryniv's father, individual arrests of members of the intelligentsia
and others thought a threat to the new regime began from the
moment the Red Army arrived. And the inherently unjust treatment of Boguslava Gryniv's father stands as an exemplar for Soviet
rule of eastern Poland.

Immediately after his arrest, Boguslava Gryniv's father was sent
to the local jail. 'It was a small cell,' his daughter remembers, 'and
it usually held drunks and petty criminals…. And we already knew
that the most important people who had stayed behind in the town
were in this prison…. They thought that it was just a temporary
misunderstanding. But about three weeks later we came to see
them and they were no longer there.' Her father had been taken to
a larger prison in Chertkov, where he still seems to have believed
that he was the victim of a 'misunderstanding'. He discovered that
'all' he was accused of was membership of the Ukrainian National
Democratic Alliance, an organization that had been legal before the
invasion and was not anti-Bolshevik. He did not realize that his
crime – in Soviet eyes – was that he was seen as a potentially dangerous member of the previous 'ruling class'. Such people were hugely
vulnerable in the new regime. And one day towards the end of
1939, Boguslava Gryniv's father simply disappeared from the
prison. It was to be fifty years before his family finally learnt that he
had been murdered by the NKVD in the spring of 1940.

THE FATE OF FINLAND

Whilst there was still no mass public outcry in Britain or the USA in the autumn of 1939 about the Soviet occupation of Poland, what had worked for the Soviets in eastern Poland – pretending that they had only moved into this territory to 'help' the local population – was not about to work in another neighbouring country, Finland.

Stalin and the rest of the Soviet leadership coveted the eastern portion of Finland for two main reasons: the existing border was only 20 miles west of Leningrad and they feared that they might one day be vulnerable to attack via this route, and they also wanted a port on the Baltic Sea. Although the Russians had previously ruled Finland as a Duchy, to the rest of the world their threatening actions now seemed more obviously aggressive than their capture of eastern Poland. In this case there was no pretence that moving into Finland would 'help' the locals at all.

In October, when it became clear that Finland was at risk of Soviet attack, British policy was confused. In spite of the Nazi–Soviet pact, the British had been trying to negotiate a trade agreement with the Soviet Union in order to acquire much-needed timber, and there was still a view that Stalin should not be confronted unnecessarily. Winston Churchill, then First Lord of the Admiralty, even went so far as to tell the Cabinet on 16 October: 'It was in our interest that the USSR [the Soviet Union] should increase their strength in the Baltic, thereby limiting the risk of German domination in that area.'[76]

But Soviet aggression also presented obvious dangers in northern Europe – not least that the whole of Scandinavia might then be at risk of Soviet attack. There was also the lingering – and ever tricky – sense of a moral issue at stake here as well. Mr Snow, the British minister in Helsinki in Finland, put it this way in a despatch of 21 October 1939: 'I assume condonation of so cold blooded a crime [the Soviet occupation of Finland] to be out of the question on the part of protagonists [Britain and France] in the idealist war against aggression and that, in view of earlier Soviet treachery [the invasion of eastern Poland], a complete breach with the Soviet government would command nation-wide support, while condonation would not only involve our profession in complete discredit in Scandinavia and elsewhere but also at home and in our hearts as well.'[77] Snow went on to conclude that, in the event of a Soviet invasion of Finland (which he called 'the iniquitous crime in question'), the choice for the British would be a 'breach of diplomatic relations with Russia or a declaration of war'.

Snow's despatch is in stark contrast, of course, to the more pragmatic views expressed by his Foreign Office colleagues over the question of the Soviet invasion of eastern Poland. And so this is an important document – not because anything came of it (nothing did), but because it demonstrates that the genuine belief that this was an 'idealist war against aggression' was not confined at the time to romantics outside the levers of power.

The British chiefs of staff were asked to consider the practical question of war with the Soviet Union in the light of the possible Soviet invasion of Finland. Their report certainly lacked the moral fervour of Snow's despatch, though it acknowledged that 'At present the sincerity of France and Great Britain is being questioned, and force is being added to German propaganda, particularly in Italy and Spain, because we have not declared war on Russia in spite of the fact that she has already interfered with the liberty of small states in much the same way as Germany.'[78] For the chiefs of staff, however, the issue at stake was not one of principle, but of harsh, practical pros and cons: 'The question thus seems to resolve itself into whether any advantage which might accrue from the support of neutrals, consequent upon a stand by us against Russian aggression, will outweigh the disadvantage which we should incur by the undoubted increase in our military commitments and by the probability that we should weld Germany and Russia more firmly together.' The conclusion was that 'we and France are at present in no position to undertake additional burdens', but that 'if' the War Cabinet decided Britain should make a stand, it was important to chose the 'right moment', when it appeared that the vital iron ore deposits of Sweden were threatened.

With the British government – unlike Mr Snow – still not certain about what their policy should be, the Soviet Union attacked Finland on 30 November 1939. The Soviets planned on the war lasting a mere twelve days, and the general assumption amongst the Western Allies had been that the Red Army – with nearly a three-to-one advantage in troops – would make short work of the Finns. But they didn't.

Mikhail Timoshenko[79] was a soldier in the Red Army's 44th Ukrainian Division and recalls how effectively the Finns used guerrilla tactics against the invading Soviets: 'In small groups, of say ten or fifteen men, the Finns were sneaking up to our bonfires, firing short bursts from their machine guns and then immediately running away again…when we sent out men to follow the tracks that we'd observed in the snow, they didn't return. The Finns lay in wait for them and killed them all in ambush. We realized that it simply wasn't possible to wage war against the Finns…personally I thought there had been some kind of misunderstanding – the decision made no sense to me. Why had they sent our division where there was no enemy, when it was so dreadfully cold? When people were freezing to death?' Only one in eight of Timoshenko's regiment of four thousand left Finland unharmed.

Meantime, in Britain there was widespread outrage at the actions of the Soviet Union. Unlike the successful Soviet campaign to confuse the West about the true nature of their invasion of eastern Poland, in the case of Finland the moral issues seemed clear. After all, what was the difference between Nazi aggression in Poland and Soviet aggression in Finland? In both instances it was an example of a strong country bullying a smaller one.

Under pressure from public opinion, and still concerned about the possible threat to the rest of Scandinavia, the British government offered some – very limited – help to the Finns in the form of a dozen Blenheim bombers and a potential loan of half a million pounds. But it soon became clear that the Finns would not be able to hold out against the Red Army for any significant length of time. The reason why they were causing the invaders problems in the early months of the war was primarily the weather – and that would soon change. The British assessment was that once the snows melted in the spring the immense manpower superiority of the Red Army would soon tell. As a result, the chiefs of the general staff were asked once again to consider direct military action in support of the Finns.

Rumours of this reached the British Communist Brian Pearce, who had recently enlisted in the Royal Northumberland Fusiliers – and the news put him, he felt, in an extremely difficult position. He had joined up because he believed that 'all Communists are supposed to take part in these wars, they must be where the workers are… the Communists always had contempt for pacifism…. The real thing, of course, is always to be where the workers are, you join the army and, of course, circumstances may arise in which your position in the army may serve the cause of the revolution very well. You know, you might even find yourself in a situation where it's up to the Communists to save the fatherland – all sorts of wonderful things could happen once a war begins.'

Pearce confesses that it 'would have been difficult' had he been sent as a member of the British army to fight Soviet forces in Finland. 'I would have had, I suppose, to cross over…. Obviously the Red Army was our army, and in a situation like that one must do everything for the Soviet Union…. Essentially we were people who had transferred our loyalty to another country. We didn't see it, of course, as another country; it was the headquarters of the world revolution. We were the British section of the Communist International – theirs was the Russian section and they happened to be the ones who made the revolution first and they were therefore in the leading position.'

He even admitted that, had he and other British Communists been called upon to instigate acts of violence in Britain in order to further the Communist cause, then 'I suppose we might have done. It's very difficult to say we wouldn't have done in those days. You know, we were so devoted to the Soviet Union. The Soviet Union was the light of the world, to put it in religious terms. And one could commit many small crimes in order to achieve a greater [goal]…you know, the end justifies the means….'

Fortunately for Brian Pearce, finally the British government decided not to mount a full-scale operation to help the Finns and so he was never placed in a position where he felt he had to desert.

However, several hundred British volunteers who, unlike Brian Pearce, passionately opposed Soviet aggression, did travel to Finland to fight alongside the Finns against the Red Army. But it was all to no avail since, as predicted, once the snow vanished so did the Finns' military advantage. The war ended in March 1940, and the Finns were forced to make peace terms with the Soviet Union along slightly worse lines than the Kremlin had demanded before the conflict started.

It may have been a small war in a far-off country, but it was nonetheless of significance. It demonstrated to keen-eyed members of the German and British High Command the ineptitude of the Soviet military. The German general staff concluded that 'The Soviet "mass" is no match for an army with superior leadership.'[80] And a British military assessment stated bluntly that, if German forces did choose at some point in the future to break the Molotov–Ribbentrop pact and invade the Soviet Union, the Red Army would not be capable of fighting back.[81] These were sentiments that Mikhail Timoshenko of the Red Army endorsed: 'The Germans, naturally enough, came to the conclusion that the Red Army was weak. And in many respects they were right.'

The Finnish war also demonstrated once again the confusion of British policy towards the Soviet Union. The British, as we have seen, sent a small amount of military aid to Finnish forces fighting the Red Army. So were the Soviets an enemy or not? Was Britain fighting – as Mr Snow memorably put it – 'an idealist war against aggression', or something much more traditional? Did the war become somehow more moral when British self-interest – in the form of Swedish iron ore deposits – was threatened? It was a confusion that was still not adequately resolved.

THE FIRST POLISH DEPORTATIONS

In February 1940, while the Finnish war still raged, the Soviets began a series of mass reprisals and deportations in eastern Poland. There were to be four major waves of deportation from Soviet-occupied eastern Poland, each separately motivated. The first began on the night of 10 February 1940 and targeted in particular a group of people against whom Stalin had a personal grudge – veterans of the 1920 war between Poland and the new Bolshevik state, known as Osadniks.

On 2 December 1939 Beria had written to Stalin about the Osadniks in a document marked 'Top Secret'. The report began with a history lesson: 'In December 1920, the former Polish government passed a decree about the settling of so-called Osadniks in border areas of the USSR [Soviet Union]. The Osadniks were chosen exclusively from former Polish military personnel, received land in the amount of 25 hectares together with livestock and equipment and settled next to the Soviet border with Belarus and Ukraine.'[82] Beria considered that the mere existence of these people in eastern Poland was a threat to the Soviet state. He claimed that they 'represent favourable soil for all types of anti-Soviet actions'. And so his conclusion was simple: 'We believe it unavoidable to deport them and their families....' Just two days later he received authorization to carry out this action; all of the Osadniks were to be deported to the remotest reaches of the Soviet Union as forced labour on 'forest developments'.[83] The 'most malicious' of them were to be singled out and separately arrested.

Nikolai Dyukarev was a member of an NKVD unit in the eastern Polish [now Ukrainian] city of Rovno and was one of those charged with carrying out the deportations. 'At the end of 1939 I was given this order to resettle the Osadniks,' he says, 'and we started to count how many families there were.... I was young at the time, only twenty years old. I did not understand much of what was happening – I had my orders from Kiev.' But he knew enough to believe that the Osadniks 'were our enemies. They

opposed the Soviet Union and they were our enemies – they
supported Poland. We knew that local people hated them, they
were rich, they had land, they had everything while other people
were really poor.'

When conducting deportations, the NKVD technique was to
move on their targets with maximum surprise and speed – but
only after a great deal of secret preparation. Nikolai spent weeks
visiting the Osadnik households in his area of operation in the
guise of an 'agricultural expert'. Invited into homes, he would
question the inhabitants about the number of people in their
family, the size of their land and the quantity of their livestock.
Only when all these details had been collected were the NKVD
ready to mount the mass deportation – with every Osadnik
targetted on one single night.

The first that Wiesława Saternus knew of the NKVD operation
was when, in the early hours of 11 February 1940, she heard a
banging on the front door of the house in which she lived with her
father, mother and three brothers and sisters. Her father had
fought in the war against the Bolsheviks twenty years before and
been rewarded with a patch of land in the district of Włodzimierz
Wołyński – they were all, therefore, classed as Osadniks by the
NKVD. Still half asleep, her father opened the door and let the
soldiers in. 'Two of them were very brutal, very aggressive,' says
Wiesława. 'They told my father when they pushed him inside to sit
down on the floor and put his hands over his neck.'

The senior of the three men, whom Wiesława remembers as
being less violent than the other two, announced that the whole
family was to be 'resettled'. Wiesława's grandmother was only
paying a visit to the family and protested that she 'shouldn't have
anything to do with this', but the NKVD officer said 'that doesn't
matter – get your stuff and you'll be resettled.' There was chaos in
the house as Wiesława's mother hurriedly tried to pack what she
could. The children were crying, and watched in terror as the
soldiers searched their father to see if he was hiding anything in his
underwear. One of the soldiers told her sister, Christina, to take a
doll with her – one she had been given for Christmas – but she

pushed it away. 'So he [the NKVD soldier] gave this doll to me,' says Wiesława, 'and told me in Polish – I don't know how he learnt Polish – he told me, "Take this doll with you, because where you are going you won't have this sort of doll." So I must have taken the doll because it was useful later when my mother used it [to barter] to get some food.'

The family were given just half an hour to pack up their belongings before being forced out of the house and on to waiting trucks. They were then taken to the local railway station and packed into freight cars: 'Then they locked the wagons – it was very noisy. I remember that noise, like the knocking on the door at night. I will never forget it. It was like lumps of iron. And we knew then we had been locked in and we were in slavery.' This first deportation took at least 130,000 people – some estimates say nearer 200,000 – to the far north on horrendous journeys that could take weeks. Wiesława Saternus and her family ended up at a logging camp in Siberia. 'The hunger was horrible,' she remembers, 'and it's a strange experience, hunger. It can't be understood by anybody who hasn't experienced it. Real hunger damages a human being – a man becomes an animal.'

'I was responsible for the deportation of one or two villages, I think,' says Nikolai Dyukarev. 'I don't know much about what happened to them. But it was very hard work [to organize the deportations]. It wasn't very pleasant. When I was young it was different, there were orders that had to be obeyed. But now I think about it, it's really hard to take the children away when they're really small and, when you come to think of it, it's not very good. I would rather not talk about it much. And, of course, I knew that they were our enemies, enemies of the Soviet Union, and they had to be "recycled".... I regret it now, but at the time it was different.'

Behind all the actions of the NKVD, as far as Dyukarev and his comrades were concerned, was the almighty figure of the leader of the Soviet Union: 'Well, Stalin was much like a god for everybody. And all of his words were the last word on any subject. You could-n't even think that it wasn't right. One did not doubt it at the time. Every decision that was made was correct. That wasn't only my opinion – we were all thinking like that. We were building Communism. We were obeying orders. We believed.'

In parallel with the deportation of these 'class enemies' went the continual monitoring of the newly Sovietized population of eastern Poland to ensure their compliance with the new political order. There was no freedom of speech, no freedom of religion, no freedom of movement, scarcely any freedom at all. And, above all, the Soviet authorities were determined to eradicate any lingering sense of nationalism.

Galina Stavarskaya[84] discovered personally how the new occupying powers would treat political dissent when, early in the Soviet occupation, she heard banging at the flimsy doors of her small cottage outside Lwów. The NKVD wanted to question her about the activities of a Ukrainian nationalist organization called AON – a political group that was now, of course, illegal. The NKVD believed that Galina, who was nineteen years old, carried messages for them. She was taken to prison in Lwów for interrogation: 'Three men were sitting there. They were strong-looking. They had big hands. Strong arms. And they asked me: "Are you in a secret organization?"

'I said: "No."

'"Are you a member of that organization?"

'"No."

'"What is your role in that organization?"

'I said, "I am not in any organization. How can I have a role if I am not a member of an organization?"

'Then they hit me from the right, then they hit me from the left and then they hit me in the head.... And they also kicked me in the back. They were healthy and well fed. They had, you know, very well-developed biceps.'

When her interrogators grew tired of using their fists, they started hitting Galina with rubber truncheons: 'They were half a metre long...and they started using these sticks. On my neck I had a black scar, like a black stripe, and it would not heal. They hit me and I got those black scars. It was like being in hell.... It is very painful to remember it. They beat me and beat me.... But I told them I would rather die than tell them anything.'

Galina pleaded with her interrogators, saying: 'You know, I am somebody's daughter. I have a mother at home, a father, friends.' But to no avail. 'They got pleasure from hitting me, it gave them pleasure.... They were sadists.... The things they called me. I was just a young girl who had never kissed a man.'

Eventually, as part of the torture, the interrogators yanked out Galina's hair: 'They ripped it out.... How young I was then. My hair was so curly. I had fair hair.'

After her 'interrogation' she was taken to a cell and crammed in with others 'like sardines in a tin'. Once in the cell 'all the other girls helped me. One of them washed me. There was a nun there.... She was very religious and she had very gentle hands. She put her hands on me and comforted me.'

In between sessions of interrogation and torture, Galina slept in the only spare space in the crowded cell – next to the bucket that served as their toilet: 'And we all just urinated around the bucket. Whoever was on cleaning duty had to clean it out. Natalia Shuhevich [a fellow prisoner] couldn't do it. She had only just had breakfast, and then she had to wipe up the urine and she vomited. And that was very tough.'

But whilst the suffering of the inhabitants of eastern Poland at Soviet hands is not generally known in the West, for a variety of reasons another related crime that the Soviets committed around the same time has penetrated the public consciousness. It is a mass murder that is collectively known – somewhat misleadingly – by one word: Katyn.

THE ATROCITY OF KATYN

On 5 March 1940 Stalin,[85] along with his fellow Politburo members Voroshilov, Mikoyan and Molotov, signed in person a proposal from Beria that led to the murder of more than twenty thousand prominent citizens from eastern Poland, many of them officers in the Polish army. The crime first became known to the world in April 1943 when the Germans, who had by then occupied the territory around the Soviet city of Smolensk in Western Russia, discovered a mass grave in a forest called Katyn (in fact one of three separate sites used by the NKVD to bury the bodies of their victims). This discovery was to haunt subsequent dealings between the Western Allies and the Soviet Union.

The crime of Katyn (the name of this one burial site where just over four thousand bodies were found became, confusingly, the name by which the entire crime was known) is significant for a number of reasons; not least because it was somewhat out of character for Stalin and his cronies. For whilst there had been isolated executions of selected groups in the Soviet Union before, certainly nothing on the scale of the extermination of an entire officer corps had ever been attempted. Until Katyn, the 'normal' way in which the Stalinist regime dealt with large groups that were considered dangerous was by deportation. The death rates in the various camps in the Soviet penal system (collectively known as the Gulag) varied, but could be as high as 20 per cent each year. The bulk of the Polish non-commissioned officers and ordinary soldiers captured by the Red Army in the autumn of 1939, for example, were sent to just such a fate.

Georgy Dragunov, as a Red Army officer in occupied eastern Poland, remembers how the deportations were 'not surprising to us because we had seen all this before. I used to live not far from the railway tracks and in the 1930s I kept seeing trains full of people.... I took it as part of the norm – if there were trains full of people sent to Siberia from Moscow, why couldn't there be people like that in western Belarus [part of occupied eastern Poland]. We had been raised to believe that these were enemies of the people and that they had to be deported. Only now, with the benefit of hindsight, I know that these were the best people – but you have to live your life to understand it.' So if deportations were a 'normal' – indeed, an often accepted – part of life in Stalin's Soviet Union, why were these Polish citizens treated differently and murdered en masse?

NKVD documents reveal several possible reasons for the crime. First, the Soviet penal system was stretched almost to breaking point by the sudden influx of Polish prisoners of war in the autumn of 1939 – around a quarter of a million were captured. Indeed, it was such a problem that orders were shortly issued permitting the release of around a third of the captured soldiers. What is significant is that only the most junior ranks were allowed to return home – none of the officers was released. Instead, the latter were mostly incarcerated in three camps – Kozelsk (southeast of Smolensk), Ostashkov (in the Kalinin region) and Sarobelsk (near Kharkov in the eastern Ukraine). Imprisoned alongside the officers were a number of other prominent citizens, such as doctors, lawyers, academics and writers. The NKVD, therefore, was clearly continuing the policy – evident in the opening days of the invasion – of targeting in particular the Polish intelligentsia.

Life in these camps during the autumn, although hardly comfortable, was not particularly oppressive by Soviet standards. The prisoners were inoculated against various diseases such as typhus and smallpox and were allowed to write and receive letters. But an NKVD document of 1 December 1939[86] shows that the Soviet authorities did not now consider these captured Poles as 'normal' POWs – they were categorized as 'counter-revolutionaries'. As such, they were liable to investigation and subsequently 'punishment' for their 'crimes'. NKVD interrogators were sent to the camps and proceeded to question the inmates over several months. They were seeing how cooperative the Poles were, and whether any might be prepared to become communists. But for the most part the Poles remained obstinate – holding firmly to their traditional belief system, rooted in passionate Catholicism, that had been so dear to them in their homeland. As late as the first weeks of 1940, and after the NKVD had completed an assessment of each of the prisoners, it still appears that the assumption within the Soviet security forces was that the Poles would be sent, as normal, to camps within the Gulag system.[87] But suddenly, by 5 March, the policy had changed to one of murder.

We know that Stalin felt passionately – in a wholly negative way – about Poland. And that predisposition to hate and distrust the Poles must have been fanned by the news from Beria in February that the Polish prisoners were, in his judgement, incorrigible. In addition, it is apparent from Stalin's subsequent statements in discussion with the Western Allies that he never had any intention of giving back to any future Polish state the territory the Soviet Union had occupied in the autumn of 1939. In such circumstances, the members of the Polish elite whom the Soviets held were considered particularly dangerous. Most of them had shown no sign that they would act in anything other than a disruptive – probably revolutionary – way if they were ever returned to Soviet occupied eastern Poland.

Another factor that could well have been present in Stalin's mind was his increasing knowledge of the actions and mentality of the Nazis. There had been contact with the Nazis, now occupying western Poland, not only via the work of the border commission, but through the exchange of thousands of prisoners. Members of the Gestapo and the NKVD even met in Lwów in October 1939 to discuss matters of mutual interest, and subsequently Heinrich Himmler, head of the SS, and Merkulov, Beria's deputy, met in Berlin in November 1940. Stalin would therefore have known of the repressive actions that the Nazis were carrying out in western Poland. In a wildly ambitious policy of ethnic cleansing, the Nazis were moving large sections of the Polish population around, deporting hundreds of thousands of people to the eastern portion of their part of Poland whilst incorporating other areas – such as Danzig/West Prussia and the area around Poznań, known to the Nazis as the Warthegau – into the Reich as part of Germany. In addition, the Nazis were confining Polish Jews to ghettos and identifying members of the Polish intelligentsia and removing them to concentration camps. Indeed, new research suggests that some actions – such as the arrest in November 1939 of Polish academics in Kraków by the Nazis, and similar arrests at the same time by the NKVD at universities in Lwów – were actually discussed and coordinated between Nazi and Soviet security functionaries.[88] All of which raises the possibility that Stalin and Beria had observed the radical way the Nazis were reorganizing western Poland and had decided as a consequence to act more radically themselves.

But whilst the precise influence of Nazi behaviour on Soviet mentality is unknown, what is certain from the available evidence is that the Soviets felt clear benefits could be derived from the elimination of the Polish leadership class. It must also have seemed a risk-free course of action – how could the crime ever be discovered? Indeed, if Beria had chosen another murder location further east, instead of the Katyn forest, the crime would never have been made public during the war – perhaps the details might still be secret even today.

So, no doubt secure in the knowledge that they were acting with impunity, Stalin and his colleagues signed the 5 March order. This called for the Poles to be cursorily 'examined by special procedure' and then shot if the investigation found them undesirable. The order extended not only to the slightly fewer than fifteen thousand Poles in the three camps, but also to around eleven thousand citizens of eastern Poland, many of Ukrainian or Belarusian descent, who had been arrested for 'counter-revolutionary activities' and were now held in prisons. The 'examination by special procedure' of the Poles in the POW camps was something of a sham. Almost all of them were condemned to die after their files had simply been read by a committee of three – Merkulov, Bashtakov and Kubulov. Fewer than four hundred of those Poles were spared the executioner's bullet – and virtually all of them had previously said, when asked by the NKVD, that they were prepared to stay in the Soviet Union.

Out of the eleven thousand held in the prisons, just over seven thousand were to be killed. Thus, in total, the Soviets' own figures – not revealed until the fall of Communism – reveal that 21,857 people were executed as a consequence of the 5 March directive.

But whilst it was one thing to give an order to kill thousands and thousands of people, it was quite another to be able to carry it out. And if Stalin and the Soviet leadership were entering new territory by ordering the murder of this number of foreigners so swiftly, then the NKVD operatives were to be even more pressed in attempting to implement the command.

An insight into how the NKVD went about this gruesome task was gained in 1991 when a Russian military prosecutor interviewed General Dmitry Tokarev, former chief of the NKVD for the Kalinin region.[89] He revealed that, together with two other NKVD colleagues, he had been called to a meeting in Moscow in March 1940 and told by Bogdan Kobulov, deputy head of the NKVD, that a decision had been taken by the 'highest echelons' that the Poles were to be shot. Tokarev then asked if he could stay behind after the meeting to have a private word with Kobulov. Once they were alone together, Tokarev claimed he said: 'Never in my life have I ever taken part in such an operation!' But he was told, angrily, by Kobulov that 'we are counting on you!'

Tokarev then returned home and ordered preparations to be made in Kalinin prison for the killings – two rooms were lined with velvet in order to muffle the noise of gunfire. Each prisoner was first to be brought before an NKVD official who would check his name on a list – to ensure they were killing the right person. Next the prisoner would be handcuffed and taken to the adjoining room, where he would be shot in the back of the head. The body would then be removed and the process repeated.

The first transport of Poles from the nearby Ostashkov camp arrived at Kalinin prison in April. 'I should tell you that the first night they brought three hundred people,' revealed Tokarev. 'This was too much. The night was too short and we had to work only at night. Then they started to bring two hundred and fifty people a night.' A number of relatively junior NKVD operatives, including drivers and guards, were told to participate in the killing. One of them, Blokhin, wore a special outfit – a brown leather apron, leather gauntlets and a leather cap. 'This made a horrible impression on me,' said Tokarev. Ironically, the Soviet killers used German pistols – Walthers – because they were more reliable than standard-issue Soviet small arms. But even the superior German weapons became worn out with so much use, and Tokarev remembered that the murderers had to take a 'suitcase' of spare firearms with them. Tokarev revealed that the killing went on for about a month – always at night. Once all the Poles had been murdered in Kalinin prison, a banquet was given to celebrate the 'achievement'. Tokarev claimed that he chose not to attend.

The killing of the Poles from Sarobelsk, the second of the three POW camps, in the Kharkov NKVD prison, followed broadly similar lines. Once again the murders took place at night, and each prisoner was shot individually in the back of the head. Their bodies were then driven away in trucks and buried – like those from Kalinin prison – in a mass grave in the nearby countryside.

But the killings of the Polish prisoners from Kozelsk camp were different. The remote forest of Katyn, which was to be their final resting place, was also the site of the murders. Nina Voevodskaya,[90] who was eleven years old in 1940, remembers seeing the Poles held in train carriages in a siding next to Gnezdovo station, just a few miles from the forest of Katyn. She had been able to enter this forbidden area because her uncle, who was an officer in the NKVD, had said to her and her young sister: 'If you want, I'll show you the Poles.' He escorted them past NKVD guards into the siding where there were several train carriages with 'latticed windows – like barred windows'. 'The Poles were waving hello to us from their train carriages,' she says. 'They were young, dressed in military uniform. I can even now remember how handsome they were.'

Previous reports had suggested that all the Poles were taken immediately from the station to the forest during the night. But one of the prosecutors appointed by the Russian authorities in 1990 to examine the Katyn case confirmed[91] the validity of Nina Voevodskaya's testimony – it now appears that occasionally the killers in the forest could not cope with the volume of people to be shot, so some of the Poles waited in the train siding at Gnezdovo station for a day or so, guarded by the NKVD. And whilst it might appear incongruous that the Poles appeared cheerful to Nina Voevodskaya, this also is consistent with the known history. The consensus amongst the Poles was that they were being taken to a work camp. And there were encouraging signs that they were about to be better treated – each of them had been given food to eat on the train and had been inoculated against illness. And who would bother to give injections to people who were about to be murdered?

From Gnezdovo station the Poles were taken in batches by NKVD trucks into the woods. And it soon became obvious to the locals what was happening there. A Russian farmer, O. Kisseljev,[92] told the Germans in 1943 that: 'In spring 1940, for approximately four to five weeks there were three to four lorries daily driving to the forest loaded with people.... I could hear the shooting and screaming of men's voices.... In my area it was no secret that Poles were being shot by the NKVD.'

No one knows for sure why the Poles were killed in the forest of Katyn rather than shot first in the NKVD prison in the nearby city of Smolensk and then taken to Katyn for burial. But it might be that the presence of a perimeter fence – this had been a secure area for some years – and the fact that there was a small house in the forest that the NKVD could use as a base meant that, uniquely amongst the three murder locations, in this instance it was thought easier to murder the Poles by their graves.

THE APRIL DEPORTATIONS

At the same time as the Polish officers and intelligentsia were murdered at Katyn, Kalinin and Kharkov, their relatives back home in eastern Poland were targeted as well. Shortly after the 5 March order, Beria gained authorization for another NKVD directive – that the mothers, sisters, children and other relations of the murdered citizens from eastern Poland should be deported.

Boguslava Gryniv, whose father had been murdered as a consequence of the 'Katyn' order, and her family heard a rumour that they were to be sent away the night before the NKVD came for them. But her mother refused to try to escape, believing that she was to be taken to be reunited with her husband who had disappeared from prison some months before: 'She immediately said,

"We are going to your father. This will demonstrate our love for your father.""

Some time after midnight on 13 April 1940 they heard a knock at the door. It was an NKVD soldier. And he turned out to be – in the circumstances – a man of some compassion: 'Mother said: "We are ready, here we are."

'He said: "What do you mean?" He went into the storage room and said, "What's all this?"

'Mother said, "It's ours."

'And he said, "Why are you leaving it?"

'He found a large basket in there. He said, "Take this." There was food, oats, everything in there. He opened the cupboards. He said, "Are these yours?" He didn't touch anything himself. He said, "Why aren't you taking this with you?"

'You know, he actually made us take [all these things with us]. He looked around [and said]: "Where is your bedlinen? Where is it? Take your bedlinen." He knew that we were being deported. You see, my mother was an idealist. We were going to suffer alongside my father. I am very grateful to this man who gave us that advice about what to take with us.'

One of the most striking aspects of testimony from deportees is the variety of attitudes they describe amongst the NKVD soldiers. Whilst Boguslava Gryniv was 'grateful' to the man who deported her and her family, Tadeusz Markow[93] had quite the opposite experience. 'We only took bread for breakfast because they told us we would be back for dinner,' he wrote. 'They [also] told us if we put on our worst clothes they would release Daddy.' (A policy of deception which meant, of course, that the best food and clothes remained behind for the NKVD to plunder.)

In the town of Rovno in the far east of occupied Poland, near what had been the border with the Ukraine, another family was awakened by the NKVD that April. Nina Andreyeva[94], a schoolgirl, lived with her widowed mother. Her elder brother, a boy scout, had been arrested the previous autumn. Her story, like that of Boguslava Gryniv, is evidence of the far-reaching consequences of the Katyn massacres, and a reminder that it was not only Polish officers and intellectuals and their relatives who were to suffer as a result of Beria's directive.

The NKVD had come for her brother in the night, six months before: 'It was terrifying because my mother woke me up. There were strangers in the room in military uniform. Yurik [her brother] was standing there in his school overcoat and said good-bye to me. That was the last time we would see him. That was our goodbye.' Her mother desperately searched for news of her son, but all she learnt was that the NKVD had conducted a mass arrest – particularly targeting boy scouts – because a commissar had recently been murdered in a nearby park: 'They were investigating if any one of the boys had participated in the murder. In short, they had arrested all of the boys for "re-education" – because they had been educated in the Polish way. And that meant they were the enemies of Soviet power.'

Like Boguslava Gryniv's family, Nina Andreyeva and her mother were given only twenty minutes to pack once the NKVD arrived to deport them. But unlike Boguslava Gryniv, they were taken away by NKVD soldiers who were less than honest. 'Don't pack a lot,' they told her and her mother. 'Don't bring anything valuable. Don't bring any gold. Don't bring any money if you have any.'

'What was essential?' says Nina. 'Well, I took my doll.'

In common with the others snatched from their homes that April, Boguslava Gryniv, Nina Andreyeva and their families were bundled on board trucks and taken to the nearest railway station to be crammed on to trains to travel east.

The conditions on board were appalling. Boguslava and her mother had to travel in a railway wagon that had two floors built into it, with all the luggage downstairs and the deportees upstairs with their bedding. This meant that everyone was pushed together, unable to stand up. 'Ever since then I have had throm-bosis in my legs from having sat like that for several days,' she says.

'It was very difficult. There was a bucket [for a toilet]. So you had to take some sort of sheet or blanket. Mother would hold it up and you would go behind it. It was very difficult to get used to this. The second thing was, of course, the fact that we could neither wash nor change our clothes. And that was for two whole weeks.... And because what was happening was so emotionally unsettling, all the women began menstruating.

'All the time we were in the wagon we all felt that some great injustice had been done to us. [We had always thought] nobody could touch your own house. A peasant once said: "Nobody will make me less than a peasant...." They thought that if you had land, if you had a house, then it was yours and nobody could ever remove you from your property. When my father built our house, he said: "This is for my children and my grandchildren...." And then suddenly all that was destroyed.'

As she looked around the train wagon, Boguslava realized that she was surrounded by representatives from the entire ethnic spectrum of eastern Poland – although most people were Polish Catholics, there were also Ukrainians and Jews. It was difficult for her to see what any of them had in common. She didn't know, of course, that they were all relatives of people who were in the process of being murdered.

It was the very old and the very young who suffered most on the trains. Nina Andreyeva watched as her neighbour's baby girl died and then the body was flung out of the door by the NKVD guard while the train was still moving. 'It's hard,' says Nina, 'to communicate what a terrifying situation it was.'

The April deportees were sent to a variety of remote places in the Soviet Union, including Siberia and Kazakhstan, although none of them was transported north to the same locations as the February deportees. Because whole families – including breadwinners – had been taken in February, many of them had been sent to forestry work camps. But since the April deportees were largely women and children, they found themselves dumped on isolated collective farms.

The train carrying Nina Andreyeva and her mother arrived late at night, after a journey of more than a week, at a remote station in northern Kazakhstan. Snow and slush lay deep all around them. There was nothing nearby but bleak forests and tundra. The deportees were crammed once more into lorries and began their journey to their final destination. 'We were driven off,' says Nina, '[but] we didn't travel for long. There was a lot of snow. And you know, in the spring the snow gets slushy. And the lorry got stuck in the middle of a field. And what fields they were! Those fields just went on and on in Kazakhstan. Somewhere in the distance there was a forest, and we saw wolves coming out [of the forest]. A pack of wolves.'

Nina and the rest of the deportees watched as the wolves attacked the lorry: 'The lorry was high up, but all the same it was so terrifying, My mother wrapped us up in a rug we had with us and we hid from the wolves. People were crying. People were screaming. The driver dipped a rag in petrol. He lit it and threw it at the wolves.' After the driver threatened the wolves with fire, they dispersed – only to regroup and attack again. 'That went on until morning,' says Nina. 'It was terrifying.'

The next morning a tractor came to pull the truck out of the snow and they continued their journey to a remote collective farm – where there was another surprise awaiting them. There didn't seem to be any village in sight: 'There were no dwellings there. And then smoke appeared…from here…from there…from over here. From all over the snow. And people began to crawl out of these dugouts.'

It was a shocking sight for Nina and her family, who were used to the relative sophistication of city life. But their arrival, already an immensely lowering experience, took another turn for the worse when the leader of the collective farm turned up on his horse: 'He said [to the villagers]: "Don't take any of them in – they are enemies of the people. These are Poles – enemies of the people."' As a result it looked as if the new arrivals would simply be left to die in the forest. But some of the Kazak villagers took pity on the deportees and gave them shelter in a barn, or on the floor of their earth dugouts.

But the woman who took in Nina and her family died a few weeks later of tuberculosis, so the leader of the collective farm turned them out into the cold once again: 'And so my mother

went to the regional centre on foot. It was about seventeen kilometres, maybe even more, I'm not sure…. And they took her on
as an auxiliary nurse at the hospital.'

As a result of the pittance she earned at the hospital Nina's
mother was able to rent a dugout house, together with other
deportees: 'The house was terrible – twelve families lived in that
house. We had a corner of the dugout and just the basket we had
taken with us from home. That was where we slept – and we lived
like that for three years.'

During the first winter, the mother of one of the deportees
who shared the dugout with them died: 'It was a very severe
winter. The frost was so bad that you could not break the ground.
We did not have a graveyard as such. The dead were simply taken
out and buried in the snow. Wild dogs and wolves would eat [the
bodies]. He [the son of the woman who had died] did not want
to do that to his mother. He asked everyone, "Please don't take
offence against me, but I do not want my mother to be torn apart
by wolves. Let her lie here [until the ground thawed and she could
be buried]. She is almost a skeleton anyway. She is like a piece of
wood. She is already completely frozen, so she cannot decom-
pose." And so they laid her out in the corridor – she was placed on
a bench. And we had to walk past her, me on the way to school
and my mother on the way to work.'

Mostly women and children, these deportees had to try to
survive in some of the worst conditions imaginable – and they
lived with the added torment of not knowing what had happened
to their husbands, brothers and fathers. In the Russian archive
rests one scrap of handwritten paper which encapsulates the long-
ing they felt to be a family again. It is a letter written by a little girl
called Krissi Mykunstkoi to 'Our kind dear father Stalin'. 'I am
currently lying ill,' she writes, 'and I'm very sad because I miss my
daddy whom I haven't seen for months. And I thought to myself
that only you, the great Stalin, can return him. He was an engineer, and in the time of war he was called to serve and he was
captured. He is currently in Kozelsk [prison] in the Smolensk
region. We have been moved from Pinska [in eastern Poland] to

the Kazak republic.... Here we have no family. My mother is very weak. Return us our father I beg you with all my heart.'[95] Stalin, not surprisingly, never replied to the little girl's plea.

There are no definitive statistics of just how many people were deported from eastern Poland that April. New work in the Russian archives has produced a figure of just under sixty thousand, but many consider this to be extraordinarily low. The previous estimate of around three hundred thousand still seems, from other evidence, to be nearer the true figure.[96]

Nor are there exact figures of how many people died as a result of the deportations, although the consensus is that around a third of those who were expelled from eastern Poland that April subsequently lost their lives. But what the documents do reveal is the clear connection between the April deportations and the Katyn massacres. After the men had been killed, their families were to be thrown into the frozen wastes of the Soviet Union. These families had committed no offence – even in Soviet eyes – other than to be related to someone who had been murdered. It was obviously a crime of monumental proportions. A crime for which no one has yet been called to account.

ALLIED REACTION TO THE CRIMES

The deportations were no secret, with newspapers in the West carrying accounts of what was happening. 'The Soviet authorities are transporting a large part of the population of Eastern Poland into inner Russia,'[97] reported the *New York Times* of 15 April 1940. 'The exiles get only fifteen minutes to leave their homes...even seriously ill persons are forced into the unheated emigration trains.' The article also talked about the night-time arrests of Poles by the secret police, the horrific conditions in Soviet prisons in eastern Poland and the fact that the region was being systematically robbed of machinery and equipment.

The British government too was well briefed on events in Poland. Sir Howard Kennard, the British ambassador to the Polish government in exile based in London, wrote a report to Lord Halifax, the Foreign Secretary, on 18 May 1940. Kennard records: 'The policy of deportations is once more being carried out on a large scale[98].... The persons arrested largely belong to the intelligentsia and include the wives and families of Polish officers who are now abroad. It is further probable that many schoolboys have also been arrested.... A similar fate hangs over the remaining Poles of the landowning class in the northern parts of the Soviet occupation, and it is all the more terrible as these survivors are mostly women and children, the menfolk of the family being in the main either abroad or in Russian prisons and internment camps.'

Just over two weeks before sending this report, Kennard had warned his Foreign Office colleagues that the Polish government in exile was considering asking the British government to condemn the 'atrocities' taking place in Soviet-occupied Poland, in order to bring home the 'indignation' they felt at these 'barbarous' methods.[99] Kennard said he had told them that he 'thought that it would be extremely difficult to secure our agreement to such a declaration. In the first place the Soviets were not at war with us and, secondly, I felt we would be loath to make any such declaration at this moment.'

A senior Foreign Office official, Sir William Strang, replied to Kennard's note on 14 May, saying that 'we quite agree with the line you took.... It is one thing for the three Allies to issue a joint declaration aimed at Germany, with whom we are all at war, and quite another for them to issue a similar joint declaration aimed at the Union of Soviet Socialist Republics, with whom only the Poles have broken off relations.'[100] The British government thus not only knew about many of the atrocities the Soviets were committing in eastern Poland, but was anxious to say nothing about them – whilst, of course, at the same time openly condemning the Nazis in western Poland for committing similar crimes.

It is not difficult to understand why the Foreign Office took this line, since it was essentially a continuation of the original policy established after the Soviet invasion of eastern Poland in September 1939. It was hard enough being at war with Germany, the British government maintained, without antagonizing the Soviet Union as well. But what this attitude of official silence meant was that the bulk of the British population never properly grasped the parallel between Nazi and Soviet actions in Poland, and that the Soviet leadership in turn came to realize that they were unlikely to be called to account by the international community – even publicly censured – for the crimes they were committing in occupied Poland.

The British attitude was predicated on the belief that the Soviet Union was not an ally of the Nazis at all, but that the Soviets had merely entered into a pact not to attack the Germans. The reality, however, was different. The Soviet Union *was* an ally of the Nazis in all but name, not just providing raw materials to help fuel the German war machine, but even – and this was, for the Soviets, one of the greatest secrets of the war – offering military assistance as well.

SECRET MILITARY HELP TO THE GERMANS

From the autumn of 1939 German merchant ships could be openly seen in Murmansk harbour, in the far north of the Soviet Union, loading up with wheat to take back to the Fatherland. German sailors wandered freely about the city and relaxed in the 'International Club', a wooden house not far from the port area. As a result, and despite official disapproval, relationships developed between some of the Germans and local girls. 'I think,' says Maria Vetsheva,[101] who was a seventeen-year-old in Murmansk at the time, 'it's a usual thing that some seamen came and found girl-friends here.'

But whilst German merchant sailors were fraternizing with the Soviets in Murmansk, there was another, secret, form of maritime cooperation taking place far from the public gaze. It had its origin in a remark Ribbentrop had made during the September 1939 meeting with Stalin and Molotov.[102] The German Foreign Minister had asked if the Soviets could provide a base in Murmansk for the repair of U-boats and, in principle, this had been agreed. But from that moment the Soviet authorities were worried that the British – or anyone else – might discover that they were providing military assistance to the Nazis.

On 5 October Schulenburg, the German ambassador in Moscow, reported that Molotov had decided that Murmansk was not 'isolated enough'[103] for the German naval base; he was now suggesting the remote harbour of Teriberka on the north of the Kola inlet. Six days later the Soviets changed plans once again and offered the nearby bay of Sapadnaja Liza instead. It was shortly confirmed by the Soviet Naval Commissariat that the Germans could use this bay as a base for repairing and supplying U-boats and possibly other naval warships. For security purposes the name of the bay was not to be used in any message – it was henceforth to be known only as 'Basis Nord' (Base North). The German supply ship *Sachsenwald* entered Base North on 1 December 1939, the first of several vessels to be stationed there. Then, on the 9th, in a development that suggested an escalation in the extent of the military cooperation between the two countries, the Soviets asked 'if German steamers going to northern Sweden could take food and fuel for Soviet submarines and then inconspicuously transfer them at sea'[104] in order to assist the Soviet navy in its blockade of Finland. But four days later the Soviets apparently thought better of the idea and withdrew the request.

The Soviet authorities' nervousness about the German military presence in this remote part of the Soviet Union continued to manifest itself in many ways. The Germans, for example, were not permitted to establish their own radio contact with base. All their messages had to be passed through the Soviet guard boat that was anchored in the bay. This proved an extremely inefficient method of communication as the Soviets were not used to writing in Latin letters and often made mistakes. As the weeks went on at Base North, a stultifying atmosphere developed. No U-boats, or any other German military vessels, arrived to be repaired or supplied. The base had been designed to service two submarines, but one was sunk before the base was up and running and the second never had cause to visit – which was perhaps just as well for the Germans since, due to the suspicion and intransigence of the Soviet officials, the supply ships themselves began to run out of supplies.

In mid-April 1940 the Germans were asked to move their base further along the coast to the even more remote Jokanga Bay. Molotov told the German naval attaché in Moscow that the move was necessary because of Soviet fears that Allied aircraft, operating in the wake of the Finnish war, might identify the German ships. When the German liaison officer, Auerbach, visited the new Base North for the first time on 20 May he found his compatriots on the supply ships demoralized. Not only had the promised relief of personnel not taken place but 'the mood grew worse, essentially because Base North had no apparent aim'.[105] Nor were the Soviets sympathetic hosts; on the boat taking him back to Murmansk, Auerbach reported, his Soviet counterpart refused to speak to him. It was all too much for the German, who had a nervous break-down shortly after his visit.

The officials at the German embassy in Moscow believed that it was faults in the Soviet system of governance that were causing the problems, rather than any direct malice from the Kremlin. The German naval attaché wrote that the 'naval Commissariat or some other Soviet departments are afraid of the head of government... they don't want to take responsibility [themselves]'.[106]

Life was grim for the German sailors at Base North. In April 1940 Dr Kampf, doctor on the German supply ship *Phoenicia*, complained in his diary about the 'Russian provisions which were suitable only to a limited extent – extremely salted fish, mouldy stinking reindeer and beef and rancid Russian butter'.[107] The combination of terrible food, immense isolation and the apparent pointlessness of the mission affected the health of the German sailors. On average they each lost more than two stone in weight and were possessed with a 'never-ending tiredness, which let us sleep for sixteen to eighteen hours a day.... In addition there was gum bleeding caused by scurvy...and another strange symptom.... Many had a constant urge to urinate which let them urinate only drop by drop.'[108]

'We feel completely abandoned and lonely,' Dr Kampf wrote on 4 May. 'The surroundings are not very attractive: flat mountains and snow. No tree. No bush.... We have nearly nothing left to drink.... The atmosphere on board is terrible, there are many disputes. Some have written letters of complaint to the commander-in-chief....'[109] And Kampf's view of the leading Soviet official, expressed in his diary entry of 29 May, is equally uncompromising: 'The Russian liaison officer is an unusually evil subject, mistrusts and harasses us whenever possible. And he always uses as an excuse "I first have to ask my High Command." As a lieutenant he gives the impression of a mentally malnourished, disingenuous servant. I am furious.'[110]

The story of Base North is significant, even though it made little contribution to the German war effort (apart from one ship based here which in April left to assist in the successful German invasion of Norway). It is important because its existence shows the schizophrenic attitude of the Soviets towards assisting the Germans. On the one hand, the Soviets undoubtedly provided the Germans with a military supply base; but on the other, ideologically the Nazis remained a possible enemy. So in effect they were allies, and yet they were potential belligerents. In order to please the Germans, the Soviets had to offer them practical help in their war effort and thus make them more powerful still. No wonder the Soviet officials on the ground were confused.

But while Dr Kampf was committing his views to his diary that May, events were taking place 1700 miles southwest of Base North that would result in a radical change in the balance of the relationship between Germany and the Soviet Union, as well as causing consternation amongst the Western Allies.

THE NAZIS ARE WINNING

Stalin's relationship with the Nazis, in the period immediately before and after the signing of the Non-Aggression Pact, was underpinned by one basic assumption – that any attempted German conquest of

France would be a protracted affair. Hitler would thus be far too occupied in the West to be able to turn his attention on the Soviet Union. But Stalin's assumption turned out to be woefully wrong.

On 10 May 1940, in pursuit of Fall Gelb (Plan Yellow), German forces advanced through the forests of the Ardennes in Belgium towards France. In one of the most dramatic military operations in history, and thanks in part to the dashing exploits of tank commanders such as Guderian and Rommel, German units managed to encircle whole Allied armies. By 16 May, with the fall of Sedan, the road to Paris lay open.

In London, following the disastrous British campaign in Norway, Neville Chamberlain had resigned as Prime Minister to be replaced by Winston Churchill. It thus fell to Churchill to lead Great Britain through one of the lowest points – if not the single lowest point – in the nation's history. In the last days of May, with the Germans on the northern coast of France and hundreds of thousands of Allied troops trapped at Dunkirk, it seemed as if little would shortly be left to defend Great Britain – except the English Channel.

Churchill later wrote in his memoirs: 'Future generations may deem it noteworthy that the supreme question of whether we would fight on alone never found a place on the War Cabinet agenda.'[111] But the truth was not so simple. In fact, in May 1940 the Foreign Secretary, Lord Halifax, suggested in the War Cabinet that an attempt be made to ask Mussolini to approach Hitler to find out what terms might be on offer. Churchill, according to the War Cabinet minutes of 27 May, went so far as to say that 'If Herr Hitler was prepared to make peace on the terms of the restoration of German colonies and the overlordship of central Europe, that was something he was prepared to accept, but he rightly thought such an offer most unlikely.'[112]

Churchill was performing a careful balancing act – he didn't want Halifax to resign, but he didn't want to pursue a negotiated peace either. He argued that, if peace was to be sought with Hitler, then 'the position would be entirely different when Germany had made an unsuccessful attempt to invade this country'. Churchill said he believed that Hitler would never let Britain carry on rearming once a peace treaty had been signed and that the country would be 'completely at his mercy. We should get no worse terms if we went on fighting, even if we were beaten, than were open to us now.' And in response to Halifax's view that there was nothing wrong with 'trying out the possibilities of mediation', Churchill stated that 'nations which went down fighting rose again, but those which surrendered tamely were finished'.

Then, on the evening of 28 May, Churchill went to the House of Commons to talk to his larger Cabinet – twenty-five strong. According to Hugh Dalton, Minister of Economic Warfare, Churchill made no secret of the gravity of the position in which Britain found itself. British troops had been forced to the French coast and would have to be rescued – perhaps a hundred thousand could be taken from the beaches. Churchill then said that 'I have thought carefully in these last days whether it was part of my duty to consider entering into negotiations with That Man [Hitler]. But it was idle to think that, if we tried to make peace now, we should get better terms than if we fought it out. The Germans would demand our fleet – that would be called disarmament – our naval bases, and much else. We should become a slave state, though a British Government which would be Hitler's puppet would be set up – under Mosley [British fascist leader] or some such person. And where should we be at the end of all that? On the other side we have immense reserves and advantages. And I am convinced that every one of you would rise up and tear me down from my place if I were for one moment to contemplate parley or surrender. If this long island story of ours is to end at last, let it end only when each one of us lies choking in his own blood upon the ground.'[113]

After he had spoken these words, wrote Churchill later, 'Quite a number seemed to jump up from the table and come running to my chair, shouting and patting me on the back. There is no doubt that had I at this juncture faltered at all in the leading of the nation I should have been hurled out of office. I was sure that every Minister was ready to be killed quite soon, and have all his family and possessions destroyed, rather than give in.'[114]

It was one of the most decisive moments of the war – perhaps the most decisive. If Churchill had wavered and agreed with Halifax that exploratory discussions about a possible peace could be pursued, it is hard to see how Britain would have continued to stand solidly and squarely against the Nazis. And peace with Britain – no doubt along the emasculating lines that Churchill had predicted – was exactly what Hitler wanted. Indeed, the Führer would ask in bewilderment a number of times during the rest of the war why Britain had not acted 'rationally', as he thought, and made peace.

Churchill can rightly be criticized for many of his later actions, but nothing takes away from the power of this one moment, in the House of Commons on 28 May 1940, when this one man gave defiant voice to righteousness, and in the process saved the independence of Great Britain. But what is also significant about this period of crisis – and often overlooked – is that Churchill believed at the time that an absolute precondition of Britain's ability to prosecute the war was the help of America. 'If this country was left by the United States to its fate,' he wrote to President Roosevelt on 18 May, 'no one would have the right to blame those then responsible if they made the best terms they could for the surviving inhabitants.'[115]

While Churchill was trying to rally support for Britain's cause, both at home and across the Atlantic, Stalin learnt with astonishment of the swift capitulation of the French. After news that the Germans had entered Paris reached Moscow on 17 June, he plaintively remarked: 'Couldn't they put up any resistance at all?'[116] Stalin's policy of standing back while Germany and France fought it out on the Western Front now lay shattered before him. Hitler was the master of continental western Europe. Only the British held out against him. And who was to say how long they would last?

Stalin's response to this worrying new development was to redouble Soviet efforts to assist the Nazis. The flow of raw material from the Soviet Union to Germany increased over the following months as he sought to demonstrate to Hitler that the Nazis could have all they needed from the Soviet Union without the necessity of war. What Stalin didn't know, of course, was the continuing depth and intensity of Hitler's hatred of Communism in general and the Soviet Union in particular. At a meeting with his military commanders on 31 July 1940 at the Berghof, the Führer's ideological conviction fused with practical necessity as he performed an astonishing volte-face and announced that German armed forces must plan for an attack on the Soviet Union.

Hitler's somewhat twisted reasoning went like this: British hopes of victory rested on the fact that the Red Army might one day offer them military assistance. So the elimination of the Soviet Union would mean that Britain would no longer have any reason to carry on fighting. It was, of course, a flawed piece of logic from the first. Britain relied on American assistance to continue fighting, not the fantasy of some eventual Soviet involvement. But the fundamental military assumption behind Hitler's words – that the Soviet Union could be crushed with relative ease – was not questioned by his military commanders. Not least because they had just defeated 3 million French soldiers – members of, in Nazi racial terms, a 'civilized' army. What opposition could the 'Bolshevik hordes' possibly provide? Then there was the question of timing. Although the Nazis were now in the ascendancy, there was no guarantee that this situation would last indefinitely. 'We knew that in two years' time,' says Hubert Menzel,[117] then a major in the General Operations Department at German army headquarters, 'that is by the end of 1942, beginning of 1943, the English would be ready, the Americans would be ready, the Russians would be ready too, and then we would have to deal with all three of them at the same time.... We had to try to remove the greatest threat from the East.... At the time it seemed possible.'

Given the subsequent destruction of much of the German army on the Eastern Front, it is easy to read into Hitler's decision to invade the Soviet Union a sense of hubristic zaniness – almost madness. But Major Menzel reminds us that at the time it wasn't perceived that way by many Germans. Yes, Hitler was influenced by ideological considerations, but in addition he demonstrated to his army commanders that the timing was right to attack the Soviet Union.

Those officers were also aware that this was not the first occasion in their lifetime when Germany had invaded the East. During the First World War the German army had conquered much of Belarus and the Ukraine. Lenin had subsequently been forced to agree at the 1918 Treaty of Brest-Litovsk to accede to German influence over not just the Ukraine and Belarus but also Poland, Finland, Latvia, Lithuania and Estonia. The fact that the defeat of Germany later that year had led to the dismemberment of this hugely advantageous deal only served to imbue the Brest-Litovsk agreement with the rosy glow of nostalgia for the Nazis. If the Germans had conquered the East once in recent memory – and in the process forced the embryo Soviet state to a humiliating peace – why couldn't they do it again?

The invasion of the Soviet Union also offered the solution to an increasingly irksome problem for the German leadership – their continued dependence on Soviet raw materials. Hitler and many leading Nazis found it almost intolerable that the future of Germany was dependent on Stalin's continued good will. As Walter Funk, the Nazis' Economic Minister, put it, Germany should not be 'dependent upon forces and powers over whom we have no influence'.[118]

THE VOYAGE OF THE *KOMET*

In the wake of the Nazi conquest of France, Stalin continued with his policy of appeasement. And one dramatic form this attempt to please his powerful neighbour took was a secret and extraordinary act of military cooperation that centred on a German ship called the *Komet*.

Apparently a normal merchant vessel, the *Komet* was actually an auxiliary cruiser armed with 5.9-inch guns, several anti-aircraft guns and a number of torpedoes, modelled on the successful Q-ships of the First World War. These vessels had been disguised as normal merchant ships in order to lure enemy submarines to the surface – submarine commanders preferred to attack unarmed merchantmen with their deck gun rather than waste a valuable torpedo. Once the submarine was on the surface, the hidden armament of the Q-ship would be revealed and the submarine sunk.

In the summer of 1940, while Hitler's generals digested the news that their Führer wished Germany to invade the Soviet Union, the *Komet* attempted one of the most daring of all wartime sea journeys.[119] Starting north of the Kola inlet, the captain of the ship, Rear Admiral Robert Eyssen, planned to sail around the top of the Soviet Union and emerge in the Pacific Ocean, where he would be able to conduct surprise attacks on Allied merchant ships. This route, known as the Northern Passage, was fraught with danger and only possible with the help of powerful icebreakers. After a month spent at various anchorages in Soviet waters, including the original proposed site for Base North at Teriberka Bay, the *Komet* set sail on the morning of 13 August 1940. By the 19th they had entered the ice-strewn Siberian Sea. 'The task was a challenge to us,' says Karl-Hermann Müller,[120] who was a member of the crew. 'We knew it could go wrong, but in every situation we were prepared to make a sacrifice.'

On 26 August, Rear Admiral Eyssen met with two Soviet pilots and two officers on the icebreaker *Stalin*. The German High Command records reveal that 'After a chat about the ice and the *Komet*'s ice reinforcement, its speed etc., they all went to the maphouse to judge the situation on a map.... At six in the morning Eyssen and Kropesch [the other German officer with him] have to drink water glasses full of vodka....'[121] The cooperation between the Soviet sailors and the Germans was amicable. 'The Russians were quiet, calm and factual,' says Müller. 'The relationship was good.... We liked them. We saw they were good people. There were no difficulties, no excitement.'

And although the *Komet* was disguised as a merchantman, its armament hidden, the Soviets knew that this was a military ship. 'Certainly [they knew],' says Müller. 'We only had military crew... they were walking round in uniform.' Nor did the Soviets appear neutral when it came to the course of the war. Not only were they physically aiding the German war effort by helping the passage of the *Komet*, but when the crew of the German ship celebrated news of a successful attack on the British, Müller witnessed how 'the Russians were happy about that as well. They joined us in that [the celebrations]. You can't fake that. That was real. They were genuine. The Russians were on our side, you can say that.'

However, on 1 September the captain of one of the accompanying icebreakers, the *Kaganovich*, came on board the *Komet* to explain that, since both American and Japanese vessels had been seen in the Bering Strait, he had received orders from Moscow not to escort the *Komet* further but to accompany the ship back. 'I took it very calmly without showing any excitement or disappointment,' recorded Eyssen.[122] 'But inside me I felt totally different. To go through all this and now very soon there will be free water in front of me. Only 400 sea miles and I would be through! And now to turn around! This is no option, even if I have to act on my own against an order of the High Command of the Navy.'

The next day Eyssen reiterated his desire to press on and even went so far as to sign a document absolving the captain of the *Kaganovich* of responsibility for any subsequent problems. The Soviets then accompanied the *Komet* for another day or so before turning back. 'There was a friendly farewell,' says Karl-Hermann Müller. 'We hooted and signalled with our ship.'

The Soviets had guided the *Komet* through the worst of the ice, and a couple of days later the Germans emerged on their own into the Bering Sea at the far eastern end of the Soviet Union. The Northern Passage had been completed in a record twenty-three days. 'I'm proud that I fulfilled my mission and we were the first German ship through the Siberian Sea path to the East,' says Karl-Hermann Müller. 'It wouldn't have been possible without the help of the [Soviet] icebreakers.' The *Komet* was now free to roam the sea lanes of the Pacific, attacking and sinking Allied vessels at will. In total the *Komet* destroyed nine ships during its months on the far side of the world, including the large food and passenger transport vessel *Rangitane*, before returning to Germany via the more conventional route around the Cape of Good Hope at the southern tip of Africa.

The German Kriegsmarine, responsible for the naval aspects of the war, was grateful to the Soviets for their assistance both with Base North and with the *Komet*'s passage. So much so that Grand Admiral Raeder wrote a thank you letter to the Commissar for Naval Matters, Admiral Kusnezow, on 16 September 1940. In it he explained that as a result of the successful German occupation of Norway it was no longer necessary to maintain Base North – explicitly stating that the 'use of the Russian bay' had been for 'German naval warfare purposes'. He also mentioned that Base North had been 'of immense value to German naval warfare' and ended the letter by writing: 'It falls to me to have the honour of expressing the German Navy's sincerest thanks to you, esteemed Commissar, for your invaluable support.' The letter was hand-delivered to Admiral Kusnezow by the German military attaché in Moscow, Baumbach, who recorded that Kusnezow received the letter with 'satisfaction'. Baumbach then told the Soviet admiral that he had been asked also to thank him in person for the 'help of the Soviet Navy in the Northern passage of our ship'.[123]

It is no wonder, given all this gushing gratitude from the Germans, that both the existence of Base North and the details of the assistance given to the *Komet* were subsequently deeply embarrassing incidents for the Soviets. After the German invasion of their country in June 1941 the fact that – beyond question – the Soviet government had rendered direct and effective military assistance to the Nazis was potentially explosive information. Even today this is still a sensitive and inconvenient part of Russian wartime history.

MOLOTOV IN BERLIN

But despite the warm sentiments of Admiral Raeder's letter, and Stalin's attempts at appeasement, tension and uncertainty remained beneath the surface in the relationship between Germany and the

Soviet Union. Stalin's own anxieties, occasioned as we have seen by the unexpected and swift German conquest of France, showed in the alacrity with which he accepted a German invitation in October 1940 for Molotov, his Foreign Minister, to visit Berlin for discussions on the way forward. Since the summer Stalin had dared to think that – just perhaps – the Germans might be planning to act Soviet Union.

The coincidence of interests that had permeated the two meetings over the Non-Aggression Pact the previous year had all but evaporated. In its place lay suspicion. For the Soviets that suspicion crystallized on German intentions regarding the fate of the buffer states between them – Hungary, Romania and especially Bulgaria – plus the overwhelming importance of ensuring that Soviet ships had free passage through the Dardanelles, the narrow stretch of water between the Black Sea and the Mediterranean. The Soviets were almost obsessed with the question of these Straits, which were currently controlled by neutral Turkey. It was an obsession based in history – Russia had been threatened a number of times in the last two hundred years by foreign incursions through the Straits, most notably during the Crimean War in the 1850s.

So as Molotov left Moscow in November 1940, he was on a mission of discovery, tasked by Stalin with finding answers to a series of practical questions about German intentions in eastern Europe and the Balkans. He was specifically forbidden to get involved in detailed negotiations, particularly on the matter of future Soviet foreign policy. The Soviet intention was that all these bigger issues should be discussed at a subsequent conference, perhaps with Ribbentrop returning to Moscow for direct talks with Stalin.

Hitler, on the other hand, had very different aspirations for the Molotov meeting. Although in July he had called for plans for an invasion of the Soviet Union, this still remained only one possible course of action – but almost certainly the one he most favoured. The Germans wanted to use the Molotov meeting to see if the Soviets could be persuaded to leave the eastern European states in German control and divert their attention to the Persian Gulf and the Indian Ocean. In these warmer climes, the Nazi leadership believed, Soviet foreign policy could happily prosper, snatching territory and influence at the expense of the British Empire.

There also remained the question of the Soviet commitment to the delivery of raw materials. What could the Soviets do to reassure Hitler and his colleagues that they would remain reliable partners for the foreseeable future?

These were the issues that concerned both sides as Molotov arrived in Berlin on the morning of 12 November. He and his personal entourage were greeted at the Silesian station by Ribbentrop and an honour guard of German soldiers, and later that same day Molotov met Hitler for the first time. This first meeting – like the subsequent ones on this trip – was not a success. Molotov, unlike Hitler, was a man of detail. Precisely and unemotionally Molotov asked a series of questions about Germany's intentions. Why were German troops in Finland? Why were German troops in Romania? What were German intentions in the Balkans? What would be Germany's response if the Bulgarians requested Soviet troops in their country?

Hitler was clearly exasperated by this detailed litany. He was a man who wanted to deal with the epic, and here he was being quizzed by a small, shabby Russian. Why, Hitler must have thought, was Molotov not quaking at the sight of German power? The very surroundings of the new Reich Chancellery, where the meeting was held, spoke of Hitler's grandiose vision. He had told Albert Speer, his favourite architect, that he had wanted a building to impress visiting diplomats. 'Hitler especially liked the long tramp that state guests and diplomats would now have to take before they reached the reception hall,'[124] wrote Speer. In fact, to reach the German leader, Molotov had been obliged to traverse a shiny marble-floored gallery twice as long as the Hall of Mirrors in Versailles. 'That's exactly right,' Hitler had said when Speer told him of his plans for the floor. 'Diplomats should have practice in moving on a slippery surface.' Speer recalled how Hitler especially liked his study in the new building: 'He was particularly pleased by an inlay on his desk representing a sword half drawn from its sheath. "Good, good [said Hitler]...when the diplomats sitting in front of me at this desk see that, they'll learn to shiver and shake."'

But Molotov was most certainly not 'shivering and shaking' in front of Hitler. And in response to the Soviet Foreign Minister's questions, Hitler betrayed his annoyance by swiftly parrying Molotov's enquiries – German troops had been in Finland only as part of the military action against Norway, the Bulgarians would never ask for Red Army troops, and so on. Hitler was only interested in the bigger picture, declaiming that the British were beaten and would soon sue for peace. So was the Soviet Union interested in joining the Axis Pact which had been agreed in September 1940 between Germany, Japan and Italy? With Britain out of the way, the whole of the British Empire would lie waiting to be despoiled. Was the Soviet Union interested in receiving its share?

It was a true dialogue of the deaf, as Molotov refused to be drawn into answering any of Hitler's wide-ranging questions. Instead, he responded with still more detailed queries about immediate German intentions. Pavlov, the Soviet interpreter, subsequently described the talks as 'tiresome and obviously pointless,'[125] and it is hard to disagree with his verdict.

In later discussions with Ribbentrop on the same visit, Molotov continued in similar vein. What exactly did Germany intend with Poland? What were German views on Swedish neutrality, on Hungary and on Yugoslavia?

Ribbentrop protested that he was being 'questioned too closely'.[126] Like the Führer, he wanted to return to the 'decisive' question, which was 'whether the Soviet Union was prepared and in a position to cooperate with Germany in the great liquidation of the British Empire.... Compared to this great basic issue all others were completely insignificant and would be settled automatically as soon as an overall understanding was reached.'[127]

The meeting culminated in the farce of Ribbentrop and Molotov closeted in a bomb shelter during a British air raid. While Ribbentrop continued to describe how the British Empire was ripe for plunder, Molotov remarked: 'You say that England is defeated. So why are we sitting here now in this air raid shelter?'[128]

The relationship between the two countries was clearly splitting apart. Hitler's obsession with pushing the Soviet Union into participating in the future dismemberment of the British Emprie was an obvious ploy to see if Stalin could be persuaded to turn his gaze away from potential conflict with the Nazis in Europe. Molotov did not pursue Hitler's offer, and his series of awkward questions demonstrated only the fragility of the relationship. Thus Hitler became certain that he was right to push forward with plans to conquer the Bolsheviks and take what he needed by force, and the formal directive for the invasion of the Soviet Union was issued on 18 December.

As for Stalin, he saw little option but to maintain the relationship with Hitler as best he could. But already, amongst his comrades in the Politburo, there were small signs that some of them believed misjudgements had been made about the friendship with the Nazis. Perhaps, for example, it had been hasty to eliminate so much of the Polish officer corps, given that if war came with Germany, the Poles might turn from enemies into allies.

That seems to have been the view expressed by the NKVD boss Beria at a bizarre dinner party held in the Lubyanka prison in Moscow in October 1940. Beria was discussing the setting up of a Polish army, loyal to the Soviet Union, with a small number of Polish officers who had demonstrated their sympathy with Communism and had therefore (unbeknownst to them) escaped the massacre at Katyn and the other murder sites. The chief Polish collaborator, Colonel Berling, asked if it would be possible to get a number of officers released from the camps in order to help form the new army. Beria, who obviously knew that virtually all the other officers had been murdered, replied: 'We have committed a great blunder.' He then repeated the same sentiment, saying: 'We have made a great mistake; we have made a great mistake.'[129]

THE AMERICANS HELP

The day before Hitler issued the formal directive to invade the Soviet Union, a momentous event that would have major repercussions on the course of the war and the relationship between the great powers took place across the Atlantic. It was at a press conference on 17 December 1940 that President Franklin Roosevelt first raised the possibility of aid to the beleaguered British war effort via a system of economic help that became known as 'Lend Lease'.

As we have seen, it had been obvious to Churchill from the moment he became Prime Minister that without American aid Britain could not continue the war. In one of his most famous letters to Roosevelt, dated 31 July 1940, Churchill had pleaded with the President to provide the British with military help, saying that 'in the long history of the world this is a thing to do now'.[130] By September that year this plea had crystallized into a deal whereby Britain was to receive fifty old American destroyers in exchange for allowing the United States the right to use a number of British possessions – mostly in the West Indies – as military bases. It was a good deal from the American point of view – and it needed to be if Roosevelt was to convince his sceptical countrymen to accept it. Whilst most of the American public wanted to help Britain, the majority also wanted to stay out of the war and, in the summer of 1940, didn't believe that Britain could ever win.[131]

Roosevelt's desire to provide more aid beyond the destroyers-for-bases deal was made especially difficult by the fact that Britain was fast running out of money. Lord Lothian, the British ambassador to Washington, put the issue succinctly on 23 November 1940 when he announced to American journalists: 'Well, boys, Britain's broke. It's your money we want.'[132]

Hence Roosevelt's dramatic announcement at his 17 December press conference.[133] 'Now, what I am trying to do is to eliminate the dollar sign,' he said. 'That is something brand new in the thoughts of practically everybody in this room, I think – get rid of the silly, foolish old dollar sign.... Well, let me give you an illustration,' he continued. 'Suppose my neighbour's home catches fire, and I have a length of garden hose four or five hundred feet away. If he can take my garden hose and connect it up with his hydrant, I may help him to put out his fire. Now, what do I do? I don't say to him before that operation, "Neighbor, my garden hose cost me $15; you have to pay me $15 for it." What is the transaction that goes on? I don't want $15 – I want my garden hose back after the fire is over. All right. If it goes through the fire all right, intact, without any damage to it, he gives it back to me and thanks me very much for the use of it. But suppose it gets smashed up – holes in it – during the fire; we don't have to have too much formality about it, but I say to him, "I was glad to lend you that hose; I see I can't use it any more, it's all smashed up." He says, "How many feet of it were there?" I tell him, "There were 150 feet of it." He says, "All right, I will replace it." Now, if I get a nice garden hose back, I am in pretty good shape. In other words, if you lend certain munitions and get the munitions back at the end of the war, if they are intact and haven't been hurt – you are all right; if they have been damaged or have deteriorated or have been lost completely, it seems to me you come out pretty well if you have them replaced by the fellow to whom you have lent them.'

It was an idea that caught the imagination of many American and British citizens. Roosevelt's folksy analogy cleverly played on the 'neighbourliness' of the two countries, and the American frontier-like quality of helping a friend in need. Only a few cynics pointed out what seems obvious today – that it was highly unlikely that any military equipment sent to the British would ever be returned. The Americans weren't lending a hose, they were lending goods that were all too likely to be consumed. But regardless, it was Lend Lease that allowed Britain to carry on fighting the war.

It was an arrangement that should not have come as a surprise to either Stalin or Hitler, since Roosevelt had consistently made the feelings of his administration clear about both repressive regimes. Nine months before, in February 1940, he had sent Sumner Welles, acting Secretary of State, on a fact-finding mission to Europe – chiefly memorable for Welles's disastrous meeting with Ribbentrop. The German Foreign Minister lectured him for two hours 'glacially...without the semblance of a smile...eyes continually closed'.[134] His verdict on Hitler's Foreign Minister was simple: 'Ribbentrop has a completely closed mind...a very stupid mind...I have rarely seen a man I disliked more.'

And whilst Welles's experience confirmed Roosevelt's views about the impossibility of a satisfactory deal with Hitler to end the war, the actions of the Soviet Union had demonstrated to the American President that Stalin was scarcely a statesman who respected the rule of law either. Roosevelt had been outraged at the Soviet invasion of Finland and, on 10 February 1940, had spoken to the pro-Communist Youth Congress of America about his feelings on the subject: 'I, with many of you, hoped that Russia would work out its own problems, and that its government would eventually become a peace-loving, popular government with a free ballot, which would not interfere with the integrity of its neighbors. That hope is today either shattered or put away in storage against some better day. The Soviet Union, as everybody who has the courage to face the fact knows, is run by a dictatorship as absolute as any other dictatorship in the world. It has allied itself with another dictatorship, and it has invaded a neighbor so infinitesimally small that it could do no conceivable possible harm to the Soviet Union, a neighbor which seeks only to live at peace as a democracy, and a liberal, forward-looking democracy at that.'[135]

These were unequivocal views – particularly from a statesman who had a predisposition towards equivocation. And Stalin would have noted them.

STALIN'S DILEMMA

It all added up to a disturbing picture for the Soviet dictator at the end of 1940. The Americans were hostile to the Soviet Union and, although unlikely to enter the war in the near future, were still prepared to supply sufficient aid to enable the British to carry on resisting the Germans, even if not enough to let them conceivably win the war; and Germany was in the ascendancy, systematically turning the eastern European countries between the Nazis and the Soviets into puppet or vassal states.

As a result of all this, one over-arching question dominated Stalin's mind – what would Hitler do next? It was clear that one possibility was a terrifying one – invade the Soviet Union. By the end of 1940 nearly three-quarters of the German army was encamped along the Soviet Union's eastern border – and Stalin knew all about it. He was receiving regular intelligence reports that revealed Hitler's intention to attack. The agent 'Meteor', for example, wrote that Karl Schnurre, who ran the Economic Division of the German Foreign Office, had said that Hitler 'intended to solve the issue in the East by military means'.[136] And Anatoly Gurevich,[137] head of Soviet military counter-intelligence in France and Belgium, sent reports back to Moscow in early 1941 saying explicitly that 'the war had to start in May 1941'.

But Stalin was not predisposed to believe these reports. It would scarcely be in Hitler's interests, he thought, to start a war against the Soviet Union when he had not yet finished a war against Great Britain. The Soviet dictator believed that the forces ranged against him in the East were designed to threaten rather than to fight. Since Stalin's views were well known to those around him, perhaps inevitably they coloured the interpretation of the intelligence material presented to him. A spiral of self-deception developed inside the Kremlin. The more obvious the reports of a possible invasion grew, the more likely were they to be dismissed as blatant disinformation. As Stalin saw it, the British wanted to provoke a war between the Soviet Union and Germany out of their own narrow self-interest, so any report that came from a source connected to the West was automatically tainted.

An element in Stalin's reasoning was simply wishful thinking. War games conducted by the Red Army in January 1941 demonstrated that Soviet forces were inadequate to hold any German advance at the borders of the Soviet Union and then conduct a counter-attack into enemy territory – the tactic of 'active defence' on which Soviet military theory was then based. The Red Army, weakened by the purges of the 1930s in which thousands of experienced military personnel had been removed from their posts, was simply not in a position to fight the Germans and win.

Aware of the failings of his armed forces, Stalin was anxious lest any obvious attempt at military preparation by the Red Army to meet a potential German attack be considered a provocation by Hitler and thus render the Soviet Union still more vulnerable. The only practicable way forward, Stalin believed, was to appease the Germans and negotiate additional diplomatic support. That was the thinking behind both the Non-Aggression Pact concluded with Japan on 13 April 1941, and of Stalin's embarrassing behaviour at a Moscow railway station the same day when, while saying goodbye to Matsuoka, the Japanese Foreign Minister, he spotted Colonel Hans Krebs of the German embassy and embraced him, saying, 'We will be your friends – whatever will come!' Stalin was visibly under immense strain. Two days later Colonel Krebs wrote to a colleague in Berlin about the incident, remarking that 'Stalin seemed to me, compared to the earlier encounters, aged. His hair was totally grey; the colour of his face looked very unhealthy. His left eye was, from time to time, closed. It can't be ruled out that Stalin was under the influence of alcohol....'[138]

The situation worsened still further once the German army had brushed aside any resistance and conquered both Greece and Yugoslavia by the end of April 1941. Somewhat belatedly, on 5 May, Stalin tried to buoy up the enthusiasm of his armed forces at a talk he gave in the Kremlin to new graduates of the Soviet military academy. 'Now that we are strong,' he told them, 'we must now go from defence to attack. In fully defending our country, we are obliged to act offensively. We most move from defence to a military policy of offensive action. We must reorganize our propaganda, agitation, and our press in an offensive spirit. The Red Army is a modern army, and a modern army is an army of attack.' This speech has sometimes been misinterpreted as evidence of Stalin's desire to attack the Germans. But it was not. It merely restated existing Soviet military theory that in the event of an attack, the Red Army should push forward in an attempt to conduct the war on enemy soil. Stalin was furious with his generals, Zhukov and Timoshenko – who were among those who had misunderstood his 5 May speech – when on the 15th they presented him with a plan to launch a pre-emptive strike into the mass of German forces on their border. 'Have you gone mad, do you want to provoke the Germans!' demanded Stalin. 'Timoshenko is healthy and has a large head but his brain is evidently tiny.... If you provoke the Germans on the border, if you move forces without our permission, then bear in mind heads will roll.'[139]

The Soviets did all they could to prove to the Germans that they were more valuable as friends than as enemies. They continued to deliver huge amounts of raw materials to the Germans (including 232,000 tons of petroleum and 632,000 tons of grain[140] in the first four months of 1941 alone), even though the Soviet economy was creaking under the strain. In return the Soviets were contracted to receive payment from the Germans, sometimes in the form of goods to the same value or technical aid, like the plans for a new battleship; but that was scarcely compensation for the massive loss to the Soviets in practical terms.

Stalin's nervous state had only been heightened by the news that on 10 May, Rudolf Hess, Hitler's deputy, had flown to Scotland. As Stalin saw it, this was obvious evidence that a secret peace treaty was in prospect between the Germans and the British. It was actually nothing of the kind and it transpired that Hess was deranged. But that was not how it appeared to the Soviet leader at the time. The British had, unwittingly, fuelled Stalin's paranoia three weeks before Hess's flight to Britain. On 18 April the British ambassador to Moscow, Sir Stafford Cripps, had written to Stalin and Molotov that 'it was not outside the bounds of possibility, if the war were protracted for a long period, that there might be a temptation for Great Britain (and especially for certain circles in Great Britain) to come to some arrangement to end the war on the sort of basis which has recently been suggested in some German quarters'.[141] Cripps had meant his letter to alert the Soviet leadership to the dangers of not forming an alliance with Great Britain against the Germans. But it had precisely the reverse effect, making Stalin believe that the British were conducting some secret deal with the Germans behind his back – a fear that Hess's arrival in Scotland only served to intensify.

Stalin now clung almost irrationally to the belief that he was not witnessing evidence of an imminent German invasion. Less than a week before the Germans launched their attack against the Soviet Union, Stalin examined a report from Merkulov, People's Commissar for State Defence, which could not have been more explicit: 'A source working in the German Aviation Headquarters reports: 1. Germany has concluded all necessary measures for war in preparation for an armed assault against the USSR and an attack can be expected at any moment.' Stalin scribbled these words across the document: 'Comrade Merkulov, you can send your "source" from his position on the staff of the German Air Force to fuck his mother. He is not a "source" but a disinformant.'[142]

There has been a recent tendency to 'relativize' Stalin's behaviour around this time – in other words, not to blame him as much as before; certainly not as much as Winston Churchill, who described Stalin and his advisers as 'the most completely outwitted bunglers of the Second World War'.[143] And, yes, it is true that events were not straightforward at the time, and, as Marshal Zhukov subsequently put it: 'There is nothing simpler than providing a new interpretation of events when the past and its consequences are already known.'[144] Nonetheless, Stalin's judgement during this period still seems exceptionally bad. The build-up of German forces was obvious, yet he remained too frightened to move the Red Army on to a sufficiently advanced state of readiness – a fundamental mistake that Marshal Vasilevsky later described as 'dangerous'.[145] As a direct result of Stalin's mishandling of the crisis, most Soviet front-line planes and much other military equipment were destroyed in the first moments of the war. If Stalin wasn't an 'outwitted bungler', then it's hard to know who in history ever was.

Shortly after four o'clock in the morning of 22 June 1941 the German ambassador to Moscow, Count Schulenburg, arrived in Molotov's office in the Kremlin to announce the news that the Soviet leadership had been dreading. German troops had crossed into the Soviet Union, Schulenburg said, because of Soviet troop concentrations at the border. It was an obvious pretext. 'After the ambassador delivered the message,'[146] recalled Gustav Hilger, who was present in the room with Schulenburg, 'there were several seconds of deep silence. Molotov was visibly struggling with deep inner excitement.... He called the German action a breach of confidence unprecedented in history. Germany without any reason had attacked a country with which it had concluded a pact of non-aggression.' (Molotov had clearly forgotten that there was indeed a historical precedent for the German action – less than two years before, in September 1939, the Soviet Union had invaded Poland, a country with whom it had signed a pact of non-aggression in July 1932.)

Finally, Molotov could think of nothing more to say to Schulenburg than the plaintive words: 'Surely we haven't deserved this?'

OPERATION BARBAROSSA, 1941

Front Lines 1941
— 21 June
—·— 1 September
— — 30 September

→ German attack

···· furthest limit of German advance December 1941

FINLAND

SWEDEN

Lake Ladoga

Helsinki

Gulf of Finland

Tallin

Narva

Leningrad

Baltic Sea

ESTONIA

Novgorod

Riga

LATVIA

Kalinin

Moscow

Memel

LITHUANIA

Vyazma

ARMY GROUP NORTH
(Leeb)

Königsberg

Vitebsk

Smolensk

Tula

ARMY GROUP CENTRE
(Bock)

Minsk

SOVIET
UNION

Warsaw

Bialystok

BELARUS

**GENERAL
GOVERNMENT
(POLAND)**

Brest-
Litovsk

*Pripet
Marshes*

Kursk

Kiev

ARMY GROUP SOUTH
(Rundstedt)

Lwów

Kharkov

SLOVAKIA

Vinnitsa

Dnieper

C A R P A T H I A N   M T S

Dniester

UKRAINE

HUNGARY

Odessa

*Sea of
Azov*

ROMANIA

Bucharest

Sevastopol

Danube

Black Sea

0   miles   100

0   km   100

N

2

DECISIVE MOMENTS

THE FIRST DAYS OF THE INVASION

The Germans launched the largest land invasion in the history of the world at just before dawn on Sunday, 22 June 1941. More than 3 million soldiers moved forward in three massive thrusts: Army Group North under Field Marshal von Leeb aiming for the Baltic states and Leningrad; Army Group Centre led by Field Marshal von Bock heading due east, aiming for the Minsk, Smolensk, Vyazma, Moscow axis; and Army Group South commanded by Field Marshal von Rundstedt targeting the rich agricultural land of the Ukraine.

The Soviet forces were little match for the Germans. And although there were isolated pockets of determined resistance, the overall picture was one of despair: 'I fought on the border for three days and three nights,' says Georgy Semenyak,[1] a soldier in the Soviet 204th Division. 'The bombings, shootings...explosions of artillery gunfire continued non-stop.' By the fourth day his unit was in disarray and falling back: 'It was a dismal picture. During the day aeroplanes continuously dropped bombs on the retreating soldiers.' In the face of the German attack, most of his commanders simply deserted their men: 'The lieutenants, captains, second lieutenants took rides on passing vehicles...mostly trucks travelling eastwards.... The fact that they used their rank to save their own lives, we felt this to be wrong. But every man has his weaknesses.'

The deadly chaos of those first moments of the invasion was also experienced by Ivan Kulish,[2] one of the Soviet soldiers who had invaded eastern Poland back in 1939: 'I never thought we would retreat from Lvov,'[3] he says, 'but instead we were retreating embarrassingly. We started running away from Lvov and there was complete chaos in the troops.... No communications; commanders of divisions, commanders of the army didn't know where their troops were or where they were... Panic. Everyone was retreating in panic.' Red Army losses were catastrophic. The Soviet air force had been all but destroyed on the ground in the first hours of the German offensive, and in less than a month Army Group Centre had captured more than three hundred thousand prisoners. And whilst German reports spoke of the 'strength and savagery' of the Soviet resistance in places like Brest-Litovsk,[4] the Red Army was clearly inferior to the Wehrmacht.

Amidst the panic, orders were issued by the NKVD to shoot the most 'dangerous' prisoners (almost certainly those detained for political offences) held near the front line. In Lwów, an estimated 4,000 people were killed by the NKVD.[5] Olga Popadyn[6] was in hospital in Lwów's Brigidki prison and remembers that in the last week of June 'there was a strong smell of dead bodies'. It clearly meant that 'they [the NKVD] were killing prisoners. With every day that passed, because it was so hot, the smell of the corpses got worse and worse....' Stalin's regime remained true to itself. The Soviets had entered Polish territory committing atrocities, and they were leaving Polish territory while still committing atrocities.

In those early moments of the war the Soviet leader showed every sign of straightforward denial. When Stalin had first been awoken in the small hours of 22 June at his dacha at Kuntsevo, just outside Moscow, he had called a meeting at the Kremlin, only to announce that this so-called attack might still just be a 'provocation', or that perhaps Hitler's generals were acting without their Führer's orders. Once it was blatantly clear that what the Germans were doing was no 'provocation', Stalin started issuing orders that bore little relationship with reality. His 'Directive Number 3', for example, called for the Red Army to push forward into enemy territory towards Lublin in implementation of the now defunct plan to conduct a defensive battle on the enemy's territory.

But Stalin's lieutenants, sent out from Moscow to learn what was happening on the front line, soon discovered the appalling truth.

Nikita Khrushchev, as a chief political officer, witnessed first hand the collapse of the officer corps when he met the desperate commissar of the Southwestern Front, Major General Nikolai Vashugin. 'I've decided to shoot myself,' Vashugin told Khrushchev. 'I'm guilty of giving incorrect orders to the commanders of the mechanized corps. I don't want to live any longer.'

'Excuse me? What is this?' demanded Khrushchev.

Vashugin began to try to explain but Khrushchev cut him short, not wanting to get into an argument, and said: 'Why are you talking such foolishness? If you've decided to shoot yourself, what are you waiting for?'

At which point Vashugin pulled out his pistol, put it to his head and pulled the trigger. He fell down dead at Khrushchev's feet.[7]

Vashugin's suicide symbolized the brittleness of the Stalinist system at this vital moment in the war. The purges of the 1930s, when Stalin had ordered the elimination of opposition – often imaginary – inside the Soviet armed forces, had grievously weakened the Red Army. Not only had some of the most talented military commanders been removed, and relatively young and inexperienced officers promoted in their place (the commander of the Soviet air force at this time, for example, was just twenty-nine years old), but the pervasive atmosphere of fear had destroyed the commanders' ability to cope under pressure.

The problem wasn't just that the Stalinist system was based on terror, it was that punishment was administered on seemingly arbitrary criteria. One of Beria's and Stalin's favourite charges against the supposed opponents of the state was 'enemy of the people'. But how was it possible to defend yourself against that charge? Many officers felt that the only way to survive was to avoid taking not only risks but any decisions at all – a damaging aspect of the Soviet system that the German liaison officer at Base North had so complained about the previous year.

Not only was the Red Army supposed to take on the Germans with inferior equipment, they were supposed to cope with a sclerotic chain of command as well. Moreover, they faced a German army that was structured in the opposite way entirely. By this point in the war the Germans had honed their Blitzkrieg tactics to a level of excellence, something that made their armoured thrusts almost impossible to defend, and their leadership theory of *Auftragstaktik* (mission command) made their entire system of leadership flexible and effective.

Unlike the Soviet battlefield commanders who feared taking responsibility for their actions, the German High Command delegated detailed decision-making down even to non-commissioned officers. The High Command set the objectives, but it was up to the actual officers and NCOs on the battlefield to decide the best way of carrying out these objectives. It was the freedom of *Auftragstaktik* that was a necessary precondition, for example, of the immense success of Heinz Guderian's Panzer army in the early days of the war. Guderian's tanks managed to push forward and capture Smolensk, deep inside the Soviet Union, less than four weeks after the start of the invasion. (It was no wonder Guderian had the nickname 'Schneller Heinz' – fast Heinz – amongst his men.)

'You thought it was a doddle,' says Albert Schneider, a member of the 201st German assault gun battalion. He and his comrades 'thought the war will be over in six months – a year at most – we will have reached the Ural mountains and that will be that.... At that time we also thought, goodness, what can happen to us? Nothing can happen to us. We were, after all, the victorious troops. And it went well and there were soldiers who advanced singing! It is hard to believe, but it's a fact.'

In the face of the dramatic German advance, Stalin was in despair. He was rendered so angry by a military briefing on 29 June, during which he was told that the Germans were about to take Minsk, capital of Belarus, that he walked out saying: 'Lenin founded our state and now we've fucked it up!'[8] He then left for his dacha. If there was ever a moment when the rest of the Politburo would have been justified in removing Stalin, it was now. After all, it had been chiefly Stalin's incompetence that had led to the Red Army's woeful lack of preparedness to face the Germans, first by denying Soviet forces some of their best commanders through the purges of the 1930s, and then by refusing to act on the myriad pieces of intelligence that made it clear that the Germans were going to invade. In addition, his behaviour during the first week of the invasion had been uncharacteristically weak. He had, for example, ordered Molotov to make the radio announcement to the Soviet people that the Germans had invaded – a moment when clear leadership from the very top had been required. The rest of the Politburo were nonplussed by Stalin's behaviour. There was even a vague suggestion by Vosnesensky that Molotov should take over as leader ('Vyacheslav [Molotov], go first, we'll go behind you!' said Voznesensky.)[9] But it was studiously ignored by the other members of the Politburo.

It was at this moment that Stalin benefited from the atmosphere of terror he had created over the previous years. Despite all the mistakes he had made, no one in the Soviet leadership was willing to come forward and replace him. Every member of the Politburo feared that the merest suggestion that they had been plotting against Stalin would mean torture and death, even with the leader in such a weakened state.

On 30 June the principal figures of the Politburo, including Beria, Mikoyan and Molotov, trooped off to Stalin's low, green-painted dacha hidden in a grove of trees just outside the capital. When they arrived they found Stalin sitting in an armchair, and he shrank back at their approach.

'Why did you come?' he asked.

According to Mikoyan, 'He [Stalin] appeared very guarded, somehow strange, and it was even stranger that he asked us that question. After all, considering the situation he should have called us himself. I have no doubt that he had decided that we had come to arrest him.'[10] Beria's son told how his father concentrated his attention on Stalin's face when they arrived, and was convinced that Stalin 'believed that they were coming to tell him that he had been relieved of his functions'.[11]

Later on, when the Red Army started to fight back against the Nazis, some people would interpret this episode as another example of the Soviet leader's shrewdness. They would point out that Stalin, an avid reader of history, was aware that Ivan the Terrible had been known to feign collapse and then withdraw, in order to identify those who then tried to plot against him. But it's an interpretation that could only have been arrived at with hindsight. In the dark atmosphere of June 1941, with the Red Army in headlong retreat and Minsk about to be captured by the Nazis, it was scarcely the time for some kind of Machiavellian plot by Stalin. No – at this, the lowest point in his leadership, Stalin thought that at last his colleagues had arrived to declare *him* 'an enemy of the people'.

But as the Soviet leader sat hunched and anxious in his armchair, Molotov told him something else entirely – that they had come because they believed it was necessary to establish a Government Committee on Defence.

'Who will head it?' asked Stalin, still clearly unsure of their intentions.

Molotov replied that they believed Stalin himself should take on this role. Relieved, he agreed, and then led a discussion about the roles each of them should take within the new committee.

Stalin returned to work in the Kremlin on 1 July. Certain of the support of his underlings, he now decided that it was time for him – the great Soviet leader – to speak to his people. So, on the 3rd, he made a broadcast that became famous not for its tortuous defence of the actions of the Soviet leadership in agreeing the pact with the Nazis in 1939, nor for its rallying cry to the various ethnic groups within the Soviet Union – Uzbeks, Tatars, Georgians, Armenians and the rest – to fight as one or risk enslavement at the hands of the fascists. Instead, the speech was chiefly remembered for the words Stalin spoke at the beginning: 'Comrades, brothers and sisters'. For many Soviet citizens these simple words epitomized a new Stalin – a leader who cared about them not only as 'comrades' but as intimate members of the same family. The words demonstrated that Stalin was calling not for an ideological battle against Nazism, but for a struggle to defend the Motherland against a rapacious invader. And this was a fight that they could understand.

STALIN AND THE WESTERN ALLIES – THE FIRST DAYS

This alteration in Stalin's rhetoric did little, of course, to stem the German advance. And, in desperation, an approach was made in late July via one of Beria's agents, Pavel Sudoplatov, to the Bulgarian ambassador to Moscow, Ivan Stamenov, to see if it was possible to discover what Soviet territories the Nazis would take in exchange for stopping the war. Molotov even thought that this offer of trading territory for peace was a 'possible second Brest-Litovsk Treaty' and added the words that 'if Lenin could have the courage to make such a step [in 1918], we had the same intention now'.[12]

Nothing came of the approach. Stamenov's view was that the Soviet Union would triumph in the end, despite any early setbacks, and even if such enquiries had been made of the Nazis, there seems no possibility, given the early victories of the German army, that Hitler would have contemplated a peace treaty at this moment of enormous success. But the fact that the Soviet leadership were prepared to investigate the possibility of a separate peace with the Nazis is significant. Not least because the suspicion that Stalin might try to opt out of the war and leave the Nazis in a position of relative stability in the East, with the ability then to concentrate all their resources on repulsing the Western Allies, was subsequently to be a recurring concern for Churchill and Roosevelt. The British signed a mutual-assistance agreement with the Soviet Union on 12 July 1941 in the wake of the Nazi invasion – one that explicitly stated that neither country would 'negotiate nor conclude an armistice or treaty of peace [with Germany] except by mutual agreement'. But the Soviet leadership demonstrably broke that agreement just two weeks later when Beria's agent met the Bulgarian ambassador.

From the beginning of the alliance there was dissembling – on both sides. Whilst Churchill had announced in a speech on 22 June that, as a result of the Nazi invasion, his attitude to the Soviet Union was that: 'The past, with all its crimes, its follies, and its tragedies, flashes away',[13] the reality was, as he had said in private to John Colville, his secretary, just before the invasion, that: 'If Hitler invaded Hell, I would at least make a favourable reference to the Devil.'[14]

It was not as if many people in power in Britain believed that the Soviet Union had much of a chance against the Germans. Many politicians and leading figures in the British military felt that the Soviets could not hold out for long. The War Office, for example, told the BBC not to give out the impression that 'Russian resistance' would last longer than six weeks.[15] And then there was more straightforward prejudice to contend with. Lieutenant General Henry Pownall, deputy to General Sir Alan Brooke, Chief of the Imperial General Staff, recorded his view of Britain's new partner in his diary on 29 June: 'I avoid the expression "Allies", for the Russians are a dirty lot of murdering thieves themselves, and double crossers of the deepest dye. It's good to see the deepest cut-throats in Europe, Hitler and Stalin, going for each other.'[16]

In the United States the immediate reaction to the Nazi invasion was almost as circumspect. Acting Secretary of State Sumner Welles (deputizing for Secretary of State Cordell Hull who was recovering from illness) issued a statement on 23 June, after close consultation with President Roosevelt, which was careful to condemn as 'intolerable' both the 'principles and doctrines of Nazi dictatorship' and the 'principles and doctrines of communistic dictatorship' – though the United States government recognized that 'Hitler's armies are today the chief danger of the Americas'. The statement left open the possibility of aid to the Soviet Union, but committed the USA to nothing.

Some American politicians openly voiced views similar to those Lieutenant General Pownall had confided to his diary: 'It's a case of dog eat dog,' said Senator Bennett Clark of Missouri. 'Stalin is as bloody-handed as Hitler. I don't think we should help either one.'[17] Another American senator came up with this intensely pragmatic proposition: 'If we see that Germany is winning, we ought to help Russia. And if Russia is winning we ought to help Germany, and that way let them kill as many as possible, although I don't want to see Hitler victorious under any circumstances.' These were the words, quoted in the American press, of Senator

Harry Truman, then a little-known politician from Missouri –
words that would come back to haunt him when he became
President of the United States in the spring of 1945 and had to
negotiate personally with Stalin. But the prize for cynicism went to
Senator Robert La Follette, a member of the tiny 'Progressive
Party' and a committed isolationist, who wrote in the magazine
The Progressive that the United States would shortly witness the
'greatest whitewash act in history' in order to get the country into
the war: 'The American people will be told to forget the purges in
Russia...the confiscation of property, the persecution of religion,
the invasion of Finland and the vulture role Stalin played in seizing hold of prostrate Poland, all of Latvia, Estonia and Lithuania.
These will be made to seem the acts of a "democracy" preparing
to fight Nazism.'

But in those early days of the invasion Stalin would have been
less concerned about how the Soviet Union might be perceived in
the future and more concerned with trying to ensure that the
Soviet Union actually had a future. And his first message to
Churchill, delivered by Maisky, the Soviet ambassador to Britain,
on 19 July reflected that reality. Stalin emphasized the difficulties
of the current military situation and asked if Churchill would help
by organizing an immediate second front in France. Churchill's
rejection of this request was to be repeated many times during the
following years; in his reply to Stalin's July communication, for
example, he emphasized the difficulties posed by the presence of
forty German divisions in northern France. It was not, of course,
to be until June 1944, nearly three full years later, that Stalin's
request was finally granted.

But the British did mount a little-known military operation to
try to help the Soviet Union that summer – on the remote island
of Spitsbergen, part of the Svalbard archipelago, just 600 miles
from the North Pole. And whilst this action was scarcely on the
scale of the second front desired by Stalin, it was hugely indicative
of the tensions that existed between the two new allies.

THE SPITSBERGEN ADVENTURE

In July 1941 a message was received in London from Sir Stafford Cripps, British ambassador to Moscow, to the effect that the Soviets would appreciate an attack on Spitsbergen, in order to make the sea route to the Soviet ports of Murmansk and Archangel more secure. After various revisions, the British eventually settled on a plan – Operation Gauntlet. The idea was that a task force of Canadian soldiers would be landed on Spitsbergen, where they would immobilize the coal mines to prevent the Germans using the island as a base for their ships and U-boats, and evacuate the two thousand Russian miners and around seven hundred Norwegians who lived there. (Although Spitsbergen was Norwegian territory, the Soviet Union operated a substantial mining concession at Barentsburg on the west coast.)

On 19 August a small fleet of three destroyers, two cruisers and the converted passenger liner *Empress of Canada* left the Royal Navy base of Scapa Flow, and after a brief stop in Iceland arrived off the coast of Spitsbergen on 25 August. It was then that the trouble began. When the Canadian soldiers landed at Barentsburg they discovered 'a dozen scowling, silent Russians, very suspicious and extremely doubtful of our intentions, though they had been advised from Moscow we were coming'.[18] In addition, 'as we got into the town our senses were assailed by a sweet, sickening smell – the scent of eau de cologne. No liquor was permitted on the island for the miners, so they imported great cases of eau de cologne and drank it wholesale. The whole town reeked of the stuff.'[19]

The Allied soldiers found the Soviet consul initially unhelpful, but he eventually agreed to cooperate in the evacuation the next day. And so, on 26 August, most of the Soviet citizens boarded the *Empress of Canada*. But there remained a small number – including the consul – who seemed reluctant to go. There was a rumour that they had been selling coal to the Germans and were, naturally enough, frightened about what would happen to them when they were returned to the Soviet Union. The consul also demanded that some of the heavy machinery at the mine be transported away on the *Empress of Canada* – something that the British and Canadians couldn't manage.

Brigadier Potts, commander of the troops, visited the consul in his cottage on the edge of the town in an attempt to break the impasse. During the meeting the consul began to drink a bottle of champagne and various other alcoholic drinks – including a bottle of Madeira ('No eau de cologne for him,' noted one of the Canadians)[20] and remained intransigent. He eventually got so drunk that he passed out and, according to a report of the incident written by Major Bruce Blake, a liaison officer, 'The Consul was [then] carried aboard [the waiting ship] on a stretcher covered by a sheet so that his own people should not know what had happened to him.'[21] The *Empress of Canada* finally left at midnight on 26 August, carrying the whole Russian population away to Archangel. On the morning of 29 August, Maisky, the Soviet ambassador in London, phoned the Foreign Office to complain about the behaviour of the British and Canadians. Charges of lack of cooperation and courtesy were staunchly rejected by the Western Allies, who must have suspected that the source of the complaint was the consul, now anxious to defend himself against news of his drunken antics.

But the behaviour of the British and Canadians at Spitsbergen was also questionable. While waiting for the *Empress of Canada* to return from Archangel, they carried out their orders and demolished mining equipment so as not to leave it for the Germans, but something else happened too – much of the town accidentally burnt down. 'The fire started at about 0600 hours on 1st September in the Terminus shed of the railway,' says a report sent by the War Office to the Foreign Secretary, Anthony Eden, on 11 September.[22] 'The fire spread very rapidly owing to the nature of the buildings, which were of wood, well soaked in oil and coal dust.... An inquiry into the incident was held but it was found impossible to discover the cause of the fire.' This idea that it was 'impossible' to discover how the fire started is surely disingenuous, since untransmitted film footage taken by a newsreel cameraman, now held in the Imperial War Museum, clearly shows the almost reckless abandon with which the Allied soldiers set fire to mining equipment and blew up communications masts. Whatever else it may have been, this was scarcely an operation carried out with military precision, and the destruction of Barentsburg was almost certainly a result of their negligence. And although the official line taken by the British government was that the operation was a success, a private Foreign Office memo sent later in September records that 'the WO [War Office] may have a guilty conscience about this [the burning of Barentsburg] as I have heard from more than one source that according to eye-witnesses the behaviour of the Canadian troops left a great deal to be desired'.[23]

The finale to this less than competent operation was a BBC radio broadcast on 9 September that called the 'daring' Spitsbergen expedition 'the first big campaign in which the Canadian troops have been employed for some time'.[24] Sir Stafford Cripps was furious when he heard about this piece of hyberbole, and complained in a telegram to the Foreign Office that 'in view of their [the Soviet Union's] recent pressure on us to do something big in the West, this will be taken as an elaborate and stupid attempt to magnify a simple and safe operation into something large and important and will either be resented or laughed at'.[25]

In terms of its importance in the military conduct of the war, the Spitsbergen action is little more than a footnote. Its significance lies in what this first attempt at practical cooperation demonstrates about the attitude of the protagonists concerned. Mutual suspicion, recrimination and lack of respect characterized the relationship on the ground in Spitsbergen between the Soviet Union and the Western Allies – qualities that were also apparent in those early months of the war between the leadership of the countries concerned.

By the beginning of September Stalin was pleading once again for an immediate second front to draw some of the German forces away from the Soviet Union. The British had supplied little practical help so far, and the only concrete gesture – apart from the departure of one small convoy to Archangel – had been an agreement to give the Soviet Union £10 million of credit at 3 per cent interest. Maisky handed over Stalin's latest missive in London on the 4th. Without the second front, claimed the Soviet leader, his country would be beaten or at best grievously weakened. When Maisky tried to browbeat Churchill over this crucial issue, the British Prime Minister replied: 'Remember, that only four months ago we in this island did not know whether you were not coming in against us on the German side.... Whatever happens, and whatever you do, you of all people have no right to make reproaches to us.'[26] But Churchill did promise an increase, albeit only a token offering, in the current trickle of British aid – to 200 planes and 250 tanks per month.

The United States initially behaved little better as far as Stalin was concerned. President Roosevelt not only ensured, as we have seen, that the American government's statement made immediately after the Nazis invaded the Soviet Union condemned both regimes as 'intolerable', but when asked by reporters if it was 'essential' to America that Russia be defended, replied equivocally: 'Oh, ask me a different type of question....'[27] And whilst, two days after the invasion, Roosevelt did allow the Soviet Union access to $39 million of assets that had been frozen, there was little other immediate sign of assistance. Part of the reason for his reticence was the prevailing view amongst his colleagues that the Soviet Union would shortly be crushed. Frank Knox, Secretary of the Navy, told him: 'The best opinion I can get is that it will take anywhere from six weeks to two months for Hitler to clean up on Russia'; and Henry Stimson, his Secretary of War, wrote to Roosevelt on 23 June, saying that 'the Germans would be thoroughly occupied in beating the Soviet Union for a minimum of one month and a possible maximum of three months'.[28] But another reason for Roosevelt's initial reticence to support the Soviet Union was almost certainly his desire not to move too far ahead of public opinion; he famously said: 'It is a terrible thing to look over your shoulder when you are trying to lead; and find no one there.'[29] And Roosevelt knew what American opinion polls were revealing: the majority of people, whilst wanting the Soviet Union to win in a direct fight with the Nazis, still did not want to offer meaningful support to Stalin.

So, as ever, Roosevelt proceeded carefully and pragmatically. He agreed that his trusted adviser Harry Hopkins should visit Moscow at the end of July. Here, in the course of two lengthy discussions, Hopkins came to the conclusion that talking to Stalin was like 'talking to a perfectly coordinated machine'.[30] But during the talks this 'machine' made an astonishing suggestion – Stalin said that American forces under American command would be welcome in the Soviet Union, as long as they came to fight the Germans. It was yet another sign of Stalin's desperation.

But whilst there was no chance of America instantly offering the immediate level of aid that Stalin sought, there were signs that summer that Roosevelt was moving closer towards fighting on the British side against Hitler.

CHURCHILL AND ROOSEVELT MEET

The American and British leaders held their first wartime meeting in Argentia Bay off the coast of Newfoundland in August 1941. Churchill had spent the journey across the Atlantic in the warship *Prince of Wales* playing backgammon with Harry Hopkins (fresh from his meeting with Stalin) and eating the caviar that Hopkins had obtained in the Soviet Union. The British Prime Minister remarked to Sir Alexander Cadogan, who was also on the *Prince of Wales*, that: 'It was very good to have such caviar, even though it meant fighting with the Russians to get it.'[31]

Roosevelt and Churchill had first met at the end of the First World War, when Roosevelt had been on a visit to Europe. He had not liked Churchill, and this negative impression was no doubt partly behind his remark to his Cabinet in May 1940, after receiving the news that Churchill had become Prime Minister, that 'he [Roosevelt] supposed Churchill was the best man that England had, even if he was drunk half of the time'.[32]

From the first, the relationship between Churchill and Roosevelt was a good deal less simple than the propaganda of the time portrayed. Whilst both of them were members of an elite –

Roosevelt a wealthy member of one of the famed 'Knickerbocker' families of Dutch descent who were much to the social fore in New York, and Churchill the aristocratic son of Lord Randolph Churchill and the rich American socialite Jennie Jerome – they each subscribed to a very different set of political beliefs. Indeed, these were two people who, in ordinary circumstances, were not likely to get on together. Churchill, for example, had written before the war about how much he disliked the 'New Deal' – the package of social reform that was central to Roosevelt's political programme.[33] Roosevelt for his part was adamantly opposed to the British Empire, something that almost defined Churchill's political vision. And in personal terms, despite each possessing an almost overbearing self-confidence and egotism, they were very different men. Churchill had demonstrated his bravery openly as a twenty-three-year-old cavalry officer in 1898 on the battlefield at Omdurman in the Sudan, whilst Roosevelt's courage, like his political mind, was much more subtle. In 1921, when he was thirty-nine, Roosevelt had been struck down by what was believed at the time to be polio – though his illness is now thought to have been Guillain-Barré's syndrome, which has much the same paralysing effect. As a result, Roosevelt lost the use of his body from the waist down. But he refused to let his disability harm his political life – or, indeed, his fundamentally optimistic and fearless temperament. Roosevelt, as we shall see, was capable of many deceptions, but perhaps his greatest was in concealing from the American public the extent of his disability. Roosevelt knew he was paralysed, but he pretended to the world he wasn't, wearing painful leg braces in public rather than using the wheelchair he used in private. Never openly – or indeed in secret as far as one can tell – did he indulge in self-pity. As he said to George Elsey, a naval intelligence officer at the White House, he was a 'happy thought' man.

These, then, were the two men who had their second meeting, now as wartime leaders, on 9 August 1941 in Canadian waters: very different people, but united in their desire to work together to defeat Germany, and determined to present a solid front to the rest of the world. The Atlantic Conference – as the meeting became known – is significant in this history for two reasons. The first is that Roosevelt hinted that he was prepared for American troops to help in the British war effort. When Churchill told him that the British planned to occupy the Canary Islands and would not then, as a result, have the resources necessary to defend the Azores, Roosevelt offered to help. The President said that America would defend the Azores if Portugal (who owned these islands) asked. Subsequently Churchill decided against the occupation of the Canaries, but this exchange showed in principle that Roosevelt was prepared to allow the American military to assist the British, even though the United States still professed neutrality. However, this somewhat tortuous level of participation did still fall short of the ringing commitment to the war that the British had hoped to hear from Roosevelt.

But this conference was memorable for an even more important reason – the Atlantic Charter. This document – a statement of agreed principles – was to cause many problems later in the war. Indeed, it came to symbolize the schizophrenia that surrounded many of the dealings between the Western Allies and Stalin; because the Atlantic Charter represents nobility of ideal, whilst, as we have already seen, much of the reality of the relationship with Stalin was pure pragmatic politics.

The Atlantic Charter laid out in eight points the principles by which the British and American leaders together based 'their hopes for a better future for the world'. But in truth this document was the brainchild of one man – Franklin Roosevelt. For Roosevelt, whilst practising day-to-day politics in an intensely practical and hard-headed way, was still driven by a sense of wider vision – a post-Wilsonian ideal (former American President Woodrow Wilson had helped establish the League of Nations after the First World War) that imagined, as point eight of the Atlantic Charter put it: 'that all of the nations of the world, for realistic as well as spiritual reasons, must come to the abandonment of the use of force'. It was this vision of a partnership within the world community that eventually led Roosevelt to push through the idea of the United Nations towards the end of the war. But it was points two and three of this idealistic document that were subsequently to cause the most difficulties. Point two stated that: 'They [Britain and America] desire to see no territorial changes that do not accord with the freely expressed wishes of the peoples concerned.' And point three: 'They respect the right of all peoples to choose the form of government under which they will live; and they wish to see sovereign rights and self government restored to those who have been forcibly deprived of them.' The trouble, of course, was that Britain's new ally, the Soviet Union, had already acted against the ideal now expressed in point two of the charter by seizing eastern Poland in September 1939, and large numbers of people – not just in the Soviet Union but also in the British Empire, notably in India – were denied the opportunity to exercise their rights under point three.

But at the time all of this appeared somewhat academic, since America was still not formally in the war and – perhaps more importantly – it seemed as though the Soviet Union was on the verge of collapse.

THE GERMANS ADVANCE TOWARDS MOSCOW

On 18 September 1941 Guderian's Panzer Corps captured Kiev, capital of the Ukraine, along with six hundred thousand Soviet prisoners of war. And this disaster – the result of the single greatest encirclement in military history – was largely the fault of Joseph Stalin, since he had insisted that Soviet troops should not withdraw from the city. Marshal Zhukov had suggested that the Red Army should pull back to a more defensible line, only to be told by Stalin that he was talking 'rubbish'. As a consequence of Stalin's rebuke, Zhukov asked to be relieved of his post as Chief of the General Staff, and Stalin granted his request. Now the German army, its southern flank secure as a result of the occupation of Kiev, moved on through the central axis of the advance towards Moscow, and in the early days of October, the 3rd and 4th Panzer Armies advanced on the cities of Vyazma and Bryansk, west of the

Soviet capital. Once again the Germans overwhelmed the Red Army. Five whole Soviet armies were encircled. Soviet soldiers tried to fight their way out of the trap, often using antiquated First World War rifles, or in some cases no rifles at all, charging the German lines empty-handed.

At the twin battles of Vyazma and Bryansk another 660,000 Soviet soldiers were taken captive by the Germans. And the combination of this victory, plus the fact that Leningrad was now under siege, led Otto Dietrich, Hitler's press secretary, to announce that: 'For all military purposes Soviet Russia is done with.'[34] But there remained the small matter of Moscow – not just the capital of the Soviet Union, but the centre of Russia's transport and communications network. So, following the triumphs at Vyazma and Bryansk, the German army moved on towards this great prize, the culmination of Operation Typhoon.

Nineteen-year-old Grigory Obozny[35] was one of the Soviet soldiers charged with the defence of the city that October. He remembers hearing the German artillery getting ever closer, and that 'there was panic'. Other eye witnesses saw some managers of shops open their doors, saying, 'Take what you want! We don't want the Germans to get these things!' 'On the one hand there were thousands who ran away, panicking,' says Zoya Zarubina,[36] a teenager at the time. 'They were taking food or whatever. [But] there was another group that was mining [the buildings]...they would come home crying that they had to mine it, but they knew they didn't want to leave it to the enemy.'

This moment in Soviet history – when Moscow seemed about to fall, with many of its citizens in a state of panic – ran completely contrary to the subsequent myth of the resolute, victorious Red Army. All mention of the reality of the situation that October was suppressed under communism. Only since the fall of the Berlin Wall have documents emerged from the Russian archives that confirm the extent of the fear that permeated the city that autumn. For example, secret document no. 34 of the State Defence Committee, dated 15 October 1941, reveals that a decision had been taken to 'evacuate the Presidium of the Supreme Soviet and the top levels of government' and that 'in the event of enemy forces arriving at the gates of Moscow, the NKVD – Comrade Beria and Comrade Scherbakov – are ordered to blow up the business premises, warehouses and installations which cannot be evacuated, and all of the Underground electrical equipment.'

It has also emerged that, at this most crucial time, Stalin himself considered fleeing from Moscow. Nikolay Ponomariev,[37] Stalin's personal telegraphist, confirmed that on the night of 16 October all the Soviet leader's communications equipment was dismantled in the Kremlin and loaded on to a train, waiting to take Stalin and his immediate entourage further east. But in the event the Soviet leader decided not to cut and run. He stayed in Moscow, imposed a state of siege on the city – which was enforced with the most brutal measures imaginable – and resolved to hold the Germans outside the capital with the help of fresh troops from far away.

That October Vasily Borisov[38] was a soldier in a Siberian division in the remote east of the Soviet Union where, he says, 'we were expecting Japan to attack'. But on the 18th his unit received orders to board trains immediately and head west to face a different foe: 'In the summer we knew the Germans were advancing very fast and were capturing Soviet territory and we knew they were technically more advanced than us...we knew that the situation was bad.' As they travelled towards the West, he and his comrades knew 'that a lot of us would be killed. We knew that the war would be hard, and that's what it turned out to be. It was very hard...we felt fear.'

They arrived to protect a defensive line that was being pushed ever nearer Moscow. 'We were retreating...we had to retreat because we were weaker...we had few weapons as good as the Germans did.... There was so much smoke and fire that we didn't even see which way to crawl – we only heard the commander saying: "Forwards! Forwards!" It's indescribable.... We saw a lot of dead bodies – both on our side and the German side.... It was frightening. Everything was on fire – the snow was black from the explosions...for me it was the most frightening point in the whole of the war.... Red Army soldiers, to tell the truth, were badly trained. They were not good marksmen because their training consisted of only a couple of days in the shooting range.... If a machine gunner was killed, I was unable to take over from him and load the machine gun because during military service I wasn't taught to do that.'

Nikolai Brandt,[39] an eighteen-year-old student called up into the Red Army to take part in the defence of Moscow, recalls how almost his whole chain of command was ignorant of the most basic military skills: 'I couldn't open the breech block on my rifle, so I was told to turn to my immediate commander and he said: "Oh, your rifle is cold – frozen. You have to warm it up." How could I warm it up in minus 30? So I turned to the platoon commander and he said the same: "You have to warm it up – the breech block has frozen." Then they said go to the battalion commander. He was a lieutenant, the only professional officer there, and he just opened the safety catch – and I felt enormous joy when the breech block opened.'

Nikolai Brandt knew that both he and his unit were able to offer little opposition to the Germans. Whilst he possessed an ancient rifle that he scarcely knew how to operate, many of the other men in his unit possessed no weapons of any kind. They planned to charge into battle behind the first wave of attack, and arm themselves from the weapons of their fallen comrades. 'To send into attack completely untrained people,' he says, 'is totally ineffective and inhuman.' He himself was badly injured within seconds of taking part in the battle for Moscow: 'I was wounded by fragments of a mortar and thrown into deep snow – and what saved me was the snow.' Cushioned by the snow beneath him he lay on the battlefield for a whole day, his trousers soaked with blood, until he was able to crawl back to the Soviet line, where he found that virtually his entire unit had been annihilated that day. 'An unseasoned soldier who comes under bombardment doesn't understand a thing,' he says. 'He goes out of his mind. But a battle-hardened soldier can get his bearings well. If a mortar explodes, he knows where to run to and from, and from where to expect the next mortar. He knows when and where to hide. So you get battle experience, which I didn't have.'

By now Stalin had few illusions about the quality of the Red Army. Many of its soldiers, like Nikolai Brandt, were ill trained and ill equipped. And in such circumstances Stalin relied ever more on a form of motivation that had served him well in the past – threat. A dramatic example of just how he sought to motivate his troops in this primitive manner is provided by a revealing phone call he made to Army Commissar Stepanov in October 1941. Stepanov had been sent to the headquarters of the Soviet Western Front at Perhyshkovo to report on the military situation. He then asked Stalin to allow Soviet forces to retreat east of Moscow. After he had made this suggestion there was a long silence, broken eventually by Stalin saying: 'Find out from the comrades if they have spades.'

'What, comrade Stalin?' said Stepanov.

'Do the comrades have spades?' repeated Stalin.

Stepanov then discussed Stalin's request with the military commanders around him before replying: 'Comrade Stalin, which spades? Sappers' spades or some other type?'

'Doesn't matter which,' answered Stalin.

'Comrade Stalin,' said Stepanov excitedly. 'We have spades! What should we do with them?'

'Comrade Stepanov,' replied Stalin, 'tell your comrades that they should take their spades and dig their own graves. We will not leave Moscow.'[40]

It was this kind of ruthlessness that was eventually to help save Moscow – a psychological toughness that was even more important than the fresh troops from the East. And as part of this approach to warfare, Stalin ordered special rearguard blocking detachments to be placed behind the Soviet front lines with orders to shoot any Red Army soldier who tried to retreat. Soviet soldiers in front of Moscow knew that they must conquer their fear or risk certain death at the hands of their own countrymen.

'These "rearguard detachments" played, I would say, a psychological, morale-supporting role,' says Vladimir Ogryzko,[41] an

NKVD officer who served in one of the units that attempted to prevent the Red Army troops retreating. 'If he [the soldier attempting to flee] resists or something or runs away, we eliminate [him]. We shot them, that's all. They weren't fighters.'

Ogryzko, like many Soviet soldiers, was inspired by the example of resistance shown by Stalin. The Soviet leader had decided to stay in Moscow and tough it out, and so, therefore, should they. The autumn of 1941 was for Stalin – as the spring of 1940 was for Churchill – the moment when true character showed through in adversity. 'Stalin did well,' says Ogryzko. 'For all his deep-seated shortcomings...Stalin will be very positively remembered in history. A strong man was required. They used fear to crush fear.'

The Germans had initially been hampered in their advance towards Moscow by the wet, slushy conditions, but by 15 November the roads were frozen and they pushed forward once again. Nearly a million Wehrmacht soldiers advanced on the Soviet capital, confronted by little more than half that number of Red Army troops. By the end of the month the 7th Panzer Division had crossed one of the last strategic barriers between themselves and the Soviet capital – the Moscow–Volga Canal. They were now just over 20 miles from Stalin's office in the heart of Moscow. But the Red Army managed to hold the Germans at the line of the canal. The invaders were reaching the end of their powers of endurance – their supply lines stretched back hundreds of miles and much of their motorized equipment no longer functioned.

A great deal has been made since of the impact of the inadequacy of the Germans' winter equipment – Hitler and his generals had planned on a short, tough war that would be finished by the autumn. And there is no doubt that the lack of warm clothing for the men and adequate cold weather protection for their guns and vehicles played a large part in stopping the Germans in their tracks. 'When the temperature dropped to below minus 30 degrees Celsius our machine guns were not firing any more,' says Walter Schaefer-Kehnert,[42] an officer with a German Panzer unit, who was encamped in front of Moscow that December. 'Our machine guns were precision instruments, but when the oil got thick they didn't shoot properly any more – this really makes you afraid.' And this failure of equipment, combined with inadequate winter clothing, made the morale amongst the invading forces plummet.

But, important as the practical problems caused by the inadequacy of the Germans' logistical preparations were, what is sometimes overlooked is that the confrontation between the Red Army and the Wehrmacht outside Moscow in December 1941 marks the first moment when the psychological difference between the two forces was starkly revealed – a difference that was to become obvious in the ruins of Stalingrad one year later. The Germans, of course, believed themselves superior to the Slavic soldiers of the Red Army. Nazi propaganda had proclaimed that this was a war of annihilation fought against a sub-human enemy. And to begin with, those racist statements seemed true enough to the German troops as they carved their way through the Soviet Union. It was the Red Army's inability to resist the Germans' motorized advance in particular that symbolized the gulf between the two sides. For many German soldiers this was obviously a war between a modern, industrialized nation and a primitive, backward one. It was an attitude summed up by Adolf Hitler, who told his colleagues that the inhabitants of the Soviet Union should be treated like 'the Redskins' of America.[43]

But in the freezing Soviet winter, all the Germans' technological advances counted for nothing. This was a more straightforward struggle – one in which the Red Army could compete on equal terms. Vasily Borisov believes that he and his comrades held firm during the battle for Moscow because of 'Siberian stubbornness.... The commanders used to say that the Siberian divisions saved Moscow....' And whilst, when they had been retreating under the constant German barrage, Borisov and his comrades had felt an element of fear, once the Red Army began to counterattack on 5 December, they started to regain their innate confidence. 'We are very strong and very fit.... This is Siberian spirit. This is how people are raised from childhood. Everyone knows that Siberians are very tough.... I am a true Siberian, everyone knows that we are tough.'

This toughness now manifested itself in the nature of the fighting: 'During the counter-attacks there was man-to-man fighting. We had to fight the Germans in the trenches. And the fitter ones survived and the weaker ones died.... We had bayonets on our rifles and I was very strong – I could pierce him [the German soldier] with a bayonet and throw him out of the trench...they were wearing coats like us, so the bayonet went through. It's the same as piercing a loaf of bread – no resistance.... It's a question of either/or. Either he kills you or you kill him. It's a real bloody mess.... I never felt proud or happy about killing a person. I just knew I achieved a small victory and I can carry on. I never felt satisfaction or joy from it.'

In the face of this physical onslaught, Vasily Borisov and his comrades noticed a change in the attitude of the Germans: 'When they saw Siberians fighting man-to-man they felt frightened – Siberians were very fit guys.... They [the Germans] had been raised in a gentle way. They were not as strong as the Siberians. So they panicked more in this kind of fighting. Siberians don't feel any panic. The Germans were weaker people. They didn't like the cold much and they were physically weaker too.' Fyodor Sverdlov, who took part in the battle of Moscow as a company commander of the Soviet 19th Rifle Brigade, confirms that: 'The German army near Moscow was a very miserable sight. I remember very well the Germans in July 1941. They were confident, strong, tall guys. They marched ahead with their sleeves rolled up and carrying their machine guns. But later on they became miserable, snotty guys wrapped in woollen kerchiefs stolen from old women in villages.'

And while the Germans shivered in their trenches and dugouts in front of Moscow, on the other side of the world an event occurred that would, within days, give Stalin a new ally and Hitler a new foe.

THE CRUCIAL MONTH OF DECEMBER

On 7 December 1941, just two days after the start of the Soviet offensive in front of Moscow, the Japanese bombed the American fleet at Pearl Harbor in Hawaii. And although the suddenness of the attack came as a surprise to the Americans, the realization that the Japanese had finally lost patience with diplomacy did not.

The relationship between the United States and Japan had been declining rapidly since the Japanese occupation of southern Indochina (today's Vietnam) that summer. The Americans had, as a consequence, frozen Japanese assets in the USA and threatened to cut off the supply of oil and other key raw materials to Japan. There followed several months of desultory and badly handled (on both sides) attempts at a compromise. The Japanese case in Washington was not helped by the decrepit state of their ambassador to the United States: the elderly Admiral Kichisaburo Nomura was partly deaf, partly blind and often confused.

The Americans did not seem to believe that they would be the victims of a Japanese attack. No doubt partly influenced by their dealings with the Nazis – who so far had been careful not to force the USA into the war – many Americans felt that the most logical scenario would be that the Japanese would attack Dutch or British colonies in the East, perhaps aiming directly at the oil-rich Dutch East Indies. But the Japanese were thinking in more epic terms. Their attack on Pearl Harbor, in the middle of the Pacific, was an attempt to push the United States out of the equation altogether. 'America is a big country and we knew that we wouldn't be able to win against them once the war was prolonged,' explains Masatake Okumiya,[44] then serving in the Japanese Imperial Navy. 'But at the time the fleet was the mainstay of military power, be it American, British or Japanese. The fleet represented a nation's military power. So if you destroyed the fleet, the damage would be huge. It would ruin President Roosevelt's reputation as a commander-in-chief and he might then be put in a difficult situation.'

It was a massive misjudgement. Far from seeking to disengage with the Japanese after the attack on Pearl Harbor, the Americans were driven on by a sense of righteous indignation to pursue vengeance against Japan. 'Remember Pearl Harbor!' became the rallying cry of American forces in the war that followed. And their determination never to trust a foe whom many US Marines now called the 'Tricky Nipper' was born in part of the American government's complacency in allowing themselves to be surprised by Pearl Harbor.

The Japanese attack on the Americans affected the Soviet Union in two important ways. First, it confirmed that Japanese forces would no longer pose any foreseeable threat to the Soviet Union in the Far East. Indeed, it had been reports two months earlier from Richard Sorge, the Soviet spy in Japan, that the Japanese intended to attack in the south that had informed Stalin's decision to move divisions from the Siberian border to help in the defence of Moscow. Second, Pearl Harbor led almost immediately to Germany declaring war on America, and so brought Stalin an ally of colossal potential power. Hitler's decision to declare war on America, made on 11 December 1941, has often puzzled people who are not aware of the details of the history. Why, as German forces faced the immensity of the challenge of the war on the Eastern Front, did Hitler voluntarily add such a powerful additional enemy to his list of adversaries?

The answer is straightforward. Hitler, like Stalin, was a political leader who had an eye for reality, not just rhetoric. And to Hitler it had been obvious that war with the United States was inevitable. The key moment on that road to war had occurred not at Pearl Harbor but several months before, when Roosevelt had ordered American warships to accompany British convoys to the middle of the Atlantic.

As Churchill noted, by the time of the Atlantic Conference in August 1941 Roosevelt was determined 'to wage war, but not declare it'.[45] This was the conclusion the German Admiral Raeder had reached too, and he had told Hitler months prior to Pearl Harbor that unless U-boats were allowed to sink American ships, the battle of the Atlantic could not be won. Inevitably, following Roosevelt's decision to order American warships to patrol the Western Atlantic in support of convoys, a series of incidents followed – notably a U-boat attack on the USS *Greer* in September and the sinking of the USS *Reuben James*, causing the deaths of more than a hundred American sailors, in November. So by December Hitler must have felt that by declaring war on America he was doing little more than accepting the inevitable – with the added benefit of retaining apparent control of events. Hitler further reasoned that the immediate entry of the USA into the war would do nothing substantively for at least a year to alter the course of the struggle in the Soviet Union – and it was this fight against Stalin that he believed would decide the entire conflict one way or the other. Moreover, he thought the Japanese would now tie down the American fleet in the Pacific and threaten British interests in the Far East.

But December 1941 was also a crucial month for less well-known reasons. On the 3rd, four days before Pearl Harbor, General Sikorski, prime minister of the Polish government in exile, together with General Anders, a senior commander in the Polish army, met Stalin and Molotov in the Kremlin. Now that Poland had become an 'ally' of the Soviet Union, Stalin was in something of an awkward position. After all, little more than a year and a half before he had ordered the murder of much of the Polish officer corps. Not surprisingly, the attitude of the Soviet authorities to the remaining Poles whom they held in captivity had suddenly changed after the German invasion. One day they had been instruments of a bourgeois state that the Soviet Union had helped wipe off the map, the next they were potential allies against the Nazis.

Tadeusz Ruman[46] experienced this near-miraculous transformation first hand. As a twenty-year-old Polish student, he had been arrested in the spring of 1940 for attempting to cross the border between the German and Soviet zones of Poland. Although he never admitted it to the Soviet guards who arrested him, he had been acting as a courier for the Polish underground and had subsequently been imprisoned under a false name. Initially he had been held in the infamous Brigidki prison in Lwów, where he had been forced into an overcrowded cell and systematically starved. From here he had been sent northeast to a labour camp in the Soviet Union, where he and a group of other Poles were told that they had all been sentenced to fifteen years' hard labour. 'There was no trial,' he says. 'You had your trial when you were interrogated...with a totalitarian system there is no need to prove [anything].' But the fifteen-year sentence did not hang over this twenty-year-old's mind because he had a more immediate problem in the camp: 'You only think – will I get enough food? When you're hungry, you don't think of anything else.'

But one day in the summer of 1941 he experienced a change in fortune. He was ordered to see the commandant of the prison, a lieutenant-colonel in the NKVD. Ruman was told to sit down and offered a cigarette. He was wary, as he knew this was the normal NKVD interrogation technique: 'Sit down, cigarette, and then you're suddenly banged in the back.' But this time the encounter was altogether more cordial. The NKVD officer explained that the Nazis had invaded the Soviet Union and that now the Poles had an opportunity to fight with the Red Army against 'our common enemy'.

'What about me?' asked Ruman. 'I've received fifteen years for fighting for the Poles.'

'Ah!' said the commandant. 'We must forget.' He took Ruman's file and put a cross on it, together with the word 'freed'.

So Tadeusz Ruman, emaciated and weak, was released from Soviet captivity, his fifteen-year sentence for hard labour dismissed as casually as it had been imposed. He thus became one of the tens of thousands of Poles who were now to be organized and trained into a fighting force to help the Soviet Union, their new ally, recover Poland.

But gathering these men together from labour camps across the Soviet Union was a huge logistical task, as was the problem of feeding and housing them. And it was practical questions like these that the Polish delegation in Moscow, headed by General Sikorski, was trying to resolve. The Polish leaders were also, of course, keen to investigate why so few of their officers had so far been released. During the meeting in the Kremlin, Sikorski explained to Stalin that the recent Soviet 'direction concerning the amnesty' for Polish prisoners of war was 'not being implemented' and that 'many of our most valuable people are still in labour camps and prisons'.[47]

'That is impossible,' replied Stalin. 'Because the amnesty applied to all, and all the Poles have been released.' Molotov nodded in agreement.

Sikorski went on to explain that he had a list of several thousand Poles who could not be accounted for. Not one of them had been released, and so, he surmised, they must therefore still be kept in captivity somewhere in the Soviet Union.

'That is impossible,' said Stalin. 'They have escaped.'

'Where could they escape to?' asked General Anders.

'Well,' said Stalin, 'to Manchuria.'

It is one of the defining exchanges of Stalin's entire war. Here was the Soviet leader, who knew better than anyone what the fate of the missing soldiers had been, calmly announcing that they had in fact escaped to a remote part of northeast Asia. It was surely one of the most cynical demonstrations of power seen in recent times. For just as the Soviet state could decree that you were an 'enemy of the people' – something was 'true' regardless of any objective criteria – so Stalin could, in what was probably a whimsical fancy, resurrect the murdered Polish officers and magic them to the wastes of Manchuria.

General Anders, who had personal experience of the Soviet judicial and penal system (all of it bad) – dared to contradict Stalin explicitly. 'All of them could not possibly have escaped,' he insisted.

'They have certainly been released,' said Stalin, 'but have not yet arrived.'

Stalin's mind was still very much on the Polish question when he held another key discussion that December – this time with the suave British Foreign Secretary, Anthony Eden. After a journey by sea to Murmansk, and from there by train to Moscow, Eden met Stalin for the first time on 16 December 1941. This too was to be a remarkable encounter, offering an important insight into Stalin's thinking. Because, with the German army still fighting near Moscow, with his country facing the possibility of extinction, with his anger still apparent at the lack of British commitment to an immediate second front, with a sense of indignation at the relatively small amount of military aid that had so far arrived, with all these pressing issues on his mind, Stalin chose to open the discussion by focusing on a question that was not immediate but important – the future post-war boundaries of the Soviet Union.

Stalin forcibly made it clear to Eden that he would accept nothing less than (with slight alterations) the pre-1941 boundaries that had been agreed with the Nazis. The Soviets thus sought to legitimize their control over a huge chunk of what before the war had been Poland. Stalin also demanded that the territorial gains he had made at the expense of the Finns should be legitimized, as well as Soviet control of the Baltic States and several other smaller territorial concessions made on the western border of the Soviet Union. The diplomat Sir Frank Roberts, who accompanied Eden, later recalled the moment Stalin made this dramatic statement: 'And when I went to Moscow with Anthony Eden in December 1941, when the Germans were still only 19 kilometres away from us as we talked, the very first thing that Stalin said at that meeting was, "Mr Eden, I want to have your assurance that at the end of the war you will support my just claim to all these areas".... And Eden said: "Oughtn't we to be thinking about how we win the war?" "No, no," said Stalin, "I would like to have this clear at the very beginning." So Eden obviously had to say we had no authority to discuss how the war was to end. And I remember I made a mental resolution – because I was dealing with Poland – I said, "We'll never be able to restore Polish independence unless we do it before Stalin is winning the war."'[48] Significantly, Stalin also suggested at the meeting that Britain and the Soviet Union sign a 'secret protocol' that would lay out post-war boundaries. The words 'secret protocol', of course, were reminiscent of the infamous deal with the Nazis, concluded in the same building little over two years earlier. Eden, for obvious reasons, considered such a suggestion 'impossible'.[49]

Eden's second meeting with Stalin, held at midnight the following day, was even more acrimonious. Eden said he was not in a position to agree Stalin's claims, as the British had agreed with the Americans that these territorial questions should be settled only after the immediate military challenges posed by the Germans had been successfully faced. Stalin was outraged, although whether his outrage was real or feigned is hard to say. All this was an indication of Stalin's preferred method of diplomacy: intimidation. The second meeting tended to be the one in which the visitor was lambasted by the Soviet leader, with the third and final encounter reserved for an attempt to mollify the previous angst caused.

And so it was with Eden. At their third and last meeting Stalin was more amiable, but he still said the same thing – he wanted an agreement on post-war frontiers that consolidated the Soviet Union's pre-1941 gains, and he wanted that agreement now.

Eden, the model of the aristocratic English gentleman, was clearly considerably disconcerted by Stalin's behaviour. Indeed, it is possible to see in this one encounter not just a clash of political ideologies but a clash of entire belief systems. Stalin – who was certainly not considered a 'gentleman' by the British – was thought to have revealed his boorish, peasant origins. His apparent lack of sophistication in diplomacy made it easy for some British people either to feel superior to him or to find him exotic and intriguing. Both approaches were mistaken. Sir Alexander Cadogan, for example, wrote in his diary after meeting Stalin on 17 December that: 'Difficult to say whether S [Stalin] is impressive. There he is – a greater Dictator than any Czar (and more successful than most). But if one didn't know that, I don't think one would pick him out of a crowd. With his little twinkly eyes and his stiff hair brushed back he is rather like a porcupine. Very restrained and quiet. Probably a sense of humour. I thought at first he was simply bluffing. But I was wrong.'[50]

The gulf between British and Soviet sensibilities was epitomized by the banquet on the last night of the talks. It was held in the Empress Catherine's rooms at the Kremlin, and Eden described it as 'almost embarrassingly sumptuous'.[51] After suckling pig, sturgeon and caviar, the serious drinking began. This soon degenerated to a level of rowdiness that surprised the visitors, although one of the junior secretaries at the British embassy did enter into the spirit of the occasion by wrestling with a drunken Marshal Voroshilov.[52] Another Soviet marshal, Timoshenko, was so inebriated that Stalin remarked to Eden: 'Do your generals ever get drunk?' Eden, ever the urbane diplomat, replied: 'They don't often get the chance.'[53]

Regardless of these alcohol-fuelled antics, the sheer power and single-mindedness of Stalin's demand that Britain must recognize the Soviet borders of 1941, reiterated again and again during the meetings in the Kremlin, did have an effect on Eden. He wrote to Churchill on 5 January 1942 that he was clear that 'this question is for Stalin [the] acid test of our sincerity and unless we can meet him on it his suspicions of ourselves and [the] United States Government will persist'.[54] Eden then outlined the 'case for immediate recognition', although he added that 'I realise, of course, that [the] great difficulty with [the] United States Government must be [the] apparent conflict with [the] Atlantic Charter'.

When Eden's suggestion reached Churchill, he was incensed and rejected Stalin's demands. 'We have never recognised the 1941 frontiers of Russia,' Churchill wrote, 'except de facto. They were acquired by acts of aggression in shameful collusion with Hitler.'[55] Churchill also reminded Eden of the circumstances in which the Soviet Union had became an ally of the British, writing that 'they entered the war only when attacked by Germany, having previously shown themselves utterly indifferent to our fate and, indeed, they added to our burdens in our worst danger'. He ended his note by saying: 'But there must be no mistake about the opinion [of] any British Government of which I am head; namely, that it adheres to those principles of freedom and democracy set forth in the Atlantic Charter and that these principles must become especially active whenever any question of transferring territory is raised.'

Churchill could not have been clearer – the principles of the Atlantic Charter, signed only a few months before, were paramount. No changes in borders could be made without the free and fair consent of the populations concerned. It was a ringing endorsement of the fundamental values for which Britain was ostensibly fighting the war. They were also words that would come back to trouble Churchill as the war progressed.

STALIN'S MISPLACED OPTIMISM

Buoyed by the success of the Red Army in holding the Germans outside Moscow, Stalin announced to his High Command (the Stavka) on 5 January that Soviet forces should simultaneously attempt to relieve Leningrad in the north, challenge Army Group Centre near the Soviet capital, and mount a major offensive in the south towards the city of Kharkov. It was a plan so wildly optimistic as to be almost a fantasy. Marshal Zhukov and the Soviet Deputy Premier Nikolai Voznesensky tried to explain to Stalin why his ideas were flawed, but to no avail. Zhukov wanted the Red Army to reinforce Moscow, but Stalin announced: 'Let us not sit down in defence,' and ordered his major spring offensive to go ahead.

Countless examples on the ground demonstrated that whilst the Red Army had achieved limited gains in the winter snow outside Moscow, Soviet units were still not in a position to mount a successful massive strategic offensive. Their units lacked the equipment, experience and, crucially, the tactical know-how to defeat the Germans in a vast, sweeping military manoeuvre. Take the experience of Vasily Borisov, for example.

After taking part in the successful defence of Moscow, Borisov and his unit were sent in early spring to support the Soviet 33rd Army on the southwest front. But almost immediately they found themselves encircled by the Germans. In conditions that once again allowed the soldiers of the Wehrmacht to use their tactical advantage in armoured warfare, the Germans managed to trap an entire Soviet army. For several weeks Borisov and his comrades tried to fight on, as the Germans gradually tightened the ring around them. 'The Germans were dropping leaflets, telling us to surrender,' says Vasily Borisov. 'And a deadline was set [by the Germans]. Those who did not surrender would get killed by artillery and machine guns.' The scenes inside the encirclement were the stuff of nightmares: 'There were a lot of wounded people on carts – some of them didn't have limbs. There was blood and parts of dead bodies, and everywhere dead horses. You would see a wounded man with his guts out asking us to either kill him or give him a hand grenade so that he could kill himself.'

Borisov's commander ordered the surviving members of the unit to assemble in a meadow within a wood. He intended, somehow, to mount a breakout. But the Germans opened fire and the Soviet commander was shot in his legs. Borisov watched as he took his pistol from his holster and held it to his head. 'I'm not going to surrender alive,' his commander said. And then he pulled the trigger and fell down dead. 'We felt very bad,' says Borisov. 'We felt it was the end for us.'

Borisov made for the woods, where, he says, the Germans 'hunted them like rabbits'. He was one of only three survivors out of the hundreds who tried to conceal themselves that day. And Borisov himself only came through the experience because he ran deep into the woods and managed to eke out an existence amongst the trees and undergrowth for thirteen months until the Red Army recaptured the area in spring 1943. Initially he lived off 'dead animals – we washed this rotting food and grilled it on the fire'. But soon he and a few other survivors made contact with local villagers and either were given food or, on occasion, stole it.

The experience of Vasily Borisov and men like him, together with the destruction of the Soviet 33rd Army, should have given Stalin cause to think carefully about his endorsement of Marshal Timoshenko's proposed massive offensive in the south, which was due to begin in early May. But he continued to ignore all warnings and ordered that it should continue as planned.

Many of the Red Army soldiers who massed in preparation for the Kharkov offensive blithely shared Stalin's optimism. Boris Vitman,[56] an officer in the Soviet 6th Army – central to the offensive – remembers that at headquarters 'those who were planning the operation were certain that it would be completely successful and the mood was very cheerful...the idea was that by 1943 the war would be finished'.

The Kharkov offensive was predicated on the assumption that the Germans were planning their own spring offensive around Moscow. But this assumption was wrong. The Germans were actually gathering their forces together in the very area around Kharkov into which the Red Army sought to attack. Soviet forces began to advance towards the German line on 12 May. Initially they believed that the lack of resistance they encountered was the result of the preceding Soviet artillery bombardment. But this was yet another misinterpretation – when they passed through the German front line they saw that the defences were empty. The barrage had destroyed nothing. As the Soviet troops advanced further, they still did not meet any resistance. 'We kept marching and marching,' says Vitman. 'We did not give much thought to the fact that there were no Germans around. We thought we were marching towards Berlin.'

Several Soviet armies (the 21st, 28th, 38th and 6th in the north, and the 57th and 9th in the south) moved blithely forward into a trap – for the further they marched, the easier it was for the Germans to mount a successful encirclement action. And once their prey had committed themselves far enough, the Germans pulled the noose tight. On 19 May General Paulus, commander of the German 6th Army, made a counter-attack in the north that took the Soviets by surprise. As the encirclement closed, the Red Army soldiers fought desperately to try and find a way out. 'They [the Red Army] couldn't believe how much ground we had made up in the rearguard of the advance of their troops,' says Joachim Stempel,[57] an officer with the German 6th Army. '[There was] the sight of thousands of Russians, who were trying to escape – a heaving mass of them – trying to reach freedom, shooting at us and being shot back at. Then, with a lot of shouting, trying to find gaps through which they could escape, and then being repulsed by the hail of bullets from our artillery and guns…. The most horrifying pictures and impressions were the ones immediately after the attempted break outs; awful, horrible wounds and many, many dead.' It was clear that the Soviet plan had led to disaster. On 28 May Marshal Timoshenko ordered a halt to the offensive, but it was too late. Most of the Red Army soldiers who had taken part in the attack were trapped in what became known as the 'Barvenkovo mousetrap', and the Germans took over two hundred thousand Soviet prisoners.

It is hard to overestimate the significance of the German victory at Kharkov. Stalin in particular had shown himself utterly inept as a military thinker. He had, after all, not just agreed and championed the initial plan of attack, but had refused the Soviet High Command's request on 18 May that the 9th Army be allowed to attempt to break out of the encirclement. But it wasn't just Stalin who was to blame for the catastrophe of Kharkov. Throughout the Red Army there had been failures in leadership, failures in intelligence, failures in strategy and failures in battlefield tactics. And perhaps even more significantly, despite the fact that – unbeknownst to them – the Red Army had attacked straight into mass German troop formations, there were at least three Soviet soldiers on the battlefield to every two Germans. What Kharkov starkly demonstrated was that the Soviet Union could not win this war merely by superiority of numbers.

Stalin, as usual, refused to take responsibility for his mistakes. Instead, Marshal Timoshenko, one of the few people who had so far survived 'friendship' with Stalin, was removed from front-line command and sidelined. And Nikita Khrushchev, the chief political commissar responsible for the attack, was recalled to Moscow to face Stalin. 'I was very depressed,' said Khrushchev. 'We had lost many, many thousands of men. More than that, we had lost the hope we had been living by.... To make matters worse, it looked as if I were going to have to take the blame for it personally.'[58] Khrushchev, who had worked slavishly for Stalin since the early 1930s, knew well that the Soviet leader 'would stop at nothing to avoid taking responsibility for something that had gone wrong'. And so he reported to the Kremlin with a sense of foreboding.

Stalin toyed with him. He acted as if he had not yet decided Khrushchev's fate. On the one hand, Khrushchev bore – Stalin clearly intimated – a large share of the responsibility for the disaster at Kharkov. On the other, he remained utterly loyal and was always happy to be the butt of any cruel joke Stalin cared to devise. Khrushchev was to escape the torture chambers of the Lubyanka, but he did not escape humiliation. Some months later, while senior military commanders watched, Stalin emptied his pipe on top of

Khrushchev's bald pate. The Soviet leader explained that he was following an ancient tradition: 'When a Roman commander lost a battle, he lit a bonfire, sat down in front of it and poured ashes on his own head.'[59]

THE ALLIED RESPONSE

But it was not just the Soviets who were tasting defeat in the early months of 1942 – so were their Western Allies. On 15 February 1942, Lieutenant General Arthur Percival surrendered Singapore to the Japanese, and seventy thousand British and Allied soldiers marched into Japanese captivity. Churchill described the event as 'the worst disaster and largest capitulation in British history'.[60] In March, the Americans too suffered a heavy defeat at Japanese hands in the Philippines – an event that necessitated the humiliating flight of the American commander, General Douglas MacArthur.

It was at this most difficult time, when the Allies were facing setbacks in almost every theatre of war, that Churchill sent a significant telegram to Roosevelt. On 7 March 1942 the British Prime Minister made a volte face from the strong sentiments of principle he had expressed just two months before in his note to Eden. 'The increasing gravity of the war,' wrote Churchill to the American President, 'has led me to feel that the principles of the Atlantic Charter ought not to be construed so as to deny Russia the frontiers she occupied when Germany attacked her.'[61] This sudden desertion of the moral position he had so recently and so boldly upheld was caused, as he saw it, by practical necessity: 'Everything portends an immense renewal of the German invasion in the spring and there is very little we can do to help the only country that is heavily engaged with the German armies.' Churchill now tried to argue that since the Soviets had already occupied the Baltic states and Poland before Britain and America signed the Atlantic Charter, their desire to retain this territory at the end of the war could conceivably be considered legitimate. It was a flawed argument, of course, since the population of the Baltic states and eastern Poland had never, in free and fair elections, consented to become Soviet citizens. And, of course, just weeks before Churchill had himself confirmed in his note to Eden that Soviet occupation of these territores was in breach of the Charter.

Churchill's attempt at joining two positions that were logically unbridgeable came to nothing. But the fact that he even attempted such circumlocution is significant because it demonstrates just how early in the relationship – when it still seemed that the Soviet Union might lose – he was prepared to break the principles of self-determination within the Atlantic Charter.

His new position did not escape strong censure from the Americans. Sumner Welles, Under-Secretary of State, said that 'The attitude of the British government is not only indefensible from every moral standpoint, but likewise extraordinarily stupid.'[62] Welles's reading of Stalin's character was that the Soviet leader demanded more when he saw weakness in negotiation, and the danger of offering the Soviets any concession over territory was that, once conceded in one instance, more demands would surely follow. These concerns were shared by others in the British War Cabinet, and the decision was finally taken to refuse the Soviet demand that any treaty signed now should contain details of post-war borders. In particular, Roosevelt's administration was not about to desert the Atlantic Charter at this stage of the war, no matter what the difficulties.

In April 1942, shortly after Roosevelt had rejected Churchill's suggestion that Stalin should be granted his wish for the 1941 borders, a young naval officer called George Elsey arrived in Washington to work in the map room at the White House at the very heart of American power. His personal experience sheds considerable light on how Roosevelt's White House operated, and offers an insight into just how the American President thought he could deal with Stalin. Whilst Elsey felt that the White House was without question 'a very exciting place to be', he did rapidly discover some surprising truths about the way the American system of supreme command functioned. 'Franklin Roosevelt had some strange habits,' he says.[63] 'He would send messages out through one department and have the replies come back through another department because he didn't want anyone else to have a complete file on his communications with Prime Minister Winston Churchill, for example.... It was a trait of his that he didn't want anybody else to know the whole story on anything.' Through his own experience in the White House, Elsey came to the conclusion that the way Roosevelt often kept his own State Department in the dark was 'disgraceful' and led to gross administrative confusion. It was a leadership technique that the President carried over into his personal dealings with his staff: 'Because Roosevelt didn't ever take people fully into his confidence, it left his subordinates always uncertain of where they stood. They had to be loyal to him, but they didn't really know how loyal he was to them. This was part of his behavioural pattern, which is hard to understand and hard to excuse except it was the nature of the man.'

Elsey's judgement is confirmed by many of those who worked for Roosevelt in more senior positions. Even a man like Henry Morgenthau, who had been a neighbour of Roosevelt's in New York State and had served him faithfully since 1933, found that he was often out of the decision-making loop – even though he was Secretary of the Treasury. Roosevelt once memorably said to him, that as President he preferred not to 'let his left hand' know what his 'right hand was doing'.[64] It is an important insight into Roosevelt's technique of leadership, and one that was to have considerable consequences when it came to the attempt to create a coherent policy for dealing with Stalin.

But this was not the only insight into Roosevelt's character and method of governance that Elsey gained in the White House map room. He also learnt about the limitless self-confidence of his new boss: 'When I was assigned to the map room in April 1942 I was frequently on a night watch, and I was alone and there wasn't much going on. [So] I would dig back into the files to see what had happened before I got there. And there were some perfectly fascinating letters and cables, copies of cables that had been exchanged with the Prime Minister.' Elsey was struck by one cable in particular that he uncovered on one of his night-time searches.

It was a confidential note sent from Roosevelt to Churchill on 18 March 1942. 'I know you will not mind my being brutally frank,' wrote Roosevelt, 'when I tell you I think I can personally handle Stalin better than your Foreign Office or my State Department. Stalin hates the guts of all your top people. He thinks he likes me better, and I hope he will continue to do so.'[65]

'That was a favourite word of Roosevelt's,' says Elsey. 'I can "handle" people. I can "handle" something. And I thought this was a pretty astonishing thing for Roosevelt to be saying to the Prime Minister. But it stuck. That phrase stuck in my mind and I kept thinking of it as the war went on. Roosevelt was always thinking he could "handle" people, no matter who or what it was. He had that self-confidence that he would be in control no matter who or where...that he would pull through as the top dog.'

Roosevelt was about to demonstrate in practical terms just how he believed he could 'handle' the Soviet leadership – with near disastrous consequences for the alliance. The occasion was the visit of the Soviet Foreign Minister, Vyacheslav Molotov, in May 1942. This was the first contact at this level between the USA and the Soviet Union, and came at a time of great tension in the relationship between the Allies.

On his way to America Molotov stopped off in London, where he met Churchill and other leading figures in the British government. It was a difficult encounter. The Prime Minister wanted to sign a formal treaty of alliance with the Soviet Union to replace the existing agreement; but there were seemingly insurmountable problems caused by the two familiar fissures between the British and the Soviets – the question of the second front and the even more intractable issue of the drawing of post-war borders. The British knew, for example, that the Soviet Union was insistent not just on consolidating its gains in eastern Poland under the Molotov– Ribbentrop pact, but on annexing the Baltic states at the end of the war as well.

Churchill could offer Molotov little hope on either of these two major issues. This meant that the meetings, which began on 21 May, were frosty. Churchill sought to emphasize the immense problems the British faced in mounting a second front, saying that he did not think it would be possible to launch a successful large-scale crossing of the Channel until 1943. Whilst he agreed in principle to an invasion of France, there remained the question of when that operation was practicable. And significantly, when the British stuck consistently to their position and refused to give ground, Molotov moved his. After consultation with Moscow, on the 26th the Soviet Foreign Minister agreed to sign a treaty that contained no mention of post-war boundaries or the date of the second front.

With the straightforward British position fresh in his mind, Molotov arrived in Washington on 29 May. During his stay he lodged in the White House. It was an extraordinary moment in history. Here was a former Bolshevik terrorist, a man utterly opposed to the values of the United States – an individual, moreover, who had personally conducted negotiations with Hitler and Ribbentrop – staying in one of the most potent symbols of a system he despised.

The incongruous nature of the occasion was symbolized by two events on the first day of his visit. Both of them occurred in Molotov's bedroom in the East Wing of the White House. First, when a White House valet unpacked the Soviet Foreign Minister's suitcase he found inside it 'a large chunk of black bread, a roll of sausage and a pistol'. These were, presumably, the essential travelling requirements of his terrorist days. Eleanor Roosevelt, the President's wife, later wrote that: 'The Secret Servicemen did not like visitors with pistols but on this occasion nothing was said. Mr Molotov evidently thought he might have to defend himself and also he might be hungry.'[66]

The second significant moment occurred after eleven o'clock that evening, when there was a knock at Molotov's door. He opened it to find Harry Hopkins, Roosevelt's special adviser, standing outside.

'Can I say a few words to you, Mr Molotov, before the meeting tomorrow?' asked Hopkins.

Molotov asked him inside.

'I can tell you that President Roosevelt is a very strong supporter of a Second Front in 1942,' Hopkins told him. 'But the American Generals don't see the real necessity of the Second Front. Because of this I recommend you paint a harrowing picture of the situation in the Soviet Union so that the American Generals realise the seriousness of the situation.'[67]

Molotov replied that the situation on the front line was genuinely serious, so, by implication, he would have no difficulty in doing as Hopkins suggested. Hopkins also recommended that Molotov find time to speak to Roosevelt half an hour before the meeting and inform the American President that he planned to take Hopkins' advice. This Molotov also agreed to do.

This exchange is not mentioned in any of the American minutes of the conference; and the content of the meeting was clearly intended to stay secret. Hopkins, in a long memo about Molotov's visit,[68] mentions only in passing that the Soviet Foreign Minister was 'put up at the room across the way' from him in the White House and that 'I went in for a moment to talk to him' – with no reference to his mission from the President.

What this bizarre nocturnal meeting in the White House offers us, of course, is the chance to see at close quarters how Roosevelt attempted to 'handle' people. (Given how close Hopkins was to Roosevelt, and that Hopkins mentioned specifically in the conversation that Molotov should approach the President before the scheduled meeting, it is clear that Roosevelt knew just what was going on.) By sending Hopkins on his own to Molotov's room, Roosevelt was able to accomplish a number of political objectives. First, he could give the impression that he was secretly on Molotov's side over the important issue of the second front and was battling against the reticence of recalcitrant generals, but more than that, he could show that he wanted to be a friend and confidant of the Soviet leadership. And, most crucially of all, he could accomplish all this in a completely deniable way.

In fact, this method of 'handling' people seems to have been not uncommon in the White House. Less than a month later, on 21 June, when the British were in Washington, General Sir Alan

Brooke (later Lord Alanbrooke), Chief of the Imperial General Staff, was surprised when Hopkins asked him to come to his bedroom for a chat. 'We went to his room,' Brooke recorded in his diary, 'where we sat on the edge of his bed looking at his shaving brush and tooth brush, whilst he let me into some of the President's inner thoughts! I mention this meeting as it was so typical of this strange man with no official position, not even an office in the White House, and yet one of the most influential men with the President.'[69]

As for Molotov, he appears to have taken the advice of the 'strange' Harry Hopkins at the crucial meeting on 30 May. In the presence not just of President Roosevelt but also of General George Marshall, the powerful Armed Forces Chief of Staff, Molotov outlined the difficulties the Soviet Union faced, going so far as to say that if the second front was delayed until 1943, it was possible that by then 'Hitler might be the undisputed master of Europe' and, by implication, the Soviet Union defeated. Molotov said he thought it only 'right' to 'look at the darker side of the picture'. He went on to state that he 'requested a straight answer' to his question about whether the Americans were prepared to establish a second front. And according to the American minutes of the meeting, a straight answer was just what he got: 'The President then put to General Marshall the query whether developments were clear enough so that we could say to Mr Stalin that we are preparing a Second Front. 'Yes,' replied the General. The President then authorised Mr Molotov to inform Mr Stalin that we expect the formation of a Second Front this year.'[70]

It was obvious to all concerned how desperately the Soviets wanted the British and Americans to mount a cross-Channel operation in order to draw off an anticipated forty German divisions from the Eastern Front. And here was President Roosevelt making a commitment that the British Prime Minister had taken great care not to make. What is also interesting, given the importance of this one exchange, is that the recently released Russian minutes of the meeting[71] do not contain the key sentence that 'The President then authorised Mr Molotov to inform Mr Stalin that we expect the formation of a Second Front this year', although they do show that General Marshall said that it was 'possible' that a second front could be opened in 1942 and that the Americans were doing 'everything possible' to achieve this end.

But whilst the Russian minutes of the meeting seem to show Roosevelt and Marshall offering less of a commitment than did the American record of the encounter, the subsequent wrangling over the wording of the communiqué to be released at the end of Molotov's visit indicates that the American records contain much of the real spirit of the discussion. When General Marshall saw the proposed statement, with explicit reference to a second front in 1942, he objected to it. He 'urged that there be no reference to 1942'[72] but Roosevelt insisted that form of words be included in order to please the Soviets.

Perhaps the possibility that the Soviets might try to extricate themselves from the war loomed large in Roosevelt's mind, and this optimistic statement about the second front was a way of offering another reason for the Red Army to keep slugging it out with the Germans. Perhaps he even – but this is extremely unlikely given the military advice he was receiving – thought that the Americans could actually deliver a second front in 1942. But what-ever the exact motives behind Roosevelt's actions – and typically he never explained to anyone why he insisted on the reference to '1942' staying in the communiqué – this was, in a profound sense, not the right way to 'handle' Stalin. The Soviet leader was a man who wanted actions to follow words. Roosevelt had utterly misjudged him.

Molotov returned to Moscow with a final communiqué containing the sentence: 'In the course of the conversations full understanding was reached with regard to the urgent tasks of creating a second front in 1942.' When Churchill learnt of this apparent commitment he was at pains once more to point out to Molotov that this statement represented only a hoped for possibil-ity, but nonetheless Molotov presented the statement to the Politburo as it stood. And the plain meaning of the words, as far as the Soviet leadership read them, was clear – the Western Allies had promised an invasion of northern France in 1942 in order to relieve the dire pressure on the Eastern Front.

It is almost impossible to underestimate the importance of this moment in the history of the Alliance. Stalin already suspected that the Western Allies were standing by on the periphery of the conflict, whilst the Soviets and the Germans bled each other to death. Now, almost worse, Stalin would come to believe that Roosevelt had added outright duplicity to the mix. When the much longed for second front was not launched in 1942, Stalin would come to believe he had been betrayed. And if he could not trust the Western Allies on this most fundamental issue, how could he trust them at all?

THE ARCTIC CONVOYS

For the Soviets, the two main priorities in their relationship with their Allies remained the demand for the opening of the second front and confirmation of the legitimacy of their pre-1941 borders, but a close third on their wish list was the continuation – and possible increase – in supplies of goods and military equipment.

But here again, as far as Stalin was concerned, the Western Allies had let the Soviet Union down. A joint British–American delegation, led by Lord Beaverbrook, Minister of Supply, and Averell Harriman, Roosevelt's special envoy, had arrived in Moscow at the end of September 1941 and signed an agreement that the Western Allies would supply a huge amount of equipment to the Soviet Union each month, including 500 tanks and 400 aeroplanes, plus quantities of tin, zinc, copper and other badly needed raw materials.[73] But this promise had not been met – only a tiny amount of aid arrived in November and December. Beaverbrook resigned from the government in February 1942, partly in protest at the 'lack' of aid to the Soviet Union and also to campaign openly for the Western Allies to mount a swift second front – a campaign that clearly touched a chord in

Britain, where fifty thousand people attended a rally in London in May 1942.[74]

In the early months of 1942 the flow of aid increased to the Soviet Union, although it never reached the optimistic levels pledged by the Moscow agreement of September 1941. Much of the supplies were sent via railway from Iran or across the Pacific to Vladivostok, but a significant amount arrived in the Soviet Union by one of the most dangerous wartime sea routes – up the coast of Norway and around the Barents Sea to the northern ports of the Soviet Union, chiefly Murmansk and Archangel.

The first convoy left Liverpool for Archangel on 12 August 1941, arriving in the Soviet Union on the 31st, but the first of the famous 'PQ' convoys (named after the first two initials of the planning officer in the Admiralty, Commander Philip Quellyn Roberts) sailed from Hvalfjord in Iceland on 29 September. Churchill promised Stalin in October 1941 that a convoy would leave every ten days for the Soviet Union, but it proved impossible to keep to this ambitious schedule – a failure that only served to irritate Stalin further.

However, the Soviet leader failed to recognize the immense difficulties faced by these convoys. At the beginning it was primarily the weather: during the winter ice formed all over the exposed areas of the ships, and the crews knew that they would survive for only a few minutes if they fell into the sea. But once the weather improved, the danger increased. The combination of the long summer nights, the concentration of German aircraft in northern Norway, the constant threat from U-boat attack and the slow speed of the merchant ships in the convoys, which were relatively unprotected from air attack, now made the voyage hazardous in the extreme. So much so that on 16 May 1942, less than a week before Molotov's arrival in London, the British Chiefs of Staff had discussed the question of whether or not to send PQ16, a convoy shortly scheduled to leave Iceland en route to Murmansk.

The fate of PQ13, which had left Reykjavik in Iceland on 20 March, was known to all the Chiefs of Staff – and the knowledge made them anxious. Five out of the twenty merchant ships on that convoy had been lost, together with one escort vessel. On one of the merchant ships, the *Induna*, out of a crew of 66 only 24 had survived – and only six of these had finished the journey with all their limbs intact. Two other Allied merchantmen were subsequently sunk by German air raids in the Soviet port of Murmansk. And although the last convoy, PQ15, had not suffered as much, the Chiefs of Staff thought this 'gave a false impression as regards the possibility of getting convoys through to North Russia'. Past experience showed, they felt, that 'unless the weather is unsuitable for flying the chances of even a ship steaming at 18 knots getting through without being attacked from the air are very remote'.[75] So on 16 May they recommended to the Prime Minister that, until the ice had receded further and the convoys could follow a more northerly route that would take them a greater distance from the German air bases in Norway, 'it would be better to defer the sailing of our convoys'. As a result, at least two planned convoys would have to be cancelled.

Since the next convoy, PQ16, was due to sail just two days later, on the 18th, the matter was clearly urgent. Churchill gave his answer on the 17th in a note to General Ismay: 'Not only Premier Stalin but President Roosevelt will object very much to our desisting from running the convoys now. The Russians are in heavy action and will expect us to run the risk and pay the price entailed by our contribution.... My own feeling mingled with much anxiety is that the convoy ought to sail on the 18th. The operation is justified if a half get through. The failure on our part to make the attempt would weaken our influence with both our major allies. There are always the uncertainties of weather and luck which may aid us. I share your misgivings but I feel it is a matter of duty.'[76]

The following day Churchill put the question of the sailing of PQ16 to the War Cabinet. But since he had already decided what the answer to the Chiefs of Staff should be, it was a foregone conclusion. Churchill first outlined in some detail the Admiralty's concerns, and then listened to a suggestion that perhaps Stalin should be asked if he really wanted these convoys to try to get through, given that half of them might be lost. This notion was quashed at once with the reply that 'the decision was one which we must take ourselves and ought not to place on other shoulders'. Churchill then reiterated that 'it was our duty to fight these convoys through, whatever the cost.... The effect on war comradeship between the United Nations, of cancellation of the May Convoy would, I fear, be very serious.'[77]

Churchill could not have made it clearer that the decision to let PQ16 sail was a political and not a military one. By explicitly announcing that he was prepared to send this convoy on the basis that 'The operation is justified if a half get through' he was demonstrating that he was ready to sacrifice hundreds of British, American and other Allied lives, plus eighteen fully laden merchant ships, in order to show Stalin that the British were serious in their desire to help the Soviet war effort. In pure military terms, contemplating sending a convoy where 'only half get through' was dubious in the extreme. But in cold political terms in the circumstances of the time, it made sense.

The timing of the decision was vital. Molotov was due to arrive in London in a few days and Churchill knew that he would be calling once again for a second front. And since Churchill was aware that he could not provide military assistance on that scale, at least, he must have thought, the British could demonstrate that they were prepared immediately to sacrifice something to help the Red Army – that they were prepared, as he put it, 'to pay the price entailed' by their alliance with the Soviet Union. And though the sailors, soldiers and airmen who waited on board the merchant ships and assorted escort vessels that constituted convoy PQ16 knew nothing of these political machinations, they did know, in the words of Eddie Grenfell,[78] a Royal Navy sailor on the *Empire Lawrence*, that 'this was not going to be a pleasant journey, because by this time we'd heard about the mass air attacks, and, of course, I knew about the weather up there'.

Neil Hulse[79] was a merchant sailor on board the same ship, and remembers that the Arctic 'didn't have a very good reputation for voyages'. So much so that he had not initially wanted to sail on PQ16: 'I went with [some] others and we decided we'd try to get a transfer to another ship because we hadn't yet signed on for this voyage. [So] I went across Liverpool, to Lime Street Station to travel home and wait for an appointment for another vessel.' But as he sat in the station buffet at Lime Street, Hulse suddenly felt 'ashamed of himself'. He thought of the example set by Captain Darkin of the *Empire Lawrence*, a man in his seventies who had volunteered to come back and serve the war effort. So he changed his mind, went back to Liverpool docks and joined the ship.

The *Empire Lawrence*, laden with tanks for the Red Army, sailed from Birkenhead and joined PQ16, which left Iceland on 21 May. The voyage across the North Sea was 'reasonably quiet', says Neil Hulse. 'But we were getting radio messages from the convoy ahead of us of the air attacks and submarine attacks which were taking place.' Eddie Grenfell was almost fatalistic about the voyage ahead: 'It was the same thing in the Mediterranean, the same thing everywhere. We always had attacks. It was the war and we just thought, well, I hope I survive it.... It was never any – honestly, I mean this – there was never any feeling about "I hope we all survive." You said: "I hope I survive. I hope I'm alive tomorrow." That was the feeling.'

PQ16 suffered its first major attack on 26 May, 370 miles off the northern coast of Norway, and was systematically targeted for the next four days. 'I've never experienced such concentrated air attacks anywhere else in the war as I did in the Arctic,' says Eddie Grenfell. 'There were days when they attacked us with 150 dive bombers and torpedo bombers, quite apart from the U-boats that were all over the place. And it was dreadful – they just came. Don't forget they were only a few minutes' flying time away from Norway and they came out in a wave of twenty to thirty at a time. And then they did their attacks, they went back, refuelled and came out again.... It was just noise all the time. Dreadful noise of guns being fired, firing all the time – and it was rather exciting.'

Kurt Dahlmann[80] was one of the German pilots who attacked PQ16. He dropped bombs on the convoy from his Junkers 88 dive bomber, whilst his comrades' Heinkel 111s made lower torpedo raids on the ships: 'The planes had different speeds. The Heinkel 111 was slower than the Junkers 88 and it was very difficult to coordinate the flights in such a way that the attacks took place simultaneously.' For the German aircrew – just as for the sailors beneath them – one of the biggest enemies was the weather: 'Of course the danger of freezing was immense – especially since we didn't have that much experience with frozen conditions.'

The *Empire Lawrence* had its own air protection – in the shape of a single Hurricane fighter flown by a South African pilot called Alistair Hay. 'They were suicide ships as far as he was concerned,' says Eddie Grenfell, 'because he was shot off [by catapult] but there was no coming back. There was no flight deck to land on. So he knew that he was either going to be killed or else he might be lucky and come down in the sea. And so long as he wasn't there more than five minutes he might be picked up.'

'If anyone was a Kamikaze,' says Neil Hulse, 'it was our pilot. He [the pilot] would talk about it to me over a dram because I was second officer. He just said, "Neil I'm going to bale out and I know you will pick me up as soon as possible." But he showed no sign of any fear whatsoever.... It was just a marvellous example of a guy who knew what he wanted to do and it didn't seem to upset him as far as his nerves were concerned.'

'We were used to people being killed,' says Eddie Grenfell. 'And we just knew that he was going out to do a job and we wished him the best of luck. We knew it was rather a dangerous job – more dangerous than anything we'd ever seen anyone else do before then. But we never thought: "Well, God, what a wonderful chap, what a brave fellow" and all that, because we were all doing the same – [and] as we realized in two days' time, we were going to suffer more than he ever did.'

On 26 May, Alistair Hay sat in the cockpit of his Hurricane on the fore-deck of the *Empire Lawrence*, gunned the engine to full throttle and released the brake. The catapult shot forward and propelled him up into the air. As he flew towards the massed German warplanes, over the radio Neil Hulse heard him say: 'I am going in, I am going in.' Single-handedly, he fought a squadron of

German Heinkels. He managed to shoot two of them down before he ran out of ammunition. Then he was ordered over the radio: 'Bale out! Bale out!'

Hay flew back towards the convoy, turned his plane upside-down so that he could more easily escape, and then dropped from the cockpit. He managed to parachute into the water near one of the escort ships, HMS *Volunteer*, and was picked up after only a few minutes in the water. Via Aldis signal lamp, the crew of the *Empire Lawrence* anxiously enquired after his fate. 'How is our pilot?' they signalled. And the reply came back: 'He is thawing out....'

But the Hurricane flight of Alistair Hay was not the only act of conspicuous bravery from the *Empire Lawrence* that day. For Eddie Grenfell volunteered to climb the ship's mast, together with another sailor, in order to try and fix the radar. This was a dangerous task to perform on a ship travelling at full speed even in good weather – but in the swelling seas of the Arctic, with the mast covered in black ice, it was perilous in the extreme. Climbing slowly, Eddie and his comrade managed to reach the top without incident and began to repair the wires. Then, suddenly, the Germans attacked again. 'We had all the blooming guns firing from our own ship,' says Eddie, 'and then there were the dive bombers coming in and firing all at the same time. Honest to God, in all my life I have never been so frightened, just crouching down there.' Then there was a sudden noise – a huge bang – as gunfire hit only a few feet or so beneath them. A hole appeared in the mainmast, damaging the access ladder – but the mast was still upright. After the attack was over, the two of them somehow managed to negotiate their way back down the broken mast and on to the relative safety of the main deck. 'Bring these boys some rum!' called the captain. 'That was the bravest thing I've ever seen.'

The next day, 27 May, the attacks increased. 'We were acting in cooperation with the German air force,' says Jürgen Oesten,[81] a decorated U-boat captain who was coordinating the operation from his base in northern Norway. 'The information we would get from the air force – about change of course and so on – meant we could place our boats in the relevant position.' And paradoxically, given the danger that the convoy crews faced, for these U-boat crews the Arctic was one of the safest places to fight: 'We lost more boats, relatively speaking, in the Atlantic than in the ice [the Arctic].'

As a general rule, U-boats did not attack British convoys in the manner of popular myth – attempting to sink the ships by launching torpedoes while submerged. 'The submarines then,' says Jürgen Oesten, 'were not actually what you would call submarines nowadays. They were surface vessels that could dive. But the problem was that when they went under the surface they were practically stationary – they could only manage very slow speeds.' As a result, the preferred method of attack was at night, on the surface. 'For instance,' says Oesten, 'with the three U-boats I had during the war, I sank twenty ships. But nineteen I sank at night on the surface.'

Pounded by German air attacks during the day, and subjected to the torpedoes of the U-boats at night, the ships of PQ16 ploughed their way towards the Soviet Union and the Barents Sea. The sailors aboard those ships wondered how many of them would make the journey alive, as each mile they steamed north seemed more perilous than the last. On the morning of 27 May Eddie Grenfell saw a whole ship on fire, lying dead in the water, and standing on the deck amidst the flames was an elderly man: 'We were close to it, and we yelled at him to jump into the sea because the whole ship was ablaze, and he wouldn't. And all we could see was this ship disappearing behind us, with this chap absolutely resigned to his fate – this look of resignation, staring into the sky. We never saw him again. That was it.'

Then, at around quarter to two that afternoon, Grenfell and the rest of the crew of the *Empire Lawrence* saw a group of Junkers 88 bombers circling overhead. They appeared to be checking whether this was the ship that had launched a fighter plane into the sky the previous day. And, once they saw the catapult on the forward deck and confirmed their suspicion, they launched an attack. The *Empire Lawrence* was hit by the first bomber, and slowly began to sink. Captain Darkin gave the order to abandon ship and the lifeboats were lowered.

Then, just as Eddie Grenfell reached the upper deck, the dive bombers attacked en masse, dropping high explosive and firing machine guns. 'And the funny thing is,' he says, 'you don't hear the explosion. The ship heaves. There's a bit of a thump. But you expect when a bomb hits to get an explosion – you don't. You just feel the thump and then the ship rises out of the water.'

Grenfell dived to the floor, and when the planes had finished the bombing run he discovered he was covered with bodies. He had to push and squeeze to escape the mound of badly wounded or dead crewmen on top of him. 'Then there was another attack – we were hit by four bombers altogether, and the last bomb obviously went into the ammunition dump and the whole ship just exploded. I shall never forget it. I flew through the air. I must have been on my back because when I was looking upwards I could see pieces of steel going through the air with me. It was like slow motion. And one of the pieces looked like the ship's funnel. And the next thing I knew I was deep down [in the sea] – I can't remember hitting the water. All I remember was being deep down in the sea.'

The ship exploded just as Neil Hulse was about to get into the lifeboat. 'I can remember being blown up into the air with ventilators, derricks, hatch-boards coming up into the air with me – and some other seamen like me were blown up. We hit the water. One of our lifeboats was upside-down, and quite a few brave seamen were hanging on to it in these icy conditions.'

Meantime, Eddie Grenfell had been pushed to the surface by the explosion of the *Empire Lawrence*'s boiler. But his troubles were not over. 'I got to the surface and I started to sink again. And I was panic-stricken. I thought: "Well, I survived that [and] here I am going down again." So I pulled...and there was something on my arm.... A head appeared with a piece of shrapnel right down the middle – there was grey matter oozing from it, obviously his brains.'

Eddie's shipmate had grabbed on to his pullover before he died and was now acting as a weight, dragging him under water. 'So I pulled him up, loosened his grip, and he just floated away.'

Once he was free of the body of his comrade, he clambered on to the top of an upturned lifeboat by pushing his fingers into the joints in the clinker-built hull and hauling himself up. But it was, he believed, only a temporary postponement of death: 'When I first got on to the lifeboat, and I couldn't see any other ships, I thought we were gone. I thought we were going to be left there, as did happen on some occasions in the Arctic.... [I was] a bit panic-stricken, thinking: "Oh, God!" I'd only just got married a couple of months before.'

Neil Hulse too had managed to get out of the water – by climbing on to a small raft. The young aircraftsman who shared his refuge said to him: 'You've got your leg off, sir. I think your leg's off.' Hulse felt down his back, and at the base of his spine 'could feel what I thought was bone... I mean, I really thought I'd lost my leg.' Summoning up his courage, he looked behind to inspect the damage. It turned out that his leg was intact, but sticking into his 'starboard buttock' was 'a small plank of wood with six-inch nails'. Then, as the minutes went by with no sign of rescue, his thoughts turned to how death in the Arctic Sea would be such a 'lonely' way to leave this world. 'I was going through the fact of having loved the sea...but I thought I would never ever have any more life.'

Eddie Grenfell and the other men clinging on to the upturned lifeboat were lucky – they were picked up by one of the Royal Navy escort vessels, a corvette: 'When we got on board we couldn't walk or anything. We were carried because we'd lost the use of our legs.' The same corvette then moved towards Neil Hulse and his companion. But the ship was under attack from Junkers 88 bombers, so the sailors on board shouted over by loud hailer that they planned to sail straight past, and the two men would get just one chance to jump and catch hold of the scrambling nets that hung down the side of the moving ship.

'Are you fit enough to jump if we come near you?' they shouted.

'I'll jump over the bloody moon if you come close – don't worry about that!' replied Neil Hulse.

But his legs were frozen, so when the ship came close some of the sailors had to lean over and help drag him, and then his companion, off the raft. Once on board, Neil's clothes were cut from him and he was wrapped in blankets and taken down to the engine room to thaw out. There he was offered several glasses of 'Nelson's Blood' (rum), and an hour later, was singing 'Nellie Dean'. Later, when he had sobered up and regained feeling in his legs, he was asked to report to the captain on the bridge: 'He said, "Well, I'm very sorry to say that you are the only surviving officer from your ship – they are all lost, including your captain who was killed in the explosion."'

Out of the thirty-six ships that sailed on PQ16, a total of six were sunk by German attack in the Arctic Sea and another ship was destroyed by air attack shortly after arrival in Murmansk. But, horrendous as the suffering on PQ16 had been, the convoy was – by Churchill's definition – a success since 'more than a half' of the ships had survived. And politically it had succeeded in demonstrating to Stalin that the British and Americans were prepared to endure hardship in order to help the Soviet war effort.

THE CRISIS GROWS

The Soviets certainly needed help because for the Red Army the next few weeks and months were to be amongst the toughest of the war. After the Soviet defeat at Kharkov, on 28 June 1942 the Germans launched Operation Blue – a massive thrust through the Soviet southern front.

The German advance prospered. It was almost a return to the glory days of the summer of the previous year. The Soviet failure at Kharkov had left a gap in the Red Army's defensive line through which the 1st and 4th German Panzer armies now charged. By the end of July, with German units having advanced as far as the river Don, Hitler decided to divide his forces. Army Group A would head south for the oilfields of the Caucasus, while

Army Group B would advance directly east in the direction of Stalingrad on the river Volga.

Anatoly Mereshko,[82] a Red Army officer, was one of those who tried – and failed – to halt the German advance that summer: 'The Germans were so confident, which was natural because they moved from Kharkov to the Don.' He recalls that they moved forward 'having rolled up their sleeves, wearing shorts and singing songs. As for our retreating units, they were really completely demoralized people. They didn't know where they were going and they didn't know where to look for their units.'

But it wasn't just the Red Army that faced defeat in the summer of 1942. The Allied force in North Africa was engaged in a fierce struggle to hold back the German Afrika Korps under Lieutenant General Erwin Rommel, with Tobruk eventually falling to the Germans on 21 June. Rolf Mummiger[83] served with Rommel, and recalls seeing piles and piles of bodies of Allied soldiers: 'They must have been lying there for days. I've never forgotten this, and it affected me emotionally very much.' Altogether some seventy thousand British and other Allied troops were killed or captured at Tobruk. It was the lowest point in the campaign in the Western Desert, which had begun nearly two years before with an Italian attack on the British in Egypt.

Churchill was in the White House when he heard the news of the defeat. This was his second wartime visit to America. He had travelled there first in the immediate aftermath of Pearl Harbor, arriving on 22 December 1941 and installing himself on the second floor of the White House. The British had been astonished at the lack of clarity in the top echelons of the American command structure. Sir John Dill, Chief of the British Joint Staff Mission in Washington, wrote to General Sir Alan Brooke, chief of the Imperial General Staff: 'There are no regular meetings of their Chiefs of Staff, and if they do meet there is no secretariat to record their proceedings. There is no such thing as a Cabinet meeting.... The whole organization belongs to the days of George Washington....'[84]

Now, in the summer of 1942, Churchill was trying once again

to keep in touch with military developments amidst Roosevelt's intentionally disorganized White House. And White House staffer George Elsey's first sight of him coincided with the news from Tobruk reaching the Prime Minister. 'I had to go to the second floor [of the private wing of the White House] to take some papers to Harry Hopkins. And as I went in with papers, trudging across the hall in his bathrobe came the Prime Minister, calling: "Harry! Harry!" Well, Hopkins wasn't there. [So] I stood very erect. I didn't have my cap on so I couldn't salute, but I said: "Good morning, Prime Minister." And all I got in return was "Harumph!!" and he turned and walked out because Hopkins was not there.... Churchill was in a foul mood that day because he'd had very, very bad news from a defeat in North Africa by Rommel.'

Despite the inauspicious circumstances of Elsey's first encounter with Churchill, 'none of this was negative: all I had was this positive feeling for this guy – here was a truly great man and I'm honoured and privileged just to be in his presence.... Churchill surprised me by being shorter than I expected – stooped and short and round-shouldered.... But all I knew was here is this God-like figure, saving the West.'

Elsey's blind faith in Churchill was touching, and it illustrated a broader point. For in the summer of 1942 it seemed as if supernatural powers might well be needed to ensure an Allied victory. For shortly after the defeat at Tobruk, the British suffered one of the greatest naval disasters in their history as convoy PQ17 was torn apart.

PQ17 was the largest convoy to set sail for the Soviet Union so far. And it received strong protection in the shape of four destroyers and ten corvettes as immediate support, with the battleships *Duke of York* and USS *Washington*, plus two cruisers and eight destroyers, sailing nearby. During the night of 4 July, the Admiralty in London received intelligence suggesting that the German warship *Tirpitz*, together with the *Admiral Scheer* and *Admiral Hipper*, had left their moorings in Trondheim in Norway and intended to attack the convoy. As a result, the First Sea Lord, Sir Dudley Pound, sent a signal to Admiral Tovey, the commander of PQ17, reading: 'Secret and most immediate: Cruiser force withdraw to westward at high speed.' Another signal was sent to the convoy twelve minutes later: 'Secret and most immediate: Owing to threat from surface ships, convoy is to disperse and proceed to Russian ports.'[85] But having sent this last signal, Pound was anxious lest the simple word 'disperse' might cause only a gradual breaking up of the convoy, so less than a quarter of an hour later he sent yet another signal: 'Secret. Most Immediate: Convoy is to scatter.' What this combination of signals caused was the sense of an imminent attack upon the convoy – something that was far from the case. Indeed, it turned out that the original intelligence was incorrect – the *Tirpitz* and the other German capital ships were not planning on attacking PQ17 at all.

PQ17 had already been under attack from German bombers and U-boats from 2 July, and on the 4th – the day Sir Dudley Pound sent his fateful signals – two ships had been sunk. So it was patently clear that the Germans knew exactly where the convoy was, and the direction in which it was steaming.

'The convoy just started disintegrating,' says Frank Hewitt,[86] who sailed on PQ17. 'And everyone was completely demoralized.' In such circumstances an order for the convoy to 'scatter' was tantamount to an order for it to self-destruct. '[We] couldn't believe it,' says Hewitt. 'Unbelievable…to think that the navy would desert a convoy. It just didn't make sense…[the speed of] the slowest ship was about four knots and they were just sitting ducks.'

Frank Hewitt was a sailor on board HMS *La Malouine*, one of the naval escort vessels that was ordered to proceed to the Barents Sea and thence to Archangel on its own: 'We felt that we were deserting them [the merchant ships of the convoy], and in fact we were.' On their way to the Soviet Union they picked up lifeboats full of survivors from the ships that had been sunk by the German bombers and U-boats, and Hewitt recalls one story told to him by the crew of an American merchantman they rescued from the sea: 'They were telling us that a submarine surfaced and the skipper said: "I'm sorry, gentlemen, I shall have to sink your ship. War is war. I will give you ten minutes to take to the boats. Have you got sufficient provisions for the journey? Good luck." And then another lot of survivors that we picked up, they said much the same sort of thing. A U-boat surfaced: "I'm very sorry, gentlemen. War is war. I shall have to sink your ship. You've got ten minutes to take to the boats. Why fight for the Bolsheviks? You're not Bolshevik, are you?"'

Hewitt had his own almost chivalrous dealings with a German U-boat when he was on anti-submarine patrol out of Archangel in the north of the Soviet Union: 'We were sailing along the edge of the ice-cap and a submarine surfaced, perhaps half a mile ahead, to charge his batteries. So, of course, we gave chase…. We took a shot at them. We had a four-inch gun, which was our biggest armament, but it fell short of the submarine. And on his Aldis lamp he flashed back: "Missed me! Try again." And I suppose our skipper replied: "We'll keep trying." And this went on for four or five hours, and then he decided he'd charged his batteries sufficiently well, so he said: "Thanks for the chase. We'll be leaving you now. Good luck." And then dived under the ice.'

Frank Hewitt's encounter with the German U-boat off the coast of Archangel demonstrated the ineffectiveness of the British navy during this crucial period of the war in the Arctic. For the reality was that the Admiralty advice about the dangers of running convoys in the long northern summer had been correct. And that, coupled with the false intelligence about the movement of the *Tirpitz*, had brought disaster. Of the 39 ships in PQ17, 24 were destroyed – more than 60 per cent of the convoy. A total of 153 merchant seamen lost their lives, and just under 100,000 tons of war material went to the bottom of the sea – including 210 bombers, 430 tanks and over 3000 other vehicles.

Not surprisingly, as a result of the PQ17 disaster, convoys to the Soviet Union were temporarily suspended.

Now, in the summer of 1942, Churchill contemplated the Allied surrender at Tobruk in North Africa, the destruction of PQ17 in the Arctic, and the swift advance across the steppes of the German army in the wildly successful Operation Blue. From the Allied perspective it was a bleak picture. Indeed, it looked as if it was perfectly possible that the Allies might lose the war.

Churchill knew that one of the keys to eventual victory was the Soviet Union. The Soviet people were bearing the brunt of the German attack. It was essential that Stalin keep the morale of the Red Army high and – most important of all – not contemplate any attempt to extricate himself and his people from the war. But Churchill was also aware of the effect that recent events would have on Stalin. The Western Allies would not open a second front in 1942 – the defeat at Tobruk, as well as other more minor military setbacks, ruled the operation out completely – and after PQ17 convoys to the north had, for the time being, ceased. The Soviet leader would not take this news well. So Churchill did what he most often did when faced with a crisis: he confronted it head on. He would, he announced, make the journey to Moscow in a converted British bomber, and explain to Stalin personally why the Allies couldn't do what the Soviet leadership had demanded. He would fly nearly 2000 miles, in great discomfort, in an attempt to preserve the vital relationship with Stalin.

3

CRISIS OF FAITH

MEETING STALIN

While the Germans were advancing through the steppes of southern Russia in the summer of 1942, Nikolai Baibakov, Deputy Minister for Soviet Oil Production, hurried to see Stalin at his office in the senate building of the Kremlin.

'I'd had about five meetings with Stalin before that one,' says Baibakov,[1] then one of the Soviet Union's top oil engineers, 'and he made a very big impression on me.... They were very business-like meetings. Joseph Stalin always showed interest in the state of affairs in the oil industry and he attached a lot of significance to its developments.' But this particular meeting was to be of more significance than the others. Baibakov was shown into Stalin's office, and in this 'calm' atmosphere waited expectantly for his leader to speak.

'Comrade Baibakov,' said Stalin, 'Hitler is rushing to the Kavkaz [Caucasus]. He has announced that if he doesn't seize the Kavkaz oil, then he'll lose the war. Everything must be done so that not a single drop of oil should fall to the Germans.' Baibakov was told that his job was to travel to the Caucasus and ensure that the Germans didn't get hold of any oil. But then Stalin added – and at this point, Baibakov recalls, his voice became 'a touch crueller': 'Bear in mind that if you leave the Germans even one ton of oil, we will shoot you. But if you destroy the supplies prematurely, and the Germans wouldn't have managed to capture them anyway and we're left without fuel, then we will also shoot you.'[2]

Perhaps surprisingly, Baibakov considers that Stalin's method of motivating him was 'justified'. 'Of course if I had made a mistake it would have been a crime,' he says. 'It would have been a crime if I had left the oilfields for the Germans. I would have gone against my country.' Yet Baibakov also admits that he would have 'done his best' to try to protect the oilfields without this blatant threat from Stalin. Intriguingly, he seems to feel that the fact that the Soviet leader had taken time in his packed schedule to threaten him personally was almost a badge of honour, a sign that he was being entrusted with an especially important task. 'Perhaps I would have said the same thing if I had been in his place,' he says. 'The end justifies the means.'

Ultimately, of course, Nikolai Baibakov survived, since the Germans never came close enough to the oilfields he was ordered to protect for him to have to make the decision whether to destroy them or not. But Stalin's method of inspiring Baibakov to do his job, together with Baibakov's total acceptance of it, is nonetheless instructive. It demonstrates the extent to which straightforward brutality was at the core of Stalin's leadership technique. He believed that if you really want someone to do something, if their task is monumentally important, you must make sure they know that if they mess it up they will die.

Around this same time, Churchill was en route to Moscow for his own series of meetings with the Soviet leader. The relationship between Britain and the Soviet Union was clearly deteriorating. On 18 July 1942 Churchill had written to Stalin and delivered the bad news about supplies and the second front. Stalin had, not surprisingly, been less than happy with this communication and had replied on the 23rd with a cold and accusatory telegram: 'I received your message of 18 July,'[3] wrote the Soviet leader. 'Two conclusions could be drawn from it. First, the British government refuses to continue the sending of war materials to the Soviet Union via the northern route. Second, in spite of the agreed communiqué concerning the urgent task of creating a second front in 1942, the British government postpones this matter until 1943.' After this devastating opening, in which he effectively accused Britain of breaking direct promises to the Soviet Union, Stalin asserted that his own military and naval experts found the reasons for the stopping of the convoys 'wholly unconvincing'. 'Of

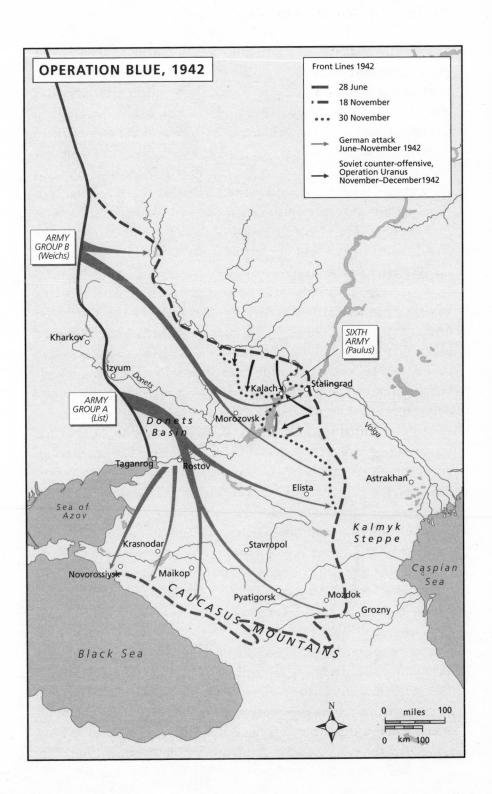

OPERATION BLUE, 1942

Front Lines 1942

- 28 June
- 18 November
- 30 November
- → German attack June–November 1942
- → Soviet counter-offensive, Operation Uranus November–December 1942

ARMY GROUP B (Weichs)

ARMY GROUP A (List)

SIXTH ARMY (Paulus)

Kharkov

Izyum

Donets

Donets Basin

Taganrog

Rostov

Kalach

Stalingrad

Morozovsk

Volga

Elista

Astrakhan

Sea of Azov

Kalmyk Steppe

Krasnodar

Stavropol

Caspian Sea

Novorossiysk

Maikop

Pyatigorsk

Mozdok

Grozny

CAUCASUS MOUNTAINS

Black Sea

N

0 miles 100

0 km 100

course,' he wrote, 'I do not think that regular convoys to the Soviet northern ports could be made without risk or losses. But in wartime no important undertaking could be made without risk or losses. In any case, I never expected that the British government would stop despatch of war materials to us just at the very moment when the Soviet Union, in view of the serious situation on the Soviet–German front, requires these materials more than ever.... I must state in the most emphatic manner that the Soviet government cannot acquiesce in the postponement of a second front in Europe until 1943.' Stalin ended with the clearly disingenuous hope that Churchill 'will not feel offended that I expressed frankly and honestly my own opinion'.

Sir Archibald Clark Kerr, the extrovert and somewhat eccentric British ambassador in Moscow who had replaced the solemn Sir Stafford Cripps in February 1942, was clear about what lay behind Stalin's harsh and non-diplomatic language. In a cable to London on 25 July he wrote that in his view the Soviet leadership didn't believe 'that we are yet talking the war seriously. They set up their own enormous losses against our (by comparison) trifling losses in men and material since the close of 1939.'[4] And three days later, on 28 July, Clark Kerr suggested that the Prime Minister should visit Moscow in an attempt to placate Stalin personally.

Churchill realized that he had to make the arduous journey, even though he did not relish the prospect of a conference with Stalin at this difficult time. Before he left he told his doctor, Charles Wilson, later Lord Moran, that he was not looking forward to the meeting because Stalin 'won't like what I have to say to him',[5] and he later wrote that he felt his journey to Moscow 'was like carrying a large lump of ice to the North Pole'.[6] But it was General Sir Alan Brooke, Chief of the Imperial General Staff, who most succinctly expressed the problem the British faced: 'We were going into the lion's den and we weren't going to feed him.'[7]

Churchill flew out in an unheated and unpressurized American bomber, wearing an oxygen mask that had a special attachment that allowed him to smoke cigars, and eventually, after a stop-over in Cairo, where he berated his commanders for their poor showing

left: The document that led to the Katyn massacre. Stalin's agreement – scrawled in blue crayon – on Beria's proposal of 5 March 1940 to 'try before special tribunals' selected Polish citizens who were 'sworn enemies of Soviet authority'.

right: Molotov (seated), Ribbentrop (standing left) and Stalin at the moment the Nazi/Soviet Non-Aggression Pact was signed in the Kremlin in August 1939. Stalin, as this picture shows, was happy and at ease with the Nazi Foreign Minister.

below: Finnish troops on exercise. They were shortly to fight during the war against the Soviet Union in the winter of 1939/40. The Finns initially had success against a Red Army that vastly outnumbered them.

above: Molotov (left) and Hitler during the Soviet Foreign Minister's visit to Berlin in November 1940. The trip was not a success.

below: Soviet troops cross into eastern Poland in the autumn of 1939. The secret part of the Nazi/Soviet Non-Aggression Pact had decreed that this area of Poland was in the Soviet 'sphere of influence'.

above: Red Army soldiers surrender to a
German tank unit in the summer of 1941.
The Germans took 3 million Soviet prisoners
in the first seven months of the war.

above: The German auxiliary cruiser *Komet*
(Comet) in a variety of different guises.
The ship, which sailed across the top of the
Soviet Union in 1940, was regularly
repainted, renamed and disguised in order
to prevent detection.

left: German officers discuss with a Soviet
officer (far left) the demarcation line between
their various pieces of conquered territory
after the signing of the Nazi/Soviet pact.

above: A vast prisoner of war camp, holding thousands of captured
Red Army soldiers in the summer of 1941. During the course of
the war the Germans took 5.7 million Soviet prisoners – 3.3 million
died in captivity.

below: Major Hugh Lunghi (centre, with moustache) in Moscow as
part of the British Military Mission. This photograph was taken after
the war when Field Marshal Montgomery (third from right) visited
the Soviet Union.

above: An Allied Arctic convoy – PQ 18 – comes under German attack. These convoys provided vital aid for the Soviet war effort.

right: The first wartime meeting between Franklin Roosevelt (left) and Winston Churchill in August 1941 aboard HMS *Prince of Wales* in Newfoundland. Here they would sign the Atlantic Charter.

below: Canadian soldiers – with British support – land on Spitsbergen in the Arctic circle in August 1941 as part of Operation Gauntlet.

Red Army soldiers fight amid the ruins of Stalingrad in the
autumn and winter of 1942. They finally defeated the Germans
here in early 1943 after Operation Uranus.

above: Valentina Ievleva, a teenager in Archangel, who became pregnant by an American sailor. She was subsequently sent to a labour camp, accused of 'spying'.

above: Sir Owen O'Malley, British Ambassador to the Polish government-in-exile based in London. He wrote two key reports about the Katyn massacre.

below: The ruins of Stalingrad. Around half a million Soviet troops died in the epic struggle to recapture this city.

left: In the spring of 1943 the Germans uncovered evidence of Soviet atrocities against Polish citizens in the forest of Katyn.

below: The first encounter between Winston Churchill and Joseph Stalin in Moscow in August 1942. Despite the smiles, this did not begin as a meeting of minds.

against Rommel, arrived in Moscow on 12 August 1942. At seven o'clock that evening he had his first encounter with the Soviet leader at the Kremlin. The setting was Stalin's office on the second floor of the senate building. In appearance it was in stark contrast to the aristocratic opulence of Blenheim Palace, where Churchill had been born, and even to Chequers, the country house retreat outside London that the Prime Minister had at his disposal. Stalin didn't just dress simply, he lived and worked simply too. His office was gloomy, with uncomfortable wooden chairs set around a rectangular conference table. In the far corner stood his writing desk, beneath a photograph of Lenin reading *Pravda*. On the other walls there were pictures of Marx and Engels. In one corner was a tiled Russian stove. Oppressive wooden panelling encased the room to shoulder height, and throughout the room there was a faint smell of polish and tobacco.

As soon as Churchill had sat down at the conference table, Stalin began by announcing that the news from the front line was 'not good' and that the Germans were forcing their way to Stalingrad and Baku. He was certain that 'they had drained the whole of Europe of troops'. Then, against this depressing background, with even the official British minutes describing Stalin as looking 'very grave',[8] Churchill launched straight into his bad news. He reiterated that Molotov had previously been told that the British could make 'no promises' about a second front in 1942 and that 'the British and American Governments did not feel able to undertake a major operation in September.... But, as Mr Stalin knew, the British and American Governments were preparing for a very great operation in 1943.'

The official minutes describe Stalin as looking 'very glum' after Churchill had finished his lengthy explanation of just why the British and the Americans were not going to help the Soviet Union with a second front in 1942. Clearly exasperated by Churchill's words, Stalin announced that 'there is not a single German division in France of any value'. Churchill replied that there were '25 divisions in France'. Stalin retorted that 'A man who was not prepared to take risks could not win a war.'

The Prime Minister tried to lighten the mood by talking about one practical way in which the British and Americans were already providing help to the war effort – the bombing campaign. Stalin immediately remarked that 'It was not only German industry that should be bombed, but the population too.' Then Churchill, in a statement at odds with his later attempt to distance himself from the 'terror' bombing campaign towards the end of the war, stated unequivocally that 'As regards the civilian population [of Germany], we looked upon its morale as a military target. We sought no mercy and would show no mercy.'

'That is the only way,' said Stalin, making virtually his first positive remark in the meeting so far.

No doubt encouraged by the Soviet leader's response, Churchill launched into an almost bloodthirsty account of just what 'more and more aeroplanes and bigger and bigger bombs' could achieve. He added that 'if need be, as the war went on, we hoped to shatter almost every dwelling in almost every German city'. 'These words,' say the official minutes, 'had a very stimulating effect upon the meeting, and thenceforward the atmosphere became progressively more cordial.'

Showing another deft politician's touch, Churchill attempted to redefine the concept of a second front. 'What was a second front?' he asked rhetorically. 'Was it only a landing on a fortified coast opposite England? Or could it take the form of some other great operation which might be useful to the common cause?' Against this background, he moved seamlessly into the one piece of good news he had to impart – that the Western Allies were planning a landing in North Africa in October 1942. To illustrate the advantages of this attack, Churchill drew a picture of a crocodile and explained to Stalin that it was the intention of the British and the Americans to attack the soft underbelly of the beast. By the end of the meeting Stalin appeared to have cheered up considerably, having grasped the benefits of an Allied landing in North Africa, and the conference ended at 10.40 p.m. on a positive note.

Churchill was pleased with this first encounter, but by the next day it was clear that he had not succeeded in 'handling' Stalin as well as he might have thought. Churchill now had to endure a meeting with the implacable and uncharmable Molotov, who almost acted as if the previous evening's converation about the North African operation had not taken place and simply reiterated the Soviet demand for a second front. Then an 'aide mémoire', written by Stalin, arrived.[9] It was a document that in effect accused the British once again of breaking their word. 'As is well known,' it said, 'the organization of a second front in Europe in 1942 was pre-decided during the sojourn of Molotov in London…. It is easy to grasp that the refusal of the government of Great Britain to create a second front in 1942 in Europe inflicts a moral blow to the whole of Soviet public opinion, which calculates on the creation of a second front, and that it complicates the situation of the Red Army at the front and prejudices the plan of the Soviet Command.'

Stalin was as truculent as ever, if not more so. And at the second meeting between Churchill and Stalin, on the night of 13 August, the Soviet leader was at his most brutally sarcastic. He suggested that the British had failed to open up the second front because they were scared of the Germans. Churchill grew angry and was visibly upset. Eventually he became so exasperated by Stalin's bitter attack that he launched into a defence of the British position so eloquent that the translators could not keep up. 'The words aren't important,' said Stalin once Churchill had finished speaking. 'What matters is the spirit.'

Churchill was dismayed by the meeting. And when he returned to his dacha, the government house just outside Moscow that had been set aside for his use, the American ambassador, Averell Harriman, who had accompanied him to the talks had to spend several hours with him to try to placate his wounded feelings. In his report to the War Cabinet written the following day, 14 August, Churchill openly questioned why Stalin's behaviour had suddenly changed since the positive first meeting. One possibility, he admitted, was that this was a straightforward Soviet tactic, one that the British party knew Eden had suffered the previous December; but Churchill also raised the possibility that the 'Council of Commissars', to whom he supposed Stalin had been compelled to report after the meeting, had disliked the news that the British had brought. (This wholly erroneous belief that there were darker forces behind Stalin, and that Stalin was not complete master of Soviet foreign policy, would reappear at various crucial moments in the relationship between the Allied leaders over the course of the war.)[10]

On 14 August, Churchill stomped furiously around the dacha in his dressing gown. He told the assembled company that he was not prepared to attend the dinner in his honour that the Soviets had arranged for that night. Clark Kerr, the British ambassador who witnessed these scenes, had little patience with Churchill's mood and wrote that he felt at the time that what the Prime Minister really required was 'good root [kick] up the arse'.[11]

Eventually Churchill was persuaded that it would be diplomatic suicide not to attend the gala dinner, and he grumpily agreed to go. But, seemingly in protest, he decided to put on 'a dreadful garment that he claimed to have designed himself to wear during air raids'. It looked, recorded Clark Kerr, 'like a mechanic's overalls or more still like a child's rompers or crawlers'. Despite their otherwise revolutionary beliefs, the Soviet leadership still maintained that suits or uniforms were the appropriate garb for formal occasions, and they were astonished at the outlandish and inappropriate attire the guest of honour had decided to wear. After this bad start the evening grew worse when many in the British party were stand-offish with the Soviets. Colonel Ian Jacob, military assistant secretary to the War Cabinet, recorded in his diary that: 'It was extraordinary to see this little peasant [Stalin], who would not have looked at all out of place in a country lane with a pickaxe over his shoulder, calmly sitting down to a banquet in these magnificent halls.'[12]

General Sir Alan Brooke complained in his diary that 'there were 19 courses and we only got up at 12.15 a.m. having been 3 and a quarter hours at table'.[13] His view of Stalin was less patronizing than Jacob's, but one still detects that he thought Stalin was not quite a gentleman. 'By the end of the dinner,' recorded Brooke, 'Stalin was quite lively, walking around the table to click glasses with various people he was proposing the health of. He is an outstanding man, that there is no doubt about, but not an attractive one. He has got an unpleasantly cold, crafty, dead face, and whenever I look at him I can imagine him sending off people to their doom without ever turning a hair. On the other hand there is no doubt that he has a quick brain and a real grasp of the essentials of war.'[14] Another member of the British party, the interpreter Arthur Bryant,[15] observed that Brooke was rather rude at dinner. The British general gave short replies to the enquiries of his dinner partner, Marshal Voroshilov, and never asked any questions himself.

Churchill left the banquet after 1 o'clock – early by Soviet standards of hospitality – and returned fuming to his dacha. He railed to his doctor, Sir Charles Wilson [later Lord Moran]: 'Stalin didn't want to talk to me. I closed the proceedings down. I had had enough. The food was filthy. I ought not to have come.'[16] Sir Charles tried to argue with him, saying, 'It wasn't a question of whether Stalin was a brigand or not, but if we did not work in with him it would mean a longer war and more casualties.' This appeal had little effect, as still the next day Churchill was furious, declaiming, 'Did he [Stalin] not realise who he was speaking to? The representative of the most powerful empire the world has ever seen?'[17] He announced he wanted to leave Moscow and had no desire to see Stalin again.

Next morning Sir Archibald Clark Kerr had to use all his considerable powers of diplomacy to convince Churchill to meet the Soviet leader again. He told Churchill, as they paced together around the garden of the dacha, that 'he [Churchill] was going about this whole business the wrong way[18].... What was wrong was that he was an aristocrat and a man of the world and he expected these people to be like him. They weren't. They were straight from the plough or the lathe. They were rough and inexperienced. They didn't discuss things as we discussed them.' Then, after this somewhat patronizing assessment of the Soviet leaders, Clark Kerr warned, as Churchill's doctor had warned the night before, of the consequences of not dealing successfully with Stalin. 'If Russia went down from want of support, his support, which only he could give.... How many young British and American lives would have to be sacrificed to make this good?' Clark Kerr admonished Churchill once again for being 'offended by a peasant who didn't know any better'. Eventually, after Clark Kerr had worked his persuasive magic, Churchill agreed to attend one last meeting with Stalin that evening.

This final encounter seemed destined at first to be trapped once again in the familiar litany of the Soviet leader demanding that the British keep their 'promise' and provide a second front during 1942, as Churchill explained once more both the difficulties of a cross-Channel crossing and that a 'promise' had never been made. When Churchill reiterated that British forces would suffer great losses in any attempted cross-Channel operation in 1942, Stalin replied that 'the Red Army was losing 10,000 people every day' and that 'without taking any risks one cannot wage war'.[19]

According to Pavlov, the Soviet interpreter, 'the atmosphere in the meeting became extremely incandescent'. But then, after the formal discussions ended, Stalin asked Churchill back to his personal apartment in the Kremlin for supper. Churchill saw this as a real sign that the ice was breaking in their relationship, especially when Stalin introduced his daughter, Svetlana, to him. But soon the Soviet leader returned to his bitter tirade against the British. 'Have the Royal Navy no sense of honour?' he demanded, referring to the cessation of Arctic convoys to the Soviet Union. Churchill replied that 'Britain was a sea power' and that 'he knew a lot about sea warfare'. 'Meaning I know nothing?' said Stalin.

But gradually, as the drink flowed and the suckling pig was eaten, the mood lightened. Churchill was bold enough to ask if the current problems of the Soviet Union were as difficult to deal with as the forced collectivization of the peasants. 'No,' replied Stalin. 'That was much harder.'

'What did you do with all the kulaks [wealthier peasants]?' asked Churchill.

'We killed them,' replied Stalin.

After this particularly revealing exchange the conversation moved on to a series of faintly disparaging comments about their own staff, with Churchill finally daring to tease the slab-faced, uncharismatic Molotov, who had joined them in the early hours and was drinking solidly.

'Were you aware,' Churchill remarked to Stalin, 'that your Foreign Secretary on his recent visit to Washington said he was determined to pay a visit to New York entirely by himself, and that the delay in his return was not due to any defect in the aeroplane, but because he was off on his own?'

'It was not to New York he went,' said Stalin. 'He went to Chicago, where the other gangsters are.'[20]

Churchill returned to his dacha at three o'clock in the morning. His spirits completely turned around in twenty-four hours. Clark Kerr was there to meet him and recorded that: 'It was clear that he [Churchill] was in triumphant mood.'[21] Churchill lay on a sofa and 'began to chuckle' and kicked his legs in the air. 'It had all been grand. He had cemented a friendship with Stalin. My God! He was glad that he had come. Stalin had been splendid. What a pleasure it was to work with "that great man". The glee of the PM was a pleasure to see...my God, he talked! Stalin this and Stalin that...' The Soviet leader was now a joy to deal with rather than a disrespectful, awkward Asiatic. The prime minister prepared to leave for London immensely encouraged at the personal rapport that he clearly felt had developed during the final night of carousing.

Churchill's conduct during the four-day visit was on occasions not just eccentric but, as Clark Kerr and others at the British embassy in Moscow noted at the time, positively childish. It is interesting to imagine what might have happened had Churchill not listened to Clark Kerr and simply departed in a huff. How can one justify the sulky behaviour of the Prime Minister at the dinner in his honour? And, perhaps more worryingly, is it not extraordinary that Churchill's opinion of Stalin could be so changed by one visit to his private apartments?

The whole episode was more like the early stages of a romance than a conversation between statesmen. Indeed, Sir Alexander Cadogan, the Permanent Secretary to the Foreign Office who accompanied Churchill to Moscow, specifically referred to these exchanges as a 'courtship'.[22] Churchill was not just intoxicated by alcohol, but by the heady prospect of intimate friendship with a man whom he knew would be recognized by history as one of the most important figures of the twentieth century. But that desire clouded his mind as to the reality. Stalin was not interested in friendship. He had no friends.

And had Churchill not been swayed by that intimate evening in Stalin's rooms, he would perhaps have taken on board two other key points from his visit to Moscow. The first was that nothing of substance had been achieved. Stalin was still angry about the cessation of the convoys and the 'betrayal' over the second front. Nothing that Churchill had said had fundamentally shifted his predominently negative view about the contribution of Britain as an ally to the Soviet war effort. And second, and more importantly, Stalin had not bothered to conceal his overt brutality from Churchill. Both in the formal meeting, talking about his desire to destroy German civilians, and in the informal setting of his rooms, where he talked about killing the kulaks, Stalin had behaved true to form. He had shown himself to be a ruthless dictator who happily admitted to killing his own people, and self-evidently presided over a system in which there was no democracy, no free speech and no rule of law. In his memoirs Churchill acknowledged that, when Stalin referred to the destruction of the kulaks, he had the 'strong impression' of 'millions of men and women being blotted out and displaced forever'.[23] But he believed that 'with the World War going on all round us it seemed vain to moralise aloud'.

Of all the important figures in the Second World War – with the possible exception of Hitler – Stalin was the one who most needed to be dealt with coolly and objectively. This was something that General Sir Alan Brooke immediately recognized on seeing Stalin for the first time during the August 1942 meeting in Moscow. 'Stalin is a realist if ever there was one,' he wrote in his diary, 'facts only count with him...[Churchill] appealed to sentiments in Stalin which I do not think exist there'.[24] As Brooke intuitively realized, Stalin was not someone with whom to attempt emotional connection. Churchill was the first Allied leader to make this mistake; Roosevelt would later be the second.

But, of course, one must not be naive. Ultimately, Churchill felt he simply had to get on with Stalin. What was the point of dwelling on the unpleasant aspects of Stalin and the Soviet Union? The bigger issue was the war against the Germans, and the Red Army was unquestionably carrying the brunt of the fighting. But all the evidence is that Churchill himself was not so hard-headed about the encounter. His happy emotions on his return from the private meal with the Soviet leader seem genuine enough. He had now convinced himself not only that Stalin was a 'great' man, but that he, Churchill, was capable of liking him as well.

FRATERNIZATION

It was not just Churchill, of course, who was forging a personal relationship with the Soviets during 1942. While Churchill and Stalin met, the seamen who had sailed on the convoys to the far north before the cancellation order of the summer of 1942 were also trying to make sense of life in the Soviet Union. Their experience, together with the personal histories of the Soviet citizens they encountered, offers a rare insight into the extraordinary collision of cultures that was the alliance between the West and the Soviet Union during the Second World War.

When PQ16 docked on 30 May 1942, the Allied seamen were shocked at what they saw: 'Murmansk was a ghost town,' says Eddie Grenfell. 'It was so badly bombed – we never suffered anything like the bombing that happened there.' The city had been devastated by Luftwaffe attacks – only Stalingrad suffered more damage in the Soviet Union during the war.

Eddie and the other survivors of ships that had been sunk were disembarked from the boats that had rescued them and taken to a warehouse on the quayside: 'There were probably about 350 to 400 survivors who were all in this big warehouse. And this is our first real experience of Russia. We had sentries – Russian sentries with rifles and bayonets – at either end of the warehouse. We were still suffering. I was bruised and cut and all the rest of it. And there were people who were very badly wounded lying there – people were moaning and so on. And we lay there for 36 hours.' As they lay in the warehouse, they heard bombs dropping on the city as the Germans began another raid. 'You've never come across anything like it,' says Eddie. 'It was really frightening.'

The British sailors were given water, but no food of any kind. Then trucks arrived to take the wounded away. Neil Hulse, Eddie Grenfell and the other injured British servicemen were taken over roads pitted with bomb craters to a hospital that had been converted from a school. But it was like no hospital that the British had ever seen before. 'The smell was dreadful,' says Eddie Grenfell, 'and the moaning and the screaming.'

'This hospital was most gruesome,' confirms Neil Hulse. 'We were glad at least to get a dry bed, [but] the poor Russians! Many were lying on the floor of the hospital. There was a lot of scream-ing [and] shouting of poor Russian soldiers who were having amputations of their limbs without anaesthetic…. Three corridors away I could hear these poor Russian soldiers bellowing and shouting, wrestling and trying to escape from this wretched type of operation.'

Neil Hulse was terrified that the frostbite in his toes might mean that he would be operated on in this Murmansk hospital – which would mean his toes would be amputated without anaes-thetic. But a ship's doctor from one of the Royal Navy vessels that had arrived in Murmansk advised him that if he kept massaging his toes he might be able to escape the surgeon's knife. So Hulse came to an arrangement with one of his shipmates who was also suffer-ing from frostbite: 'I was busy massaging one chap's fingers, he was busy massaging my feet, for quite a few days at regular inter-vals. Thank God I've still got my toes on me, and he's still got his fingers on him.'

At night, while others tried to sleep, Eddie Grenfell stared at the wall and saw that it was 'absolutely covered black with cock-roaches and lice and every horrible thing you could think about.'

And so he decided to try and escape the hospital. He lobbied the aide of Admiral Bevan, the senior British naval officer in the Soviet Union, and eventually managed to get a transfer to a naval camp further down the Kola inlet at a city called Vaenga.

On board the tug that took him and a number of other British sailors to Vaenga he saw first hand how the Russians on board 'were just like our own merchant seamen.... Out came the vodka, they'd put on gramophone records and they were just as nice as could be. So we began to realize that the Russians were quite ordinary people.'

But for Eddie the naval camp at Vaenga was scarcely an improvement on the hospital in Murmansk: 'When you consider the danger we'd faced, not only in the Arctic [but] everywhere else, you'll probably laugh at this, but I was scared to hell by one thing – the rats. The rats jumped from body to body at night-time. They were looking for any scrap of food we had.... You felt these blooming things jumping on your body, plopping and squeezing in between you at night. It was terrible.'

Eddie Grenfell was also shocked to discover how the Soviet authorities at Vaenga dealt with breaches in discipline amongst their own men. One night a petty officer in the Soviet navy, who had become friendly with some of the British sailors, started banging on the barrack door. He was clearly extremely drunk – something that was frowned upon by the Soviet authorities, especially in front of foreigners. When the Allied sailors opened the door to let him in, he was immediately seized and taken away by one of the Soviet sentries stationed at one end of the hut. 'Half an hour later we heard a volley of shots,' recalls Eddie, 'A little bit later there was a hammering on the door of our hut and we went to the door and there was a [Soviet] commissar – the ugliest-looking man I've ever seen in my life. Bloody stern face – not a soldier, probably never heard a shot fired in his bloody life, but he was a commissar, he was just in charge of something or other. And he just said in good English: "We are sorry that you were disturbed like this. It was dreadful that this man should behave as he did. You'll be glad to know we shot him." Just like that! He was shot!

And, of course, we were astounded. We were not accustomed to this sort of thing.'

Incidents like this summary execution led Eddie Grenfell and his comrades to form the conclusion that 'the ordinary Russian was a damn nice fellow, but they were under the thumb of pretty horrible people.... So therefore we realized that it was a pretty horrible regime, but we had to accept it because they were fighting on our side.'

And it was not just British sailors who experienced this kind of radical awakening when confronted with the realities of life in the Soviet Union. American seamen too underwent a similar initiation. Jim Risk[25] arrived in Murmansk on board an American merchantman, the *City of Omaha*. Born in Florida, he had never even seen snow until he journeyed to New York to board his ship. But snow and ice had accompanied him across the Atlantic and up the coast of Norway to the north of the Soviet Union. His relief at reaching Murmansk was palpable, not least because just off the Kola inlet his ship had nearly been destroyed: 'It was at night-time, about one o'clock in the morning, the lookout on the starboard wing yelled: "Mate!" That means you've got trouble. So I ran out on the starboard wing and there was a ship closing right alongside of me. Now ships are pretty strong in all kinds of ways, except if you put two ships together broadside – then they're both going to go down.... So I yelled to the helmsman: "Hard to port!", which he did. And, thank goodness, the other ship must have yelled: "Hard to starboard!" and they pulled away and we survived. But that was the closest I've ever come to losing a ship in all seven years I was at sea.'

The Murmansk Jim Risk witnessed, as the *City of Omaha* steamed into harbour, was 'a shambles – just nothing going on around there at all'. And if the bombed-out devastation of the Soviet port was his first surprise, his second was that women were charged with the task of unloading the ship, supervised by a fearsome matron called Olga. 'All of a sudden,' says Risk, 'the captain of the ship yelled around, and he couldn't find any of the crew, and the armed guard commander couldn't find any of the crew either. And so being the

youngest officer, of course, my job was to find them – and do whatever the captain wanted. So I started searching the ship.'

Eventually, down in the bowels of the ship, on a grating in a
space above the engines, he saw an astonishing sight: 'I found the
crew. They were all in there with Olga. She had gotten a mattress
from somewhere and she was charging two packets of cigarettes a
throw...[for] having sex, yeah.... Certainly I'd never run into
anything like that before in my life. Neither had anybody else on the
American ships or English ships either.... So I had to throw Olga off
the ship.' But whilst he condemned Olga, Jim Risk did have some
sympathy for his crew: 'These boys had been through pretty much
hell, and they needed release any way they could get it.'

There was a strange postscript to the Olga story – the reaction
of the Soviet authorities: '[They] came back aboard the ship and
they raised hell with us – the officers – for throwing her off the
ship.' And even though the Americans explained what happened,
telling them about the reprehensible conduct of their female long-
shoreman, this did little to assuage the Soviet anger. Moreover,
Olga wasn't punished, and Jim Risk saw her working on the other
ships that came in behind them.

Across the other side of the Kola inlet, at the port of
Archangel, a teenage Russian girl called Valentina Ievleva[26]
welcomed the arrival of the Allied sailors as a kind of 'holiday'. 'It
was very exciting,' she says. 'It meant something new. There were
naval officers, speaking a foreign language – [they were] cheerful.
It made you forget about the war.' In Archangel the Allied sailors
frequented the International Club, where they relaxed and
mingled with invited locals – most of them female. 'I went there
to the International Club every day,' says Valentina. 'I couldn't live
without it. They showed films like *Lady Hamilton* or *Pinocchio*, or
films with Bing Crosby – I liked all the melodies of his songs at the
time.' For Valentina the place soon took on the status of a paradise
on earth: 'I'd never seen such comfort as I saw in the International
Club. It was inside an old merchant's house, and when you came
in there was carpet and it was so soft that you didn't even hear
your footsteps. Then there was a library, and I loved books and

music and somebody always sang and read. There was a place to play chess, there was a dance hall and there was a screening hall where you could see films. Once a week there was a dance, and I danced from 8 p.m. to 4 a.m. and at 5 a.m. I came home. I danced every dance. I never sat down.'

Her social life in the International Club inevitably led to Allied sailors taking an interest in her: 'They were very courteous. One naval officer's name was Christopher. He took me as far as the tram stop, kissed my hand, saluted and bade me goodbye. And everyone was looking surprised at this scene. I got on the tram and I felt very flattered.' This chivalrous behaviour from a British officer contrasted dramatically with her experience of Soviet men. 'If a Russian took me home, he took it for granted that I would invite him inside. Once, when I didn't let a Russian officer come into my home, he got very angry. They didn't want to waste time. If they met someone they liked, they didn't want to waste any time on courtship, they just wanted to have this girl, whereas the Westerners were different.'

And, as many inhabitants of Archangel and the other Soviet ports remember, there was also a clear difference in attitude between British and American sailors. 'The British were somewhat more closed,' says Maria Vetsheva, who in 1942 was a teenage Soviet sailor. 'The English came from a country at war and their mood was very depressed. The Americans weren't from a country at war – they did not have bombing, and so if they survived on their way here then they were very happy.' This notion that the British appeared more reserved than the Americans is confirmed by Alexander Kulakov,[27] who used to watch the sailors as they walked the streets of Archangel: 'My impression was that the Americans were more loose and the British were more inside themselves.'

Maria Vetsheva experienced first hand the 'more loose' attitude of the Americans when she was unloading goods from Allied ships in Murmansk harbour. She was operating a primitive rope-and-pulley system to haul the supplies out of the ship's hold and swing them over to the quay, when one day an American sailor sat down next to her and started to ask her questions. After a few minutes he tried to 'hug' her, but she rebuffed him and then asked a Soviet frontier guard what she should do if the American made advances again. He gave her a big stick and said she should keep it by her side.

'Then this American became more blatant,' says Maria. 'He said: "Jiggy, jiggy?" and he unbuttoned his trousers and took out his assets. So I took the stick and hit him. He screamed, and then a frontier guard came and asked what was the matter.'

Much to the amusement of his comrades, the American was thrown off the ship by the guard. 'So he received what he deserved,' says Maria. 'It was a strong hit – I did my best. These things happen.'

Valentina Ievleva had precisely the reverse problem with a British sailor called Bill, whom she fell in love with in 1943 – because he wouldn't make the advances she wanted. 'Bill and I met and started dancing and then dating. But one day he said: "I'm leaving tomorrow," and he gave me the home address of his aunt. And he came to say goodbye and brought a tin of cocoa and some food…. I said to him: "Bill, I want to have your baby, because I'm not going to love anyone any more." And he said: "Val, you're a good girl, I don't want to ruin you. I believe in God and I don't want to be responsible for your ruined reputation."

'I was very hurt by what he said,' says Valentina, 'because I wanted to be a woman. And I was hurt by his refusal. A Russian wouldn't have…well, wasted his time in such a way.'

But although there were clearly some Soviet women, like Valentina Ievleva, who were ready to have sex with foreign sailors, the experience of many British sailors was that a larger number were certainly not prepared to have a physical relationship. That was most definitely the experience of Eddie Grenfell and his comrades. They were taken by lorries every Tuesday from their camp to the nearby town to participate in a tea dance. 'In this very large hall where we danced, at one end there was a proper orchestra [and] at the other end was a gramophone, so you could dance around. And at one end you were dancing a waltz, then [when] you got over to the gramophone it was a foxtrot, so you had to change your step…. There were all these Red Army girls, perfectly nice, they danced with us – but that was all.'

In fact, the problem for these British sailors was that there simply weren't enough girls to dance with – a ratio of one girl to every five or six men. And so the men danced with each other. 'And I shall never forget it,' says Eddie Grenfell, 'because I've never experienced it in my life before. Ginger Bailey – one of my friends from HMS *Edinburgh* [the ship he had sailed on before the *Empire Lawrence*] – he had a red beard. And the Russians loved red beards, you know, and he just never had a moment's peace because he had these smart Russian officers coming up to him and asking to dance with him.'

A VOYAGE TO NEW YORK

While the Allied sailors whiled away their time in the far north of the Soviet Union as they waited for their return convoys to form, a number of Soviet ships made the reverse journey from Murmansk to New York. And in the late spring of 1942 Maria Vetsheva was on board one of these Soviet merchantmen taking timber, as ballast, to America. Once across the Atlantic, they expected the ship to be loaded with military equipment for the return journey. She was one of four women on board, and worked as a cleaner and caterer: 'Of course, for a woman on board a vessel it is very tough – lots of work, for one thing – and morally one should have willpower. I was very young and the captain instructed how one should act. He told me that the engine room and deck crew will be courting you but you should not break down.... One should protect oneself. If you defend yourself then they will respect you.'

'Men and women have different psychology,' she says, 'and a woman should have her pride. She should be a woman. And if she is proud then she will be more desired.' She had already witnessed, before the boat sailed, the consequences of not keeping this female 'pride' intact. A new girl, called Nina, had joined the ship as a caterer and shared a cabin with her. But early one morning Maria awoke to find Nina absent. When she went out on deck to search for her room-mate, she saw her walking away from the cabin of one of the crew. Nina was drunk and naked, carrying her clothes in her hands: 'And, of course, the master dismissed her and that afternoon she had to leave the vessel.... As they say, one black sheep soils the whole family.'

Maria Vetsheva arrived in New York in the late spring of 1942. It was her first trip abroad – and her first taste of capitalism. 'We were kids there,' she says. 'It was paradise.' They walked around Manhattan, and saw the Statue of Liberty and the Empire State Building. On Broadway and in Times Square they marvelled at the flashing neon signs and the advertisements – all completely new to them. But they could only look – not buy. Maria Vetsheva was given just $3.70 spending money during her three-month stay in New York. When she and a few of the other women from the ship visited Macy's on Seventh Avenue, they made straight for the shoe department and looked longingly at the expensive goods on offer, but it was all light years beyond Maria's reach. However, the staff took pity on the female Soviet sailors and gave each of them a pair of sandals – a souvenir from New York.

But Maria saw another side to immigrant life in America when she visited a club for people who had managed to leave Russia before the formation of the Soviet Union in 1922: 'Of course, when they left they were young and now they were old. And they cried and they asked us to bring them some Russian soil and they said our children are no longer Russian...so they really missed their Motherland.' She claims that these experiences made her feel that, although America was a good place to visit, 'it was impossible to live there'. 'We missed our Motherland,' she says. 'Like the words in the song: "Bulgaria is good but Russia is better." This is the Russian spirit. We have this spirit, and that's good.'

But that was clearly not the whole story. When pressed, Maria revealed that she and her comrades feared that if they had decided to stay and seek political asylum in America then, 'For sure we would be returned. If we had valuable brains, then we would be received with our valuable knowledge, but there were too many people like us. We would be returned and then there would be

Siberia and life would be over. So one had not only patriotic feelings but also fear, of course.' And so it was with a mixture of feelings that Maria watched the skyscrapers of New York City recede in the distance as her ship left America in August 1942. She felt envy for the lifestyle of the capitalists, but was certain in her own mind that a combination of homesickness and straightforward 'fear' meant that her decision not to defect had been the right one.

Her merchant ship, the *Friedrich Engels*, was making the long journey back to Murmansk without the protection of a convoy. In the immediate aftermath of the disastrous PQ17, the few Soviet and other merchant ships that made the journey did so alone. All seemed to go well until they reached the northern coast of Norway. Suddenly, out of the fog, appeared a German heavy cruiser, the *Admiral Scheer*, with its guns turned on the Soviet merchantman: 'We were quickly gathered together and ordered to burn all the documents.' Minutes passed and still the German ship did not fire. 'Then suddenly we came into very thick fog and we stopped the engines. No motion, no noise – like we are dead.... We stood there for forty minutes, and then the captain reversed course for about two hours.' Once they had cleared the fog banks they found the German warship had vanished. An officer on Maria's ship explained that he believed he knew why the Germans had not attacked. The crew of the Admiral Scheer must have mistakenly believed that this one merchantman was the lead vessel in a larger convoy. So the Germans clearly hadn't wanted to alert the other ships by firing just on this one.

This was by some measure the most frightening moment of Maria Vetsheva's life: 'They [the Germans] are aiming at you with all sorts of cannons...and we looked overboard and knew that the water was cold – and we just looked at our own death.' Back in the Soviet Union the stress and pressure of the journey – in particular the memory of the encounter with the German warship – became too much for Maria. 'I had a nervous breakdown,' she says. 'I was sick for a very long time. It's the most frightening thing when a person is not in control – if they had hit us with just one torpedo we would sink, and this anticipation is very frightening.... You look into death's eye and your death is looking at you. Every seaman knows what I'm talking about.'

FIGHTING THE GERMANS ON THE VOLGA

As Maria Vetsheva was wrestling with her emotions in the Arctic Sea, Joseph Stalin was watching with growing anger the German advance in Operation Blue. In just two months the 6th Army covered some 400 miles, reaching the city of Stalingrad on the river Volga during the last week of August 1942. German soldiers were exultant. It seemed as if the new strategy of their High Command – attempting to capture the raw resources of the Soviet Union in the south instead of a direct assault on Moscow – would succeed. The Volga was, they believed, the boundary of their new empire. Now, they felt, they had practically won the war. 'The Volga! It was within our grasp!' said Joachim Stempel, an officer in the 6th Army. 'The Volga was a very impressive sight in the autumn sun – a river of a width that we don't know in Germany. And this incredible view into the depths of Asia – nothing but forests, more forests, plains and the endless horizon. It was an inspirational feeling.... We thought it can't take much longer now – we're here.'

At whatever cost, Stalin was not prepared to give up the city that bore his name; Hitler, equally intransigent, announced on 30 September that it was certain that Stalingrad would fall into German hands. That autumn this one place became a microcosm of the immense destructive capacity of modern warfare. The Germans launched bombing raids on a scale not previously seen on the Eastern Front, and their artillery bombarded the city to rubble. By October there was little left standing. But still the Soviet forces, led by Major General Vasily Chuikov of the 62nd Army, would not surrender the ruins of Stalingrad on the western bank of the Volga.

Chuikov's tactics played perfectly to Soviet strengths. He called on his troops to stay as close as possible to the German front line.

That meant that it was hard for the Germans to use their artillery or bombers. 'Don't get too far from the enemy,' says Anatoly Mereshko, who worked in Chuikov's headquarters. 'That was our motto. The gap between you and the enemy should not be more than 50 or 100 metres.'

The Germans were at first bemused and then distressed to discover that they had come to the ends of the earth only to find it protected by people who fought with a personal ferocity they had not encountered before. Helmut Waltz,[28] a soldier in the German 305th Infantry Division, recalls fighting through a 'desert of rubble' and seeing a Red Army soldier shooting a German officer at close range so that 'his head was open and I could see his brain, on the right, left and in the middle – there was water but no blood. He looked at me and then he fell into the rim of the crater.' Waltz witnessed, during the course of one day in Stalingrad that October, the destruction of his entire company of more than seventy men: 'Nobody was left – they were all either dead or wounded. The whole company was gone.' The German forces were sustaining so many casualties that, as Joachim Stempel put it, 'it was possible to work out that soon there won't be anyone left. And we knew that the Russians at night were taking people [reinforcements] across the Volga, but we had nothing left, so we had to keep going. Nailed to the spot.'

Even today, if you walk the hills around Stalingrad just after the winter snow has melted, you can see fragments of bone littering the fields. The human losses here were immense. No one knows exactly how many people died at Stalingrad, but the best estimate is that the Red Army lost nearly five hundred thousand and the Germans around two hundred thousand. And to put those figures in the context of the Western Allies, in this one battle the Soviet Union suffered more dead than either the British or the Americans did in the entire war.

It was against this background that Stalin reviewed the course of the war in a speech on 7 November 1942.[29] 'At the start of this year,' he said, 'during the winter, the Red Army inflicted heavy blows on the German-fascist troops. Having repulsed the German attack on Moscow, it took the initiative itself, went on to the offensive and forced the German soldiers westward, liberating a number of areas of our country from German slavery. The Red Army therefore showed that under certain advantageous circumstances it can destroy the German-fascist troops.' After this optimistic version of the history of the first six months of 1942, Stalin went on to give a more sobering version of what had happened since: 'But in the summer, the situation on the front altered for the worse. The Germans took advantage of the absence of a second front in Europe, and they and their allies gathered all their reserves, threw them against our Ukrainian front and pushed through it. With the cost of heavy losses the German-fascist soldiers succeeded in moving towards the south and causing a threat to Stalingrad, the coast of the Black Sea, Grozny and the approaches to Transcaucasia.... However, having been stopped at Stalingrad and having lost tens of thousands of troops, the enemy has hurled into action fresh divisions, exerting his last efforts. The fight on the Soviet–German front is growing in intensity. On the resolution of this fight depends the fate of the Soviet State, the freedom and independence of our country. The Red Army bears most of the burden of the war against Hitler's Germany and her allies.' Stalin's bitterness at the lack of a second front was evident both in the overall tone of his speech and in the bald statement that the Red Army was currently bearing 'most of the burden'. But the day before, in a speech made to the Congress of Soviet Deputies, he had been a good deal more explicit, warning the Western Allies that: 'The absence of a second front against fascist Germany may end badly for all freedom-loving countries, including the Allies themselves.'

Just two days later, 8 November, the Western Allies did launch a second front – of a kind – with Operation Torch, the invasion of North Africa. This was not, of course, what Stalin had always explicitly understood as a 'second front' – by that he meant a substantial cross-Channel invasion that would draw German forces directly away from the war in the East. And although, in pursuit of Operation Torch, around six hundred ships had crossed the

Atlantic carrying nearly a hundred thousand men, Stalin believed this Allied effort was insignificant compared to the great struggle that the Red Army faced: 'Why were they able to do this?' he asked rhetorically. 'Because the absence of a second front in Europe enabled them to carry out this operation without any risk.'[30] He emphasized that whilst the Red Army were facing 240 enemy divisions in the East, the Western Allies were confronting a total of 'only 15 German and Italian divisions'.

This difference in scale between the Soviet and Allied contributions to the war was further emphasized, as far as Stalin was concerned, by the launch of Operation Uranus on 19 November 1942. More than a million Red Army soldiers took part in this attempt to cut off the German forces in Stalingrad, and they all listened as their leader's words were read to them at six o'clock on the morning of the attack. 'Today you start an offensive,' Stalin told his troops, 'and your actions will decide the fate of the country.'

For many of the troops who listened to these words, Stalin was almost a supernatural being. They had been brought up with propaganda newsreels in the cinema, and teachers in their schools, all spouting the same refrain: Stalin was more than a mere leader, he was a figure of ultimate certainty and trust. His presence, many believed, had inspired the defence of Moscow a year before and now his hopes would carry them forward towards Stalingrad.

And this time it was the Soviet forces that had the advantage of surprise. The Red Army had managed to keep preparations for the attack secret, deploying techniques of deception that went beyond anything previously seen in the war. Ivan Golokolenko,[31] for example, an officer with the 5th Tank Army, was ordered to build phoney offensive positions: 'There were fake bridges as well as fake areas of troop concentration far from the direction of the attack.' As for the real bridges needed to mount Operation Uranus, they went undetected by German reconnaissance aircraft: 'Some of the bridges were built as underwater bridges. They were built at a depth of 50 to 70 centimetres down in the water. From the air it was more difficult for the reconnaissance planes to spot the presence of such bridges.'

The Red Army had managed to keep the build-up of more than a million men secret from the Germans, who now watched in disbelief as Soviet forces burst through their flanks, pushing aside the Hungarian, Italian and Romanian forces that defended them. The bitterness that German soldiers of the 6th Army felt towards these allies, who they believed had not fought as fiercely as they should have, was still evident sixty years after the battle. 'Heard the joke about the new Italian tank?' one veteran of the 6th Army said. 'It has six gears. Five of them reverse!'

But regardless of the disputed performance of the German allies, the Soviet forces themselves were now much improved, for Operation Uranus marked another turning point. Stalin had recently started taking more advice from his military experts, notably Marshals Zhukov and Vasilevsky, rather than trusting his own instincts as he had at the disastrous battle of Kharkov earlier in the year. Stalin would never be anything other than the decisive force in the formation of Soviet military strategy – but now, at least, he was listening to others. On 9 October he had even restored 'unitary command' to his generals, freeing them from 'dual command', which had necessitated frequent consultation with political officers. The result of this and other improvements in supply, tactics and administration was an astonishing success. Just four days after the launch of Operation Uranus, in a military manoeuvre of tactical brilliance two Soviet pincer thrusts from either side of the German line met up near Kalach. The 6th Army was now encircled – trapped in Stalingrad.

Their fate had not been helped by the seeming inability of Adolf Hitler to grasp what was happening. Unlike Stalin, who as the war went on interfered less and less with detailed tactical decisions, Hitler was travelling on the opposite trajectory. And before any response to Operation Uranus could be contemplated, the Führer had to be consulted. But the Führer had chosen exactly this time to take a break from his military headquarters at the Wolf's Lair in East Prussia and was relaxing at the Berghof in Bavaria,

1400 miles from the front line. Even when he heard the news of the Soviet offensive, he reacted slowly – what could the Red Army possibly achieve, he must have thought, against the demonstrably superior might of the German armed forces? These complacent feelings had been endorsed by the sycophantic General Zeitzler, newly appointed Chief of the Army General Staff, who had told him only the previous month that the Red Army 'were in no position to mount a major offensive with any far-reaching objective'.[32]

As a result of all this, the initial German response to Operation Uranus was inadequate. And when the enormity of the problem facing the 6th Army was finally realized by the German leadership, the solution proposed was almost laughably optimistic. Hermann Göring promised Hitler that his Luftwaffe could mount an air bridge to supply the 6th Army until they were relieved by land forces. Such an action had successfully managed to supply German forces trapped at Demyansk earlier in the year, but that operation had been on a fraction of the scale now needed to supply the 6th Army. And while Göring's air bridge was supposed to keep the troops fighting inside Stalingrad, Field Marshal von Manstein was ordered to mount a relief operation on the ground in Operation Tempest. Both the air bridge and Operation Tempest were catastrophic failures. The 6th Army never received adequate supplies from the Luftwaffe – to the extent that by Christmas 1942 they were reduced to eating their own horses – and von Manstein's rescue mission was beaten back by the Red Army.

On 1 February 1943 the 6th Army surrendered at Stalingrad. Much to Hitler's fury, Field Marshal Paulus was captured alive by the Red Army. Hitler had promoted him to field marshal just two days before, in a clear signal that he should take his own life, since no German field marshal had ever previously been taken prisoner. Instead, Paulus became one of over ninety thousand Axis soldiers taken at Stalingrad.

It was a defining victory for the Red Army and for Stalin's leadership. But the cost had been so huge, the battles so bloody, that there was little feeling of sustained joy. Instead, many Soviet people felt that Stalingrad was symbolic of their virtual abandonment by the Western Allies. 'It was obvious to us that the burden of the war was carried on the shoulders of the Soviet Union,' says Grigory Obozny,[33] a member of the NKVD during the war. 'If the second front had opened in 1942 then things would have gone differently because 1942 was a difficult time…. We knew that only we could win the war, and only by sacrificing our own lives. So this is definitely why we felt that we won the war. It was clear to everyone that we were the leading force.'

In an attempt to shame the West into opening a second front, the Soviet creative community was told in the autumn of 1942 to try to influence foreign public opinion. 'Artists, writers and journalists were given an assignment,' says cartoonist Boris Yefimov,[34] 'to appeal to our colleagues abroad. Writers had to send letters to English writers, musicians to English musicians [and so on], all asking the question: where is the second front?'

Yefimov, as one of the Soviet Union's leading cartoonists, wrote to his famous counterpart in Britain, David Low. He received an answer a month later, explaining that 'whilst England had great military power, this power was only "potential" as he described it'. Having now witnessed personally the equivocation of the West on this most vital subject for the welfare of the Soviet Union, Yefimov decided to fight back in 1942 with the weapon he was most familiar with – the cartoon – and created a number of visual attacks on the British. The first featured six fat British generals in a military conference. Each carried a different caption, reading: 'General Don't Hurry, General What if We Get Beaten' and so on. Opposite them across the table were two colonels, on their helmets the words 'Courage' and 'Determination'. 'The implication was that in England there were proponents as well as opponents of the second front,' says Yefimov. 'This cartoon was sent, and Stalin approved it, and it was published in *Pravda*. Such a delicate issue as the discontent with our Allies needed Stalin's approval.'

Yefimov then felt that Soviet discontent about the lack of a second front could be personified in dislike and distrust of one person – Winston Churchill. 'There was a feeling of disappointment about Churchill's behaviour,' he says. 'My feelings about

Churchill were commonplace. He was seen as a man whom it was difficult to trust…. He had the reputation of a cunning, cynical politician.' And so Yefimov drew a variation of the first cartoon which included an attack on Churchill. The overweight generals remained from the original version, but the two brave colonels were replaced with a caricature of Churchill next to two bottles of whisky, and happy not to open a second front: 'It was just characteristic of Churchill. Everyone knew that Churchill started every morning by drinking a big portion of whisky…. It wasn't a secret to anyone that he had a weakness for drinking. I didn't see anything humiliating about it for Churchill as he didn't hide it – the fact that he liked to have a drink in the morning.'

This harsher attack on the Western Allies, specifically targeting Churchill, would also have had to be approved by Stalin, and it is significant that he was prepared to let such ridicule be published in the Soviet press. It is one more example of the importance that the Soviet leadership in general and Stalin in particular attached to the opening of the second front. 'Everyone used to say that the Americans were delaying the opening of the second front in order to wear out both the Germans and the Russians,' says Vasily Borisov, by now a member of the NKVD. And this was clearly Stalin's suspicion as well. Vladimir Yerofeyev,[35] a Soviet diplomat who worked for a time as a translator for him, recalls the Soviet leader expressing his views on the subject immediately after the war to a French visitor to the Kremlin: 'Stalin said we had been hopeful that the second front would be opened, but it was opened [only] at the moment when our allies felt threatened by our presence in Europe, when they were concerned that we would penetrate too far into Europe.'

Indeed, the Soviet victory at Stalingrad only served to increase Stalin's desire for an immediate second front. For whilst the German 6th Army had been destroyed, the task facing the Red Army remained gargantuan. German Army Group A had skilfully retreated from the Caucasus and continued to represent a formidable force in the southern sector of the front. The Soviets still had to fight over nearly 1000 miles of their own territory just to force the Germans back to the June 1941 border. And then there was another worry, less of a practical nature but more insidious, for the Soviet leadership. Was the Red Army trapped in a disastrous cycle in which it could hold – even defeat – the Germans in the winter, but would then be pushed back by the Wehrmacht in the spring and summer? The Red Army had won victories in the winter of 1941 at the gates of Moscow and now in the winter of 1942 at Stalingrad, but everyone remembered all too clearly the failures of the Soviets at Kiev and Minsk in the summer of 1941 and the disaster of the spring offensive at Kharkov in 1942. What chance would the Red Army now have in the spring and summer months of 1943, once the steppes hardened and the Germans could play to their military strengths once more?

THE WESTERN ALLIES, THE SECOND FRONT AND KATYN

Such was Stalin's concern about the challenges and dangers the Red Army would face in 1943 that on 14 December 1942, as Roosevelt and Churchill were about to meet at the Casablanca Conference, he almost pleaded for the Western Allies to fulfil what he regarded as their absolute commitment to the second front. 'I feel confident', he wrote, 'that no time is being wasted, that the promise to open a second front in Europe, which you, Mr President, and Mr Churchill gave for 1942 or the spring of 1943 at the latest, will be kept and that a second front in Europe will really be opened jointly by Great Britain and the USA next spring.'[36]

In mid-February Churchill replied, on behalf of the Americans as well as the British, that the long-awaited cross-Channel invasion would take place in August or September 1943, but that the exact timing would depend on 'the condition of German defensive possibilities...'.[37] This was still consistent with the assurance the British Prime Minister had given the previous August, when he met Stalin in Moscow, that 'the British and American governments were preparing for a very great operation in 1943'. But Stalin would thus not get the second front he craved by 'the spring of 1943 at the latest', and his feelings of suspicion and bitterness continued to fester. And it was in this uneasy period in the weeks immediately after the Soviet victory at Stalingrad that the alliance between the Western Allies and the Soviet Union was to be further tested – almost to breaking point – by the discovery of a crime that the Soviet Union had committed three years before, in the spring of 1940.

On 9 April 1943, Joseph Goebbels wrote in his diary that 'Polish mass graves have been found near Smolensk. The Bolsheviks simply shot down and then shovelled into mass graves some 10,000 Polish prisoners.' Radio Berlin announced the news to the world two days later. Eight mass graves had been found in the depths of the Katyn forest, varying in depth from 6 to 11 feet, and each was crammed with human remains. Every one of the victims had been killed by a shot in the back of the head. And by their uniforms and clothing they were all clearly Poles – the majority of them Polish officers.

The Germans did all they could to publicize the crime. Dimitry Khudykh,[38] then a teenager living nearby, was one of a group of Russian civilians whom the Germans took up to the forest to witness their gruesome discovery. 'We saw the exhumation,' he says, 'and the stench was terrible…there were bodies in coats and the Germans were feeling in these bodies, checking the pockets, removing flasks and watches and setting up a museum [near by]. The faces [of the bodies] were black.' He viewed this macabre sight with a certain amount of insouciance: 'We were young, we were not particularly interested. We had seen death inflicted by the Germans. We had seen that Russian prisoners of war were dying in the camps.'

Taken at face value, the German discovery showed evidence of a terrible war crime. Agents of the Soviet Union had apparently murdered the officers of an ally. For the Polish press in Britain – and indeed for the Polish government in exile – it was obvious that the Soviets had a case to answer. They knew all too well the prehistory of this crime: that in the aftermath of the Soviet invasion of eastern Poland, officers and other members of the Polish elite had been imprisoned and that subsequently the majority of them had disappeared in the spring of 1940. Since then there had been no letters from them, no sightings or contact of any kind. The Polish government in exile also remembered the evasive and, they now suspected, immensely cynical way in which the Soviet authorities, and Stalin in particular, had dismissed all enquiries about the whereabouts of the officers.

In the light of the anti-Soviet publicity that was appearing in the Western press, much of it fuelled by the justifiable suspicion of the Poles, the Soviet authorities decided to fight back in the most cynical way imaginable – they attacked the Polish government in exile. In *Pravda* on 19 April 1943, under the headline 'Hitler's Polish Collaborators!' the Soviet case against the Poles was made explicit. Since both the German and Polish media had, not surprisingly, refused to accept the Soviet version of events, then this was, according to *Pravda*, clear evidence of collusion between them. The Polish Minister of Defence must have offered 'direct and obvious help to Hitlerite provocateurs'. In addition, the suggestion that the Polish government in exile might in any way participate in the inquiry the Germans proposed to hold into the details of the mass murders was to strike 'a treacherous blow at the Soviet Union'.

The Soviets thus sought to conceal their guilt by a straightforward lie, and in the process they deliberately misrepresented the position of the Polish government in exile in London. Whilst it was true that the Prime Minister, General Sikorski, had raised the possibility of an independent inquiry into the affair to be conducted by the Red Cross, he had never suggested colluding with the Germans; but *Pravda* elided this suggestion with a proposed German-run investigation – presumably to blacken the Poles still further. The line taken in *Pravda*, just six days after the Germans revealed the crime, would be stuck to by the Soviet authorities – in spite of all evidence to the contrary – for nearly fifty years until Mikhail Gorbachev authorized the truth to be told to the world.

The British government moved swiftly to try to stifle the protests of the Poles. Churchill wrote to Stalin on 24 April:[39] 'I am examining the possibility of silencing those Polish papers in this country which attack the Soviet government and at the same time attack Sikorski for trying to work with the Soviet government.' He also did his best to explain away the coincidence of the Polish government in exile's call for an inquiry with the Germans' own moves to push forward with an investigation: 'Sikorski stated [to Foreign Secretary Eden] that so far from synchronising his appeal to the Red Cross with that of the Germans, his government took the initiative without knowing what line the Germans would take. In fact, the Germans acted after hearing the Polish broadcast announcement.' Churchill's telegram to Stalin demonstrates how effective the immediate Soviet strategy of outright attack on the Poles had been. Much to the surprise of the Polish government in exile, its members were now the ones who were being berated for complaining about a crime that – at first sight – seemed might have been committed by one of their allies. Only one small reference in Churchill's telegram – to the fact that Sikorski had said he had 'several times raised this question of the missing officers with the Soviet government, and once with you personally' – gave any clue that Churchill was not siding wholly with the Soviet Union in this row.

The defensive nature of Churchill's telegram allowed Stalin to take the high ground in his reply the next day.[40] He coolly announced that he thanked the Prime Minister for his 'interest in the matter', then stated that 'the interruption of relations with the Polish Government is already decided' and that 'I was obliged also to take into account the public opinion of the Soviet Union which is deeply indignant at the ingratitude and treachery of the Polish government.' It is worth noting the lengths to which Stalin now felt confident to take this device of protesting at being accused of a crime that he knew he had committed. For the idea that he was swayed in his decision-making by 'public opinion' was perhaps the most blatant lie of all.

Molotov's letter to the Polish ambassador in Moscow, dated 25 April,[41] which formally broke off diplomatic relations was just as breathtaking in its audacity in the face of the facts he personally knew – since Molotov had been one of those who had signed the order that had led to the deaths of the Polish officers. He accused the Polish government of having 'failed to offer a rebuff to the vile fascist calumny' that the Soviets had murdered the Poles. Furthermore, Molotov ascribed to the Poles a wholly discreditable motive for their action – one that points strongly to the Soviet concern at the time: 'The Soviet government are aware that this hostile campaign against the Soviet Union has been undertaken by the Polish government in order to exert pressure…for the purpose of wresting from them territorial concessions at the expense of the interests of the Soviet Ukraine, Soviet Belorussia and Soviet Lithuania.' Thus Molotov claimed a linkage between issues that did not exist, and in the process used the Katyn controversy not just to sever relations with the Poles but to restate Soviet demands for Polish territory.

So, just twelve days after the Germans had announced the discovery of the bodies at Katyn, the Soviet leadership had managed to produce a position of strength from a potential position of great weakness. And in the process Stalin had clarified his own views about the ultimate usefulness of the Polish government in exile – something about which he had always had severe doubts. The previous year, Stalin's ambivalence about the Poles had been demonstrated by his treatment of the Polish army that had been formed in the Soviet Union after the German invasion. When it became clear that General Anders and his men were not malleable to Soviet will and were not prepared to fight as disparate units within the Red Army, they had been permitted to leave the Soviet Union and fight on the side of the Western Allies. However, a 'free' Polish army fighting in the West was always going to be an eventual problem for the Soviet Union, as would a 'legitimate' government of Poland based in London. Now, in one bound, Stalin had found the way to free himself of both these troublesome issues. The fissure that Stalin opened here, in the opportunistic moment of the German discovery of his war crime, would cause far-reaching problems for the Western Allies.

But in the crisis of the moment in April 1943 Churchill had no doubts about where his primary political interests lay. He referred disparagingly of the Poles to Stalin, remarking that 'If he [General Sikorski, leader of the Polish government in exile] should go, we should only get somebody worse.' And his confidential government minutes in the aftermath of Katyn were even more brutally pragmatic. On 28 April 1943, for example, Churchill wrote to Eden: 'There is no use prowling morbidly round the three-year-old graves at Smolensk.'[42]

Meantime, the Germans revelled in their propaganda coup and pushed forward swiftly with their own investigation into the crime. The International Commission they appointed consisted of a number of world-renowned forensic experts, but only Dr François Naville from Switzerland came from territory outside Nazi control. These twelve experts worked at Katyn from 28 to 30 April and were given access by the Germans to forensic evidence and to eye witnesses. No doubt the Germans, who knew for certain they had not committed the crime, were working on the basis that this was one of the rare cases of a war crime on the Eastern Front where they had nothing to hide.

The report,[43] agreed unanimously by all the members of the Commission, pointed unequivocally to the fact that the Poles had been murdered three years before – which meant that it was the Soviets, without question, who had committed the crime. The experts pointed to a number of pieces of evidence that, cumulatively, had removed all doubt from their minds. First, the documents found on the bodies of the Poles – the letters, photographs, identity documents and so on – contained no date later than April 1940. Second, the spruce trees growing on top of the mass graves were considerably younger than the surrounding trees in the forest, and a forestry expert confirmed that these new trees must have been planted around spring 1940. Third, eye witnesses confirmed NKVD activity in the forest in April 1940, and stated that they had seen lorry-loads of Poles transported into the forest followed by the noise of gunfire.

On 24 May 1943 Sir Owen O'Malley,[44] in his capacity as

British ambassador to the Polish government in exile in London, sent a long report to the Foreign Secretary, Anthony Eden, about the Katyn affair. This followed his despatch of 29 April, in which he had laid out much of the background to the disappearance of the Polish officers. His second report is one of the most remarkable documents in the wartime history of Anglo-Soviet relations.

O'Malley was a fifty-six-year-old British career diplomat of Irish descent when he wrote his report on Katyn. Although his education was conventional for his class at that time – Harrow and Oxford – he was of somewhat independent mind. He later wrote that he had been surprised when, at the end of his career, he had been appointed merely as ambassador to Portugal, since 'Lisbon is a most enjoyable place but in the estimation of the Foreign Office only of third-class importance'. He asked a number of colleagues 'what was the reason [for] my relative unsuccess in that Service bearing in mind that nothing I had done had ever met with explicit criticism or disapproval'. One of them told him that he 'had been too often too right too soon'.[45] That was certainly the case with O'Malley's judgement on Katyn.

In his report,[46] O'Malley analysed the available evidence in an attempt to reach an – albeit preliminary – view as to who had committed the crime. And his conclusion was devastating: 'But though of positive indications as to what subsequently happened to the 10,000 officers there was none until the grave at Katyn was opened, there is now available a good deal of negative evidence, the cumulative effect of which is to throw serious doubt on Russian disclaimers of responsibility for the massacre.' O'Malley clearly did not accept the Soviet claim that they had transported the Poles to the Katyn region in the spring of 1940 to work in labour camps, and that all these prisoners had then been killed by the Germans in the summer of 1941. This explanation lacked credibility – not least because the Soviets had failed to mention it when the Polish government in exile first enquired about the fate of the officers. If this was the reason for the disappearance of the Poles, why come up with the nonsense about 'escaping to Manchuria'? Especially since, as O'Malley put it, 'it is notorious that the NKVD collect and record the movement of individuals with the most meticulous care'.

The cool analytical method by which O'Malley took apart the ludicrous Soviet claims about Katyn is in stark contrast to the tone of the last paragraphs of his report – words that are worth quoting at length. Having said that he was 'inclined' to believe that the Soviets committed the crime (obviously a deliberate diplomatic understatement, since the evidence he laid out in the preceding paragraphs was compelling), O'Malley wrote: 'In handling the publicity side of the Katyn affair, we have been constrained by the urgent need for cordial relations with the Soviet government to appear to appraise the evidence with more hesitation and lenience than we should do in forming a common sense judgement on events occurring in normal times or in the ordinary course of our private lives; we have been obliged to appear to distort the normal and healthy operation of our intellectual and moral judgements; we have been obliged to give undue prominence to the tactlessness or impulsiveness of Poles, to restrain the Poles from putting their case clearly before the public, to discourage an attempt by the public and the press to probe the ugly story to the bottom. In general we have been obliged to deflect attention from possibilities which in the ordinary affairs of life would cry to high heaven for elucidation, and to withhold the full measure of solicitude which, in other circumstances, would be shown to acquaintances situated as Poles now are. We have in fact perforce used the good name of England like the murderers used the little conifers to cover up a massacre; and in view of the immense importance of an appearance and of the heroic resistance of Russia to Germany, few will think that any other course would have been wise or right.'

Eloquent words, indeed; and they expertly outlined the dilemma the Western Allies faced in their relationship with the Soviet Union. For although Western leaders – and explicitly Churchill – knew about the brutal nature of Stalin and the Soviet regime before the war started, it was one thing to know that your ally is capable of evil acts, quite another to cover up those acts for him. This was a point that O'Malley made with pinpoint accuracy:

'This dislocation between our public attitude and our private feelings we may know to be deliberate and inevitable; but at the same time we may perhaps wonder whether, by representing to others something less than the whole truth as far as we know it, and something less than the probabilities so far as they seem to us probable, we are not incurring a risk of what – not to put a fine point on it – might darken our vision and take the edge off our moral sensibility.'

After so clearly outlining the problem O'Malley was a good deal less successful in proposing any solution. He stated that, whilst he was a supporter of the dictum that 'what in the international sphere is morally indefensible generally turns out in the long run to have been politically inept', he nonetheless recognized that there was little alternative than to pursue the current course of dissembling, and not to tell the public the whole truth. But he did make a heartfelt plea in the final paragraph of his report that 'since no early remedy can be found in an early alteration of our public attitude towards the Katyn affair, we ought, maybe, to ask ourselves how, consistently with the necessities of our relations with the Soviet government, the voice of our conscience is to be kept at concert pitch. It may be that the answer lies, for the moment, only in something to be done inside our own hearts and minds where we are masters. Here at any rate we can make a compensatory contribution – a reaffirmation of our allegiance to truth and justice and compassion. If we do this we shall at least be predisposing ourselves to the exercise of a right judgement on all those half political, half moral questions (such as the fate of Polish deportees now in Russia) which will confront us both elsewhere and more particularly in respect to Polish–Russian relations as the war pursues its course and draws to an end.'

It was demonstrably an impassioned report, but it is important to reiterate that, despite the clear moral sense that ran through it, O'Malley recognized that there was no viable alternative to the policy the government was already pursuing. In such circumstances it is easy to imagine how those who were charged with making the political decisions about the Allied response to Katyn, together with a number of O'Malley's colleagues at the Foreign Office, were liable to find his note somewhat indulgent – to see it as a vain attempt to seek the moral high ground while simultaneously accepting that the course ahead would be one of almost cynical pragmatism.

And although those sentiments were never explicitly expressed, the confidential comments of some Foreign Office mandarins certainly show that O'Malley's note was – to say the least – unwelcome. For example, after calling it 'a brilliant, unorthodox and disquieting despatch', Sir William Denis Allen at the Foreign Office went on to warn that: 'In effect Mr O'Malley urges that we should follow the example which the Poles themselves are unhappily so prone to offer us and in our diplomacy allow our heads to be governed by our hearts.'[47] Meantime, Sir Frank Roberts noted that O'Malley's report pointed to difficulties that might occur when the victors came to dispense justice on the vanquished: 'It is obviously a very awkward matter when we are fighting for a moral cause and when we intend to deal adequately with war criminals that our Allies should be open to accusations of this kind.'

But the response to O'Malley's report that offers us perhaps the greatest insight into the 'sophisticated' thinking of some members of the Allied elite came from the powerful Permanent Secretary and head of the Foreign Office, Sir Alexander Cadogan: 'I confess that, in cowardly fashion, I had rather turned my head away from the scene at Katyn – for fear of what I should find there.... I think no one has pointed out that, on a purely moral plane, these are not new. How many thousands of its citizens has the Soviet Union butchered?... Quite clearly, for the moment, there is nothing to be done. Of course it would be only honest to circulate it [O'Malley's report]. But as we all know (all admit) that the knowledge of this evidence cannot affect our course of action, or policy, is there any advantage in exposing more individuals than necessary to the spiritual conflict that a reading of the document excites?'

Cadogan's comments on the O'Malley report are a masterpiece of diplomatic realpolitik. But his inclination to suppress the document did not prevail, and the report was circulated first to the

Prime Minister and then widely within the British government. Churchill even asked for copies to be sent to the King and Mrs Churchill, calling it a 'lamentable tale'.[48] But there remained the question of whether the O'Malley report should be shown to President Roosevelt. The Foreign Secretary, Anthony Eden, wrote to Churchill on 16 July that 'The story has not been sent to the President but the Embassy at Washington have a copy of the despatch and can send it round to the President if you wish. On reflection I should be against this: the document is pretty explosive and in some respects prejudiced...if it were to find its way into unauthorized hands the reactions on our relations with Russia would be serious.' Eden also added in his own handwriting the note: 'The document might well be shown to the President when you next meet him.' Churchill clearly felt it important that Roosevelt saw the O'Malley report, and he sent it to him on 13 August.[49] In the note he enclosed with the report, the Prime Minister called it 'a grim, well written story, but perhaps a little too well written'. He added: 'I should like to have it back when you have finished with it as we are not circulating it officially anyway.'

It is interesting to observe that both Eden and Churchill felt uneasy about the O'Malley report. As we have seen, Eden called it 'in some respects prejudiced' and Churchill 'perhaps a little too well written'. But what exactly did they mean? It is likely, surely, that they judged it somewhat politically naive. And although admittedly it contained no inaccuracies or substantial errors of fact, the problem remained that it was simply inconvenient. O'Malley had shown that, on a balance of probabilities, the Soviets were guilty of an immense war crime. And that was news that few people at the time wanted to hear.

It is probable that President Roosevelt soon joined the growing band of people who wished O'Malley had never committed his views to paper. That judgement can be inferred from the chain of notes that followed the delivery of the report to him. Some months after Churchill sent him the report, his secretary wrote to the White House asking if it could be returned. Further polite requests followed. But the report never came back. Roosevelt treated it, as he did so much material that he believed was 'unhelpful', with complete disdain. No comment from him on the O'Malley report has ever been found – an eloquent statement in its own right.

THE RELATIONSHIP WITH STALIN WORSENS

It is not hard, of course, to understand why the President of the United States might have wanted simply to wish away the issue of Katyn, because at the same time as the Western Allies were wrestling with this potentially explosive problem they were also walking towards a political crisis with Stalin over the wartime policy that continued to be closest to the Soviet dictator's heart – the second front, or rather the lack of it. In August 1942 Churchill had announced to Stalin that the Western Allies were planning 'a very great operation in 1943'. This very specific promise had been designed to soften the blow that there was to be no second front in 1942. And now, five months into 1943, Stalin was demanding to know, once again, exactly when the second front would be opened.

Roosevelt was intensely aware of the deteriorating relationship with Stalin; and he decided that whilst he had nothing of substance to offer – he certainly could not guarantee the imminent launch of a second front – he could attempt to 'handle' the situation by using his strongest personal attribute: his charm. But it was obviously difficult to charm Stalin at a distance of several thousand miles, so Roosevelt focused his attention on attempting to persuade the Soviet leader to attend an intimate meeting at which the two of them could become personally acquainted. And to deliver this invitation the American President carefully selected a special envoy.

Joseph Davies was a wealthy lawyer from Wisconsin, and a personal friend of the President's. He had served as American ambassador to the Soviet Union in the late 1930s and witnessed personally some of the infamous show trials during the Stalinist purges. Significantly, he had formed the erroneous view that most of those who were on trial had genuinely been guilty of plotting against the Soviet state – a view that others in the American embassy in Moscow found bizarre given the true nature of the regime.[50] Davies wrote a book about his experiences as ambassador, *Mission to Moscow*, which was made into a Hollywood film in 1943. In both book and film, Stalin is portrayed as the father-figure of the Soviet Union – a giant of a man responsible for massive projects of industrialization. And the purges are glossed over as implicitly necessary for the security of the state. The film was condemned as crass pro-Soviet propaganda during the 1950s, but during the war it was a hugely influential piece of work.

Davies arrived at the Kremlin to hand-deliver Roosevelt's invitation on 20 May 1943. And so secret was the message that Davies carried that the current American ambassador, William Standley, was not allowed to accompany him into the meeting with Stalin. Standley was furious when Davies told him that he was excluded: 'I felt as if I had been kicked in the stomach,' he wrote. 'In plain language he [Davies] meant that a letter, which not only Mr Stalin and Mr Molotov, but also the interpreter, Mr Pavlov, would read, by the President's orders, could not be read or even discussed in the presence of the American ambassador, the regularly accredited representative in the Soviet Union. A pretty state of affairs!'[51] The next day Standley revealed his feelings to his wife: 'I don't know anything about what was in the letter or what went on in the Kremlin. I lay awake half the night wondering what I should do; that's why I'm disgusted, more so than usual.'[52]

As soon as he was closeted in Stalin's office, Davies explained to the Soviet leader that, although he personally did not believe in Communism, he felt that 'it was vital to the war and to a post-war peace, that our governments, despite ideological differences, could and should work together'.[53] He then went on to reveal that he believed that since 'Britain, after this war, would be financially "through" for a long time', the reality of world politics was that the 'post-war peace depended on the unity of our two countries in this situation'. Davies expressed sympathy over the delay of the second front, and remarked that it had been 'most unfortunate' that Stalin had not been able to meet President Roosevelt personally. He said that whilst he had 'only admiration and respect' for Churchill and Eden, 'they were both adherents of an Imperial Policy, ingrained in their history'. And it was because the President thought it so vital that a meeting be arranged between the two leaders that he, Davies, had come on this new mission and carried a personal and special message from Roosevelt. He then handed over the letter he had carried from Washington and Pavlov, Stalin's translator, read it out in Russian. 'During Pavlov's translation,' recorded Davies, 'Stalin didn't flicker an eyelash. Grim and forbidding, he looked down at a sheet of paper on which he was "doodling".'

The letter related 'solely to one subject'[54] – the proposed meeting between Roosevelt and Stalin that summer. The President outlined some possible locations for this intimate encounter, remarking that 'Iceland I do not like because for both me and you it involves rather difficult flights and in addition would make it, quite frankly, difficult not to invite Prime Minister Churchill at the same time.' So Roosevelt suggested that the best place to meet would be 'either on your side or my side of Bering Straits'. Stalin, naturally enough one might think, immediately pounced on the one glaring revelation in the letter – the deliberate exclusion, and by implication deception, of Churchill. Why was the British Prime Minister not to be invited to the proposed meeting? Davies replied that, whilst Roosevelt and Churchill 'were strong and loyal allies, who respected each other and admired each other', they 'did not always see eye to eye'. Davies reiterated that the President was a firm believer in the second front and that he thought it the 'quickest and most direct way to defeat Hitler'.

The conversation then moved on to a discussion of the kind of post-war world that Stalin envisaged. And here the Soviet dictator used a form of words that would remain remarkably consistent through the next few years of the conflict. He said that the Soviet Union 'wanted all European peoples to have the kind of government they themselves chose, free from the coercion of any outside power; that they [the Soviet Union] had no aggressive intent, and would perpetrate no aggression, external or internal, except as it might be a military requirement to protect themselves. But they insisted that the governments of countries on their border should be really friendly, not professionally friendly and secretly hostile, prepared to stab the Soviets in the back, as they have in the past.' It was this formula – 'really friendly, not professionally friendly' – that was later to cause so much trouble.

Towards the end of the Davies meeting, Stalin announced that he would be 'very glad' to meet with Roosevelt. But although Davies managed to force from him a provisional date of 15 July, Stalin was careful to say that he could only confirm the exact details later, since his movements were circumscribed by 'the military developments of the summer'. This was a theme he developed in his formal reply to Roosevelt's offer, in which he expressly linked his inability to confirm a date for the meeting with the threat to the Soviet Union of an imminent massive summer offensive from the Germans. The implicit link was also clear – that the Soviet Union continued to carry the brunt of the war on its own, and the Western Allies, by continually delaying the second front, were daily increasing the cost of the war to the Soviet people in both material and human terms.

At the same time as Davies was in Moscow for his meeting with Stalin, Churchill was in Washington for a series of meetings with Roosevelt at the Trident Conference. Significantly, during that conference Roosevelt did not tell Churchill about Davies' mission, but focused instead on the broad question of Allied military policy. And central, of course, to the discussion was the question of the second front. Here there were clear differences between the Western Allies. The Americans believed an invasion of northern France was the quickest way to end the war, but Churchill remained wary of a cross-Channel operation and pressed strongly for the Allied forces to continue to attack the 'soft belly' of the Axis instead. In practical terms this meant mounting an invasion of Italy during 1943. To Churchill, the dangers of a cross-Channel operation were not so much the commonly perceived problem of establishing a foothold in northern France after landing on the beaches, but rather the danger of a subsequent influx of German military resources from the East via their 'excellent road and rail communications'. Later that year, in October 1943, Churchill revealed his fears that, if the Allies landed in France, the Germans would be able to 'inflict on us a military disaster greater than that of Dunkirk. Such a disaster would result in the resuscitation of Hitler and the Nazi regime.'[55]

Churchill had even previously wondered whether an invasion of Germany might be necessary in order to win the war. He remembered how Germany had collapsed from within at the end of the First World War, broken by blockade while German soldiers still remained in France; and perhaps a similar result could be achieved in the current conflict by destroying Germany from the air. 'In the days when we were fighting alone,' Churchill wrote on 21 July 1942, 'we answered the question: "How are you going to win the war?" by saying: "We will shatter Germany by bombing."'[56] And a few days later, on 29 July 1942, Churchill had remarked to his colleague Clement Attlee: 'Continuous reflection leaves me with the conclusion that, upon the whole, our best chance of winning the war is with the big bombers. It certainly will be several years before British and American land forces will be capable of beating the Germans on even terms in the open field.'[57]

Although this does not suggest that Churchill was implacably opposed to a second front, it does suggest that he saw an Allied invasion of France as something that should be considered only once Germany was considerably weakened – 'several years' hence. And although it would be harsh to allege that Churchill deliberately lied to Stalin during his meeting in August 1942, when he led the Soviet leader to believe that there would be a second front in 1943, he certainly – by saying in 1942 that it would happen in 1943 – gave himself room subsequently to conclude 'reluctantly' in 1943 that circumstances were not now as propitious as he had hoped. Which is what happened at the Trident Conference. Churchill and Roosevelt now considered a second front impossible during 1943 for several 'practical' reasons. The German resistance in North Africa had been stiffer than anticipated, and the Western Allies had failed to take Tunis before the winter storms had made the roads impassable. More resources than had at first been anticipated had been needed in the Pacific theatre of the war. And, finally, the early months of 1943 had seen terrible losses in the Atlantic: in March alone the Western Allies had lost twenty-seven merchant ships.

A combination of these factors, allied to Churchill's own unbending fear of the consequences of a cross-Channel attack, meant that the Western Allies now had the unenviable task of communicating their decision to Stalin. George Elsey was one of the first to learn of this tricky mission when Churchill, Roosevelt and a 'whole gaggle' of other people burst into the map room in the White House early in the morning of 25 May 1943: 'They'd had a very convivial dinner upstairs – very convivial I might say from their appearance – but they had to settle down and answer this latest demand [from Stalin about the second front]. It wasn't a request from Stalin, it was almost a demand: "What are you going to do next?" And the debate went on...they couldn't answer Stalin. Sir John Dill, who was Chief of the British Mission in Washington, drafted an evasive reply, passed it across the desk. General Marshall and Admiral Leahy did some tinkering with the words and then it was Leahy who handed it to me to type and he read it aloud to the group and they all agreed that this would not satisfy Stalin because it was an evasive answer.'

The cable to Stalin was eventually finalized with the help of General Marshall and was transmitted on 2 June. It was a somewhat pusillanimous document in which the issue of the second front was not addressed with any clarity. Only towards the end of the cable was any reference made to this most vital issue: '...the concentration of forces and landing equipment in the British Isles should proceed at a rate to permit a full-scale invasion of the continent to be launched, at the peak of the great air offensive in the spring of 1944'.

Stalin's reply to Roosevelt, on 11 June, was ice-cold. He pointed out that 'these decisions are in contradiction with those made by you and Mr Churchill'[58] and that 'the opening of the second front in Western Europe, which was postponed already from 1942 to 1943, is being postponed again, this time until spring 1944'. Stalin further stated that this decision would create 'exceptional difficulties' and a 'painful and negative' impression on the people of the Soviet Union. He also noted that the decision had been taken without discussion with the Soviet leadership. This news that the second front was to be delayed yet again would lead, not surprisingly, to the dropping of any idea of a meeting between just Stalin and Roosevelt. And it was only now, after Stalin's devastating telegram, that Roosevelt thought Churchill should be told the details of the Davies trip to Moscow.

The smooth and emollient American aristocrat Averell Harriman was chosen by Roosevelt for the delicate task of breaking the news to the British Prime Minister. During a meeting with Churchill in Downing Street in the early hours of 24 June, Harriman emphasized that there was great value in allowing the President and Stalin to establish an 'intimate understanding' and that this was 'impossible' if the three of them got together. He then gave a straightforwardly political explanation for the meeting – that an encounter between the two of them, excluding Churchill, would play better with the American public, since any meeting on 'British soil' involving the three of them would make it appear as if Churchill had been the 'broker' and arranged it all. Harriman reported that he believed Churchill, although not agreeing with this course of action, would 'accept it in good part'.[59]

Harriman was wrong: Churchill didn't take the news 'in good part' at all. The next day he sent a devastating note to Roosevelt. 'You must excuse me expressing myself with all the frankness that our friendship and the gravity of the issue warrant,' he wrote. 'I do not underrate the use that enemy propaganda would make of a meeting between the heads of Soviet Russia and the United States at this juncture with the British Commonwealth and Empire excluded. It would be serious and vexatious, and many would be bewildered and alarmed thereby.'[60]

Roosevelt's reply, on the 28th, was an almost half-hearted attempt to justify the meeting *à deux*, but the momentum behind the idea was clearly dying, not least because of Stalin's fury at the news that the second front was to be delayed yet again. The reply is nonetheless a remarkable document for its opening sentence, which read: 'I did not suggest to UJ [Uncle Joe, FDR's pet name for Stalin] that we meet alone but he told Davies that he assumed (a) that we would meet alone and (b) that he agreed that we should not bring staffs to what would be a preliminary meeting.'[61]

It is not often that a man with the illustrious reputation of Franklin D. Roosevelt is caught out in a straightforward, bare-faced lie – but this is one such moment. In fact, that single sentence contained two lies. The suggestion for the meeting excluding Churchill had been Roosevelt's, not Stalin's, and Roosevelt had never told the Soviet leader that the proposed encounter would merely be some kind of 'preliminary meeting'. Roosevelt then left it to Churchill to defend to Stalin the decision not to mount a second front in 1943. The correspondence grew so fractious that Churchill felt forced into changing his position on any talks, and asked Roosevelt to meet one-to-one with Stalin in order to repair the relationship – a suggestion that came to nothing.

This episode demonstrates in stark terms how Roosevelt worked his politics. By using emissaries, such as Davies, Hopkins and Harriman, he provided a barrier of deniability between himself and any idea he floated. Moreover, these emissaries, as can be seen in the prickly relationship between Ambassador Standley and Davies, often operated outside conventional diplomatic channels, with the salaried diplomats kept in a state of ignorance. Even more noteworthy, of course, is Roosevelt's easy recourse to duplicity over the idea of the Stalin meeting.

The President's behaviour was based partly on his habit of concealment – of never letting his right hand know what his left hand was doing. But there was a second reason why he was prepared to lie to Churchill about his dealings with Stalin: the anxiety, especially during the first six months of 1943, that the Soviets might be considering another deal with the Nazis that would extricate them from the war. At first sight such an idea seems ludicrous – the Red Army had just won the battle of

Stalingrad, an event that, with hindsight, signalled the start of a relentless march to Berlin. But that was not how it seemed to many at the time. Stalin had good reason to suspect that the Western Allies might never mount a second front – had they not already, as he saw it, reneged twice on their promise? And the cost to the Soviet Union of pushing the Germans back would clearly be immense, in both manpower and other resources. Why not see if the Germans would agree terms in 1943?

Both the British and Americans were clearly aware of this danger. In January 1943, Sir Archibald Clark Kerr believed that 'Stalin may make a separate peace if we do not help him'.[62] And there is evidence, not just in the memoirs of Peter Kleist, the shady former associate of Ribbentrop, but also in British and American intelligence reports[63] that contact between German and Soviet representatives occurred in neutral Stockholm that year. News of these peace feelers was even reported in the press, with the Swedish paper *Nya Dagligt Allehanda* announcing on 16 June that German and Soviet diplomats had met just outside the capital.

Although both the Germans and the Soviets denied that there had ever been any such negotiations, Molotov admitted to Harriman in November 1943 that the Nazis had tried to make contact but had been rebuffed.[64] The evidence about the precise meaning of these alleged contacts in Sweden remains inconclusive – was Stalin really trying to make peace with Hitler, or was it just a provocation? But the significant point in the context of this history is that both the British and American leaders were aware of the potential danger that Stalin might extricate the Soviet Union from the war. The possibility might have been small – how could Stalin ever trust Hitler again, after the destruction of the Non-Aggression Pact? And Hitler always seemed opposed to such a compromise. Nonetheless, for the Western Allies there was a genuine perceived risk, and fear of what Stalin might do was a persistent worry lurking in the minds of Roosevelt and Churchill.

THE REALITY OF SOVIET LIFE

Tensions existed not only at the highest level in the relationship between the Western Allies and the Soviet Union: strain was also apparent much lower down the hierarchy of power. As Stalin, Roosevelt and Churchill danced warily around each other during 1943, Hugh Lunghi,[65] a twenty-three-year-old British officer, was posted to Moscow as part of the British military mission. Before he arrived he had viewed the Soviet Union through 'rose-tinted glasses. We had great admiration for what the Red Army had, by then in 1943, achieved.' He was also influenced by 'the way the media was reporting not only Russian military achievements, but, of course, was writing up the success – as they put it at that time – of this wonderful socialist experiment, the first socialist country in the world. So I thought we would see, when we got there, laughing, happy people.'

It was not surprising that Hugh Lunghi had these preconceived ideas since, especially during the first half of 1943, the Western media was full of praise for Stalin and the Soviet Union. In Britain, Lord Beaverbrook's *Daily Express* in particular was hugely supportive of the Soviet war effort, whilst in the United States the January 1943 edition of *Time* magazine put Stalin on the cover as 'Man of the Year' for 1942. 'The year 1942 was a year of blood and strength,' reported *Time*. 'The man whose name means steel in Russian, whose few words of English include the American expression "tough guy", was the man of 1942.... He collectivized the farms and he built Russia into one of the four great industrial powers on earth. How well he succeeded was evident in Russia's world-surprising strength in World War II. Stalin's methods were tough, but they paid off.' And in a still more positive article in *Life* magazine in March, the Soviet Union was painted as a quasi-America, with its citizens portrayed as 'one hell of a people...[who] to a remarkable degree...look like Americans, dress like Americans and think like Americans'. Beria's NKVD was even described as 'a national police similar to the FBI'.[66]

But instead of finding people in Moscow who 'look like

Americans, dress like Americans and think like Americans', Hugh Lunghi witnessed poverty, hunger and fear amongst the ordinary citizens of this supposed workers' paradise. And as for the 'official' relationship with the Soviet authorities, it was, as far as he was concerned, 'an absolute freeze'. The strictly controlled Soviet media were 'hostile to us, and certainly played down any achievement that we might have gained on the field of battle with the Germans in the African campaign, or with bombing and so on'.

Throughout the war the British were suspicious that their military mission in Moscow was bugged by the Soviets – so much so that if they had anything of particular importance to discuss they would go into the bathroom and turn on the taps in an attempt to drown out their words. It was a precaution that they later discovered was fully justified, because immediately after the war Lunghi, now promoted to assistant military attaché, discovered surveillance equipment hidden underneath the parquet floor. He subsequently contacted 'friends' in the American military mission, who came round with a 'box of tricks' in an attempt to de-bug the whole building. Lunghi was intrigued to discover that they found bugs in all the rooms: 'Now when I say all of them, every [single] room was bugged, even our cipher room. And it was either bugged under the ventilators or in the skirting boards.' The presence of newspapers around the electronic surveillance equipment which dated back to the 1930s confirmed that the Soviets had been listening to the British for years.

The disillusionment that Hugh Lunghi experienced – between the propaganda image of the Soviet Union disseminated in the West and the harsh reality – was something felt by many Allied servicemen. Jim Risk, for example, then an American merchant marine officer in his early twenties, was astonished by life in the port of Molotovsk (now Severodvinsk) east of Murmansk. During his stay in the city he was shocked by evidence of the oppressive nature of the Soviet state. He managed to talk to some of the dock labourers, and discovered that they were political prisoners. 'We're anti-Stalin,' they told him. 'And they [the Soviet authorities] are not going to kill us – they're just going to work us to death.'

Every morning a column of several thousand political prisoners would march through the town from the prison camp on the outskirts to the docks, and the Allied sailors would stand and watch. One morning Risk saw a fellow American seaman throw a cigarette butt into the gutter. Suddenly one of the political prisoners broke from the column, and as he reached down to pick up the smouldering butt, he was shot by a guard. 'And he was left to lie there – that was the thing that got me more than anything else. Dead!' says Risk. 'Just lying there on the side of the street!'

He soon discovered that dead bodies were a common sight in the streets of Molotovsk: 'Several times in the morning we'd get up early and walk up to the town, and then in the gutters you'd see a body lying there – an old body. Grandfathers etc., they couldn't work...and didn't have enough to eat.'

'It was a big shock,' says Risk. 'I had no idea that people could be treated that way and still not do something violent in return.... We had learned that Stalin was a brute just like Hitler was a brute. They were just brutes in a different language. [When] I came back I was interviewed in New York on a radio station about the trip and one of the questions was: "How do you feel about the future of Russia?" And I said: "Well, you know, all those millions of people they have over there are treated like animals. They're prisoners in their own country. They have a commissar that rules them day and night and they can only do what he or she says. And they're going to rise up in righteous indignation and overthrow Stalin. Well, they didn't – but that was my attitude. I said I cannot conceive of people being treated this way and still not doing something violent in return.'

But although Risk found 'the system' in the Soviet Union repulsive, he discovered that the 'ordinary' citizens could be generous and friendly. He remembers that there was 'lots of fraternization going on'. The most noticeable sign of this – clearly visible to him on his second trip to the city, later in the war – was the sight of 'black babies'. 'We had black crew on board ships, mostly in the storage department, and they went ashore and connected. Not very many of them, you know, but there were a few black babies. There could have been some white babies, but we would not recognize that.'

On his first trip to the Soviet Union, Risk and his shipmates were waiting nearly nine months for a return convoy. As a result, the food on the American ships began to run out, and eventually all they had left was their emergency supply of Spam. The paucity and monotony of the diet, combined with the intensely depressing atmosphere, began to turn a few American minds to thoughts of self-harm. 'We had two suicides in our four American ships tied up there,' says Risk. 'We had no idea when we were gonna go home – if we were ever gonna go home. As far as we knew, we might just become Russian citizens!'

Risk witnessed at first hand the attempted suicide of one seventeen-year-old sailor on his own ship: 'We had a guard on the top of the flying bridge of the ship – that's 45 feet above the water level. And his job is to walk back and forth and survey everything that's going on and make the ship secure.... He was walking back and forth and my state room was right under that section of the bridge...and as I stepped out of my state room I could hear him walking and then all of a sudden I heard a scuffle and I looked up and he was on the edge of the bridge [and] jumped into the water.... And I yelled to the bosun to launch the lifeboat and I dived after this kid. It was so cold! Anyway, we both came to the surface and I grabbed him and he was willing to be grabbed, and by that point they'd launched a lifeboat and they came and picked us up.' So severe was the young sailor's depression that he was immediately sent home on an American merchantman sailing from Britain to the United States. But the story has a sad end: 'He managed to jump off the side of that ship on the way [back] and committed suicide,' says Risk. 'He was from Georgia – a farm boy.... He was just despondent, despondent...it was such a waste.'

The personal experience of these American sailors in the Soviet Union was so searing that previously held allegiances changed completely. 'Aboard my ship, for instance,' says Risk, 'when we went to Russia we had six members aboard who were red [Communists] – "pinkies", we called them. And when we got back to Philadelphia Navy Yard at the end of the year they were no longer pinkies. They had learned what a mistake it was.' And as for Stalin, Risk had formed the view, as a result of his acquaintance with the Soviet regime – that he was 'the dirtiest, filthiest personality in the world'.

The Allied sailors, of course, experienced life in the northern ports of the Soviet Union and in due course returned home. But for the women who fraternized with them, life was altogether different. Valentina Ievleva, for example, who loved to frequent the International Club and flirt with foreign sailors, faced vilification because of the life she now led: 'Everybody, from children to elderly people, they called me an "English doormat". Not American, but English – I think it was easier to pronounce.' In addition her 'girlfriends stopped being my friends' – they were 'jealous of me because I could dance with any man I liked and I took their men away from them. I came to the club in a very plain cotton dress, and from all corners of the room immediately three or four people got to their feet and came up to me. I was a great success.' This 'jealousy' that Valentina experienced was not, however, occasioned entirely by envy of her beauty and charm. There was also a more practical reason: 'In the International Club it was chocolate and chewing gum and cigarettes only. But if they came to your home they brought you soup and canned meat and sausage and whatever they had. I remember there were biscuits. I will remember it for ever. There was peanut butter in those biscuits. It was so delicious. I still remember this.'

She recognizes that some people might feel her actions came close to prostitution – a charge she denies. 'I'm not excluding the material factor', she says, 'but I think the main driving factor was fondness – liking.... I don't think we were selling ourselves. But I'm not denying the material factor. It was also important to get something material. Let's face facts – it helped you survive the next day.' And then, almost inevitably given the circumstances, Valentina became pregnant. She had met, on one of her frequent visits to the International Club, an American sailor from Brooklyn. 'We slept together,' she says simply. 'He said: "We are married –

you are my wife, I am your husband."' The relationship lasted for four months until the sailor returned home. And the baby was born in February 1945.

Valentina dreamt of living a new and glamorous life in America: 'Everyone was saying: "You're so beautiful – if you came to Hollywood you would become famous." I just wanted to be an actress. I had no idea whatsoever about American life. I was very young and I was thoughtless...everyone was admiring me. Everyone was open and I greeted them in the same way. The world looked wonderful.'

But her 'wonderful' life and dreams of America were destroyed when the NKVD began to take an interest in her. Stalin had always been suspicious of contacts between foreigners and Soviet citizens and anyone who had spent time with a foreigner was a suspect. In such an environment Valentina Ievleva, with her baby fathered by an American, was more at risk than most, and when her flat was searched by the NKVD they found a diary she had been writing. It was merely a collection of girlish dreams and longings, but sections of it were underlined by the investigators as incriminating. They included sentiments such as: 'I want to go to America so much. I dream about it day and night. To be an actress in America you only have to be beautiful. And here? To be beautiful is not enough, you have to have ten years of schooling.'[67] And so, armed with these devastating discoveries, the NKVD accused Valentina of 'spying for two intelligence services – of being both an American and a British spy'.

'My investigator was saying: "Tell me about your spying activities", and I was only smiling at him. What could I have seen? What could I have done? How could I be guilty? Of loving someone? I loved a man, so what was wrong with that? Who did I harm? I didn't harm anyone, only myself!' Her interrogator followed normal NKVD practice in such circumstances and asked Valentina the same question over and over again: 'What were your spying activities? What were your spying activities?' During the 'investigation' – mostly conducted at night – Valentina was deprived of sleep. When her investigator was bored with his single question he read the paper or talked to his wife on the phone, but ensured that Valentina stayed awake. The interrogation normally ended at about five in the morning, and only then was Valentina taken back to her cell. But she was forced to get up again at seven and, like the rest of the prison population, was not allowed to sleep during the day. All this left her with lifelong insomnia.

Once during the interrogation, tired and frustrated, she spoke angrily back to her tormentor, saying: 'How did you help your Soviet Motherland? By arresting and interrogating people! Is that how you helped your Motherland?' For this crime Valentina was sentenced to several days in the punishment cell – a tiny, concrete-floored cage about 6 feet by 9 feet. She survived by singing songs in English she had learnt from the movies she had watched at the International Club. She refused to stop when ordered to, and as a result was forced into a straitjacket: 'After that I burst into tears and they told me to stop crying, which I couldn't. But soon the doctor came and they untied me. That's how I suffered for my resistance.'

Valentina was sentenced to six years in a Gulag for the 'crime' of fraternization and 'spying'. But her fundamental optimism and humanity were not crushed by the experience of working in a penal camp, dragging logs in the icy north of the Soviet Union. Instead she focused on the positive gains from her wartime experience, which included the ability to belly-dance, a skill she had first seen in a Hollywood movie at the International Club. 'After that film I stood in front of the mirror and practised belly-dancing, and so I learnt to do it...[then] in the Gulag it helped me because no other woman could do belly-dancing and they [the other prisoners] asked me to demonstrate it again and again. "Do you have any artificial parts?" they asked. And everyone was surprised.'

And still, with the knowledge of hindsight, Valentina Ievleva would not have chosen to act differently: 'I remember those years [visiting the International Club] as the best years of my life. I would be ready to go to the Gulag for ten more years if I could spend three years living like that – the love, the admiration, the compliments. It's like a drug.'

THE KURSK OFFENSIVE

As spring turned to summer in 1943, Stalin and the rest of the Soviet leadership anticipated a massive German offensive in the centre of the front around the city of Kursk, 400 miles south of Moscow. And still in 1943 the signs were that the Germans had not lost their ability to destroy the Red Army once the snows melted. During February and March German troops under Field Marshal Erich von Manstein had managed to retake Kharkov in the Ukraine, and now they had assembled a massive attacking force near Kursk. Their plan was simple. Around the Soviet-held city there was a bulge in the front line that contained nearly 20 per cent of the Red Army. The Germans planned to attack simultaneously north from Kharkov and south from Orel in a gigantic encirclement, reminiscent of the glory days of Kiev and Vyazma in 1941. The scale of this encounter dwarfs the imagination. Three times more tanks would fight at Kursk than participated in the battle of El Alamein, the most famous armoured encounter in the West, and the battlefield was spread over an area as large as Belgium.

But the German attack lost all element of surprise because the operation was delayed until July, when new armaments – in particular the powerful Panther tank – were expected to arrive. And, unbeknownst to the Germans, the Soviet High Command already knew from intelligence sources the details of the offensive. In particular John Cairncross, the Soviet spy who worked at the British decoding unit at Bletchley Park, provided intricate information that officially the British would not give their Soviet ally for fear of compromising the source – 'Ultra', gained from breaking German Enigma codes.

As a consequence of all this fore-knowledge, the Soviets dug massive defence works just behind their lines – more than half a million mines were laid and elaborate anti-tank ditches were prepared. But still the Red Army soldiers were insecure – after all, uppermost in their minds was the knowledge that they had never successfully held a German summer offensive. 'I often had shivers down my spine,' says Mikhail Borisov,[68] a Soviet artilleryman at

Kursk, 'the result of fear. I didn't know what would happen if we had to come face-to-face with the German tanks.'

By contrast, the mood amongst German tank crews was high: 'The Tiger [tank] was good,' says Alfred Rubbel,[69] a tank commander who took part in the German assault on Kursk from the south. 'We had good leadership...there wasn't much you could do against the Tiger – that made us a bit reckless sometimes.' But as soon as the battle began, Rubbel realized that Kursk would be a different kind of encounter from the easy victories of 1941. 'The Russians shot – we'd never experienced it before – such an initial barrage.... it was so dense.... We crossed the river and immediately afterwards we came into a minefield. All fourteen vehicles got stuck there. The second company never had a very good reputation, so twelve Tiger tanks were gone.'

During the intense fighting the officer in charge of Mikhail Borisov's artillery battery was killed and he had to take over command. He and two comrades fired shell after shell: 'I found the tank in the sighting device and fired. And the tank caught fire. Then I loaded the next shell and released the second...and I was lucky again.... And I set the next tank on fire...the hatch opened and the tank driver, a tall guy, young, very thin, wearing black overalls, he stood on the turret and he shook his fist in our direction.... He was no threat to me. But I shot directly at him and I killed him.'

'It was non-stop shooting,' remembers Wilhelm Roes,[70] a tank driver with the SS Leibstandarte Adolf Hitler. 'We at that time were not aware it was such a huge tank battle, but we thought: "God! How many tanks are shooting off?" When a [Soviet] T34 tank explodes the turret flies off and a huge ring of smoke goes up, [and] we saw these rings of smoke coming up. We thought: "How many more are coming? All these rings of smoke going up to the sky!"' During the battle of Kursk, Roes took part in one of the most famous tank encounters of the war. At Prokhorovka, a small town on the main railway line to the city, 600 Soviet tanks faced 250 German.[71] 'The Russian scenery, the landscape, that had been beautiful before was [now] complete chaos,' recalls Roes. 'Everywhere burning tanks, smoke everywhere, smell of ammunition, smell of burning corpses. It was like an inferno. It was Hell.' Such was the impact of Prokhorovka on his imagination that he 'dreamt after the war, not once but a hundred times, that I was again and again on the battlefield of Prokhorovka. But I was alone, and I had to get home from Prokhorovka, through 1500 kilometres of enemy territory. I was constantly thinking: "How can I do it?" In my dream there were always burning tanks.... I was alone, wondering how I could get back home through the forests, how I could hide. Then my wife would wake me and say, "You're dreaming of Russia again".'[72]

The Red Army lost nearly three hundred thousand dead at Kursk, the Wehrmacht about one hundred thousand. It was an immense encounter that left both sides momentarily stunned. But the Red Army could claim victory. They had, for the first time, held the German summer advance, a fact that led Alfred Rubbel to this conclusion: 'It wasn't until then that we truly understood how strong the Russians were.... One didn't want to believe it before [but] now the pessimistic view was that the war was lost. It was over.'

Mikhail Borisov was decorated as a Hero of the Soviet Union for his exploits during the battle of Kursk. He claims that it was simply 'love for the Motherland' that motivated him to 'fight to the last breath – that is how we were brought up. And this feeling remained with us for the rest of our lives. I keep saying to myself: "If Russia finds itself in hard times again, even now I can do something to defend it."... I come from a Cossack family and my ancestors were all Cossacks. And love for the Motherland and love for weapons came with a mother's milk.'

Now, as the Germans began a slow fighting retreat that would last almost two years, until the Red Army reached the gates of the Reich Chancellery in Berlin, the Allied leaders had to discuss not just the strategy for the remainder of the war, but also the shape of the post-war world and the new boundaries of Europe. So as one war entered its last phase, a new one began – this time a fractious and divisive political struggle. What had united the three Allied leaders was the desire to defeat Hitler. But what would hold them together once the threat from Hitler started to disappear?

4

THE CHANGING WIND

FIRST MOMENTS AT TEHRAN

It is the Yalta Conference in January 1945 that has come to symbolize the controversial division of Europe at the end of the war. 'The agreement at Yalta followed in the unjust tradition of Munich and the Molotov–Ribbentrop Pact,' said President George W. Bush, speaking in Latvia in May 2005 on the sixtieth anniversary of the end of the war in Europe. 'Once again, when powerful governments negotiated, the freedom of small nations was somehow expendable.'[1]

Whether President Bush's words represent an accurate judgement on Yalta or not is something that the reader must decide, having read the evidence in Chapter 5. But what is certain is that the focus of the world on Yalta as the moment of key decision-making at the end of the war is mistaken. The first meeting between Roosevelt, Stalin and Churchill, held in the Iranian capital, Tehran, in November 1943, was of much greater significance. This initial encounter not only established the dynamic of the personal relationships between the so-called 'Big Three', but determined the answer to many of the key questions facing the post-war world that would merely be tinkered with or rubber-stamped at Yalta just over a year later.

Roosevelt had wanted a face-to-face meeting with Stalin for years; the Davies visit to Moscow was only the most recent attempt to arrange the encounter. He had suggested several times in 1942 that the two of them should meet, and had even asked Stalin to attend the Casablanca Conference at the start of 1943 – this was the conference at which Roosevelt had first announced that the Allies should only accept 'unconditional' surrender from the Germans.

For Stalin, the ability to reject or accept an invitation to a summit with Roosevelt was one of the easiest levers of power he had in the relationship. Stalin was quick to couple the question of whether or not he would agree to meet Roosevelt and Churchill with the perennial issue of the second front. Although in August 1943 Stalin had written to Churchill and Roosevelt agreeing that a meeting of the three of them was 'desirable at the first opportunity',[2] he made it clear that if the imminent summit was not convened on his terms then he would insist it was postponed until after the long-awaited second front had been launched.

This did not suit Roosevelt at all. He wanted to establish a personal relationship with Stalin, something that could only be achieved if the two of them were in the same room. It was uniquely within this intimate zone that Roosevelt believed he could work his magic of 'handling' people. And there were also vital questions of substance that the President wanted to discuss – questions that he felt could best be resolved to his advantage only after his personal chemistry had charmed the Soviet dictator. Two of these issues were, as far as Roosevelt was concerned, more important than all the others. First, he wanted to know whether or not the Soviet Union would commit to breaking its treaty of non-aggression with Japan and come into the war in Asia on the side of the Western Allies, and second, he wanted to judge the extent to which Stalin was prepared to participate in American plans for a post-war world of collaboration and peace (a policy that would eventually result in the formation of the United Nations).

Roosevelt suggested meeting Stalin in Cairo, but this location – along with a string of others that the Americans subsequently put forward, including Beirut and Basra – was rejected by the Soviets. Stalin, not for the first time, used the excuse that he could not stray far from his country while his people were still facing the might of the German army. Eventually Stalin suggested Tehran, but the Americans thought this impractical. While Congress was in session the President was constitutionally obliged to sign or veto legislation within ten days of it being presented to him – something he could not do from the Iranian capital.

TEHRAN CONFERENCE, 1943

N

SWEDEN

Tallinn

Ventspils

Riga

Liepája

Baltic Sea

Western Dvina

Kaunas

Kaliningrad

Vilnius

Minsk

Gdańsk

Vistula

EAST
GERMANY

Oder

Bialystok

BERLIN

Poznań

POLAND

Bydgoszcz

SOVIET
UNION

WARSAW

Oder

Łódź

Brzesć

Wroclaw

Lublin

PRAGUE

Kraków

Lwów

CZECHOSLOVAKIA

Stanisławów

Danube

VIENNA

Bratislava

Miskolc

AUSTRIA

BUDAPEST

HUNGARY

ROMANIA

Zagreb

0 ___ miles ___ 100

0 ___ km ___ 100

YUGOSLAVIA

BELGRADE

Territory annexed by Poland
in 1945

Territory in Poland annexed
by Soviet Union in 1945

The Curzon Line

Roosevelt therefore wrote to Stalin on 21 October, stating simply: 'I cannot go to Tehran.'[3]

Stalin insisted: if the meeting was not held in that city, there would be no meeting at all. The Soviet leader was attracted to Tehran not only because of its proximity to the Soviet Union but also because he felt safe quartered within the guarded compound of the Soviet embassy. On 8 November Roosevelt caved in and agreed to meet Stalin in Tehran later in the month – thus his first concession to the Soviet leader was made even before the meeting began. A contingency plan was developed to enable Roosevelt to deal with his constitutional responsibilities; if he needed to sign any legislation he would leave the conference, fly to Tunis – which was more than two thousand miles west of Tehran – and then return.

This was not, of course, just to be a meeting between Stalin and Roosevelt: Churchill was invited as well. After the debacle of the secret approach to Stalin in May, the Americans knew that the British Prime Minister could not be excluded from this encounter. Roosevelt and Stalin would thus meet for the first time with Churchill present – but with the British Prime Minister as something of a gooseberry. Roosevelt knew that just because Churchill was to be physically present at the meeting, it did not mean that he could not still be marginalized. After all, just six months before, Joseph Davies, acting as Roosevelt's agent, had explicitly told Stalin that after the war 'Britain will be financially through for a long time' and that the two most powerful nations in the post-war world would be the Soviet Union and the United States. And these were truths Roosevelt still believed. Subsequently, one wit referred not to the 'Big Three' but to the 'Big Two and a Half'; and it was the 'Big Two and a Half' who met together from the beginning.

Even before the Tehran Conference began, Roosevelt was careful not to create the impression that Britain and America were somehow ganging up on Stalin. When the British and Americans met in Cairo before travelling on to Tehran, Churchill was disappointed by his lack of contact with the President. Instead of holding meetings with the British Prime Minister, Roosevelt preferred to while away the time talking to the Chinese Nationalist leader Chiang Kai-shek about the war in Asia – meetings that Churchill believed were 'lengthy, complicated and minor'.[4]

All this was exasperating for Churchill. He had important strategic matters he wanted to discuss with Roosevelt – chiefly the war in Italy, which was not going as well as expected. Although the Italians had surrendered on 3 September 1943, the German commander in the country, Field Marshal Kesselring, had moved swiftly to disarm the Italian army and rush reinforcements to the south. The Germans now held the Allies near Salerno, and were clearly prepared to fight a slow war of retreat. The most effective way to deal with the Germans, given Italy's long seaboard, was by a series of amphibious landings further up the coast in order to bypass their defences. But such an operation needed landing craft, and these were in short supply. The American Admiral King had insisted on large numbers for the war in the Pacific – a war that could only be conducted amphibiously – and the demands of the forthcoming Operation Overlord (as the long-awaited second front was now called) meant that there were precious few landing craft in Europe that were not already committed for D-Day.

At the first Quebec Conference in August 1943 (there was to be a second, held in the autumn of 1944) the Western Allies had agreed to launch Overlord in the spring of 1944. But now, because of the slow progress of the Italian campaign, Churchill wanted to revisit the whole schedule. On 20 October he wrote to Roosevelt, asking for a detailed discussion of the options at their meeting in Cairo. But this was a matter Roosevelt and the American military leadership did not want to open up once again. Churchill, it will be recalled, had on several previous occasions announced that despite agreeing with the second front in principle in practice there was always one more operation that needed to take precedence; and the Americans had at last run out of patience with him.

Churchill had thought that he would have three clear days alone with Roosevelt in Cairo to discuss all of this before the Chinese arrived, but the Americans juggled the schedule at the last minute to eliminate this possibility. Indeed, Roosevelt had been so

anxious to avoid the impression of an Anglo-American cabal forming in Cairo that he had even wanted the Soviets to be represented
at the meeting – with their delegation arriving on the same day as
the British and Chinese – but Stalin had decided not to allow
Molotov to participate. He explained to the Western Allies that it
was inappropriate, given the Soviet Non-Aggression Pact with
Japan, to have a Soviet voice at a meeting attended by Chiang,
whose troops were fighting the Japanese in China.[5]

At a meeting on 24 November in Cairo, Churchill finally
seized the opportunity to plead with Roosevelt and the American
military leadership for more resources for the Mediterranean. But
– predictably – the Americans would not countenance a delay in
Overlord. Towards the end of the meeting Roosevelt reminded
Churchill of the relative troop numbers now committed to the
overall conflict: very soon more Americans would be involved in
the war than troops under British command.

On the 26th, Roosevelt and Churchill left for Tehran. In the
plane Churchill gloomily confided to his doctor, Charles Wilson
(later Lord Moran), that the campaign in Italy had been put 'in
jeopardy'[6] by the American desire to invade France on the schedule
drawn up at Quebec. Moran also gives an insight into the American
mind-set just before the Tehran Conference by quoting a revealing
conversation he had with Harry Hopkins, Roosevelt's close adviser:
'Harry tells me the President is convinced that even if he cannot
convert Stalin into a good democrat he will be able to come to a
working agreement with him. After all, he had spent his life managing men. And Stalin at bottom could not be so very different from
other people. Anyway, he has come to Tehran determined, if I can
trust Hopkins, to come to terms with Stalin, and he is not going to
allow anything to interfere with that purpose.'[7]

Roosevelt was immediately presented with an unexpected
opportunity to spend more time at the conference with Stalin. On
24 November the Americans had enquired of the Soviets about
safety in the city – there was a fear that 'Axis agents' might be
operating in Iran. And since the American legation was the other
side of the city from the Soviet compound, where the meetings

were to be held, the Soviets suggested that Roosevelt should place his safety in their hands and stay in a building within their security zone.

There was some truth in the Soviet claim about the dangers of Tehran. Iran had privately supported Germany earlier in the war, although officially remaining neutral, and the British and Soviets had responded with an invasion, Operation Countenance, in August 1941 in order to protect their own interests in the country. As a result, Iran was now backing the Allies, and the important supply route to the Soviet Union – known as the Persian corridor – had been safeguarded. But the legacy of the early years of the conflict, and the sympathy with Germany, remained in some quarters.

Roosevelt swiftly accepted the suggestion that he stay in the Soviet compound, no doubt also thinking that this would be seen as a physical statement of his desire to build a relationship with Stalin. Churchill, meantime, stayed in the British embassy next door. Roosevelt's decision to reside under Soviet control meant that his premises were bugged – something that Sergio Beria, son of the NKVD chief Lavrenti Beria, later confirmed.

'I'm sure that the leaders of both the Allies understood they might have been bugged,' says Zoya Zarubina,[8] who was a Soviet intelligence officer, liasing with the press in Tehran at the time. 'But there was nothing to be done, you can't avoid that....You bugged our hotel rooms when we came to Britain – don't tell me that it's not proper.'

At a quarter past three on 28 November 1943, Roosevelt and Stalin met for the first time when the Soviet leader came to call on the American President as he settled into his rooms in the Soviet legation. Superficially, two more different leaders it is hard to imagine. Zoya Zarubina, who saw both in Tehran, describes Stalin as having 'a tired face...and if you are closer you can see [his] smallpox spots. And the one thing that surprised you is the eyes. His eyes were, I don't know...well, golden yellowish, let's call it that way. But once, all of a sudden, you get eyeball to eyeball it is scary – scary in the sense that he just pierces through you.'

Roosevelt, on the other hand, 'his eyes were always smiling at you. I don't know what he thought, but you know, [his eyes were] sort of inviting you to come on, speak up.'

Roosevelt greeted Stalin with the words: 'I am glad to see you. I have tried for a long time to bring this about.'⁹ Stalin pointedly replied that he was to blame for the delay since he had been 'very occupied because of military matters'. That first encounter lasted about an hour, and is notable chiefly for the way Roosevelt was prepared to criticize the absent Churchill. The President mentioned that Churchill's attitude to India (the Prime Minister was opposed to Indian independence) meant that 'it would be better not to discuss the question of India with Mr Churchill, since the latter had no solution of that question, and merely proposed to defer the entire solution to the end of the war'. Stalin agreed that India was Churchill's 'sore spot'. Then, in an overt attempt at ingratiating himself with Stalin, Roosevelt suggested that India should be reshaped 'somewhat on the Soviet line'. Stalin remarked that this would mean 'revolution'.

It is not surprising that Roosevelt used the question of India, and thus implicitly the British Empire, in an attempt to create an immediate bond with Stalin. The American President had always disapproved of the British Empire – as far as he was concerned, the sooner it was dismantled the better. Indeed, it is important to remember, says George Elsey, that whilst the Americans recognized that Stalin's regime was 'pretty despicable' it was also the case 'that in the United States there were a significant number of people who were not very comfortable with the British Empire either. There was a sizeable vocal minority who questioned whether we should be spending so much to preserve the British Empire. So there was scepticism about Britain, there was scepticism about the Soviet Union.' At the Yalta Conference, just over a year later, Roosevelt was to demonstrate further his anti-colonial stance by suggesting to Stalin that Britain should give up Hong Kong to China.

Churchill, wholly committed to the British Empire, did little to hide his views on the subject – views that he knew were anathema to the American administration. He memorably remarked to Charles Taussig, one of Roosevelt's foreign policy advisers, that: 'We will not let the Hottentots by popular vote throw the white people into the sea.'[10] This, naturally, was an attitude which fuelled Roosevelt's suspicion that the British were fighting the war – in part at least – to preserve the empire. In the autumn of 1944 Roosevelt said to Henry Morgenthau, the Secretary for the Treasury, that 'he knew why the British wanted to join the war in the Pacific. All they want is Singapore back.'[11]

At Tehran, straight after their tête-à-tête, Roosevelt and Stalin moved on to the first plenary session of the conference, which opened at 4.30. Here the stark difference in political styles between the Western Allies and Stalin became immediately evident. Roosevelt remarked that 'the Soviets, the British and the United States were sitting round the table for the first time as members of the same family'; Churchill added portentously that 'the meeting probably represented the greatest concentration of worldly power that had ever been seen in the history of mankind. In their hands almost certainly lay victory: in their hands beyond any shadow of a doubt lay the happiness and fortunes of mankind.' He added that he 'prayed that they might be worthy of this wonderful God-granted opportunity of rendering service to their fellow-men'.[12] Stalin, who in his entire life would never make a speech like the one he had just heard from Churchill, contented himself with thanking the President and Prime Minister for their remarks and said merely that he hoped that the three of them would 'make good use of this opportunity'.

At this first full meeting, Stalin made an immediate concession. Instead of berating the Western Allies for the lack of a second front or insisting on the 1941 borders with Poland – the two subjects that, as we have already seen, were highest on his personal agenda – he announced that he 'would first address himself to the question of the Pacific'. He said that 'unfortunately it was impossible for the Soviets to join in the struggle against Japan at the present time, since practically all their forces were required to be deployed against Germany'. However, Stalin went on, 'the moment for their joining their friends in this theatre would be the moment of Germany's collapse: then they would march together'. It was a clever tactic. Stalin immediately placed the Americans in his debt. But what, in practical terms, had he conceded? Only an agreement in principle to attack Japan once the war in Europe had been won. And what was crucial, in Stalin's mind, to help the war in Europe to be over swiftly? Why, the second front of course.

It was clear from Stalin's subsequent words that his single-minded focus on the importance of the second front had not diminished. The British and Americans had gained the impression, from a meeting of Foreign Ministers in Moscow in October, that the Soviets might possibly call at Tehran for both Overlord and an increase in Allied resources for the Mediterranean theatre. But Stalin now made his wishes clear. Overlord was pre-eminent – a view that coincided exactly with American plans.

Churchill was not about to give up, and he launched a spirited attack, outlining once more the benefits of more resources for the Mediterranean. But to no effect. Stalin saw no benefit in dispersing the Allied effort. He wanted one strike against the beaches of northern France with – just possibly – a landing in support of Overlord in the South of France. The session broke up with Churchill dismayed – he confided to Lord Moran immediately afterwards that 'A bloody lot has gone wrong.'[13] But, tough as he was, Churchill pressed on, holding one more crucial meeting with Stalin later that day – this time on the question of Poland.

From the first moment of the Soviet invasion of eastern Poland there had been an acceptance in the British Foreign Office that it would be difficult ever to get this portion of Poland back, but Churchill had been outraged when Stalin told Eden in December 1941 that he wanted to claim this territory as his own. However, by now the Prime Minister had come to the conclusion that, politically, there was no alternative but to give the Soviets what they wanted. At Tehran, late at night, he and Stalin discussed the fate of Poland in what must surely rank as one of the most important – yet seemingly casual – conversations of the war. It was Churchill who raised the question of Poland, and Stalin was careful to say nothing until he heard what the Prime Minister proposed – this despite Churchill's attempt to get the Soviet leader to disclose first 'what he thought about it'. Stalin revealed nothing, saying that 'he did not feel the need to ask himself how to act' and waited for Churchill to show his hand.[14] Churchill said that after the war 'the Soviet Union would be overwhelmingly strong and Russia would have a great responsibility for hundreds of years in any decision she took with regard to Poland. Personally, he thought Poland might move westwards like soldiers taking two steps close. If Poland trod on some German toes, that could not be helped, but there must be a strong Poland. This instrument was needed in the orchestra of Europe.'

The significance of Churchill's words should not be underestimated. For he had just proposed – via the almost comic simile of 'soldiers taking two steps close' – one of the largest and most fundamental population shifts of the twentieth century. As a consequence, millions of people would either be uprooted if they sought to keep their previous nationality, or subsumed into another country. At a stroke, Germany would lose more territory than had been lost as a consequence of the Versailles Treaty. Meantime the Poles, Britain's ally, might lose in the East around 40 per cent of the country that had existed before the war – the very land, moreover, from which came the majority of Polish soldiers who were currently fighting in the British army in Italy.

Anthony Eden, the Foreign Secretary, said in the same meeting that he was 'encouraged' by the idea that 'the Poles should go as far west as the [river] Oder'. But Stalin was careful not to commit himself, merely asking Eden 'whether we [the British] thought he was going to swallow Poland up'.

Eden replied that 'he did not know how much the Russians were going to eat. How much would they leave undigested?'

'The Russians did not want anything belonging to other people,' said Stalin. 'Although they might have a bite at Germany.' The notes of the meeting conclude: 'The Prime Minister demonstrated with the help of three matches [to mark the new border] his idea of Poland moving westwards, which pleased Marshal Stalin.'

Rather than looking at the subsequent conference at Yalta for the moment when the Allies demonstrated their power to determine the fate of post-war Europe, it is better to focus on this late-night meeting on 28 November 1943 in Tehran. By the use of similes, metaphors and, ultimately, props in the form of matches Churchill and Eden reshaped the boundaries of Poland and Germany – significantly without the presence of representatives from the two countries involved in this demographic and geographical upheaval. Indeed, Churchill said to Stalin that his idea was to see, 'if the three Heads of Government, working in agreement, could form some sort of policy which might be pressed upon the Poles'.

Churchill was perfectly aware that the suggestions he made to Stalin were diametrically opposed to the views he had expressed two years before. A clue as to the reasons why he changed his mind can be found in a letter he wrote to Eden after the conference in January 1944. Principally, Churchill felt that the Soviet demands were in fact a *fait accompli*. 'We are now about to attempt the settlement of the eastern frontier of Poland,'[15] he wrote, 'and we cannot be unconscious of the fact that the Baltic States, and the questions of Bukovina and Bessarabia, have largely settled themselves through the victories of the Russian Armies.' But there was more to the Prime Minister's change of heart than a mere acceptance of the inevitable. He revealed that 'undoubtedly my own feelings have changed' over the last two years. 'The tremendous victories of the Russian armies, the deep-seated changes which have taken place in the character of the Russian State and Government, the new confidence which has grown in our hearts towards Stalin – these have all had their effect.'

Churchill was clearly influenced by the fact that 1943 had been a year of transformation in the fortunes of the Soviet Union. At the start of it the Red Army had been battling with the Germans in Stalingrad; now the Germans were in retreat. And this change in fortune on the battlefield had been accompanied – at least in the view of some leading figures in the British Foreign Office – by a number of signs that the Soviet regime was altering for the better.

For example, the Comintern – the body dedicated to the imposition of Communism on other countries – had been abolished in
May 1943. (Its aims were simply too incompatible with the reality
of the strategic alliance with the Western Allies.) And there were
also indications of a new religious tolerance in the Soviet Union
when in September 1943 Stalin permitted the Russian Orthodox
Church to appoint a new patriarch.

Roosevelt too hoped for the best. 'The revolutionary currents
of 1917 may be spent in this war,' said the American President in
April 1943 when talking of future Soviet intentions, 'with progress
[in the future] following evolutionary constitutional lines'.[16]

In addition, in purely practical terms, Churchill must have
thought that the Poles would never be able to live at peace with
their powerful neighbour if they kept the eastern portion of their
country – territory that Stalin had so persistently demanded.
Earlier discussions with the Soviet leader had made clear his obsession with ensuring post-war security on his borders, and perhaps,
Churchill believed, if the Soviets were given eastern Poland, then
they would feel more secure and thus more disposed to cooperate
with the new independent Poland. As for the Poles, as Churchill
was later to reiterate, they were, as far as he was concerned, gaining industrial land in the West – such as the port of Danzig –
which was far more useful than the primarily agricultural land they
were being asked to give up in the East.

And then there was another mood in the air, one fanned by
the pro-Soviet tone of much of the reporting in the West in the
wake of the Red Army's victories and sacrifices. It was a sense that
the Soviet Union might have something to teach the world; that
after the war a form of 'socialism' might be possible that took the
'good things' from the Soviet experience (a sense of 'togetherness', the goals of free education, healthcare for all, and full
employment) and eliminated the 'bad things' (the lack of freedom and the corruption of the rule of law). Indeed, Churchill
himself observed to Stalin at Tehran that the British were becoming 'a trifle pinker'. And Stalin had retorted: 'That is a sign of
good health.'[17]

The question was, did all this really amount to 'deep-seated changes…in the character of the Russian State and Government'? Probably only if one ignored the contrary evidence. For example, Churchill knew that earlier in 1943 Sir Owen O'Malley had reported that on a balance of probabilities Stalin's regime had been responsible for the murders at Katyn – a crime that the Soviets were now actively covering up.

More important still, where was the practical evidence that Stalin would allow 'democracy', as the West understood the concept, in any of the states that he was soon likely to control? Recent history had demonstrated that the Soviets were much more practised at organizing fake 'elections' as they had during their occupation of eastern Poland four years before. But Churchill felt he had little alternative but to accept the Soviet annexation of eastern Poland. Neither he nor Roosevelt was prepared to 'turn them out' with military force – indeed, it would have been impossible to do so while the war was still raging, and in the immediate aftermath of the conflict public opinion in Britain and the USA would hardly have supported the idea of a Third World War over the question of the boundaries of Poland and the Soviet occupation of the Baltic states.

However, if Churchill had stated, in effect: 'We accept that the Soviet claims for Poland and other disputed territory such as the Baltic States are wrong – they are unjust – but there is no practical method of putting this right', that would have been the reality. But he felt he could not say that – this was, remember, a 'moral' war – and it was thought essential for the Allies to present a united front to the world in order to prevent their enemies gaining heart from public discord between them. So Churchill persuaded himself that Stalin and the Soviets had changed. He (and Roosevelt) leapt on any sign that Stalin was a person who kept his word and who wanted to deal cooperatively and honestly with the West to make a better post-war world.

'We have been constrained,' wrote O'Malley in his Katyn report, 'by the urgent need for cordial relations with the Soviet government to appear to appraise the evidence with more hesitation and lenience than we should do in forming a common sense judgement on events occurring in normal times or in the ordinary course of our private lives; we have been obliged to appear to distort the normal and healthy operation of our intellectual and moral judgements.' And despite all the recent scholarly work[18] that suggests possible reasons why the British might have believed that Stalin was trustworthy, or that the Soviet regime was softening in some way, it is O'Malley's words that still best explain the thought process of Churchill and many of his Foreign Office advisers.

It is also significant that Churchill discussed Poland with Stalin in the absence of Roosevelt, who had gone to bed. This was a moment when the British Prime Minister could still demonstrate that he was a power in the world, able to negotiate epic deals. It was a rare moment at the conference. Because, as events the next day would demonstrate, Churchill was to be increasingly pushed aside.

ROOSEVELT MOVES ON STALIN

The second day of the conference opened with a meeting of military experts. It was a curious affair. Both the British, with General Brooke and Air Chief Marshal Portal, and the Americans, with a delegation led by General Marshall, had brought their finest military minds to Tehran. But Stalin had only taken the elderly and somewhat inept Marshal Voroshilov. A cavalry officer during the Russian Revolution, Voroshilov had proved his incompetence twice in recent years: first by commanding the Red Army during the disastrous Winter War against Finland, and second by failing through his tactical mistakes to prevent the Germans advancing on the Leningrad front. 'Here was Voroshilov,' remembers Hugh Lunghi, who was present at the meeting as an interpreter, 'faced by this phalanx of Western Allies, and I suppose he did his best – but his best wasn't very good at all because he really was very thick-headed and couldn't really understand much about strategy.'

The official minutes[19] reveal a number of almost surreal moments during the meeting. Voroshilov was either unable to accept or to comprehend the difficulties of a cross-Channel operation. 'Marshal Voroshilov agreed that the launching of such an operation [the second front] was more difficult than the crossing of a big river,' record the minutes, 'but somewhat similar. During recent operations the Russians had crossed several big rivers and in each case they had been defended by the enemy who held the higher west bank. With the help of artillery, machine guns and mortars, the German defences had been overcome. He thought that with such help, and with the aid of mine throwers, the difficulty confronting the cross-Channel operation could be overcome.'

'That wasn't very productive,' recalls Lunghi, with considerable understatement. In the face of Voroshilov's attempt to compare crossing the English Channel with crossing a big river both the British and Americans initially did their best to try to humour him. General Brooke even acknowledged that amphibious landings 'should have the mortar support of which Marshal Voroshilov had spoken'. But eventually General Marshall cracked. 'The difference between the river crossing and a landing from the ocean,' he said, 'was that, whereas the failure of a river crossing would be a reverse, the failure of an amphibious landing would be a catastrophe for it would mean the utter destruction of the landing craft and the troops involved.' In response to Marshall's comments, Voroshilov said 'quite frankly' that he 'did not agree'.

Stalin's attitude to Voroshilov bordered on open contempt as Lunghi witnessed: 'Stalin was generally treating him...rather like an old dog.' Why Stalin chose to bring Voroshilov to Tehran as his sole military representative is something of a mystery. The Soviet leader remarked during the conference that he had not expected military men to hold separate meetings, which could possibly be true – on many occasions Stalin asserted that it was the duty of political leaders to decide and military commanders to implement. And perhaps he had wanted to ensure that the Soviet Union's best military brains were kept far from the decision-making forum.

If the military meeting on the morning of 29 November was something of a dialogue of the deaf, a conversation between

Roosevelt and Stalin after lunch the same day was a good deal more productive.[20] Significantly, as on the previous day, Churchill was deliberately excluded (indeed, Roosevelt had so far declined the opportunity to meet the British Prime Minister on his own at the conference). During his private conversation with Stalin, the American President outlined his idea for the new organization that was dearest to his heart – the United Nations. He talked of his plans for what would eventually become the General Assembly of the UN and the Security Council. What is remarkable is that, even though there were subsequent changes in detail and composition of the two bodies, the shape of the United Nations as we know it today was clear in Roosevelt's mind at this moment in November 1943.

Stalin's response was relatively amenable. He clearly had what for him were more important matters on his mind – notably the practical matter of how first to win the war and then to ensure the security of the Soviet Union in the immediate post-war world. Indeed, it is possible to see in this brief encounter the essential political character of each of these massive twentieth-century icons. Stalin was practical, suspicious and looking for the advantage of the moment; Roosevelt presented an extraordinary mix of crafty, workaday politician and idealistic dreamer. For whilst the visionary Roosevelt had outlined to Stalin his world-changing plans for the future of the planet, the politician in him had recognized the value of keeping Churchill out of the meeting. Not only did this prevent any impression that the Western Allies were 'ganging up' on the Soviets, it also allowed Roosevelt an opportunity to work his charm on Stalin – something that did not, as yet, appear to be having much effect.

After their meeting, Stalin and Roosevelt attended the ceremonial handing over of the sword of Stalingrad by Churchill to the Soviet leader in the hall of the embassy. This was a gift from King George VI to the people of Stalingrad in recognition of their extraordinary tenacity and bravery during the siege of their city. Etched in acid on the 36-inch blade were the words: 'To the steel-hearted citizens of Stalingrad, the gift of King George VI, in token of homage of the British people.'

'There was an honour guard of the Buffs, a British regiment,' recalls Hugh Lunghi, who witnessed the ceremony. 'The NKVD provided their own honour guard with Tommy guns. Our honour guard simply had fixed bayonets.' When Churchill formally presented the sword to Stalin, 'he was clearly very moved, kissed the hilt and took the sword over to show it to Roosevelt, who was quite rightly taking very much a back seat at the side of the hall, and then brought it back and handed the sword to the only senior military that he had there – to Voroshilov – who took the sword, but he let it slide out of the scabbard. He clutched it to his chest and that didn't help – it fell on to his toes. He blushed all over his face, looked very discomfited, managed somehow to put it back into the scabbard again, then looked at Stalin from under his eyes and was obviously afraid he was going to get a real ticking off.'

As Lunghi left the hall after the ceremony, 'I heard a sort of shuffling noise behind me, and someone [was] tugging my sleeve. I was following Churchill who was just in front of me, and the person who was tugging my sleeve, of course, was Voroshilov. And I turned around, and he said: "Can you help me?" And I said: "Yes, of course, sir. What can I do?" And he said: "I'd like to speak to your Prime Minister." So we caught up with Churchill and I said: "Excuse me, sir", and Churchill turned round, looked a bit discomfited, and looked at Voroshilov and smiled, and Voroshilov mumbled his apology, and Churchill sort of just waved his hands…and then he [Voroshilov] wished him a happy birthday.'

But Voroshilov had got the date wrong. The Prime Minister's birthday was the next day. 'Churchill walked over to the legation, where he was staying,' says Lunghi, 'and I followed him – and it was just across the road, only a few yards across the road dividing the two. And he said to me: "He [Voroshilov] must be angling for an invitation [to Churchill's birthday party the next night]. He got the date wrong, and he couldn't even play a straight bat with the sword." So that was Churchill's verdict on Voroshilov.'

Zoya Zarubina too was present when the sword was handed over, and she recalls the Soviet leader's emotional acceptance of the King's gift: 'Stalin, I will tell you, never showed any outward feeling, but the one thing that really touched him was the way Churchill presented that sword.... His voice wavered...and he just said thank you.' For Zoya, a Soviet intelligence officer who was helping with press arrangements, the ceremony had special significance. She knew that a group of Allied delegates – both military men and diplomats – had flown to the conference from Moscow, stopping en route at Stalingrad; and she recalls the delegates' 'feeling of guilt' when they saw the devastation of the city. Moreover, she believed they were 'right' to feel guilty – by delaying the second front, the Western Allies had let the Soviets carry the chief burden of the war. For her, the ceremony of the handing over of the sword of Stalingrad was almost open recognition by the Western Allies of their culpability. Yet she says she felt no bitterness: 'I will tell you, the Russian people are a special type of people – they never expect too much of anybody.'

At four o'clock that afternoon the three leaders sat down with their advisers – political and military – for the second plenary meeting of the conference. There were no surprises in substance – Stalin simply reiterated once again that he wanted a second front and he wanted it in May – but there were a few surprises in tone. When Stalin learnt that no commander had yet been appointed for Overlord he remarked dismissively that 'nothing would come of the operation'.[21] Although it had been agreed that an American would be in command, Roosevelt had doubts about appointing the obvious candidate – General Marshall. So the American President was unable to commit to a name at the conference – much to Stalin's irritation.

The Soviet leader grew still more annoyed when Churchill launched into his idea for an advance on both Rome and the island of Rhodes. Stalin finally asked point-blank: 'Did the British believe in Overlord, or were they just saying so in order to pacify the Russians?' Churchill replied that the British did believe in Overlord, but only if the right conditions were met – an answer, not surprisingly, that did little to appease Stalin.

This heated exchange was the background to one of the most extraordinary moments in all of the conferences between Stalin,

Roosevelt and Churchill, an incident that occurred that night at a dinner attended by all three leaders. The minutes of the encounter stress the '[bad] attitude of Marshal Stalin toward the Prime Minister'.[22] Stalin inferred that the British were trying to deceive the Soviets. 'Just because Russians are simple people,' he said, 'it was a mistake to believe they were blind and could not see what was before their eyes.' Stalin also implied that Churchill had a 'secret affection' for Germany. Stalin's remarks were thought at the time to be motivated by 'his displeasure at the British attitude on the question of Overlord'. But the Soviet leader was also indulging in what might best be termed 'tactical teasing'. He was watching to see not just Churchill's reaction to his remarks, but also the extent to which Roosevelt defended or supported him.

Stalin gained his greatest insight that night into the respective characters of the two Western leaders when he remarked that, in order to subdue Germany after the war, 'At least 50,000 and perhaps 100,000 of the German Commanding Staff must be physically liquidated.' Churchill, in his post-war writings, said that he had not resented any of Stalin's remarks until this last one about the killing of Germans at the end of the war. 'The British parliament and public,' said the Prime Minister, 'will never tolerate mass executions.'[23] And when Stalin still insisted that 50,000 'must be shot', Churchill lost his temper. 'I would rather,' he said, 'be taken out into the garden here and now and be shot myself than sully my own and my country's honour by such infamy.'

At this point Roosevelt intervened – but in an oblique way. Instead of supporting Churchill, or simply changing the subject, he said that his compromise was that '49,000' should be shot. The American President clearly intended this remark as a joke. But, knowing as he did Stalin's track record in matters of mass murder, it was a strange kind of jest. Others present took Stalin's words at face value. Elliott Roosevelt, the President's thirty-three-year-old son who was also at the dinner, said: 'Look: when our armies start rolling in from the West, and your armies are still coming on from the East, we'll be solving the whole thing, won't we? Russian, American and British soldiers will settle the issue for most of those fifty thousand in battle, and I hope not only those fifty thousand war criminals will be taken care of but many hundreds of thousands more Nazis as well.'[24]

This was too much for Churchill. It was bad enough being teased and harassed by Stalin, but to have to listen to the uncongenial views of a relatively junior American air force officer was more than he could stomach. The British Prime Minister stood up and left the table, stomping off into the room next door. Moments later Stalin and Molotov followed him, smiling, and the Soviet leader announced that he had only been 'playing'.

It was a watershed moment; not so much in the context of the relationship between Stalin and Churchill – the Soviet leader had verbally attacked the British Prime Minister before – but in the context of the relationship between Churchill and Roosevelt. Stalin had bullied Churchill in front of an entire dinner party, and Roosevelt had not come to his aid.

Churchill returned in a melancholy mood to the British legation, and remarked around midnight to his doctor, Lord Moran: 'There might be a more bloody war. I shall not be there. I shall be asleep. I want to sleep for billions of years.' And later, 'I believe man might destroy man and wipe out civilisation. Europe would be desolate and I may be held responsible.... Stupendous issues are unfolding before our eyes and we are only specks of dust that have settled in the night on the map of the world.'[25]

Moran wrote that he 'lay awake for a long time, frightened by his [Churchill's] presentiment of evil'. And it was clear what the source of the Prime Minister's ghastly vision of the future had been. It was a world in which the democracies would not stand firm in the presence of dictators. 'Now he sees he cannot rely on the President's support,' wrote Moran. 'What matters more, he realizes that the Russians see this too.' And, in the last entry in his diary for 29 November, Moran records perhaps his most poignant insight of all: 'The PM is appalled by his own impotence.'

That same day the British Chief of the Imperial General Staff, General Sir Alan Brooke, gave vent in his diary to his own feelings about the conference so far. 'After listening to the arguments put forward over the last two days,' he wrote, 'I feel more like entering a lunatic asylum or a nursing home than continuing with my present job. I am absolutely disgusted with the politicians' methods of waging a war!! Why will they imagine they are experts at a job they know nothing about! It is lamentable to listen to them!'[26]

The next day, 30 November, began with a meeting of the British and American Chiefs of Staff. General Brooke and the other members of the British military delegation managed to convince the American military chiefs that a small delay in the date of Overlord would benefit them all – and a new date of 1 June was finally agreed.

After their meeting the British and American military leaders went to report this new date to the President and Prime Minister. Roosevelt made one alteration to their conclusion – a small but significant one. He said that instead of announcing that Overlord would take place on '1 June', they should tell Stalin that it would take place 'during the month of May'. After all, wasn't 31 May nearly 1 June and yet still in 'the month of May'? It is a minor moment amidst the epic decisions these statesmen were making at Tehran, but one that nevertheless shows the subtle way in which Roosevelt's mind worked. By coming up with this form of words the President must have felt that he had squared the circle between Stalin wanting Overlord on 1 May and the generals wanting it to be launched at the earliest on 1 June.

Hugh Lunghi, who observed Roosevelt at the conference, thought that he detected signs of the scheming mind behind the bonhomie: 'He seemed at first to be very sort of hail fellow, well met. He was smiling and cheerful and slapping people on their back – but from a distance, metaphorically – and smiled and nodded to me, but as time went on I got an impression that he was rather cold and insincere. I don't know why – this was the feeling that I got. His laughter and his jokes, such as they were, seemed rather forced – as though he was pushing it.'

The final plenary session of the conference was held that afternoon, and little of substance was added to the decisions that had already been taken. Overlord would take place 'in the month of

May' and a commander for the operation would be named within the next few days.

That evening a dinner was held at the British legation to celebrate Churchill's sixty-ninth birthday. There were many courses and a complex layout of cutlery – something that seemed, momentarily, to fox the Soviet leader. 'All seemed to be going well,' says Lunghi, '[when] I saw Churchill's chief interpreter, Arthur Birse, pointing something out to Stalin with the cutlery. And I learnt afterwards from Arthur Birse that Stalin had been puzzled to have all this vast amount of cutlery on either side of his plate, and he actually asked Arthur Birse: "What do I do with them?" And Arthur Birse said to him: "Just proceed as you want. It doesn't matter at all which one you pick up – whatever you're comfortable with", to put him at his ease.'

It was moments like this that made Stalin appear almost a comforting figure to the sophisticated Westerners. He could be admired as the leader of a nation fighting back against the Nazis, but still gently patronized. As one British correspondent put it: Stalin 'looks like the kindly Italian gardener you have in once a week'.[27] And so his occasional breaches of good taste – like his aggressive taunting of Churchill the previous night – could be put down to bad manners and lack of 'class'.

The evening proceeded in a relaxed and happy way, marred only by a remark that Stalin made as he proposed a toast to General Sir Alan Brooke. Stalin's suspicions that it was the British who had, as he saw it, consistently been obstructive over the launch of the second front had been confirmed by the way the conference at Tehran had proceeded. So he made a sly dig, remarking that he hoped Brooke would 'no longer look upon the Russians with such suspicion'[28] and adding that if he really got to know them he would find them good people to deal with. Brooke, the most forthright of men, was not about to keep silent in the face of such a comment. He stood up and told Stalin that he had been deceived by appearances. Just as earlier in the day the Soviet leader had talked of the importance of 'dummy tanks, aircraft and airfields' in the deception of the Germans, so Stalin had mistaken

Brooke's genuine desire for a closer working relationship with the Soviets with the belief that he viewed them with 'suspicion'. The speech seemed to mollify Stalin. But it did nothing to alter the substantive criticism, because Stalin was right. It had been the British – and in particular Churchill – who were least enthusiastic about the second front.

A small moment of comedy was provided towards the end of the evening when the dessert was brought in by a Iranian waiter, dressed in formal uniform with white gloves. According to Hugh Lunghi, the waiter 'looked rather nervous' and 'was holding aloft a creation which I eventually realized was ice-cream – which I could hardly believe because it had some night lights burning under it. He moved towards Stalin, wanting to serve Stalin first.' But since the Soviet leader was speaking the waiter paused behind him with the salver on his right shoulder. Gradually it started tipping as the ice-cream began to melt. 'I saw this wonderful creation slipping off the salver,' says Lunghi, 'and about to descend on Stalin, but in fact the waiter moved suddenly to the side where Pavlov, Stalin's inter-preter, was sitting, and this ice-cream fell all down the shoulder of Pavlov's new uniform – which was the new Soviet diplomatic uniform – so it ruined that. But Pavlov went on interpreting quite happily. And I heard Sir Charles Portal [the head of the RAF] whis-per in a loud whisper: "Missed the target", but it was a wonderful occasion. The party broke up quite happily after that.'

The following day, 1 December, the American and British mili-tary delegations left, leaving the politicians to discuss further – amongst other things – the potentially contentious issue of the boundaries of Germany and Poland. Originally these discussions had been scheduled to last several days, but the prospect of bad weather that might affect their flight plans made the leaders decide that they would attempt to resolve any difficulties during this one day and leave the next.

Roosevelt later revealed that by this fourth day of the conference he was 'pretty discouraged'. He felt he had still not made the 'personal connection with Stalin' that he craved. Stalin, he felt, was 'correct, stiff, solemn, not smiling, nothing human to get hold of'.

So on the morning of 1 December, the American President hit on a new tactic: he would ingratiate himself with Stalin by insulting Churchill. 'On my way to the conference room that morning I caught up with Winston and I had just a moment to say to him: "Winston, I hope you won't be sore at me for what I am going to do." Winston just shifted his cigar and grunted. I must say he behaved very decently afterwards. I began almost as soon as we got into the conference room. I talked privately with Stalin. I didn't say anything that I hadn't said before, but it appeared quite chummy and confidential, enough so that the other Russians joined us to listen. Still no smile. Then I said, lifting my hand up to cover a whisper (which of course had to be interpreted): "Winston is cranky this morning, he got up on the wrong side of bed." A vague smile passed over Stalin's eyes, and I decided I was on the right track.'[29] Roosevelt carried on teasing Churchill – 'about his Britishness, about John Bull, about his cigars, about his habits' – and the Prime Minister was visibly discomfited. Eventually Stalin started laughing. This, Roosevelt believed, meant that he and the Soviet leader could talk for the first time 'like men and brothers'. So much so that he subsequently told his son, Elliott Roosevelt, that he both liked Stalin and found him 'altogether quite impressive'.[30]

Now that Roosevelt felt he had established the all-important personal connection with Stalin, he was not anxious to prolong the official talks. Stalin had already agreed to enter the war against Japan once Germany was defeated, and also to cooperate – albeit so far only in general terms – with Roosevelt's vision for the United Nations. Alongside these massive gains for the American President, the prospect of poring over maps and discussing exact boundaries seemed not only laborious but potentially divisive.

The first official meeting on 1 December discussed – somewhat inconclusively – the question of how to try to force Turkey into the war, and then the extent of reparations to be demanded from Finland once the war was over. Stalin, true to form, said that as regards the Finns he would be satisfied with the '1940 border' – that is to say, the agreement the Soviets forced on the Finns after the Winter War – with perhaps some minor adjustments.

There was then a brief break in the talks, during which Roosevelt had a private conversation with Stalin and Molotov.[31] Aware that the contentious issue of Poland was about to be raised, the American President confided to Stalin that since he 'might' stand for re-election the following year, he had a problem – the several million Americans of Polish ancestry. As 'a practical man', he had to be conscious of their feelings – they could decide to vote against him if they disliked any deal he did over the future of their land of origin. But Roosevelt said he could tell Stalin secretly now that he agreed with moving the whole of Poland west and allowing the Soviets to keep the territory gained as a result of their invasion in September 1939. It was a significant exchange. Stalin now knew he had, at last, gained the land he had been demanding from the first moment of the forced alliance with the West. In 1942 the Americans had reacted with outrage at any suggestion that the Soviets could retain this territory; but now here was Roosevelt giving it away without a murmur. The President must have felt he had to balance the question of the future boundaries of Poland against the other key issues over which he had already reached agreement with Stalin. In addition, as Churchill had admitted, what could the Western Allies do in practice to get this territory back for the Poles?

This secret conversation with Stalin was yet another example of Roosevelt's hard-headedness. It was Stalin who had taken the *nom de guerre* 'Steel', but it was also an epithet that could on occasion apply to Roosevelt – at his core, and despite the patina of jokes and charm, he had an ice-cold, almost ruthless sense of political realities.

Two of Roosevelt's most important colleagues – Averell Harriman and Charles 'Chip' Bohlen – heard him give Stalin this secret assurance over Poland. Both recorded afterwards that they believed he had made a mistake. Harriman felt that Roosevelt had at this moment just given the Soviets the right to impose whatever system they wished on Poland, and Bohlen confessed he was 'dismayed' for much the same reason.

Harriman was subsequently called to task for the American decision to let Stalin keep eastern Poland when he appeared before the US Congress committee on the Katyn forest massacre just a few years after the war. When asked how it was possible to reconcile the decision to let Stalin have this territory with the principles of the Atlantic Charter, he replied: 'The Russians had contended – and I am not justifying the contention, but I am merely stating the fact – they had contended for a considerable period of time that the eastern borders of Poland had been unfairly made and that ethnologically there was a larger percentage of white Russians and Ukrainians in that area and that the agreement at the end of World War I was unfair to the Soviet interests. I assume that was the reason why this discussion took place and was not to be considered to be perhaps a violation of the Atlantic Charter.'[32] Given that the position of the American administration in 1942 had been that the Soviet claim on eastern Poland was in clear breach of the Atlantic Charter, Harriman's argument was specious. (As Churchill wrote to Eden in January 1942: 'We have never recognized the 1941 frontiers of Russia, except *de facto*.')

Sumner Welles, who had served as American Under-Secretary of State until just before the conference, was someone else who thought the President had made a mistake about Poland at Tehran. When giving evidence at the Katyn massacre hearings he was asked: 'Don't you think that if we had adopted a more firm policy toward Soviet Russia and particularly toward its demands with regard to Poland and other similar situations that we could have avoided much of the trouble of the world today?' Welles replied unequivocally: 'As it has turned out, the answer to your question, I think, is clearly "Yes".'[33]

But just what would this 'more firm policy' towards the Soviet Union have consisted of in practical terms in 1943? An outright confrontation with Stalin over the issue of the borders of eastern Poland might well have been immensely damaging to the war effort. By now it was unlikely in the extreme that Stalin could possibly make a separate peace with Hitler, but the potential of the Soviet Union to cause problems over a range of issues – not least refusing to come into the war against Japan once Germany was defeated – was huge. But there was, perhaps, a middle way on offer that Roosevelt spurned. He could have refused to make any commitments on borders until the end of the war, when a peace conference could be convened with the participation of all the parties involved, crucially the Poles themselves. This had been the position of both the Americans and British earlier in the war, but they altered their policy, as they saw it, because circumstances had changed. At such a post-war conference the Poles might well still have objected to the border changes, but at least the matter would have been dealt with honestly and in the open.

What would Stalin have done if the Western Allies had kept to their original line and postponed any commitment on borders until the war was over? There were other things that Stalin wanted from the United States and Britain at this stage in the war apart from firm agreement on borders – most particularly, of course, the second front. Would he have thrown away all cooperation with Churchill and Roosevelt merely because they would not – without the consent of the Poles – agree to move the borders of the whole country? That is surely unlikely.

But, it might be argued, what would have been the point in causing this angst when Stalin would shortly have possession of all this territory and could do what he liked anyway? There was never any serious chance of the West fighting the Red Army to get this land back.

However, there is a clear difference between recognizing that one country has occupied another country by *force majeure*, and legitimizing that occupation. Maybe it is naive to expect politicians to stick to the principles they have freely signed up to – like those enshrined in the Atlantic Charter – but the corrosive cynicism that results when they don't is often worse.

In Tehran, after Roosevelt's private chat with Stalin in which he said he wouldn't cause trouble over the Soviet demand to keep eastern Poland – a conversation the British didn't find out about until long after the conference was over – the American President then expressed 'officially', once representatives of the three governments had all sat down together, the hope that Stalin might reach some accommodation with the Polish government in exile in London.

THE CHANGING WIND | 239

Stalin quashed this notion at once – even suggesting, shamefully, that the London Poles were 'in contact' with the Germans and had 'killed the partisans'.[34] He went on to say that 'the day before yesterday (when Churchill had his "matchstick" conversation with him about the shifting borders of Poland) there had been no mention of re-establishing relations with the Polish government. It had been a question of prescribing something to the Poles.' Significantly, neither Churchill nor Roosevelt uttered a word in defence of the Polish government in exile. There was no evidence to support Stalin's ludicrous charge that 'the Polish Government and their friends in Poland were in contact with the Germans'. Yet the British Prime Minister and the American President did not protest.

Churchill did try to explain to Stalin, with great patience, how important the fate of Poland was to the British. 'We felt very strongly about it,' he said, 'because it was the German attack on Poland which had led us into war.' The three leaders then gathered around a map of Poland to discuss the border the Soviets wanted – along what Eden called 'the Ribbentrop–Molotov line' and what Molotov swiftly remarked 'was generally called the Curzon line'. 'Call it whatever you like,' said Stalin.

After a 'prolonged' study of the map, Churchill announced that he 'liked the picture' and that he 'would say to the Poles that if they did not accept it they would be fools, and he would remind them that but for the Red Army they would have been utterly destroyed'. Crucially, Churchill then volunteered that he believed the new Polish state would be 'friendly' to Russia. Stalin agreed that the Soviet Union wanted a 'friendly' Poland. This apparently throwaway line from the British Prime Minister was almost as damaging to the interests of the Polish government in exile as the unilateral decision of the Big Three to shift their country to the West. The problem was that it was impossible to define 'friendly' – if the Poles ever did anything the Soviets disliked, they could be accused of acting in an 'unfriendly' way. The only way the Polish state could be permanently 'friendly' was to be a puppet of the Soviet Union. And so it was eventually to prove.

The meeting then moved on to the final subject to be discussed at Tehran – the question of the future of Germany. Everyone present wanted to break up post-war Germany – the dispute was over the question of how many pieces it should be split into. Churchill suggested that Prussia, which he saw as the most dangerous region – should be detached from the rest. Roosevelt then launched into a plan to split Germany into five separate parts, plus two areas, the Kiel Canal and the Ruhr, which would be controlled by the international community. It was an astonishing idea; and one that came as a shock to Churchill, who had never heard such a wide-ranging plan suggested before.

Stalin, not surprisingly, liked Roosevelt's proposal more than he did Churchill's. He wanted Germany so fragmented as to present no military threat for the foreseeable future. Churchill, on the other hand, was alert to the danger of central Europe lacking strong states. Who, he must have been thinking, would stand in the way of the Red Army and the English Channel, once the war was won and the Americans had withdrawn?

The policy of the Big Three on the future of Germany – unlike the future of Poland – was not resolved at Tehran, although the relative positions of each of the protagonists had certainly been demonstrated. After this final meeting Roosevelt, Churchill and Stalin attended a farewell dinner, said their goodbyes and left for home early the following morning.

The meetings at Tehran had lasted only from 28 November to 1 December, but in these four days historic decisions had been taken. The conferences that followed, at Yalta and Potsdam, would both exist in the shadow of Tehran. It would have proved virtually impossible – even if Roosevelt and Churchill had desired it – to backtrack on the fundamental issues of principle that had been decided here in Iran; most notably, of course, that Poland would shift to the West.

But Tehran is important not just for the epic political and military questions that were resolved, but also for the way both Churchill and Roosevelt – in particular Roosevelt – sought to make themselves amenable to Stalin. Partly, as we have seen, they felt it was essential to get on with the Soviet leader. Red Army

soldiers were still fighting the majority of the German forces –
indeed, they would continue to do so until the end of the war in
Europe. And during 1943 more Soviet lives were lost at Kursk and
elsewhere on the Eastern Front than the British lost in the entire
war. The Western Allies thus needed the Soviets to keep fighting –
and consequently to keep dying.

But there was also a sense in which Roosevelt and Churchill
must have felt constrained by their respective governments' own
previous half-truths about Stalin. During 1943 Allied propaganda
had continued to churn out wildly positive material about the
Soviet Union and Stalin, of which *Mission to Moscow* was the most
glaring example. Robert Buckner, the producer of the film, later
described it as an 'expedient lie for political purposes'.[35] The trouble was that the general public formed their own upbeat view of
Stalin and the Soviet Union based on 'expedient lies' such as this.
Consequently Roosevelt – with an election coming up in less than
a year – would have felt it unhelpful to his own political chances to
contradict the positive gloss.

In any event, Roosevelt seemed happy enough to stick to the
previous propaganda line on his return from Tehran. When asked
by a journalist what 'type of person Marshal Stalin' was, he
replied: 'I would call him something like me...a realist.'[36] And in
his 1943 Christmas Eve broadcast to the American people,
Roosevelt remarked: 'I must say I got along fine with Marshal
Stalin. He is man who combines a tremendous relentless determination with stalwart good humour. I believe he is truly representative of the heart and soul of Russia; and I believe that we are
going to get along very well with him and the Russian people –
very well indeed.'[37]

But Stalin was, as Roosevelt knew full well, a 'realist' who had
shown in the past that he rejected the values that the American
President held most dear – freedom of speech, freedom of religion
and freedom from fear, to name but three. Roosevelt had openly
condemned Stalin's regime just three years before, and although
there were now straws in the wind to suggest that the Soviet
system might possibly become less draconian in the future, the

American President ought to have known full well that Stalin was not a man 'like' him at all.

But the signs are that Roosevelt's gushing words about Stalin were not just politically expedient. As he had told his son, Elliot, in private at Tehran, he had genuinely found something to 'like' in Stalin and thought him 'impressive'. Perhaps it was because the Soviet leader was a great listener – an attribute that suited the garrulous President – and, as we have seen, in manner and style Stalin did not seem to be a bloodthirsty tyrant at all. It was only if you discarded the surface appearances and listened carefully to what Stalin said that a darker picture appeared. At Tehran, the two Western leaders either didn't choose to see this, or else simply couldn't see it.

THE RETURN OF KATYN

While Stalin dined with Roosevelt and Churchill at Tehran, his security forces were hard at work trying to cover up the mass murder they had committed three years before at Katyn. The Red Army liberated Smolensk and the surrounding area in late August 1943, in the aftermath of their victory at Kursk. Within days the Soviets fenced off the murder site at Katyn once again, and the NKVD began excavating the bodies that had been reburied by the Germans after their own investigation into the crime earlier in the year had been completed.

The Soviet authorities knew they faced two practical problems in trying to pretend that the Germans had committed the murders. First, the Germans had gathered eye-witness testimony that blamed the Soviets for the shootings; and second, no documentation had been found on any of the Polish corpses that dated from after April 1940 – something that was at odds with the Soviet claim that the Poles had been murdered in the summer of 1941.

But neither of these difficulties was insurmountable for the Soviet secret police. First they added false documents to the genuine ones the Germans had already found. These included a receipt for 25 roubles from Starobielsk camp in the name of Vladimir Arashkevich, dated 25 March 1941, and an icon on the reverse of which were an illegible signature and the date '4/9/41'. And it was an equally simple task for the secret police to deal with the matter of the incriminating testimony. One of the Germans' star witnesses had been a local forester, P. G. Kiselev,[38] who had told of hearing 'screaming' and 'shooting' coming from the forest in the spring of 1940. Now Kiselev and his son were arrested by the NKVD and charged with collaborating with the Nazis. This was a serious charge, punishable by a death sentence or a long period of imprisonment.

A number of witnesses confirmed to the NKVD that Kiselev had given his testimony 'freely' to the Germans, and that no violence had been used to get him to tell his story. But in the face of threats from the NKVD, both Kiselev and his son changed their story and stated publicly that their testimony to the Germans had been forced out of them and that everything they had said was untrue. They now claimed that the Poles had been murdered by the Germans in the summer of 1941, not by the NKVD in the spring of 1940 as they had originally stated. As a result, the charges against Kiselev and his son were dropped. And the NKVD worked similar magic on other locals after charges of collaboration with the Nazis were set aside – people like Yefimov, Zubkov and Bazilevsky all now gave evidence that the Germans had committed the crime.

For five months the rewriting of history at Katyn was pursued by the NKVD. Only in January 1944 were the results made known to the world through the propaganda mouthpiece of an 'investigation' led by Nikolai Burdenko, the President of the Soviet Academy of Medical Science. The title of his commission of investigation is instructive, demonstrating as it does that the conclusion was predetermined before the investigation began. It was called 'The Special Commission for Determination and Investigation of the Shooting of Polish Prisoners of War by German-Fascist Invaders in Katyn Forest'. Documents[39] reveal that Burdenko was kept away from the forest until the NKVD had finished planting their false evidence: he was not allowed to approach Katyn until January, and his report – based heavily on the 'preliminary' work by the NKVD – was then completed in a matter of only a few days.

The next stage in the Soviet deception involved publicizing the falsehood to the world. For that purpose the Soviet authorities needed the unwitting cooperation of foreign journalists. Just over a dozen – mostly Americans and British – made the journey to Katyn between 21 and 23 January 1944. They were accompanied by John Melby, third secretary at the American embassy in Moscow, and by Kathleen Harriman, the twenty-five-year-old daughter of the new ambassador, Averell Harriman, and were transported from Moscow in considerable style. 'No press excursion to any part of Russia has been arranged with greater luxury than the Katyn party,'[40] a report from the British embassy to the Foreign Office recorded. 'The correspondents travelled in electric train, comfortable sleeping compartments and large saloon car. They were given very good food, and supplies of vodka, wine and cigarettes were plentiful.' Then, in a somewhat bitchy aside, the report concluded: 'No doubt some of these amenities were provided for the benefit of Miss Harriman (now described here as the poor man's Mrs Roosevelt).' A previous telegram from the British embassy to the Foreign Office, on 23 January, had already warned: 'It is hard to believe that the Russian propaganda machine will refrain from drawing the obvious conclusion from the association of these two "official" Americans with the enquiry.'[41] (The 'obvious conclusion' was that the presence of these two Americans would give the impression that the American government endorsed the Soviet view of Katyn.) At the bottom of the note a Foreign Office official scrawled: 'This is not my business but it doesn't seem very wise.'

The correspondents, together with John Melby and Kathleen Harriman, arrived in Katyn between seven and eight o'clock in the morning on 22 January and left in the early hours of the following morning – so they had less than twenty-four hours to evaluate the 'evidence' the Soviets had uncovered. Immediately after the visit, Melby wrote a lengthy report describing the Soviet attempts to blame the Germans for the crime and pointing out the obvious deficiencies in their case. In particular, the 'witnesses' produced by the Soviets were clearly problematic. It was obvious, wrote Melby, that 'the witnesses were merely repeating stories that they had already told the Commission. The show was staged under hot and blinding klieg [film] light and motion picture camera.... Attempts by the correspondents to question the witnesses were discouraged.... All the statements were glibly given, as if by rote.' Melby formed the view that: 'It is apparent that the evidence in the Russian case is incomplete in several respects, that it is badly put together and that the show was put on for the benefit of the correspondents without opportunity for independent investigation or verification.'[42] Yet, incredibly, after stating these reasons why the Soviet investigation into Katyn was untrustworthy, Melby concluded: 'On balance, however, and despite loopholes, the Russian case is convincing.'

After the war Melby was questioned about this report at the congressional hearings into the Katyn massacre, and was asked: 'Why did you come to a conclusion when, on your own evidence, you could not reach a conclusion?'

'Because,' answered Melby, 'I had no other basis on which to go except the Russian side of the story.' Some members of the congressional committee were incredulous at Melby's position, and he was repeatedly asked if he hadn't just reached the conclusion that he felt his superiors wanted – a charge he denied.

Kathleen Harriman too wrote a report after her visit to Katyn – and again it supported the Soviet view. Like Melby, she was asked at the congressional hearings how it was possible for her to conclude that the Soviet case was sustainable when her 'reasoning destroys' her 'conclusion' because her 'report had more reasons why the Russians did it and not the Germans, than you have that the Germans did it'.[43] Her position was that, although the Soviets had put on a 'show' for the correspondents, she still believed that it was the Germans who had committed the massacre – not least because of 'the methodical manner in which the murder was committed'.

Despite the denials of John Melby and Kathleen Harriman, there was inevitably suspicion that they were reporting to the State Department what the administration wanted to hear, since it was scarcely credible for either of them to have reached the conclusion they did from the facts in their own reports. As for the correspondents who visited the burial site with them, the British embassy report stated: 'I [the British embassy official, Mr Balfour] have discussed the excursion with several correspondents who went to Katyn. Although they are by no means reluctant to accept [the] Soviet version of the affair, they are not altogether satisfied with what they saw and heard. Some of the American correspondents told the Press department for the People's Commissariat for Foreign Affairs that they were not very impressed.'[44]

When Churchill learnt of the Soviet report he wrote to the Foreign Secretary: 'I think Sir Owen O'Malley should be asked very secretly to express his opinion on the Katyn Wood Inquiry.'[45] Significantly, he ended his brief note with the sentence: 'All this is merely to ascertain the facts, because we should none of us ever speak a word about it.'

O'Malley reported back with a lengthy despatch on 11 February 1944. In another brilliant analysis of the claim and counter-claim now surrounding the Katyn massacre, he mentioned and then set to one side both the interview testimony and the forensic evidence since these elements could have been tampered with by either the Soviets or the Germans. Instead, O'Malley focused on facts that were indisputable. First, he pointed out that the Soviet version of events made 'at least one essential assumption which is incredible'.[46] The 'incredible' assumption was that thousands of Polish prisoners could, in the chaos of the summer of 1941, have been somehow transferred from Soviet captivity to German captivity without a 'single one of them having escaped and fallen again into Russian hands or reported to a Polish consul in Russia or to the Polish Underground Movement in Poland'. Second, O'Malley reiterated that there remained an 'unexplained set of facts' that have 'dominated this controversy throughout, namely that from April 1940 onwards no single letter or message was ever received by anybody from the Poles'. The combination of these two factors made O'Malley feel that his original 'tentative conclusion' that the Poles had been murdered by the Soviets was correct.

No one reading O'Malley's report could doubt either the sincerity with which it had been written or the damning verdict that had to be taken from it – the Soviets had committed a terrible crime and had now sought to cover it up with a fictitious 'Special Commission'. O'Malley ended his despatch to Anthony Eden with these poignant words: 'Let us think of these things always and speak of them never. To speak of them never is the advice which I have been giving to the Polish Government, but it has been unnecessary. They have received the Russian report in silence. Affliction and residence in this country seem to be teaching them how much better it is in political life to leave unsaid those things about which one feels most passionately.'

And silence was what now emanated from both the British and the American governments on this subject. Despite the knowledge that the Soviet report was based on an 'incredible' assumption, the Western leaders still stuck to Churchill's rubric that 'we should none of us ever speak a word about it'. And when Averell Harriman was asked directly at the Katyn hearings: 'As far as you know, at Tehran, at Yalta, and Potsdam, did you engage in any discussion at all, with any of our officials or foreign officials, with reference to the missing Polish officers, or their problem?' he replied: 'No; I do not recall the subject came up.'[47]

A direct insight into Roosevelt's attitude to Katyn – and indeed one of the only recorded occasions on which he was compelled to mention the subject – comes from a meeting he held in May 1944 with George Howard Earle III, a former governor of Pennsylvania and friend of the President's during the 1930s. Earle was a colourful character, fond of the good life. 'Twenty-four hours a day he was on the go,' says Lawrence Earle,[48] his son. 'He was an adventurer. He was a pilot of aircraft – he was game for anything – and he loved fishing and hunting. After the First World War he became a wonderful polo player, and he played with some of the best teams in the world and was captain of the Philadelphia polo team.... He's mentioned in the book of polo as being one of the best polo players in the world.'

Earle had served as American diplomatic minister in Bulgaria, and more recently as the President's special emissary for Balkan affairs based in Turkey. Now, in 1944, he returned to Washington to give Roosevelt the benefit of his views on the Katyn massacre. Earle had been briefed by a number of intelligence contacts in eastern Europe about the killings and had come to the firm view that the Soviets were responsible for the crime. Before meeting the President, Earle had been warned by an 'old friend' of his, Joe Levy of the *New York Times*, 'George, you do not know what you are going to get over there [in the White House]. Harry Hopkins has complete domination over the President and the whole atmosphere over there is "pink".'[49]

Once in Roosevelt's presence, Earle outlined the evidence that had made him certain in his own mind that the Soviets had committed the murders at Katyn – evidence that included testimony from Bulgarian and 'White Russian' agents, as well as a number of photographs from the burial site. 'About this Katyn massacre, Mr President,' said Earle. 'I just cannot believe that the American President and so many people still think it is a mystery or have any doubt about it. Here are these pictures. Here are these affidavits and here is the invitation of the German Government to let the neutral Red Cross go in there and make their examination. What greater proof could you have?'

'George,' said President Roosevelt, 'they could have rigged things up. The Germans could have rigged things up.' Roosevelt was adamant that 'this is entirely German propaganda and a German plot'.[50]

'Mr President,' insisted Earle, 'I think this evidence is overwhelming.'

Earle also made it plain during the meeting that he was 'very much worried about this Russian situation. I feel that they are a great menace, and I feel that they have done their best to deceive the American people about this Katyn business, and, also primarily the most important of all, by this dreadful book of Joe Davies' *Mission to Moscow* which made Stalin out to be a benign Santa Claus. We never recovered from that. It made such an impression on the American people.'

'George,' said Roosevelt, 'you have been worried about Russia ever since 1942. Now let me tell you. I am an older man than you are and I have had a lot of experience. These Russians, they are 180 million people, speaking 120 different dialects. When this war is over, they are going to fly to pieces like a centrifugal machine cracked through and through travelling at high speed.' This, Earle said, was Roosevelt's 'stock in trade' answer: 'We have nothing to fear from the Russians because they would fly to pieces.' Earle felt 'hopeless', and his last words as he left Roosevelt were: 'Mr President, please look those over again.'

The Earle story has a revealing postscript. In March 1945 he decided that he ought to tell the world his view about the Soviets, but as a loyal friend of the President's he first asked for permission to make his observations public. Almost by return he received a note of admonition from Roosevelt. 'I have noted with concern your plan to publicize you unfavourable opinion of one of our allies,' wrote the President on 24 March 1945, 'at the very time when such a publication from a former emissary of mine might do irreparable harm to our war effort.... To publish information obtained in those positions without proper authority would be all the greater betrayal.... I specifically forbid you to publish any information or opinion about any ally that you may have acquired while in office or in the service of the United States Navy.'[51]

'I think that he really basically felt that my father had let him down by not staying with the team,' says Lawrence Earle. 'And Roosevelt was a man that demanded a team effort. I mean, he wanted people around him to...when he said jump, they jumped.'

Just a few days later, Earle learnt in practical terms what the President thought of him. He was on a boat, fishing in a remote lake in Maryland, when suddenly he looked up and saw another boat coming towards him. On board were two FBI agents. They came alongside and said: 'Mr Earle, we have a letter for you.' It contained the news that – with immediate effect – Earle had been appointed assistant head of the Samoan Defence Group. This meant he had to leave for the Pacific at once – all because the President had directly ordered the Navy Department to send him 'wherever' they could made use of Earle's services. His son Lawrence, then an officer with American forces in the Pacific, was able to visit his father in this remote outpost. He found him 'bitter; he was very disappointed – he was very upset that the President had done that to him'.

Roosevelt wanted rid of George Earle. And that remains hard for his son to take. 'I think it was very unusual and very autocratic,' says Lawrence Earle. 'Because I mean in a democracy you don't do that sort of thing, but the President thought in wartime he could do it and he did it. Of course, he got away with it.'

PUNISHMENT DEPORTATIONS

In May 1944 – the same month as George Earle had his fruitless meeting with Roosevelt in the White House – Stalin was considering a proposal to deport an entire ethnic group within the Soviet Union. The document, dated 10th May,[52] was from Beria, head of the NKVD, and concerned the fate of the Crimean Tatars. Around two hundred thousand of them lived in the Crimea, on the north shore of the Black Sea, alongside the Russians. The Tatars had their own language, customs and dress; they were also followers of Islam. In the 1930s they had suffered Soviet persecution[53] and now, during the German ocupation, many of their villages had been raided by ethnic Russian-dominated partisan units.

Without question, a number of Tatars had collaborated with the Germans during their occupation between November 1941 and spring 1944. Nearly twenty thousand of them, selected from prisoners of war, had served in German-organized self-defence units. But although it is true that the German military commanders considered the Tatars as more likely to collaborate than the ethnic Russian population of Crimea, it is also the case that tens of thousands of Tatars served loyally in the Red Army.

Now that the Crimea had been recaptured, Stalin had to decide how the Tatars should be treated. Would it be possible to see in Stalin's response evidence of 'the deep-seated changes which have taken place in the character of the Russian State and Government' that Churchill claimed to have detected?

No, not at all – Stalin acted true to form by authorizing Beria to deport the entire Crimean Tatar nation into the wasteland of Uzbekistan in the Soviet interior. Every single one of them would suffer because of the actions of a minority. And whilst it was certainly a monumentally unjust method of dealing with the 'problem' of the Tatars, it had the benefit, as far as the Soviet authorities were concerned, of being swift and decisive.

The plan was to arrest the entire nation in little more than one day. 'It was a big operation,' says former NKVD Lieutenant Nikonor Perevalov,[54] who took part in the action. 'The Crimea is a big area, and in order to evict them you need a lot of people.' Around twenty-three thousand NKVD troops took part in the action, and, just as they had in eastern Poland in 1940, the NKVD first carried out a careful reconnaissance of the area for several weeks before the day appointed for the arrests. When the locals asked why so many troops were suddenly stationed in the Crimea, behind the front line, the NKVD were told to reply that they were 'just on leave from the front'.

At dawn on 18 May 1944 the NKVD entered every Tatar village. 'I came and knocked on the door [of the first house targeted],' says Nikonor Perevalov. 'The light switched on and they asked: "Who is it?"' Perevalov told them he was a representative of the Soviet state and they should open the door immediately. Once inside, he read out the decree announcing their deportation: 'And of course they all started crying and screaming, and the people were frightened. But they didn't fight against us. They didn't put up resistance. No one tried to run away. They received us in an obedient way.' Perevalov says he felt personally 'unhappy' as he saw the devastated Tatar family in front of him:

'I was sorry for them on a personal level because, for example, an elderly person was carried out on a stretcher to the truck.... She was so weak that she didn't utter a single word. She didn't even move. She was very old.' It was obvious, of course, that this sick old lady could not have collaborated with the Germans. 'That old woman wasn't guilty of anything,' confirms Perevalov. 'Most people were not guilty of anything – I have to be frank about it.'

Kebire Ametova[55] was still a young girl when the NKVD came to take her and the rest of her family away. Her father, ironically, was away fighting for the Soviet Union in the Red Army. But that meant nothing to Stalin or the NKVD. Nor did it matter that she had previously witnessed her mother helping the local partisans: 'We prepared some food for some partisans who were passing by – I used to give them pies. At that time we weren't expecting anyone to come, so my mother invited them to sit at our table.' But then they saw Germans in the street outside, about to enter their house. Quickly, the partisans opened the window and climbed into the well in the garden. Kebire's mother hid them until the Germans had gone. If the partisans had been found, she would have been shot.

But on 18 May all that concerned the NKVD was that the family – Kebire, her mother, three sisters and brother – were on their list as Crimean Tatars. 'Two middle-aged soldiers arrived,' says Kebire. 'They told us that we were being thrown out of our house and had fifteen minutes to get ready.' Her mother 'started to rush about and weep' and tried to gather together whatever belongings she could: 'Of course there was a lot of shouting and noise, that's for sure. There was shouting, noise and pain. And bitter tears.... We had some boiled milk on a three-legged stand on the floor. My mother asked them to wait so that she could give the children some milk to drink. But he [one of the soldiers] kicked it over with his foot and spilt it all. He wouldn't allow us to drink any milk.'

The NKVD soldiers then searched for gold – Tatars tradition-ally kept any wealth they possessed in the form of gold jewellery and concealed it somewhere in their house or garden. The Ametov family kept theirs hidden under the stove in the kitchen. The

NKVD failed to find it, so, no doubt disappointed, the soldiers carried away the Ametovs' sewing machine instead.

The family were taken to a nearby Muslim cemetery, which was used as an assembly area for all the families from the surrounding villages. The scenes were heartbreaking. 'The noise and the shouting were indescribable,' says Kebire. 'All you could hear throughout the village was crying. People lost their daughters, their sons, their husbands. The chaos was deafening and very frightening.' The families were confined in the cemetery for most of the day, and of course the children needed to go to the toilet – but their faith forbade them to desecrate the cemetery by using it in this way. Nonetheless, the NKVD refused to let anyone out to relieve themselves in the field next door. And so, adding to the humiliation of the day and much to their shame, 'We children could not bear it. We did it all in our knickers, in whatever way we could.'

In the late afternoon the NKVD moved into the cemetery and started dragging people on to trucks to take them to the nearby station, where they were herded into freight wagons. The whole process was conducted swiftly and brutally. No care was taken to ensure that families were deported together: 'They [the NKVD] threw [people's] things in one vehicle and the people themselves into another. They scattered everything around. They put children in one vehicle and the adults in another…. So when we were taken to the station, lots of people were running around like mad, trying to find their children…. As for us, our mother did not allow us to move away from her – she did everything herself and we just stayed in one place. And when they were loading us, they just took us by the scruff of the neck and threw us in a carriage…they flung us like kittens, grabbed us by the neck, kicked us. They treated us as cruelly as they liked – they did not take pity on one single child.' Many of the carriages had previously been used for transporting cattle, and were full of lice-infested straw. 'The stench was indescribable,' says Kebire. 'It was terrifying – a nightmare.'

As the train pulled away, they heard the noise of the abandoned dogs and cows in the deserted villages. Just hours earlier the Tatars had been celebrating the end of the conflict in the

Crimea and dreaming of a return to normality. Now they were being transported like animals to an unknown destination. And as she stared into the night through the slats in the freight truck, one thought obsessed Kebire Ametova. 'I didn't know what we had done,' she says. 'We were children – how could we know? Even today we still don't know what we were being punished for.... I have never considered myself to be guilty. What could these old people and children have been guilty of? What had we done in our lives that justified being given just fifteen minutes in which to get ready to leave?'

But however confused Kebire remains about the reasons why she and her family were so brutally evicted from their homes and deported, one emotion still boils within her – the desire for revenge: 'If I met that soldier [who evicted her and her family] I would cut him into pieces and hang him.... I would rip his medals from his chest and shove them in his eyes. Because he did things that he should not have done. He should have been fighting the war, not evicting innocent children.... I would knife that soldier – even though my blood pressure [today] is 220, I would still knife that soldier myself.'

Eleven-year-old Musfera Muslimova[56] was another child thrown with her family on to one of the deportation trains on 18 May: 'Many people began saying: "Surely Stalin doesn't know about this? If Stalin knew [about it], this would never be happening." And during the journey rumours began that Stalin had found out [about what was happening] and that we would soon be going back home again.... Stalin liberated us from the Germans, so there was a kind of trust in him.'

But if the mass deportation was designed to punish those Tatars who were guilty of collaborating with the Germans, then it was a failure. Many of the Tatars who were serving with the enemy simply retreated with their units, leaving large numbers of innocent people behind. And amongst those deported by the NKVD were around nine thousand Tatars who had been serving in the Red Army, together with over seven hundred Tatar members of the Communist Party.[57]

Not surprisingly, the apparently illogical nature of the deportations has led some who have studied the subject to suspect a
hidden motive.[58] The key to understanding the action, so this
theory goes, was the Soviet attitude to Turkey. Stalin made no
secret of his desire to exercise greater influence over the
Dardanelles, which linked the Black Sea to the Mediterranean.
This narrow sea lane was historically controlled by Turkey – a
country that, much to the irritation of the Allies, remained neutral
during the war. The Soviets wanted to place military bases in the
straits, as well as to occupy nearby Turkish territory. The persecution of the Tatars, with their historical links to the Turks, was – it
is speculated – part of the growing anti-Turkish movement within
the Soviet Union. Subsequently other nationalities, such as the
Chechens and Ingush, were deported supposedly for similar anti-
Turkish reasons.

It is an interesting theory – but almost certainly mistaken. The
deportation of the Tatars in fact fits a broader pattern of mistreatment of ethnic minorities within the Soviet Union – one that has
nothing to do with the undoubted Soviet desire to put pressure on
Turkey. For example, on 28 December 1943, over four months
before the deportation of the Tatars, the NKVD deported just
under a hundred thousand Kalmyks. Descended from nomadic
Mongols who had settled the steppes hundreds of years earlier, the
Kalmyks lived south of Stalingrad in a bleak landscape stretching
to the Caspian Sea. Like the Tatars, they were accused of collaborating with the Nazis; were deported en masse; and the deportation order encompassed people who could not by any logic be
considered 'collaborators'. Aleksey Badmaev,[59] for instance, had
fought in the Red Army on the Stalingrad front and received
awards for bravery. In January 1944 he was in a military hospital
recovering from wounds received in battle when he was ordered to
report at once to the railway station. He was then immediately sent
north to a labour camp in the Ural Mountains. There he watched
as other Kalmyk soldiers in the camp died of hunger and disease.
It all seemed crazy. 'Of all people,' he says, 'I know very well that
we were short of soldiers at the front, and to take these people

away was beyond stupidity. And secondly, the deportation of the whole nation was a crime. To punish one innocent person is enough of a crime, but to deport the whole of the people and to doom them to dying of extinction – well, I don't know what to compare it with.'

The deportation of the Crimean Tatars was therefore part of an overall policy of punishment – one that removed entire ethnic groups from their homelands and banished them to labour camps and collective farms in the furthest reaches of the Soviet Union. The exact number deported in these various actions may never be known, but it certainly exceeds a million and may be closer to 2 million.

And far from there being any Machiavellian reason behind the deportations, the motivation was a plain and simple desire to suppress dissent and take revenge. And in the process it was immaterial to Stalin and Beria whether the innocent suffered along with the guilty. 'If Stalin had begun to sift things,' says Vladimir Semichastny,[60] a post-war head of the KGB, 'and to discover who was guilty and who wasn't guilty, who fought at the front, who worked in the Communist Party organizations and so on, it would have taken twenty years. But the war was on, and if Stalin had begun to investigate he might not have finished until now. This was Stalin's way to tackle problems.... To send away a million people meant nothing to him.'

It was impossible, of course, for the Soviet authorities to hide from the West these massive population shifts. But, just as with the Katyn massacres, this was not a subject that either the British or the Americans thought it fruitful to pursue. But there was one group of people who had been victims of Stalin's deportation policy but who were impossible for the West to ignore – not least because at the same time as the Crimean Tatars were being deported to Uzbekistan, they were helping to win for the Allies one of the fiercest and most brutal battles of the war.

THE POLES AND MONTE CASSINO

As we have already seen, Churchill was anxious about the progress of the Allied action in Italy at the time of the Tehran Conference. For this attack on the 'soft underbelly' of Axis Europe was not going to plan. The greatest problem the Allies faced was simple – geography. The harsh reality that the Allied troops had learnt in the months since the September 1943 landing at Salerno was that the terrain as they advanced north towards Rome was ill suited for an invading army. The combination of steep-sided mountains and swift-flowing rivers meant that progress was painfully slow. 'Taking one mountain mass after another gains no tactical advantage,' wrote Major General Frederick Walker, commander of the American 36th Division, in his diary for 22 December that year. 'There is always another mountain mass behind with Germans on it.'[61] The Allies were discovering the accuracy of Napoleon's judgement: 'Italy is a boot. You have to enter it from the top.'[62]

A German propaganda leaflet of the time sums up the difficulties faced by the Allies. Above the caption 'The mountains and valleys of "Sunny Italy" want to see you' it depicts a series of mountains with salivating mouths and pointed teeth preparing to gobble up Allied troops – and the largest and most dramatic of the mountains is labelled 'CASSINO'.[63]

The monastery of Monte Cassino, founded in the sixth century by St Benedict, stood on a high peak above the small town of Cassino. The mountain was a crucial part of the German defence line south of Rome – the Gustav Line – and before they pushed on north towards the capital the Allies wanted to remove the enemy from this defensive position. It would prove to be one of the most difficult and bloody tasks faced by the Western Allies in the entire war.

The problem of the geography of southern Italy – which so massively favoured the defending Germans – was exacerbated by Churchill's impatience. He had placed much personal political capital behind the invasion of Italy, and now saw it being – in his view – squandered. He was immensely disappointed by the failure of the Allied landing at Anzio, north of the Gustav Line, on 22 January 1944. This operation, for which Churchill had obtained extra landing craft after much badgering at Tehran, had been intended as a thrust on Rome from behind the German lines. But it had become bogged down as the German defences swiftly regrouped. Churchill famously said of the Anzio operation that he had hoped 'we were hurling a wild cat on the shore, but all we got was a beached whale'.[64]

All of which meant that the pressure on the Allied armies to make progress in the advance on Rome was immense. But taking Monte Cassino presented enormous problems. One of the most insidious was psychological. Even though the monastery had been declared sacrosanct by the Germans, and the Nazis claimed that no Axis troops were occupying it, the high walls still presented a seemingly impregnable barrier to the troops below. There was also a fear that the Germans might place artillery spotters inside the monastery – something that Allied intelligence suggested they had already done (although subsequent investigations showed that the Germans had kept to their promise and not placed troops inside the building).

So, in one of the most controversial military actions of the European war, on 15 February 1944 the Allies bombed the monastery of Monte Cassino. 'We assumed that it wouldn't be bombed,' says Joseph Klein,[65] then a twenty-three-year-old German paratrooper, 'because after all it was the oldest monastery in Europe...and we were totally surprised when aeroplanes flew towards the monastery.... We could already see that when the bombs were released that they would hit the monastery. We couldn't believe it. We were flabbergasted. We never thought it possible. Because [even though] the Germans had this reputation of not being pious – that these Christian people would do this? We'd never have believed it!'

A combination of bombing and artillery turned the monastery to rubble. The *New York Times* described the operation as the 'worst aerial and artillery onslaught ever directed against a single building'.[66] But whilst the propaganda effect on the Allied troops below was undoubtedly strong, the destruction of the monastery presented the German defenders with an unexpected opportunity. 'A fixed building in the middle of terrain normally doesn't offer any possibility of defence,' says Klein. 'We would never go into a complete building because you can be seen, [but] once the building is destroyed, then the human being is blurred into the ruins and becomes part of the terrain. This monastery as long as it stood there and was undamaged was totally useless.... [But] when the monastery was destroyed, we immediately occupied it.... I was up there a few times and it was excellent protection. It offered wonderful possibilities of defence.'

In all, the Allies were to mount four separate operations in their attempt to take Monte Cassino. The first predated the bombing of the monastery by a month. On 17 January British troops from X Corps had crossed the Garigliano river on the left of the battle front, and were then supported by a crossing of the Rapido river made by the American 36th Division in the centre. Both actions failed. A combination of bad weather, lack of armoured support, difficult terrain and powerful German counter-attacks forced the Allies back. Subsequent fighting in the hills alongside Monte Cassino was just as ineffective, and the attack was called off before the bombing raid. The Allied attackers suffered much greater losses than the German defenders – one American Division, for example, with more than two thousand casualties lost about 80 per cent of its fighting strength.[67]

The second attempt to capture Monte Cassino, mounted in the days immediately after the bombing, was no better. Units of the Royal Sussex Regiment, the Rajputana Rifles and the Gurkhas all tried to dislodge the Germans, but to little effect. Similarly the third battle, launched on 15 March and involving New Zealand troops among others, was also a failure. The German defenders – notably the 1st Parachute Division, described by British Commander General Alexander as 'the best Division in the German Army'[68] – had held firm. Joseph Klein was a member of this 'elite' group 'formed from the soldiers that had been in Crete and then in Russia'. And he believes that one of the greatest – and most obvious – advantages the Germans possessed was the power of their defensive positions: 'I thought: "What nonsense!" How can you send people up this mountain [to attack] – 45 degrees steep! So we often asked ourselves why they chose that way.... They always attacked on the broadest side and on the most impossible terrain.'

The final attempt to capture Monte Cassino was made in May 1944. The delay of nearly two months between the third and fourth assault had allowed the Allies time to benefit from better weather and to prepare a larger and wider military operation against the German line. This time the task of disabling Monte Cassino fell to the 2nd Polish Corps under the command of Lieutenant General Władysław Anders. They were ordered to 'isolate' the monastery by attacking the heavily defended mountains alongside. Anders immediately understood that for the Poles this attempt to capture the 'Monte Cassino heights' would be more than just a military operation: 'I realised that the cost in lives must be heavy, but I realised too the importance of the capture of Monte Cassino to the Allied cause, and most of all to that of Poland, for it would answer once and for all the Soviet lie that the Poles did not want to fight the Germans. Victory would give new courage to the resistance movement in Poland and would cover Polish arms with glory. After a moment's reflection I answered that I would undertake the task.'[69]

On the 11th May Polish troops mounted their first attack on Monte Cassino as part of the overall Allied offensive on the Gustav Line. For the men of Anders' army it was, as Wiesław Wolwowicz[70] describes it, 'a christening of fire'. Wolwowicz, then a twenty-two-year-old junior officer in the 16th Lwów Rifle Battalion, had come on a typically lengthy and circuitous journey to be here in Italy. In the autumn of 1939 he had been captured by the Soviets just outside Lwów while trying to escape wetwards to join the Polish Army. After interrogation by the NKVD in the notorious Brigidki prison in Lwów he was taken by train to the Soviet Union in the spring of 1940 where he was sentenced to five years' imprisonment and confined in a camp in the Ural Mountains. After some months cutting trees in the forest as a forced labourer, he was released following the German invasion of the Soviet Union and joined Anders' army. He subsequently left the Soviet Union as part of the II Polish Corps and started training first in Iraq and then in Palestine. Now he listened as 'thousands of guns started shelling Monte Cassino' and the first wave of Polish soldiers climbed the mountains to attack: 'Monte Cassino is known as a very difficult battle,' Wolwowicz says. 'Yes, it's true. Can you imagine rocks? When the German army started shelling us there was no green grass, there were no bushes, there was just rocks and rubble.... It wasn't easy.... When the guns were shelling the rocks, the rocks used to break up.' The Poles moved forward in the darkness, but the lack of cover and the murderous German fire from above wreaked havoc on the advancing troops. Still they pressed on, reaching the ridge on top of the mountain adjacent to Monte Cassino, where they fought the Germans hand-to-hand.

Tomasz Piesakowski[71] learnt of the carnage in the mountains around Cassino from his position commanding a mortar troop behind the lines. Like Wolwowicz, he came from eastern Poland, now claimed by Stalin as Soviet territory, and had previously been imprisoned in the Soviet Union. He describes the battle as a 'hell on earth' as the Poles tried to seize the high ground from the Germans. 'When [after the battle] I went to the cemetery – the provisional cemetery – to find out where the graves of my friends were, I couldn't believe my eyes! So many graves were there!'

The Poles were unable to hold the territory they had captured, and Anders was forced to order his men back. Just as before, the defenders of Monte Cassino – by now fewer than a thousand of them – had proved too strong. And Anders was clear why the attack had failed: 'Enemy reserves would suddenly emerge from conceal-ment in caves to make a series of powerful counter-attacks which were supported by accurate fire from guns...it soon became clear that it was easier to capture some objectives than to hold them.'[72]

But even though the initial attack had failed, the Poles had earned the respect of their opponents. 'They were brave soldiers,' says German parachutist Joseph Klein. 'They were the bravest of them all, in fact. But it was more like an inner drive that went almost to the level of fanaticism.... They looked at death but marched ahead nevertheless, which nobody else did.... This was a devastating thing – the order and sense of duty the Poles had. The thinking that: "We have to get through. We have to show the Allied forces that we are worthy of belonging to them. We must make the breakthrough."... We often couldn't believe it.'

On 16 May the Poles mounted another attack, and this time Wiesław Wolwowicz and his unit moved forward into battle: 'There were many people who died, many wounded. Being in charge of a unit I tried to help them as much as I could.... Being a commander you don't really think much about danger. In fact, you do think about it at the back of your mind, but you don't believe that you will be wounded or you will die. But in practice, of course, it's not always the case.'

Conditions on the battlefield were appalling. Wolwowicz could 'smell the decomposing bodies of our soldiers, of the animals in the sun. All the bodies of the dead soldiers were swollen and they looked almost like barrels. We could smell the terrible, terrible smell of dead bodies. You could smell this smell later on for a long time afterwards. It was like a nightmare haunting you...the smell coming from the dead bodies of the soldiers lying in the open sun.'

This time the Poles managed to hold their forward positions against a German force that – though still resisting fiercely – was now considerably depleted. Elsewhere on the front, Allied troops had succeeded in advancing through the Liri valley, which meant that the Allies now had the opportunity to skirt around Monte Cassino, and by 17 May the mountain was all but encircled. As a consequence, the German commander Field Marshal Kesselring ordered the 1st Parachute Division to withdraw.

The remaining German soldiers on Monte Cassino – those who were too sick or too badly wounded to evacuate – surrendered to the Poles on the morning of the 18th. Just before ten o'clock Anders' men raised a makeshift red and white Polish flag over the ruins of the monastery: it was a famous victory. But a victory won at massive cost. Several thousand Poles were killed or wounded in the battle for Monte Cassino. And the majority of these Poles – like the majority of the soldiers in Anders' army – came from the very areas of eastern Poland that Stalin now claimed as his own.

As they fought and died in the rocky outcrops and gorges of the heights of Monte Cassino, these Poles hoped that their sacrifice would help Poland to become a free and independent land. As it turned out – tragically – they were mistaken.

THE SECOND FRONT IS LAUNCHED AT LAST

At half past seven in the morning on 6 June 1944, tanks of the British cavalry regiment the 13th/18th Hussars pushed forward over the sandy beach of Ouistreham in Normandy. They were part of an invasion force of over 160,000 Allied troops targeting five main beaches, codenamed Utah, Omaha, Juno, Gold and Sword. This was D-Day – the first opposed amphibious landing in strength on the coast of France for nearly a thousand years. It was also the start of the second front that Stalin had been calling for since the summer of 1941 – something he believed Roosevelt had promised would be mounted two years earlier.

'We kept going in and in, and all of a sudden we hear these pings on the steel-hulled landing craft,' says Sid Salomon,[73] a member of the US Rangers who took part in the attack on Omaha beach, where the Allies faced the toughest resistance. 'And the guy said: "The Germans are firing at us." We could see them in the distance up on top of the cliffs. Something landed in the water and the concussion hit and it flipped me over and I heard somebody yell: "Keep moving! Keep moving! ...I reached over and grabbed him by the jacket ... pulled him out from the surf. And just then a mortar shell landed behind me – knocked me flat on my face and I thought: "What the hell! I must be dead.".…And there were guys lying on the beach dead. Shells hitting it, machine gun fire ripping across it, an LST off to our right – they got a dead hit as they were unloading. These guys were coming down and just blew that sucker right out of the water. Hell of a sight. Awful.'

But on the other beaches the landings went more smoothly. 'I can remember talking it over with a fellow company commander and reckoning our chances of getting across the beach alive were going to be pretty small,' says Peter Martin,[74] then a major with the Cheshire Regiment. 'But in fact everything by that time had quietened down and we weren't under fire of any sort...and it was one of those very rare occasions in war when the plan goes absolutely according to plan.'

As soldiers of the Western Allies battled to establish a foothold in Normandy, the Red Army prepared to launch a massive attack on German Army Group Centre in an attempt to recapture Minsk and push the Wehrmacht back out of the Soviet Union. This operation, which had been agreed at Tehran, dwarfed D-Day in scale. The Germans had 30 divisions in the West to face the Allied onslaught following D-Day, but concentrated 165 divisions against the Red Army in the East. Over 2 million Red Army soldiers would take part in the June offensive, codenamed by Stalin 'Operation Bagration' after the Georgian military hero who had fought against Napoleon.

'For Bagration we were preparing very carefully,' says Veniamin Fyodorov,[75] then a twenty-year-old soldier with the Soviet 77th Guards infantry regiment. 'Whatever resources the Soviet Union had were concentrated in this direction. Big numbers of artillery, tanks and ammunition. And big numbers of infantry.' On 22 June 1944 (the third anniversary of the German invasion) Fyodorov watched the initial bombardment from his own side with a sense of awe: 'When you look ahead, you see bits of earth flying up into the air and you see explosions. As if you light a match. Flashes, flashes. One flash, another flash. And bits of land [are thrown in the air]. After the bombardment, planes came, flying low. We felt more cheerful because we had a lot of military equipment.'

For the Germans, on the other hand, Operation Bagration marked the lowest point in their military fortunes so far – lower even than Stalingrad in terms of military losses. Seventeen divisions were destroyed completely, with another fifty enduring losses of 50 per cent. And it was Hitler who was largely to blame for this defeat. No longer did he trust his generals to take the initiative on the battlefield as he had done in the early days of the invasion of the Soviet Union in 1941. Now he gave direct tactical orders to the commanders of the 9th Army who faced Operation Bagration – and increasingly these orders seemed disconnected from the realities of modern warfare. One of Hitler's most debilitating instructions, for example, was to establish *Feste Plätze* (Fortified Places) that would act as fortresses behind the lines when the Red Army moved forward.

On the eve of Bagration General Jordan, commander of the 9th Army, wrote these words: '…The Army believes that even under the present conditions, it would be possible to stop the enemy offensive, but not under the present directives which require an absolutely rigid defence…. The Army considers the orders establishing *"Feste Plätze"* particularly dangerous. The army looks ahead to the coming battle with bitterness, knowing that it is bound by order to tactical measures which it cannot in good conscience accept as correct and which in our earlier victorious campaigns were the cause of the enemy defeats.'[76]

This sense that the Germans were contributing to their own defeat now pervaded even the most junior ranks. 'Sometimes…you just received orders that were so nonsensical from behind you,' says Heinz Fielder,[77] then a twenty-two-year-old private with the 9th Army, 'from the division or from the army corps. I remember once that one position had definitely to be taken back again, and the young second lieutenant had refused to attack again because more than half of his men had already died and they were just all sacrificed. They attacked again and again until the very last one died and that of course makes you wonder. But those were the men of the General Staff. They had their little flags and they put them on the map and then they say, this absolutely has to be restored, no matter what the sacrifices are.'

Fielder was one of the Germans ordered to defend the *Feste Plätz* of Bobruisk in the wake of the Red Army attack: 'Everywhere dead bodies are lying. Dead bodies, wounded people, people screaming, medical orderlies, and then there were those who were completely covered, who were not taken out at all, who were buried there straight away by the bunkers and trenches that collapsed. You don't have any feeling any more for warmth or coldness or light or darkness or thirst or hunger. You don't need to go to the loo. I can't explain it. It's such a tension you're under.... Everything was simply shit. Everything was shit.'

Only after the *Feste Plätz* was completely encircled and had been subjected to continuous bombardment was Fielder's unit at last told it could try and escape: 'And then the last command arrived. Destroy vehicles, shoot horses, take as much hand ammunition and rations with you as you can carry. Every man for himself. Well, now go on and rescue yourself.'

Fielder joined a group of other German soldiers who were trying to fight their way through the Red Army troops ahead of them and reach the retreating German line. He 'headed west – towards the setting sun' and saw sights that haunt him still: 'There was a private, a young boy, who sat at a very big birch tree – you know in Russia there are lots of birch trees. So that's where he was sitting, and from his tummy his intestines were streaming and he was crying, "Shoot me, shoot me" and everybody just ran past him. I had to stop – but I could not shoot him. And then a young second lieutenant from the Sappers came. He took off his headgear and gave him the *coup de grâce* with a 7.65 into the temple. And that's when I had to cry bitterly. I thought if his mother knew how her boy ended [here], and instead she gets a letter from the squadron saying, "Your son fell on the field of honour for great Germany".'

In July 1944 the German army on the Eastern Front lost nearly two hundred thousand men killed or wounded; in August it was nearly three hundred thousand. In total, German losses as a result of Operation Bagration would be calculated at around 1.5 million. There had never been a defeat like it for Hitler and his generals.

The Red Army made swift progress against the Wehrmacht, retaking Minsk, capital of Belarus, on 3 July. 'Gradually the Germans were losing morale and losing their belief in victory,' says Fyodor Bubenchikov,[78] then a twenty-eight-year-old Red Army officer. 'Germans no longer cried: "*Heil Hitler!*" On the contrary, they were surrendering. They were crying: "*Hitler kaputt!*"' That summer, Bubenchikov says he felt as if he was 'flying': 'Victory always makes you feel like [you are] flying. It makes everyone feel this, from ordinary soldier to the commander, and all our units were filled with this sensation.'

Operation Bagration – still not as known in the West as it should be – marked the end of a transformation in the fortunes of the Red Army. Not just tactically and strategically, but also in terms of sheer military hardware. The Soviets had managed to increase their manufacture of military equipment – often in the most difficult of circumstances – so that they were now out performing the Germans. There had been signs that this would happen for some time – in 1942, for example, the Soviets made twenty-five thousand aircraft, ten thousand more than the Germans produced that year. And, subsequently, in both 1943 and 1944, the Soviets produced more tanks and self-propelled guns than their enemy.

It had been Stalin's drive to industrialization via the five-year plan in the 1930s that had prepared the way for this massive expansion in production. And added to Soviet output, of course, were the benefits of aid from the Western Allies – the vast majority of it from America. Although this remained only a small percentage of total Soviet military equipment, it was important because of the often superior technology the Western Allies offered – for example, the Studebaker US6 truck, used by the Red Army for the launching of Katyusha rockets.

But elsewhere in the Soviet Union, as the Red Army celebrated victory after Operation Bagration, some of the many people whose lives had been changed for the worse by this reoccupation of Soviet territory were just beginning their new and bitter existence.

THE TATARS IN EXILE

The majority of the Tatars deported by the NKVD from the Crimea were sent to Uzbekistan. And the story of what happened to them there is important – not only because it represents the climax of one of the most ruthless acts of ethnic cleansing in history, but also because it demonstrates the attitude of the Soviet authorities at a time when the West was about to discuss with Stalin the fate of those eastern European people shortly to be under Soviet occupation.

The journey to Uzbekistan took several weeks on board the freight trains commandeered by the NKVD. Conditions were so bad that a large number of people – particularly the old and the young – died en route. One estimate is that as many as seven thousand Tatars lost their lives in the transports[79] before they reached Uzbekistan. 'In our wagon…one small child died,' says Musfera Muslimova, who was eleven at the time. 'And so as not to upset us, the others in the wagon [said]: "Children, don't look in that direction."' The child's body was left by the railway track at the next stop.

And when the Tatars arrived at the 'special settlements' in Uzbekistan they faced persecution from many of the indigenous population. 'The Uzbeks were told: "The people who are being brought here are cannibals",' says Musfera. '"They eat people, especially children. Don't let them see them [the Uzbek children]! They suck the blood of children." And the people believed this. Neither the Uzbeks nor us Tatars were very literate.'

'The Uzbeks didn't like us,' confirms Nazlakhan Asanova,[80] who was fourteen when she was deported to Uzbekistan. '[They used to say]: "There go the traitors!" And who were we really? Honest people…. It was truly terrible. It's not even possible to describe it. There isn't enough paper to do that.'

Even without the antipathy of the local population, life for the Tatars in Uzbekistan would have been grim. They had swapped one of the most fertile parts of Europe – a region famous for its temperate climate and aromatic wine – for a dry and arid wilderness in which little could grow. In the summer the temperature in Uzbekistan could easily exceed 40 degrees Celsius. In winter it would drop regularly below minus 20.

'Special settlements' for the Tatars had been established by the NKVD. They were little different from labour camps – though there was no need for barbed wire. The nature of the wilderness, plus the presence of regular NKVD guard posts, meant the Tatars were effectively imprisoned anyway. The Tatars were made to work long hours, in cotton fields on collective farms or in factories, but no matter how hard they tried to stay alive, the conditions were such that many of them began to die.

The combination of lack of medicine and proper food was devastating. 'They forced us to work for ten hours at a time – hard agricultural labour,' says Refat Muslimov, who was twelve years old in 1944. 'Well, after that the diseases began. One of the most dangerous diseases was dysentery, which came from filthy water. People [also] began dying from the disease malaria. There was no medicine. There were no doctors. There was no hospital. And people just began dying. My grandfather died after a week. My mother's sister, my favourite aunt, survived for about twenty days. And then one day she just died because of the climate – from the heat, you understand…. And when my brother [who was fifteen years old] could no longer work they began to beat him, and we complained to the commandant. We said: "Look how badly they have beaten him up!" And he said: "They shouldn't have just beaten him up – they should have killed him! They should kill you all!"'

Starving as they were, the Tatars were ripe for exploitation. 'My cousin,' says Refat, 'went up to an Uzbek and she asked him for some bread. And he was married. He forced her to come home with him, raped her and then gave her a small pie. And she thought this behaviour was normal because she was so hungry. She would have agreed to anything.'

The majority of Tatars deported to Uzbekistan were women and children. And they suffered in particular because – not surprisingly – the young children found it hard to function as manual labourers, and the mothers often could not work because they had to look after their small children or babies. As a result, Kebire Ametova and her mother, three sisters and brother soon found themselves starving: 'When you don't eat for a week, your mind is there, your head is working, but your tongue won't move any more.'

Her mother sold anything she could in order to buy food for

her family – her earrings and other jewellery were the first possessions to go – but after a few months she had nothing left to sell.
And Kebire's younger sister, Ziver – who was only two and half
years old at the time of the deportation – began to starve to death:
'My sister was so swollen that, had it not been for her hair, it
would have been impossible to know where her face was.
Everything was swollen. It was only her hair that enabled one to
tell the difference between the back of her head and the front.'
Ziver died when she was three years old. Her mother bathed her
body and wrapped her in a cloth, and then the whole family helped
dig a grave in the hard earth.

Kebire's mother tried to earn money to feed her surviving
family by digging turnips on the collective farm, but in the frozen
winter she got frostbite on her leg, which then became sore and
inflamed. In desperation, she told Kebire and her brother that their
best chance of survival was to leave her, walk to the next village, and
see if there was anyone there who would take pity on them. Kebire
was just ten years old when she left her mother and started wander-
ing. As children, she and her brother were able first to pass the
NKVD checkpoint at the border of the collective farm and then to
enter the nearby forest. Here they came across an Uzbek man who
took pity on them. He took them home, fed them and told them
that their only chance of survival was to become beggars. 'He
explained what we should say [when we begged],' says Kebire. "In
the name of Christ, please give us something to eat – we haven't
got a father and our mother is ill." And he told us where to go. He
told us to save ourselves, and not feel bashful about doing so. He
told us that begging was not stealing, and that it is not a sin to ask
people for food…. And we started going around begging. We went
round the houses begging for something to eat in the name of
Christ. Sometimes we even lied and told them that we had no
father or mother and they gave us food…[then] we brought our
mother the potatoes or whatever we had been given.'

Kebire and her brother would sleep rough, often in empty
barrels, when they were out begging, but occasionally Uzbek
villagers would take them in for the night: 'When they [the

villagers] undressed us and put our clothes on the stove to dry there were so many lice they [seemed] to weigh more than we did!'

Although she managed to survive in this way, Kebire was denied an education and grew up illiterate – something that still embarrasses her to this day. Her childhood, she says, was stolen from her. 'We did not know what life was – we never saw it…. We went around homeless…. Of course it's very painful.'

The NKVD's own figures show that within eighteen months of arriving in Uzbekistan, over 17 per cent of the Tatars were dead.[81] The overall death toll during their entire period of exile – which lasted officially until 1989 – is harder to establish precisely. Some believe that nearly half of the Tatars died as a result of the deportations. What is certain is that this is a crime – together with the deportation of the other ethnic groups like the Chechens and Kalmyks, all of whom suffered in a similar way – that ranks alongside some of the worst atrocities committed during the war.

Even after years of exile, some of the Tatars still believed rumours that Stalin had 'made a mistake' in sending them away from the Crimea. 'We were thinking that the next day we would be put back in those trains again and would return to our homeland…that someone had made him [Stalin] do it or that he hadn't understood,' says Refat Muslimov. 'I'm telling you in all truth that people even packed up to leave, and were saying: "We're leaving. The order has already been given. Stalin has already given the order and we are waiting for the train."'

But today, now that they know for certain who was responsible, the Tatars direct their anger at the man who authorized the deportations, and who never sent the train to rescue them – Joseph Stalin. 'He was a butcher,' says Muslimov. 'Millions and millions of people were killed by him. That butcher. He should be put on trial. People have forgotten about him, but because of what he did he should be put on trial. I demand that he be put on trial! He may be dead but he should be put on trial. He should be punished!'

THE RED ARMY RETURNS

In the wake of the attack on German Army Group Centre in Operation Bagration, the Red Army moved forward into eastern Poland and mounted the Lwów–Sandomierz assault. This powerful thrust involved over a million Soviet soldiers of the 1st Ukrainian front under the command of Marshal Konev.

In July 1944 the Soviets approached Lwów, a city they had first seized in September 1939 in agreement with the Nazis. 'In 1944, when the Red Army came for a second time, it was, of course, worse,' says Anna Levitska, then a teenager living in the city. 'Because we already had an idea of what the consequences might be, because of all the arrests there had been in 1939 and 1940.... So of course it was terrifying.'

Anna recalls one old man coming up to her and her family in 1944 and saying: 'This is the second time [the Soviets have come]. It was better the first time.'

'Why?' they asked him.

'Because the first time, they came and they went. But this time when they come there is no way they will be leaving.'

Vyacheslav Yablonsky[82] was part of the great Soviet assault on Lwów that summer. But he was no ordinary soldier: as a member of an elite NKVD squad he had a very specific role. Together with two dozen other members of the secret police, and a squad of Red Army soldiers, he entered Lwów just before the Germans retreated from the city. Travelling in American Studebaker trucks they plotted a route via the back streets of the city to the Gestapo headquarters. The location was familiar to the Soviets, since the German secret police had merely taken over the old NKVD headquarters – a building that in turn had previously housed the Polish secret police and before that the Austro-Hungarian intelligence agency (today, the same building is used by the Ukrainian police).

The task facing Yablonsky and his comrades was straightforward, but considered vital. They had to capture the Gestapo headquarters before the Germans left, and steal intelligence information that their superiors hoped would reveal just who had been collaborating with the Nazis.

They arrived just as the Germans were packing their files into trucks. The Soviet force scaled the wall surrounding the Gestapo headquarters, shot the German guards and prevented the trucks from leaving. Hurrying into the building, they made straight for the cellars, where they knew the intelligence files were stored. While the remaining Germans, panic-stricken, sought to escape, the NKVD swiftly made the building secure and started examining the files they had found. They then immediately sought out anyone whom the German documents had named as an informer. Yablonsky also relied on pro-Soviet informers to tell him who had been collaborating with the Germans or was simply 'anti-Soviet': 'We got to know about the dangerous people from these other people [informers]. They told us that somebody hated Soviet power and was a threat to us and then we would arrest him...they could be saying bad things about us or just thinking we were bad.' Once arrested for the crime of 'saying something bad' about the Soviet occupation, Yablonsky recalls, the 'normal' sentence was 'about fifteen years of forced labour'.

'Now I think it was cruel,' he says. 'But at that time, when I was young, twenty-two or twenty-three years old, I didn't.... Now I understand that it's cruel because I'm older. I don't think it was a very democratic time. Now you can say anything, but at that time you couldn't. At that time most things were censored and nobody could say anything bad about the Soviet Union. So we all thought it was normal at the time.'

Despite feeling now that Soviet policy was 'very cruel', Yablonsky looks back on his years as a member of the NKVD in Lwów with affection. 'I'm proud of it. I feel I was doing the right thing. I felt that I was alive. I was starting. I was learning something. I loved my country and I felt it was right. We won such an incredible war. I'm proud of the Soviet Union and I'm proud I was part of it and brave enough to go through the war and not let my country down.'

It was clear that Soviet soldiers like Vyacheslav Yablonsky

believed they were reclaiming Lwów as part of Soviet territory – and they never intended to give it up again; and it was members of the underground Polish Home Army who were some of the first to learn this dispiriting truth. These were volunteer soldiers who had remained hidden under the Nazi occupation, waiting for the moment to strike back, and they played an important part in the battle for Lwów. Around three thousand soldiers led by Colonel Władysław Filipkowski had supported the Red Army during the fierce fighting that lasted from 23 to 27 July.[83] But once the battle was won the Soviet authorities arrested the officers and then forced the ordinary soldiers to join units of the Red Army.

In parallel with the elimination of the underground Polish Home Army, the Soviet authorities immediately sought to re-establish the institutions of control that they had created during their first occupation. 'In 1944 they set up their rule again,' says Anna Levitska. 'They organized schools according to their own system. It was obligatory that every student belonged to the Young Communists. And, of course, there were no religious classes. Just those lectures on atheism. And studying the history of the Communist Party was obligatory. The fundamentals of Marxism and Leninism – those were the main subjects.' And as she saw the Soviet hold on eastern Poland strengthening, Anna didn't just blame Stalin and the rest of the Soviet leadership for her plight. 'We felt betrayed,' she says, 'because we had hoped that the West would react differently.... We were even hoping that England and France [would help us], but that didn't happen.'

On 26 July 1944, while the battle for Lwów still raged, at Perugia in Italy General Anders was presented to King George VI. The British monarch had flown to Italy under the pseudonym of 'General Collingwood' in order to congratulate Allied forces on their progress. During dinner he listened to the regimental band of the II Polish Army Corps, and remarked that he found one song particularly attractive. He asked what the song was called and was told that it was a particular favourite of theirs: 'And if I ever have to be born again, then let it happen only in Lwów.'[84]

5
DIVIDING EUROPE

THE WARSAW UPRISING

It was not just eastern Poland that was within Stalin's grasp as a result of the summer offensive of 1944, but the rest of the country too – territory that even he did not claim as part of the Soviet Union. And although not seeking to incorporate western Poland into the Soviet Empire, Stalin still wanted to exercise 'influence' over this land. As a result, this was a moment of immense potential conflict.

The Soviets persisted in their mantra that they wanted a 'friendly' Poland and still – as a result of the controversy over Katyn – refused to recognize the Polish government in exile based in London. Now they moved to install their own tame administration in western Poland. On 28 July 1944 they transferred from the Soviet Union to Chem in Poland a collection of little-known Polish politicians who were prepared to collaborate with them. This group, officially called the Polish Committee of National Liberation but later known as the Lublin Poles (the committee moved to the Polish city of Lublin in early August 1945), had declared in a 'manifesto' issued in Moscow on 2 July that they were in favour of a variety of leftist policies such as nationalization, as well as a 'fair' border with the Soviet Union (which actually meant the Curzon Line). And as far as they – and their Soviet masters – were concerned, they were now the de facto government of 'liberated' Poland. Nikolai Bulganin, a leading member of the Soviet State Committee of Defence, was sent from Moscow to be Stalin's representative to the Lublin Poles, and effectively the puppet government reported to him. Accompanying Bulganin was Ivan Serov, a senior member of the NKVD who had masterminded the deportations from eastern Poland during the Soviet occupation between 1939 and 1941; his task was to 'help' the Poles administer the newly liberated territory.

Of course, the imposition on Poland of a regime controlled by Stalin was not something that either the Western Allies or the official Polish government in exile could accept. And the situation was further complicated by the presence on Polish soil of four hundred thousand members of the Polish underground – the Armia Krajowa or Home Army – who owed their allegiance to the government in exile in London. Stalin's attitude towards this underground resistance force had been made plain at Tehran, where he had dismissed them as bandits. And the stance of the Red Army on the ground had already been demonstrated in Lwów, where the soldiers of the Home Army who had helped the Soviets liberate the city from the Germans had been subsequently disarmed. This kind of persecution was clearly part of a broader pattern. Also in July, for example, the Home Army units that had helped the Soviets capture Vilno were disbanded, the officers arrested and the men sent off to join collaborating Polish units within the Red Army.[1]

It was against this background that the focus of all the various competing parties now turned to the fate of the capital, Warsaw. What would happen here, when the population of Warsaw rose up against the German occupiers in the summer and early autumn of 1944, would expose to the world the tensions and conflict within the West's relationship with Stalin and the Soviet Union that Churchill, Roosevelt and their respective propaganda machines had tried so hard to hide.

In the process, a number of myths would grow up around the Warsaw Uprising. The most prevalent of them was that the Poles had been lured into insurrection by direct blandishments and promises of assistance from the Soviets.

But although it is certainly true that radio broadcasts were made under Soviet auspices that encouraged the people of

SOVIET ADVANCE WEST, 1942–4

——	Front line December 1942
┅▬	Front line July 1943
▬ ▬ ▬	Front line December 1943
• • •	Front line August 1944
⟶	Soviet advances

FINLAND

SWEDEN

Lake Ladoga

Helsinki

Gulf of Finland

Baltic Sea

Tallin

Narva

Leningrad

Novgorod

ESTONIA

Kalinin

Moscow

Riga

LATVIA

Dvina

SOVIET UNION

Memel

LITHUANIA

Vyazma

Königsberg

Kaunus

Smolensk

Tula

Vistula

Minsk

BELARUS

Bialystok

Kursk

Warsaw

Brest-Litovsk

GENERAL GOVERNMENT (POLAND)

Pripet Marshes

Kiev

Kharkov

Lwów

Vinnitsa

Dnieper

CZECHOSLOVAKIA

Dniester

UKRAINE

CARPATHIAN MTS

HUNGARY

Odessa

Sea of Azov

ROMANIA

Sevastopol

Bucharest

YUGOSLAVIA

Danube

Black Sea

BULGARIA

0 miles 100

0 km 100

N

Warsaw to believe that liberation was near, it is not the case that this was a direct attempt by the Soviet military to agree a joint attack on the Polish capital with the Home Army. The appeals were much less specific. On 29 July, for instance, Radio Moscow announced that 'the hour of action has already arrived' for Warsaw, and that 'those who have never bowed their heads to the Hitlerite power will again, as in 1939, join the struggle against the Germans, this time for a decisive action'. And a broadcast from the PKWN Soviet-authorized radio station the following day announced that Soviet forces were approaching and were coming 'to bring you freedom'.[2] But this fell far short of a direct instruction to the Home Army to rise up in Warsaw in a coordinated way and link up with the advancing Red Army. So far, it was all just encouraging rhetoric.

The Home Army in Warsaw, together with the Polish government in exile in London, faced a difficult political dilemma. They knew that if they did nothing, and the Red Army liberated Warsaw before they could rise up, then the Soviets would be in a still more dominant position when it came to any post-war negotiations. After all, wouldn't the Home Army have then shown the very ineffectiveness that Stalin had always said characterized them? But, on the other hand, if the Home Army rose up long before the Red Army arrived, then they would be annihilated by the Germans. The timing of any rising was thus crucial.

What was obviously important, therefore, was to try to coordinate any rising with the imminent arrival of the Red Army. But the distrust between the two sides was so great that this was the one thing that the Polish government in exile did not feel able to do. On 26 July the leader of the Poles in London, Prime Minister Stanislaw Mikołajczyk, authorized the Home Army in Warsaw to 'pronounce the Rising at a time to be determined by you'. But this was an instruction that went directly against the advice of the Polish commander-in-chief in London. He had said that 'Insurrection without a fair understanding with the USSR and honest and real cooperation with the Red Army would be politically unjustified and militarily nothing more than an act of despair.'[3]

Nonetheless, the commander of the Home Army in Warsaw ordered 'W' hour – the launch of the uprising – to take place (without notifying the Soviets beforehand) at 5 p.m. on 1 August. He was aware that not only were the Red Army closing on Warsaw, but that on 27 July the Germans had called for a hundred thousand Polish civilians to surrender themselves and help build the defences of the capital. The Home Army, not surprisingly, was suspicious of this German order and urged people not to come forward. It thus made sense to senior figures in the Polish resistance to start the uprising at this moment. It was a gamble. And it wouldn't pay off.

Zbigniew Wolak[4] was one of the first to start fighting. He was nineteen years old and a unit commander in the Home Army. His father, a major in the regular Polish army, had died in 1939 and his mother had been killed in a Nazi concentration camp. For the previous two years he had worked as a porter at Warsaw central railway station, and during his free time he had trained with the Home Army. Now he and his colleagues had heard how the Soviets were oppressing other members of the Home Army elsewhere in Poland, and it was this news that, in his mind, predominantly dictated the timing of the rising. At seven o'clock in the evening of 1 August, Zbigniew and his unit emerged on to the streets in the suburbs of Warsaw, wearing headbands with the colours of the Polish flag – white and red. 'Just imagine,' he says, 'after four years of occupation we come out on this fragrant August day full of people, the women with children, people going back home from work, and all of a sudden there's sixty-four armed insurgents in the street. In a moment they would start dying.'

Zbigniew's unit was part of a larger group ordered to attack a German military barracks. Lacking heavier weaponry, they were only armed with pistols, rifles and hand grenades. And as they prepared to fight the Germans, one of Zbigniew's closest friends, a young man called Zazek who was studying electrical engineering, stood alongside him. Zbigniew remembers how he had encouraged his friend to take part in the battle: 'The recruitment of the Home Army was based on trust, absolute trust – you could introduce someone to the army only if you know them very well. This was my close friend, but he was not interested in the underground struggle. He was a pupil at the university and he was in love with a girl and he wanted to become a scientist. And in 1943, during a walk we took together, I told him something – and I regret it to this day. I was learning English from books at the time, and I borrowed a book about the First World War and there was [a picture of] a typical English living room, and there was a staff sergeant from the First World War sitting at the fireplace and he held a child on his lap and his child was asking: "Father, tell me, what you did during the war?" And I told Zazek, "Look, the war will be over, your son or daughter will ask what you did, you'll say, 'Nothing – I just studied.' And you'll regret it until the very end of your days." So this was moral blackmail. [As a result] he said yes, and joined the Home Army.'

However, on 1 August, because there were not enough weapons to arm each of the Home Army volunteers, Zazek wasn't selected to take part in the attack. As the unit was about to leave on its mission, Zbigniew saw his friend watching from the window. 'Ah!' he shouted up. 'You want to get out of it again!' Stung by this remark, Zazek went to the local Home Army commander and begged for two hand grenades so that he could participate. Five minutes later, Zazek was alongside Zbigniew when the attack began. 'He walked one step in front of me,' says Zbigniew, 'and a series of bullets from a machine gun hit him in the chest and he fell on his back holding those two hand grenades.... The feeling that you see somebody alive – you're talking to a handsome, beautiful boy – and [moments later] he's lying there like this! And the worst thing was that I got him into it!'

It was a devastating introduction to the realities of battle for Zbigniew. As for Zazek's family, they never recovered from the loss of their son. After the war, when Zbigniew visited them, he saw in their apartment a 'big photograph' of his friend, draped in black and garlanded with flowers. His mother looked at Zbigniew and asked: 'Why did he die? Why didn't you die?' 'These,' says Zbigniew, 'are the most difficult things.'

Within the first few days of the rising, and despite their lack of heavy weapons, the Home Army managed to take control of a number of key districts of Warsaw, in particular the narrow streets of the old town in the centre of the city. However, on the east bank of the river Vistula the rising was much less successful, since this was the area of greatest German troop concentration. The Home Army knew that it would only be a matter of a few days before the Germans counter-attacked in strength. Moreover, the Polish fighters held only isolated pockets of the city and it was already proving hard to establish proper communications between them. What they needed now was what they had needed all along – help from outside.

The head of the Polish government in exile knew better than most that the Warsaw Uprising could not succeed without the practical assistance of the Allies. But Mikołajczyk had decided that it was best to approve the insurrection first and then – effectively as a fait accompli – push for cooperation. He ought, perhaps, to have known beforehand that this was not a strategy calculated to work on the predilections of Joseph Stalin.

Mikołajczyk, who had been active in the Peasants' Party in Poland since the 1920s and was still only forty-three, had travelled to Moscow to meet Stalin after authorizing the uprising but arrived on 30 July before it had been launched. For him, time was of the essence. He urgently needed to obtain an agreement from Stalin that the Red Army would help the insurgents in Warsaw. Unfortunately, both for Mikołajczyk personally and for the Home Army generally, Stalin did not see it that way at all. To begin with, as we have seen, the Soviets did not recognize the government in exile and were trying to break the power of the Home Army in the sections of Poland that the Red Army had liberated so far. And although Stalin realized that it would be seen as offensive to the British and Americans to refuse to meet the London Poles, he knew that he was under no obligation to be accommodating when he did see them.

The Poles were treated with great rudeness from the moment of their arrival – they were snubbed at the airport, and then told that Stalin was 'too busy' to see them. When Molotov met them on 31 July he simply said: 'Why have you come?' and suggested that they meet with the Lublin Poles – Stalin's tame Polish government – instead. They didn't manage to get an audience with the Soviet leader until the evening of 3 August, by which time, of course, the rising was already in progress and lightly armed Poles were dying on the streets of Warsaw, desperately in need of help.

The day before the meeting with Stalin, Churchill had given a resolutely upbeat assessment of the situation in a speech in the House of Commons. He talked of having done 'our best' to get Stalin to receive the Polish Prime Minister, pointing out that the 'Russian Armies...bring the liberation of Poland in their hands' while 'we have several gallant Polish divisions fighting the Germans in our Armies'. Now, he said, 'Let them come together.'[5] But a necessary precondition of this togetherness, he went on to say, was the old proviso that 'there should be a Poland friendly to Russia'. Given the immensity of the gulf between the Polish government in exile, who thought the Lublin Poles were stooges, and Stalin, who had asserted that the London Poles had collaborated with the Nazis, Churchill's statement in the House of Commons was wishful thinking of the most momentous kind.

The detailed minutes[6] of the meeting between Mikołajczyk and other representatives of the Polish government in exile on the one side and Stalin and Molotov on the other make for insightful – if painful – reading. Almost certainly, given the entrenched positions of each of the parties present and the massive disparity in real power, it was destined to be a failure. But what is remarkable is the way in which Mikołajczyk seems to have misjudged the reality of the situation. He knew that, as he talked to Stalin in the Kremlin, the fate of millions of people in Warsaw rested on the result. Yet in his initial long and somewhat ponderous statement he mentioned a four-point 'programme' that he wished to discuss with the Soviet leader – and the Warsaw Uprising was only listed as point 4, after such matters as 'the widening of the scope of the Polish–Soviet Agreement of 1941' to relate to the administration of the liberated Polish territories. And even when the Warsaw

above: George Elsey, a naval officer in the White House Map Room during the war, briefs President Harry Truman.

below: Soldiers from the Polish II Corps patrol amongst the ruins of the town of Cassino, at the foot of Monte Cassino, in the aftermath of the battle in May 1944.

above: A street in Warsaw. The Germans destroyed the city in the summer and autumn of 1944.

left: Lieutenant General Władysław Anders, commander of the Polish II Corps in the British army. He had successfully negotiated the release of thousands of his fellow Polish soldiers from the Soviet Union.

above: Nikonor Perevalov, an officer in the NKVD, who took part in the deportation of the entire Tatar nation from the Crimea in May 1944.

below: The 'Big Three' – Stalin, Roosevelt and Churchill – meet for the first time at the Tehran Conference in November 1943. This – not Yalta – was the most decisive Allied meeting of the war.

above: The remains of Tadeusz Ruman's plane, which he just
managed to crash-land back at his RAF base in southern Italy
after a tortuous trip to Warsaw to provide aid during the uprising.

below: Zbigniew Wolak (bottom left) with friends in Britain
immediately after the war. Shortly after this picture was taken
he decided to return to Soviet-controlled Poland.

above: Soviet forces in front of the ruins of the German parliament, the Reichstag, in May 1945.

left: Halina Szopińska, a member of the Polish underground Home Army, who was captured and tortured by the NKVD in December 1944. She then served ten years in prison.

below: John Noble and his father. Both of them were imprisoned by the Soviet authorities after the war in 'Special camp Number 2' – the Soviet name for the former Nazi concentration camp, Buchenwald.

left: Two soldiers of the Red Army during the Battle for Budapest in the early weeks of 1945. The behaviour of some of the Soviet troops in the aftermath of this battle would become infamous.

below: Dinner at the Yalta Conference, February 1945. Churchill is flanked by Molotov (far right) and a sick-looking President Roosevelt. The latter's poor condition was remarked on by many who attended the conference.

VE (Victory in Europe) Day in London, May 1945. These happy scenes were far removed from the reality that prevailed in much of Eastern Europe, particularly Poland, where, under the Soviet occupation, there was a good deal less to celebrate.

The Victory Parade held in London on 8 June 1946. Notable by their absence from this vast celebration were the fighting forces of Poland. The Polish soldiers who had fought with the British were not invited to participate.

Uprising was mentioned, it was in the context of a desire to carry
out elections in Poland based on 'universal suffrage'. At the end
Mikołajczyk did say directly to Stalin: 'I now have to ask you to
order help to be given to our units fighting in Warsaw', but the
force of the appeal had been blunted by all the preceding verbiage.

Stalin replied: 'I shall give the necessary orders'. (Those who
were familiar with Stalin would have noted the presence of the
word 'necessary' – after all, what constituted a 'necessary' order in
these circumstances would be a matter of individual interpretation.) He then remarked that he had noticed the absence in
Mikołajczyk's remarks of any reference to the Committee of
National Liberation – the Lublin Poles – with whom the Soviets
had already concluded an agreement. 'Could you not,' asked
Stalin, 'possibly realize the importance of this fact?'

Mikołajczyk's reply was lengthy and emotional, including the
plea that: 'The four main Polish political parties which are represented in this government [the London Poles] and have for five
years carried on the struggle against Germany should have a say
in the matter.' But all this was wasted on Stalin, who, when
Mikołajczyk had concluded, coldly asked: 'Have you finished?'

Stalin then said that he had agreed to meet the Poles, at the
instigation of Churchill, in order to discuss a 'union' with the
Lublin Poles. Mikołajczyk answered with the extraordinary request
that he be allowed 'to go to Warsaw'. It took Stalin to remind him:
'The Germans are there.'

Stalin and Mikołajczyk essentially then restated their respective
positions. Stalin wanted the London Poles to deal with the Lublin
Poles, and Mikołajczyk reiterated that, although he was willing to
cooperate, the Lublin Poles 'represent but a very small section of
Polish opinion'.

The two sides may have been talking to each other, but there
was certainly no meeting of minds. Stalin felt he could speak
progressively more frankly, openly revealing his scorn for the
Polish Home Army: 'What is an army without artillery, tanks and
an air force? They are even short of rifles. In modern warfare such
an army is of little use. They are small partisan units, not a regular

army. I was told that the Polish government had ordered these units to drive the Germans out of Warsaw. I wonder how they could possibly do this – their forces are not up to that task. As a matter of fact these people do not fight against the Germans, but only hide in woods, being unable to do anything else.'

Just over an hour into the meeting, Stalin showed his contempt for the Poles by taking a phone call from one of his colleagues. When he had finished, he reiterated his position that what the Soviets faced was the danger that 'the Poles quarrel amongst themselves', adding ominously that: 'We shall never allow this.'

Stalin was, of course, deliberately misrepresenting events – as the Poles in the room with him knew very well. Mikołajczyk had stated the truth. There was no comparison in terms of political experience or political popularity between the representatives of the Polish government in exile and the group that the Soviets had sanctioned in Lublin. Stalin was not comparing like with like. But the Soviet leader never had any problem with basing an argument on a falsehood and then forcefully sticking to it. It was brutal politics based on enormous military power – and immensely effective. Indeed, so intransigent was Stalin on the question of the need for the London Poles to negotiate with the Lublin Poles that the conversation reached a point where the minute-taker felt compelled to write: 'There is a general feeling that the discussion has become futile....'

Next, Mikołajczyk tried to reason with Stalin on the question of the position of the eastern border of Poland after the war. But Stalin, who had proved firm on this question in the face of Roosevelt and Churchill, was certainly not going to alter his position on the modified Curzon Line now. Flying on a wave of self-righteousness, he remarked portentously that: 'I am too old to act against my conscience.'

Then, once again, Stalin interrupted the meeting to take a phone call. Shortly afterwards he asked, clearly wanting to end the meeting, if the Poles had 'any other subjects to discuss with me'? Mikołajczyk said he hadn't, 'apart from these two major issues concerning Polish–Soviet relations and the frontiers'. And so the meeting ended just before midnight.

It had been a remarkable encounter. The relatively inexperienced Mikołajczyk had been humiliated by Stalin, but he himself had been partly to blame. Instead of focusing the meeting on the one practical measure that was needed at that moment – support for the Warsaw Uprising – he tried both to pretend he was dealing with an equal, one political leader talking to another, and to use this encounter to discuss matters that he already knew from a briefing from the British ambassador to Moscow were anathema to the Soviets.

In sharp contrast to Stalin's reticence to help the Poles, Churchill reacted quickly to the plight of the inhabitants of Warsaw. Their fight in the streets and parks of the city was precisely the sort of romantic endeavour that would appeal to him. On 4 August, the day after Stalin had met the Polish delegation in Moscow, Churchill sent a cable to the Soviet leader saying that: 'At the urgent request of the Polish underground army, we are dropping, subject to weather, about 60 tons of equipment and ammunition into the south-western quarter of the city, where, it is said, a Polish revolt against the Germans is in fierce struggle. They also say that they appeal for Russian aid, which seems very near. They are being attacked by one and a half German divisions. This may be of help to your operations.'[7]

Tadeusz Roman[8] was one of the Polish RAF pilots who tried to help the insurgents in Warsaw. Twenty-five years old, he had served time in a Soviet prison after being caught trying to flee from eastern Poland. After the armistice of 1941 he had made his way west and, always a keen flyer, joined RAF Bomber Command. He was now based at Brindisi in southern Italy as part of the Polish Flight. For him it was a matter of honour – and familial love – to help: 'They were my friends there [in Warsaw]. My brother was there [in Poland] in the underground army – he could have been [though he wasn't] in Warsaw. Nobody refused [to help], not a single person.'

It was a long and dangerous flight from southern Italy to Warsaw – one of the longest and most dangerous of the war, taking between ten and eleven hours. Starting on 4 August, flights left both Bari and Brindisi, with the airmen of the 1568th Polish Flight initially dominating the operation. Between then and the end of September more than two hundred flights were made – dropping a total of more than 100 tons of supplies.[9] Around 80 Polish airmen lost their lives in the operation, together with more than one hundred other Allied flyers – many of them South African.

The danger for the bombers was not just the air defences around Warsaw but the lengthy and tortuous route over German-occupied territory on the way to the Polish capital and back again. 'It was a long trip,' says Tadeusz Roman, 'and the Germans knew we were coming.' Tadeusz's own luck ran out early in the morning of 28 August. Just after he and his comrades had dropped their supplies over Warsaw – flying low, at around 2000 feet – and as they began the journey back, anti-aircraft fire smashed into one of their engines. They kept going, but near Kraków they were hit again. Even so, Tadeusz and his crew managed to coax the plane back to base in Italy, crash-landing on the airport perimeter – with just five minutes' fuel left in the tanks. 'I went on my knees,' says Tadeusz, 'and kissed the mother soil. You know our Pope [John Paul II], when he was going to various [places] always kissed it [the ground]. I said he took this from me!' For his skill and bravery in piloting the damaged plane home, Tadeusz Roman was awarded the Distinguished Flying Medal. The other three planes that accompanied him on the mission to Warsaw that night never returned.

Meantime, Prime Minister Mikołajczyk had left Moscow and returned to London. His last meeting with Stalin, in the Kremlin on the evening of 9 August,[10] had been bizarre. After Mikołajczyk had told the Soviet leader that his talks over the last couple of days with the Lublin Poles had convinced him that 'we shall eventually reach an agreement' he asked Stalin once again for 'immediate assistance' for Warsaw. 'All these struggles in Warsaw seem to me unreal,' replied the Soviet leader. 'It would be different if our armies were approaching Warsaw, but unfortunately this is not the case.' He went on to explain that 'a vigorous counter-attack' by the Germans had prevented the Red Army moving towards the Polish capital. 'I am sorry for your men who started the battle in

Warsaw prematurely and have to fight tanks, artillery and aircraft with rifles....What can an airlift do? We can supply a certain quantity of rifles and machine guns but we cannot parachute cannons.... Are you quite sure that arms parachuted from the air will reach the Poles?' None the less, added Stalin, 'We must try. How much assistance are you asking for and where would you like us to drop the arms?' The discussion then moved on to examine the practicalities of the air drop – there was even a suggestion from Stalin that a Soviet officer with a codebook be dropped into Warsaw in order to allow secure communication between the Home Army and the Soviet troops outside.

All of which raises the important question: how is it possible to reconcile Stalin's sudden promise on 9 August to help the Home Army in Warsaw with what actually happened? After all, just four days later the Soviet TASS news agency announced that, since the London Poles had not notified the Soviets in advance of the uprising, all responsibility for what was now happening in Warsaw lay with them. And then, on the night of 15 August, the American ambassador, Averell Harriman, had a meeting at the Kremlin with Soviet Foreign Ministry officials, which led him to send a telegram to the USA saying: 'The Soviet Government's refusal [to help the uprising] is not based on operational difficulties, nor on a denial of the conflict, but on ruthless political calculations.'[11] Finally, on the 22nd, Stalin made his position clear personally in the most strident and insulting terms possible. He described the Home Army as a 'bunch of criminals', and stated that the Soviets would refuse to help the Western Allies with the airlift.

So was this change in position just another straightforward example of Stalin's mendacity? Significantly, towards the end of the last meeting with Mikołajczyk, when the Polish Prime Minister asked: 'Would you tell us something to comfort the Polish hearts at this difficult time?' (the kind of emotional request that Churchill could always fulfil with immediate and often lachrymose power), Stalin replied: 'Surely you attach too much importance to words? One should distrust words. Deeds are more important than words.'

And, clearly, as far as 'deeds' were concerned, Stalin failed the Poles in Warsaw. But it is possible that when Stalin met Mikołajczyk on 9 August he had still not definitively made up his mind. He had, as yet, given no reply to the Western Allies about his position on the uprising. One possible reading of the history is that between the meeting with Mikołajczyk on the 9th and the TASS statement on the 13th Stalin changed his mind. On 9 August he was inclined to help; by the 13th he had decided he wouldn't.

At first sight such a reading of the evidence seems hardly persuasive. Hadn't Stalin already shown that he wanted to destroy the Home Army? But we must not read back into history what we know subsequently happened. In August 1944 Stalin knew he faced battles ahead with the Western Allies over the composition of any future Polish administration. He had no reason to suppose that the British and Americans would eventually go along with his wishes and recognize a modified version of his puppet government. Maybe he felt that summer that if the London Poles agreed to be subsumed into the Lublin Poles then he had to offer some kind of assistance to the Warsaw Uprising as a kind of primitive quid pro quo.

We can't know for sure. Probably, Stalin was always inclined to act as he did and refuse help to the Poles in Warsaw. That refusal fits a consistent pattern of behaviour, one in which the Soviet leader had demonstrated time and time again his distrust of the Poles and his desire to see the Home Army disbanded and 'neutralized'. But if Stalin did always intend to dismiss the Poles' request for help, then there was no need for him to go as far as he did in appearing to accede to their requests at the meeting of 9 August. In his first meeting with Mikołajczyk on the 3rd Stalin had been careful only to say he was issuing 'necessary' orders about the uprising. And he could have been just as evasive on the 9th.

In any event, by 13 August Stalin had made up his mind, and during August, the crucial period of the rising, the Soviets refused to offer any assistance with the air supplies. And although it is arguable whether or not the Red Army could have reached Warsaw in August – they faced a military setback on the 2nd when the Germans mounted a counter-attack on the front line east of the city – what is certain is that they could have made the air bridge work much more successfully if they had wanted to. But they didn't. In fact, a statement made by an official from the Soviet Commissariat for Foreign Affairs to the American ambassador on 18 August made their policy quite clear: 'The Soviet government cannot, of course, object to English or American aircraft dropping arms in the region of Warsaw, since this is an American and British affair. But they decidedly object to British or American aircraft, after dropping arms in the region of Warsaw, landing on Soviet Territory, since the Soviet Government do not wish to associate themselves either directly or indirectly with the adventure in Warsaw.'[12] In the light of Stalin's position, Churchill tried to enlist Roosevelt's help in sending a combative reply, only to be told on 26 August by the American President that: 'I do not consider that it would prove advantageous to the long-range general war prospect for me to join you in the proposed message to UJ (Uncle Joe, i.e., Stalin).'[13]

Hugh Lunghi, as a member of the British military mission to Moscow, went with the chief of staff of the mission to the Soviet Ministry of Defence to try to get the Soviets to help with the air supplies: 'I must have gone there with him almost daily for the first two weeks, and afterwards it became sort of hopeless. We realized they were not going to allow either us or the Americans to land on Soviet territory. And this seemed to us the most terrible betrayal, not only of the Poles but of the [Western] Allies. And again, another example of Stalin cutting off his nose to spite his own face, because it meant the Germans would put down this uprising more easily and then the remaining Germans would be available to oppose the Soviet army. So it seemed quite crazy to us, but also terrible. We were fuming. We were absolutely furious in the military mission.'

Of course, there was a sense in which Stalin's action was not 'cutting off his nose to spite his own face', because if he stood back and did nothing, then the Home Army, which he openly dispar-aged, would almost certainly be annihilated. And that is what was now happening inside Warsaw. During August, German SS soldiers, supported by various collaborators – including Cossacks from the

15th Cossack Cavalry Corps – conducted a brutal house-to-house war in the Polish capital.

The most notorious SS unit in Warsaw was led by Oskar Dirlewanger. This ruthless commander (who, although a brute, was certainly not an ignorant brute – he gained a PhD in political science in the 1920s) presided over a gang of ill-disciplined and bloodthirsty soldiers. Most of them were convicted criminals released from captivity and they were already infamous for their mistreatment of civilians in the occupied Soviet Union.

Matthias Schenk,[14] a Belgian conscripted into the German army, was eighteen years old when he served as a demolition engineer in Warsaw alongside the SS Sturmbrigade Dirlewanger, and the sights he saw haunt him still: 'Once we went towards a house [which served as a school] with 350 children. We went upstairs and the children came down – children of nine to thirteen years old. They held up their hands [and said]: "*Nicht Partisan!*" [Not Partisan!] and they stood on the steps. And the SS started to shoot. And then the commander said: "No ammunition – use the butt of the gun!" And the blood spilled down the stairs.'

This was not an isolated crime, for the Axis units in the city committed a whole series of atrocities. And many of them witnessed by Matthias Schenk seem purely sadistic: 'In front of my position was a little girl, ten or twelve years old and she had probably lost her way and stood there frightened. She looked at me, lifted her hand and said "*Nicht Partisan!*" And I asked her to come towards me and then her small head burst in the air. And then [the SS officer next to him] said: "Wasn't that a master shot!"'

In other incidents during the uprising, Schenk witnessed members of the SS demonstrating their warped sense of 'fun'. Early in the uprising, the unit had 'adopted' a Polish boy of about twelve or thirteen who was disabled. He only had one leg and would hobble about on crutches performing menial tasks for the soldiers: 'One day, they [the soldiers] asked him to come close to them, and I saw that they stuck something into his trouser pocket and then I saw the signal and then they asked him to move very fast – run away. The boy was jumping around and then he flew up in the air. They had put hand grenades in his pocket. And that's how it was every day in Warsaw.... Women and children were absolutely slaughtered.'

When a hospital held by the Home Army was stormed by the Dirlewanger brigade, he saw, in the aftermath, Polish nurses sexually assaulted by the SS: 'They tore the clothes off these women and jumped on top of them, held them down by way of force...then they were raped.' That night half a dozen nurses were subjected to a final, gross assault when they were paraded with their hands above their heads in the 'Adolf Hitler Platz' in the centre of Warsaw: 'Then Dirlewanger drove them through the [German] crowd, which cajoled and applauded them to the gallows.'

The appalling actions that Matthias Schenk witnessed were not isolated incidents of brutality, but part of a systematic German plan to crush the uprising. Under the overall command of SS General Erich von dem Bach-Zelewski, who had previously overseen the shooting of Jews and partisans in the occupied Soviet Union, the Germans targeted civilians as well as members of the Home Army. By 8 August, in one district of the city alone, the Germans had killed at least forty thousand civilians.

The overall atmosphere of the German action against the Poles was captured by the SS commander-in-chief Heinrich Himmler, who later stated that he had told Hitler at the time of uprising that: 'From the historical point of view the action of the Poles is a blessing.... Warsaw will be liquidated; and this city which is the intellectual capital of a sixteen to seventeen million strong nation that has blocked our path to the east for seven hundred years...will have ceased to exist. By the same token... the Poles themselves will cease to be a problem, for our children and for all who follow us.'[15]

Himmler's use of language is significant. The phrase 'the Poles themselves will cease to be a problem, for our children and for all who follow us' is reminiscent of the 'justification' he gave to senior Nazis for the extermination of Jewish children. They had to be killed along with their parents, said Himmler, because otherwise they would only cause problems for future generations of Nazis. (At Poznań in Poland in October 1943, Himmler had said in a speech to SS officers: 'We come to the question: how is it with the [Jewish] women and the children? I have resolved even here on a completely clear solution. That is to say I do not consider myself justified in eradicating the men – so to speak killing or ordering them killed – and allowing the avengers in the shape of the children to grow up for our sons and grandsons.')[16]

Danuta Gałkowa[17] was twenty years old at the time of the uprising, fighting the Germans in the centre of Warsaw. And on 2 September she experienced personally the brutality of the German troops and their auxiliaries when she took a wounded comrade to the 'hospital under the lantern', a makeshift medical station just outside the walls of the old town. Inside the hospital, in the dark basement rooms where the wounded were treated, she heard German auxiliary soldiers arriving outside. A male friend said: 'Lie down on this stretcher – I'll cover you with a blanket', and she hurriedly managed to hide as the soldiers stormed into the hospital. The first group of soldiers searched for valuables on the wounded, such as gold crosses and watches, but those that followed – many of whom were drunk – came in and raped the women: 'It was for them, and I am sorry that I use this word, it was for them entertainment. They were excited by the fact that the people were yelling.... I was in despair, I was afraid only of rape, because I wouldn't be able to live through that.'

Danuta managed to remain concealed, but she 'heard these voices. "Sister, help!" The tragic voices. "Colleagues, don't abandon me!" I felt helpless.' Inside the cellar the soldiers rampaged around in a frenzy of sadistic sexual excitement. The wounded men of the Home Army who were present could do nothing to protect the women: 'Normally every boy defends a girl, but here when he was wounded in the stomach or his legs were broken and he had only one hand he could move, what could he do? Nothing!'

All this horror lasted 'from eight in the morning until it became dark.... When it was getting dark they left.' As they went, the German auxiliaries set fire to the hospital. Danuta then tried to escape, dragging with her the wounded Home Army officer who had protected her on the stretcher: 'I pulled him to the entrance, and in front of us there was a fourteen-year-old boy who was also crawling up the steps to the street. And this one enemy soldier, he shot him in the head and the boy just said: "Oh, mamma!" and he fell right in front of our feet.' The German auxiliary then turned his gun on Danuta but it jammed, and in the chaos and smoke she managed to get away and find another door that led on to the courtyard of the hospital: 'I opened it and there was a terrible sight of executed people – girls without gowns who had been raped and murdered.' In the darkness she made her escape, together with her wounded companion. Eventually, after many adventures, this man who had saved her became her husband.

CHURCHILL MEETS ANDERS

While the battle for Warsaw raged, Winston Churchill met with General Anders at Polish military headquarters in northern Italy. In the context of the controversy over the future of Poland, this meeting, on 26 August, was one of the most revealing of the war. Churchill, who knew that this would be – at the very least – an awkward encounter, began by congratulating Anders on the performance of the Polish II Corps during the campaign in Italy[18] and enquired about the 'mood' of the soldiers 'given what they are going through at the moment'.

Anders replied that the spirit of his men was 'excellent', but that their 'one great concern is the future of Poland, and at the moment, the current situation in Warsaw'.

'I realize this too,' said Churchill. 'Together with President Roosevelt I asked Stalin to help those fighting in Warsaw: our first request was met with no answer at all, our next request met with a negative response.... We are not ready for action over Warsaw, but we are currently doing everything in our power to provide aid via the air route.'

Churchill then referred to his 'speech last winter' when, in the House of Commons, immediately after the Tehran Conference, he had said that the Poles must be prepared to negotiate away some of their eastern territory in exchange for an agreement with the Soviet Union.

'We were and still are upset with you about this, Prime Minister,' said Anders.

'In entering into a pact with Poland,' replied Churchill, 'Great Britain never guaranteed Polish borders; we guaranteed and made a pledge to Poland as to its existence as a free, independent state, totally sovereign, strong, large, that the citizens living within it might live happily and with the possibility of free development without any foreign influences threatening from the outside.' (This was certainly disingenuous, since Churchill himself had written to Eden in 1942 that the Soviet occupation of eastern Poland was contrary to the 'principles of freedom and democracy set forth in the Atlantic Charter'.)[19] The Prime Minister then expressed to Anders the same view he had voiced at Tehran, that the Poles would receive 'much better lands in the west' in exchange for the eastern territories of the 'Prypet marshes'.

Anders replied that 'the issue of borders can be definitively sorted out only at a Peace Conference, after the war is completely over'. Churchill agreed that 'these issues can only be decided at a peace conference' and assured Anders that he would be invited to that conference, adding: 'You must trust us. Since Great Britain entered this war to defend your independence, then I can assure you that we will never abandon you.'

These words were similar to those that Churchill had spoken to Anders at their last meeting in Cairo, straight after the Tehran Conference. And once again Anders reiterated his warning about the Soviet Union – a warning given with the authority of a man who had tasted Soviet injustice first hand in the cells of the Lubyanka. 'We cannot trust Russia,' said Anders, 'since we know it well, and we know that all of Stalin's declarations that he wants a free and strong Poland are lies and fundamentally false…. As they enter Poland, the Soviets arrest and deport our women and children deep into Russia as they did in 1939; they disarm the soldiers of our Home Army, they shoot dead our officers and arrest our civil administration, destroying those who fought the Germans continuously since 1939 and fight them still. We have our wives and children in Warsaw, but we would rather they perish than have to live under the Bolsheviks. All of us prefer to perish fighting than to live on our knees.'

The minutes record that Churchill was 'very moved' by these words and emphasized once again that Britain would never abandon Poland, before adding: 'I know that the Germans and Russians are destroying all of your best elements, especially intellectual spheres. I sympathize deeply. But you must trust – we will not abandon you and Poland will be happy.'

Anders, not surprisingly, was somewhat suspicious of Churchill's words. He reminded the British Prime Minister that the Soviet Union would be immensely strong after the war; but then Churchill, in a curious answer, talked of the 'capabilities of Britain and the United States' being 'unlimited' and that after the war 'the United States and Britain will have vast supplies of planes, guns and tanks'. He was not saying directly that the Western Allies would go to war with the Soviet Union, once Germany was defeated, if Stalin refused to allow for a free and independent Poland; but his reply certainly implied the possibility of military action – something that Churchill had explicitly ruled out earlier in the year.

THE END OF THE UPRISING

Stalin may have decided at the latest by the middle of August that the Soviet Union would not support the Home Army in Warsaw, but his policy towards the uprising was still not completely coherent. On 18 September the Soviet authorities surprisingly allowed one flight of American bombers en route to Warsaw to refuel on Soviet territory. In addition, for two weeks, between 14 and 28 September, the Soviets themselves dropped supplies on Warsaw. But since the drops were conducted without parachutes, much of the 50 or so tons that the Soviets provided was destroyed on landing.

It appears that Stalin, as he must have been during the 9 August meeting with the Polish Prime Minister in exile, was once again concerned about the effect on world opinion of Soviet inaction in the face of the destruction of Warsaw. His solution to this propaganda problem seems to have been to demonstrate public support to the Home Army but without offering any effective assistance.

And then there was the most curious action of all. On the night of 14 September several patrols from the 1st Polish Army, serving with the Red Army and commanded by the Polish collaborator General Zygmunt Berling, landed on the western bank of the Vistula in the suburbs of Warsaw, and then made contact with Home Army soldiers. Several more landings were attempted on successive nights until around three thousand men of the 1st Polish Army were in contact with the Poles fighting in Warsaw. Fewer than one in three of Berling's men ever made it back across the Vistula.

Zbigniew Wolak was one of the Home Army soldiers who watched as Berling's men tried to establish a bridgehead on the riverbank. His emotions were mixed. Although he appreciated any help from whatever source, he was shocked to see that a number of the officers of this 'Polish' army were Russian. He felt a 'strong feeling of humiliation' at the sight. 'Making such a parody! You dress up a Russian who doesn't even speak Polish....' They were unruly. They were not elegant. They had no discipline. They looked more like riff-raff.... You see, a few months earlier he was a forestry worker and [now] has to pretend he's a captain, a major, a colonel! And they would address themselves "comrade", stressing the political character of the army. Just imagine someone in a British uniform, and he is a staunch enemy of the British. Just imagine such a person, and he is a superior of the Polish officers!'

It proved impossible for Berling's men to hold the bridgehead, and by the last week of September those who were still able retreated across the river. This was the only attempt made on the ground to help those fighting the Germans in the Warsaw Uprising, and it was a costly failure. It was clear that only a massive and coordinated assault by the Red Army could shake the Germans – something that was clearly not going to happen. That autumn Marshal Rokossovsky, commanding the Red Army outside Warsaw, didn't even bother to reply to the increasingly desperate requests for help from the Polish insurgents inside the capital.

The troops of the 1st Polish Army, fighting with the advancing Red Army, were themselves devastated by the fate of Warsaw. 'We waited. It was very tense,' says Jan Karniewicz,[20] then a young soldier in Berling's army. Like many ordinary Poles, he had ended up fighting with the Red Army by accident rather than intention. He had been deported from eastern Poland along with the rest of his family in February 1940. Then, after the German invasion in June 1941 and the subsequent armistice, he had wanted to join Anders' army but had been too young, and so a year later he joined Berling's men. He had joined the Polish unit that fought with the Red Army not out of political commitment to the Communist or Soviet cause – he describes himself at the time as a 'simple soldier, a marksman' – but because it was the only way he could fight to liberate his native land. Now he watched as 'the Germans set fire to buildings, all autumn...there was an aura over Warsaw in the evening – a red aura, a pink aura.... I felt like the capital is burning. If the capital is not liberated, it will be burnt down at any minute.... Warsaw is dying. National culture – Polish culture – is dying. You feel all this will be lost and destroyed and won't be regained.'

On 2 October General Tadeusz Bór, commander of the Home Army, signed an instrument of surrender with General von dem Bach-Zelewski, and the Warsaw Uprising was over. In order to end the bloody house-to-house fighting, the Germans had been forced to concede that any Home Army prisoners they took would be regarded as captured combatants, not 'bandits', and that they would treat the civilians with humanity – a promise that was, most certainly, not universally kept. The Germans then proceeded to destroy Warsaw, brick by brick, until when, early in 1945, Jan Karniewicz finally entered the city he found that 'Warsaw was just a lot of rubble. There were some walls and the burnt-out skeletons of buildings the Germans hadn't bothered or hadn't had time to dynamite. It was terrible.... You know there must be sacrifices – there's no war without sacrifices and without victims. Warsaw made the sacrifice. I felt like a person does when he sees a boat go down in the open sea and there is nothing you can do. You can't help. The same with Warsaw. Warsaw was being destroyed and there was nothing we could do, because there was no order and that's why we couldn't help.'

Without support from the Red Army, the Warsaw Uprising was always doomed. And despite his promise to help, given on 9 August, and despite the equivocal and limited Soviet actions in September, it is clear that Stalin had decided he was going to stand back and let the Home Army be destroyed by the Germans. Churchill described the Soviet behaviour at the time as 'strange and sinister',[21] but it was nothing of the kind. It was purely – and brutally – pragmatic. The Soviets had already shown by their arrest of Home Army officers their feelings about this powerful and independent partisan force, and now Stalin simply seized the opportunity to have one enemy, the Germans, eliminate another, the Polish Home Army. This cynical political decision had been demonstrated in the form of military action when, towards the end of August, the Red Army under Marshal Tolbukhin moved to attack Romania rather than Warsaw. Militarily, it was obvious that the Soviets had decided to leave the Polish capital for another day – when the opposition inside, both Polish and German, was spent.

As for the decision to launch the uprising without first obtaining a commitment from the Soviet Union to coordinate an attack, that turned out to be, as the Polish commander in chief back in London had feared, a terrible mistake – though it was an understandable mistake. Even if the uprising had not occurred the Home Army would almost certainly have been subsequently eliminated by the NKVD. But the cost of the decision to try to take the Polish capital was immense. Around 220,000 Poles died (200,000 of them civilians) as a result of the uprising, and all that was accomplished – in practical, if not romantic, terms – was the destruction of both Warsaw and the Home Army that sought to liberate their capital.

It is hard not to agree with the judgement of General Anders, expressed in a letter in the autumn of 1944: 'It [the Warsaw Uprising] didn't have the slightest chance of success, and exposed all parts of the country still under German occupation to new and appalling repressions. No one who is not dishonest or blind could have had the least illusion that everything which had happened was always going to happen: i.e. not only that the Soviets will refuse to help our beloved heroic Warsaw but also that they will watch with the greatest pleasure as our nation's blood is drained to the last drop.'[22]

The practical attitude of the Soviet authorities in the aftermath of the uprising can be seen in their treatment of Halina Szopińska,[23] then twenty-four years old. She had fought with the Home Army in Warsaw and, as the moment neared for their capitulation, had felt betrayed by the Soviets. Not only had the Red Army not come to their rescue, but she and her comrades believed that the air drops organized by the Soviets in the last days of the uprising had been a sham: 'They had these small planes and would throw dry bread without a parachute and when it fell down it would just break into powder.... They would drop guns without a parachute – ammunition as well. There was no way we could repair it. So they pretended they were helping. They were doing it in such a way that it wouldn't really help us.'

Once the uprising was over, Halina, who had served both as a fighter and then as a nurse for the Home Army, pretended to be a civilian and left the city amongst the non-combatants. She then managed to escape and made her way home to her mother-in-law's house. But a few weeks later one of her Home Army superiors ordered her to move back towards Warsaw. It was there, by the frozen Vistula, that she was captured by the Red Army. She was taken to a nearby house and interrogated by an NKVD officer in his early twenties.

By the end of August the NKVD had been told to detain and interrogate all Poles who had taken part in the fight for Warsaw and who had managed to 'escape' into the Soviet part of occupied Poland.

'What were you doing in the uprising?' the NKVD officer asked her. 'If you lie, then I'll prove you are lying because I know everything.'

Halina said nothing 'concrete' to him. And as a result: 'He would hit me, beat me.... He called me "whore". "Bloody whore" in Russian. "You'll die," he said.... He kicked me and I fell off [the chair] on to the floor and then he kicked me and beat me [again]. He hit me in the back of the head [but] he kicked first and foremost....He had hatred – hatred, hatred – to Poles. That's how he was brought up.'

On her second day in captivity she was called into a room where three Soviet officers – one of them a woman – were waiting for her. What happened next, she feels even today, was the most degrading moment she faced in what turned out to be a long period of captivity. They told her to take her clothes off, and when she was naked, and in full view of the male officers, the female officer gave her a 'gynaecological check-up'. When she was finished she cleaned her fingers on a newspaper, lit a cigarette and told Halina to go to the toilet – but the toilet door had to be kept open so that they could check that she 'didn't kill herself'. All of this process, she says, 'was maybe the worst and most humiliating [ordeal] for a woman'.

Several days later, the young NKVD officer who had beaten her placed food in front of Halina – sausage, wine, tea, buns and sugar. 'He thinks I'll speak for that price,' thought Halina. She leaned forward and drank the tea, then said: 'I won't speak.' He hit her hard and she started crying and sobbing once more. But then she saw a mouse in the room, feasting on a lump of sugar, and this sight made her suddenly laugh. 'He thought I was crazy,' she says, 'but in such a misfortune – such a funny incident.'

It was clear to Halina from her interrogation just what the Soviet authorities thought of both the Home Army and the Western Allies: 'For them [the NKVD] we were spies. They said we [in the Home Army] were cooperating with the English and the Germans – that together with the English and the Germans we were fighting the Russians.' Halina was sentenced to ten years in prison. '[They said] that I was spying for the Germans and the English. That's what I was accused of.... It was enough for you to be a member of the Home Army. You were abandoned.' In Lublin

Castle prison she learnt how other Poles – some former members of the Home Army – were executed by firing squad. She heard how the officer in command of the execution squad would shout out: 'Shoot at the traitor of the motherland.' And then, 'When we went for a walk [in the exercise yard], after the execution, you could see human brains on the wall.'

One day, early in her sentence, Halina was given a further insight into the mentality of the people who held her captive. A Soviet commission arrived and enquired whether anyone had any complaints about the way they were treated. 'I said: "Yes,"' says Halina. 'In the basement – it was December – there were three water taps and three toilets and twenty-something people had to wash and piss in ten minutes. Is it possible? No.' After she had complained, one of the prison guards came to see her and said: 'OK, now you will have time to wash.' She took Halina and the other women who had complained down to the freezing basement that contained the toilets and water taps, and told them to strip naked and stand there all night. Next morning a senior officer arrived and asked them: 'Did you wash now?' The women didn't reply. They were then paraded in front of the other cells so that 'all the inmates would see what happens if you complain to the authorities'.

In the damp and unhealthy atmosphere of the prison, Halina contracted tuberculosis and was lucky to survive. But she was sustained by regular visits from her mother-in-law, who never gave up on Halina during her ten years in various Polish prisons. Halina's husband never came to visit her. After serving her full ten years, on the morning of her release Halina finally learnt from her mother-in-law the reason why: 'She said, "Child, you can't return there [back to her home]. There's another woman there with one child already and another on the way."'

Halina tried her best to begin a new life – without her husband and without her health. She was just one human casualty of the Soviet occupation of Poland. There were many, many more.

AN ENCOUNTER IN QUEBEC

In September 1944, Churchill and Roosevelt met in Quebec. This encounter in Canada is not known today as one of the iconic meetings of the war – not judged as important as Tehran, Yalta or the Newfoundland conference that spawned the Atlantic Charter. Nonetheless, it was a highly significant moment in the relationship between the two leaders – one that belies the mythical sense of chummy friendship between them that, fanned by rose-coloured wartime propaganda, has grown to be the dominant feature of their relationship in popular consciousness today.

Quebec was initially important because of something that was not discussed in any detail. Even though the Warsaw Uprising was still in progress and the insurgents were clamouring for more help than ever, the fate of Poland and Stalin's intentions for the future of the country did not figure prominently at the talks. Roosevelt was – true to form – dealing with this unpleasant political reality by largely ignoring it. The Home Army's fight inside Warsaw, like the death of the Poles at Katyn, was an inconvenient – though no doubt regrettable – smudge on the bigger picture. And Roosevelt was a big picture man.

And what was prominently discussed at Quebec was certainly big picture stuff – most notably the future of post-war Germany. This vital question had proved divisive at Tehran, as evidenced by the infamous dinner at which Stalin had called for at least fifty thousand Germans to be shot in the immediate aftermath of the war. And here at Quebec the issue of Germany's future was just as contentious. During dinner on 13 September – an encounter that rivalled the Tehran dispute for sheer emotion – Roosevelt asked his Secretary of the Treasury, Henry Morgenthau, to outline for Churchill just what the Americans had in mind. It was a strange request from the start, because the question of the future of Germany should have been a matter for the State Department, not the Treasury.

Morgenthau proceeded to describe one of the most radical and destructive proposals ever formulated by a democratic state in the twentieth century. Not only was Germany to be split into two countries, but all its industrial capacity was to be destroyed. Later in the twentieth century an American general threatened to bomb the Vietnamese 'back to the stone age'[24] – and economically at least, Morgenthau's plan for Germany was the equivalent during the Second World War.

Churchill, who trusted his emotional responses, was outraged. 'I had barely got under way,' recorded Morgenthau, 'before low mutters and baleful looks indicated that the Prime Minister was not the most enthusiastic member of my audience.... I have never seen him more irascible and vitriolic than he was that night.... After I finished my piece he turned loose on me the full flood of his rhetoric, sarcasm and violence. He looked on the Treasury plan, he said, as he would on chaining himself to a dead German.'[25]

Churchill further told Morgenthau that he felt his proposal was 'unnatural, unchristian and unnecessary'.[26] And according to his doctor, Lord Moran, who witnessed Churchill's protest, the British Prime Minister was clear that: 'I'm all for disarming Germany, but we ought not to prevent her living decently. There are bonds between the working classes of all countries, and the English people will not stand for the policy you are advocating.'[27]

There could scarcely have been a greater point of division between Britain and America over future policy than was evident that night. But then something quite extraordinary happened. Two days later Churchill withdrew his strident objections and endorsed the substance of Morgenthau's radical plan.

On 15 September, Churchill signed a continuation of a Lend Lease agreement with America that guaranteed the British $6.5 billion. This was the second great issue discussed at the talks, and one of vital importance to the British economy, which, as everyone knew, had been devastated by the war. According to Morgenthau's own notes, 'Churchill was quite emotional about the meeting and at one time had tears in his eyes.'[28] After the signing of the agreement, Churchill turned to Roosevelt and said how grateful he was – thanking him 'most effusively'. Then Churchill asked Morgenthau and Professor Lindemann (later Lord

Cherwell), the Prime Minister's scientific adviser: 'Where are the minutes on this matter of the Ruhr?'

Eventually Churchill ended up dictating his own version of the Morgenthau Plan, based on Morgenthau's notes, which retained the essential destructive character of the original. Memorably, Churchill added one key word to the line: 'This programme for eliminating the war-making industries in the Ruhr and the Saar is looking forward to converting Germany into largely an agricultural country.' In Churchill's version it became: 'This programme for eliminating the war-making industries in the Ruhr and the Saar is looking forward to converting Germany into a country primarily agricultural and pastoral.' The use of the word 'pastoral' – which became infamous – was probably intended to suggest 'an idealized view of agricultural life' and thus 'give a rose-tinted view of the plan's drastic implications'.[29]

Anthony Eden, the Foreign Secretary, was astonished at Churchill's volte face and remained adamantly opposed to the Morgenthau Plan. 'It was as if,' he wrote, 'one were to take the Black Country and turn it into Devonshire. I did not like the plan, nor was I convinced that it was to our national advantage. I said so....'[30] The Americans – including President Roosevelt – watched as the British Prime Minister and Foreign Secretary had a public row about the Morgenthau Plan in front of them. Churchill first tried to convince Eden of the advantages for British exports if the plan was implemented and Germany would no longer be an industrial competitor, but ultimately he said: 'After all, the future of my people is at stake, and when I have to choose between my people and the German people, I am going to choose my people.'[31]

Churchill had thus changed his position from believing that the American plan to destroy German industrial capacity was 'unnatural, unchristian and unnecessary' to one of steadfast support. It is scarcely credible that he made this reversal merely because of a sudden realization that Morgenthau's proposals benefited British industry – after all, the 'advantages' to British industry had been obvious when he had first heard the plan outlined. Much more likely is the straightforward explanation that Churchill went along with what the Americans wanted after they had signed the additional Lend Lease agreement.

That was certainly the view of one of the creators of the American plan, Morgenthau's assistant Harry Dexter White. He explicitly linked Churchill's difficulties in the negotiations with Roosevelt over Lend Lease (at one point Churchill was reduced to saying to the President: 'What do you want me to do, stand up and beg like Fala'[32] – Roosevelt's dog) with his immense gratitude once the deal was signed and his immediate desire to agree the Morgenthau Plan in return.

As for Roosevelt, there is little doubt that he wanted to be hard on Germany out of personal conviction. For years he had been wary of what he believed were the military tendencies of the Germans. The actions of the Nazis, following on from German aggression in the First World War and back into the nineteenth century, were – as he saw it – all part of a pattern. And the Nazis had as little time for Roosevelt as he did for them. Just before the war, in a speech made in 1939, Hitler had openly ridiculed Roosevelt's appeal for a Nazi commitment not to attack a number of specific countries. And Roosevelt would also have been aware of both Hitler's contempt for America as a racially 'impure' country and his disdain for its President as an individual – his physical disability would have clearly demonstrated his inferiority as far as Nazi ideology was concerned.

At the Casablanca Conference in 1943, Roosevelt had insisted that the Allies accept only 'unconditional' surrender from the Germans; and now, just before the Quebec meeting, on 19 August, Roosevelt had told Morgenthau: 'We have got to be tough with Germany and I mean the German people not just the Nazis. We either have to castrate the German people or you have to treat them in such a manner so they can't just go on reproducing people who want to continue the way they have in the past.'[33] And although Morgenthau swiftly replied that 'nobody is considering the question along those lines', the strength of the President's desire to be 'tough' on the Germans could scarcely have been more apparent.

But there was another dimension to Roosevelt's support for the Morgenthau Plan that must not be forgotten. The American President was acutely aware that another powerful world leader too wanted Germany drastically weakened after the war – Stalin. The Soviet leader had emphasized this desire not just at Tehran, but also more recently during his last meeting with the Polish Prime Minister in Moscow on 9 August, when he had closed the meeting with the words: 'I stand for all possible and impossible repressive measures against Germany.'[34] Consciously or unconsciously, Stalin's views were on Roosevelt's mind during the initial conversation about the Morgenthau Plan with Churchill at Quebec. The American President remarked that the de-industrialization of Germany was necessary because 'a factory which made steel furniture could be turned overnight to war production'.[35] This was exactly the sentiment he had heard Stalin express at Tehran. 'Are you going to let Germany produce modern metal furniture?' demanded the Soviet leader. 'The manufacture of metal furniture can be quickly turned into the manufacture of armament.'[36]

The Morgenthau Plan was thus exactly the kind of repressive measure against Germany that Stalin craved. Which makes it all the more significant that one of the authors of the plan – Harry Dexter White – was a Soviet spy, raising the intriguing possibility that Stalin, far from being absent from Quebec, had actually played a part in the creation of the Morgenthau Plan in the first place. White was named as a Soviet spy by the defecting Soviet agent Elizabeth Bentley as early as November 1945, but it was not until the release of the Venona decrypted Soviet intelligence material years later that his culpability was established beyond any reasonable doubt – something that the American Commission on Government Secrecy, chaired by Senator Daniel Patrick Moynihan, confirmed in 1997.

Thus the potential chain of causation is clear. White was one of the leading creators and proponents of the Morgenthau Plan, and through his Soviet handlers would have had knowledge of the views of the Soviet government – and Stalin – on the future of Germany. And although no one document in the Venona collection specifically links a message from White (variously codenamed Jurist,

Richard and Lawyer) to the Soviets on this exact subject, it is hardly credible that the subject was not discussed between him and his Soviet minder.

What is certain is that through his spies Stalin was informed about the nature and detail of Morgenthau's proposals. On 18 October the Venona code-breakers detected a message from Nathan Gregory Silvermaster, an economist at the War Production Board, to his Soviet spymasters that outlined the plan ('The Ruhr should be wrested from Germany and handed over to the control of some international council. Chemical, metallurgical, and electrical industries must be transported out of Germany.')[37] Silvermaster was one of the most productive of all the Soviet spies in the USA and helped to coordinate a large group of agents within the United States government. He had been suspected of being a Soviet agent as far back as 1942, but when confronted, he appealed to his bosses, including Harry Dexter White, who vouched for him. As a result, far from being removed from a position of influence, Silvermaster was promoted.

Within days of the Quebec Conference there was a storm of protest about the Morgenthau Plan. The American Secretary of State, Cordell Hull, was appalled not only that Morgenthau had been allowed to trespass so blatantly on an area of policy that did not belong to him, but that a plan had been proposed that would, in his judgement, so clearly result in the Germans resisting more fiercely. His health failing, Hull resigned in November 1944.

The press was just as antagonistic. The *New York Times* and *Washington Post* both attacked the plan as playing into the hands of the Nazis. And in Germany, the Morgenthau proposals were a gift for the Nazi propagandist Joseph Goebbels. 'In the last few days we have learned enough about the enemy's plans,' said Goebbels in a radio broadcast that autumn. 'The plan proposed by that Jew Morgenthau which would rob 80 million Germans of their industry and turn Germany into a simple potato field.'[38]

Roosevelt was taken aback at the scale of the attack on the Morgenthau Plan. He had – a rarity for him – misjudged the mood of his own nation and allowed a Nazi propaganda triumph. By the end of September he was back-tracking. On 29 September he told Cordell Hull that 'no one wants to make Germany a wholly agricultural nation again.... No one wants "complete eradication of German industrial production capacity in the Ruhr and the Saar".'[39] That same day, Roosevelt sent a letter to the press in which he said that nothing about Germany's post-war future had finally been agreed. Then, in early October, the President remarked to Henry Stimson, Secretary for War, that he 'had no idea how he [Morgenthau] had initiated this'.[40]

The Morgenthau Plan was quietly dropped in the radical form that had originally been proposed at Quebec, although the punitive philosophy behind it later found expression in the Joint Chiefs of Staff directive 1067, which stated that occupation forces should 'take no steps looking toward the economic rehabilitation of Germany [or] designed to maintain or strengthen the German economy'.[41]

CHURCHILL AND STALIN – MOSCOW IN OCTOBER

As we have seen, the summer and early autumn of 1944 were a time of conflict between the Allies – not just over what seemed the eternal question of Poland, but also over the question of the post-war shape of Europe, and, most particularly, Soviet intentions towards the eastern European countries they were shortly to occupy. And in the face of these difficulties Churchill resorted to the tactic he had first used in August 1942 during the row over the second front – he got on a plane and went to Moscow.

Perhaps surprisingly, Churchill was now to be at his most emollient towards Stalin. He had good cause to be angry – the Soviets were continuing to shun the Polish government in exile, and as he had said to Anders just a few weeks before, the 'Russians' were 'destroying' all of the 'best elements' in Poland, 'especially intellectual spheres'. But during these talks it was as if the row over the Warsaw Uprising had never happened.

In the Kremlin, at ten o'clock in the evening of 9 October,

back in the now familiar shabby surroundings of the Soviet leader's office, Churchill met Stalin once again. The Prime Minister suggested beginning with 'the most tiresome question – Poland'.[42] He remarked that 'at present each [of us] has a game cock in his hand' (meaning that the British were linked to the Polish government in exile in London and the Soviets to the Lublin Poles). Stalin laughed, and replied that 'it was difficult to do without the cock – they gave the morning signal'.

Churchill then said that the question of the post-war frontier of Poland was 'settled'. This was a strange remark given that the Polish government in exile, which the British recognized as the 'legitimate' government of Poland, still vehemently disagreed with the Soviet claim over eastern Poland. Stalin merely replied that 'if the frontier was agreed on the Curzon Line, it would help their discussion'.

Churchill added that if at some future peace conference 'some General Sosnkowski' objected, it 'would not matter' because the Americans and British thought the new border 'right and fair'. (Sosnkowski, as commander in chief of the Polish armed forces, had been outspoken in his attacks on Soviet policy towards Poland. Indeed, at a meeting held in Downing Street in May 1944, Churchill had even advised the Polish Prime Minister to drop Sosnkowski from his Cabinet – referring to him as 'Sozzle-something'.)[43]

Churchill asked Stalin if he thought it was 'worth while' to get the London Poles to fly to Moscow, saying that he had them 'tied up in an aircraft'. If they came to Moscow, he said, then 'with British and Russian agreement' they would be 'forced to settle'.

Stalin responded that he had no objection to the London Poles coming to Moscow, but stuck to the line he had used with the Poles a few weeks before, adding that Mikołajczyk 'would have to make contact with the committee [the Lublin Poles]'. After all, Stalin said, the Lublin Poles 'now had an army at its disposal and represented a force'.

What Stalin did not mention was the nature of the new Polish army at the 'disposal' of the Lublin Poles. Because at the same moment as Churchill was meeting with the Soviet leader in the

Kremlin, members of the Red Army like Georgy Dragunov were receiving rather bizarre instructions – direct from Stalin.[44] Dragunov was a pilot with a forward unit of the Soviet 6th air force in eastern Poland. Everyone in his unit was a Russian. But then one day in October 1944 'we were told that from tomorrow we had to fight under the flag of Poland. Some of them [his unit] said: "No. I would rather kill myself than fight as part of the Polish army."' But there was no choice. Dragunov's unit was to become 'Polish' overnight. Their planes were immediately painted in Polish colours and the squadron became part of a new Polish air force. However, there was a problem. None of the members of this new unit spoke a word of Polish. So they immediately enrolled for a crash course in the language. The Soviets were aware of the danger of dressing up their pilots as Poles – if they were shot down by the Germans, their enemy would have 'guessed everything'. So a rule was imposed. The planes became Polish immediately, but the pilots would only be allowed to dress up as Polish flyers once their language skills were good enough for them to pose as Poles. And within months 'the majority or our pilots were wearing Polish uniforms, and all our documents were in Polish'. Dragunov did not consider his actions in any way disreputable, believing merely that he was helping to start up a new Polish air force. This, then, along with Berling's units within the Red Army (which were to a large extent already staffed by Russian officers in Polish uniforms), was the new and suitably compliant 'force' that would be at the disposal of the Soviet-backed government of 'liberated' Poland.

But back in Moscow, when Stalin referred to the Soviet-controlled 'Polish' army, which in his eyes lent legitimacy and power to the Lublin Poles, Churchill was swift to point out that the 'other side' had an army as well. Part of it had 'held out in Warsaw', but 'they also had a brave army corps in Italy where they lost seven or eight thousand men. Then there was the armoured division, one brigade of which was in France.... They were good and brave men. The difficulty about the Poles was that they had unwise political leaders. Where there were two Poles there was one quarrel.' Stalin quipped 'that where there was one Pole he would begin to quarrel with himself through sheer boredom'.

The two leaders then moved on to discuss the future shape of much of the rest of Europe. It was during this discussion that Churchill produced what he called a 'naughty' document. This has become an infamous moment in the history of the war. As he took the paper out, Churchill said to Stalin that 'the Americans would be shocked if they saw how crudely he had put it. [But] Marshal Stalin was a realist.'[45] Churchill jokingly added that he himself was not sentimental 'while Mr Eden [who was also present] was a bad man'.

The handwritten document contained a series of percentages, outlining how much influence 'Russia' and other countries should have over specific European territory. The list was as follows:

'Romania: Russia 90%, the others 10%.

Greece: Britain (in accord with USA) 90%, Russia 10%.

Yugoslavia: 50/50%.

Hungary: 50/50%.

Bulgaria: Russia 75%, the others 25%.'

Stalin made one change to the document. He crossed out the percentages for Bulgaria and changed them to Russia 90 per cent and 'the others' 10 per cent.

It was at first sight an extraordinary moment. Here was one of the leading statesmen of the democratic world secretly bandying percentages of 'influence' over the countries of eastern Europe with a man who was recognized as a tyrant. It seemed almost reminiscent of the first meeting with Ribbentrop back in August 1939, when the Soviets had bargained with the Nazis over the fate of weaker countries who could not resist.

And this apparently callous way of trading other people's destinies continued in discussions held between Molotov and Eden the next day.[46] Here, in a series of meetings that are not as well known as the initial 'percentages' conversation, but are in their own way at least as revealing, the two foreign ministers swapped percentage figures as if they were used car dealers discussing prices. Molotov asked if they could not now agree to 'Bulgaria, Hungary and Yugoslavia, 75/25 per cent each'. Eden replied that such figures 'would be worse than the previous day', so Molotov countered with '90/10 for Bulgaria, 50/50 for Yugoslavia, and Hungary subject to amendment'. Molotov later bargained that 'if Hungary was 75/25, then Bulgaria should be 75/25 and Yugoslavia 60/40'. This, he said, was the 'limit' to which he would go. Just what, it might reasonably be asked, was going on?

Given that much of eastern Europe was to suffer under Soviet domination for most of the second half of the twentieth century, it is not hard to condemn the British for talking in such apparently heartless terms. But we must remember that Churchill and Eden could not be sure how matters would turn out. Moreover, there was enormous pressure on the British to get on with Stalin.

As Churchill talked with Stalin in the Kremlin, Soviet forces were about to liberate and then occupy Romania, Hungary and Bulgaria. So given this hard reality, Churchill must have thought he had to try and salvage something from the Red Army's rush into Europe. Gaining any immediate Western influence over these countries represented an advance on the current situation.

And then there was the question of the Americans. After the war American forces were to have a seemingly permanent presence in western Europe via their membership of NATO, but it is easy to forget that neither Roosevelt nor Churchill anticipated this development. Quite the reverse, in fact. At Tehran Roosevelt had emphasized to Churchill and Stalin that the Americans would only send 'planes and ships' to Europe in the event of any 'future threat to peace'.[47] In the context of this lukewarm American commitment to Europe, much of the responsibility for making any post-war European settlement succeed would fall to the British. And no post-war settlement could truly work without the cooperation of the Soviet Union.

Added to that straightforward political necessity, as the British saw it, was Churchill's continued perception of Stalin the individual. Stalin remained essentially quiet and thoughtful in meetings. Any vitriol that suddenly appeared could continue to be dismissed as part of the – utterly mistaken – belief that there were other people behind Stalin who occasionally intervened and forced him to be less accommodating. Indeed, in a telegram sent to the War Cabinet in the context of this very trip to Moscow, the Prime Minister wrote: 'There is no doubt that in our narrow circle we have talked with a...freedom and beau gest[e] never before attained between our two countries. Stalin has made several expressions of personal regard which I feel sure were sincere. But I repeat my conviction that he is by no means alone. "Behind the horseman sits dull care."'[48] This convenient method of dealing with any unwelcome news that emanated from the Kremlin had, it will be remembered, first been expressed by Churchill during his initial meeting with Stalin in the summer of 1942. It was a theory that evened out the inconsistencies and also, crucially, allowed Churchill and the British to give Stalin the benefit of the doubt. When he was relatively accommodating, this was the 'real' Stalin. When he was difficult and harsh, he was acting on the instructions of the dark forces behind him. But there was no 'dull care' sitting behind this 'horseman'. That such a misguided theory was accepted by Churchill reflects not only how little was known about how the Soviet state functioned but also, it must be said, a predisposed desire in the circumstances to see something that just was not there.

It was against all this background that Churchill sat down with Stalin to discuss 'percentages' of influence. And as the detailed bargaining between Molotov and Eden that followed the introduction of Churchill's 'naughty' document showed, this was a serious attempt – though also a crude and first draft one – to solve the new foreign policy issues in eastern Europe that the post-war world would throw up. But after the Molotov discussions had demonstrated the alacrity with which the Soviets wanted to bargain, and also exposed the immense ambiguity of the term 'percentages of influence' – which nobody who was involved defined exactly – any attempt to take the proposal further in any formal way was dropped. Nonetheless, Churchill believed that the 'naughty' document did inform Stalin's subsequent actions. Later in the year, for example, the Soviets did not interfere in British action in Greece (a country that Churchill had written was '90%' part of a British sphere of influence). But there is evidence that Stalin may have already decided that the Soviet Union should not try to influence the fate of Greece before Churchill ever raised the question.[49]

During this first meeting of the trip – the same one in which Churchill raised his 'naughty' document – the discussion also turned to the future of Germany. Churchill said he was all for 'hard terms' and Stalin added he wanted German 'heavy industry' destroyed. Molotov then, perhaps disingenuously, asked Churchill his 'opinion' of the Morgenthau Plan. Churchill said that Roosevelt and Morgenthau were 'not very happy about its reception'. And when Stalin spoke of his belief that 'a long occupation of Germany would be necessary' Churchill replied that 'he did not think the Americans would stay very long'.

It was this realization that the Americans were not liable to participate long-term in European affairs that also partly lay behind Churchill's desire to resolve the Polish question on this visit to Moscow if he possibly could. Deals needed to be done – and they needed to be done swiftly. For this reason Churchill had pressed Stalin to allow the Polish Prime Minister in exile, Stanislaw Mikołajczyk, to come to Moscow. And at five o'clock in the afternoon of 13 October he duly walked into the Spiridonovka Palace in the Kremlin to begin discussions with Stalin and the British Prime Minister.

It is not hard to imagine Mikołajczyk's emotions as he met Stalin once again, especially as any assurances he had received from the Soviet leader little more than two months before about the Warsaw Uprising had come to nothing. But no matter how badly he felt at the start of the meeting, worse was to follow. To begin with, Stalin reiterated the demands that he had expressed back in August.[50] 'One could not shut one's eyes to the facts,' he said. And the facts, as far as Stalin was concerned, were clear. 'The Polish Committee' (the Lublin Poles) were overseeing 'much work' in Poland and – a familiar theme – had 'a large army'. They therefore had to be involved in any discussions about the future of Poland. In addition, the London Poles must recognize the 'Curzon Line' and relinquish eastern Poland – without accepting Soviet demands here, 'there could be no good relations'.

Mikołajczyk made the understandable point that 'Polish soldiers abroad who were fighting against the Germans thought that they were fighting in the hope of returning to that territory', [meaning the land that would be lost in eastern Poland if the Curzon Line was accepted]. Stalin retorted that 'Ukrainians and White Russians' were also fighting for this land but 'Mr Mikołajczyk perhaps did not know of it. They had suffered much more than all the Poles put together.'

Churchill did his best to act as mediator, saying that 'they all knew of Poland's sufferings'. He then made a long and emotional statement in which he argued that they all – including Marshal Stalin – wanted Poland to be a 'free, sovereign and independent state, with the power to lead its own life', as long – and here came the familiar qualifier – as Poland was 'friendly' to the Soviet Union. But on the crucial question of the eastern Frontier of Poland the British government supported the border the Soviets wanted, 'because they felt it their duty. Not because Russia was strong but because Russia was right in the matter.' Mikołajczyk replied that 'he did not know that they now had to divide Poland before dealing with other questions'.

Then came a devastating moment for the Polish Prime Minister. After Churchill had 'appealed' once more to Mikołajczyk to make a 'beau gesture' and give up eastern Poland, Molotov intervened. He had clearly had enough of Churchill's emotional speeches and wanted to return to hard realities. Molotov reminded everyone 'what was said in Tehran upon the Polish question'. President Roosevelt had 'agreed to the Curzon Line' but 'did not wish it published at the moment' and so they 'could [all] conclude that the points of view of the Soviet Union, Britain and America were the same'.

It was the diplomatic equivalent of a mugging. For although Mikołajczyk had known that Churchill had wanted the Poles to agree to the Curzon Line, he had not known that the matter had been discussed – and seemingly agreed – at the Tehran Conference without the Poles being present. Nor had he realised that Roosevelt had also been party to this agreement.

Churchill said: 'I hope you will not hold against me these

unpleasant but frank words which I have spoken with the best of intentions.' Mikołajczyk replied: 'I have already heard so many unpleasant things in the course of this war that one more will not let me lose my balance.'

The next day, at the dacha outside Moscow where the British were based, Churchill once again pressed the Poles to change their minds and consent to the movement of the frontier. It was here that the strain on Churchill began to show. He simply could not believe that the Poles would not do as they were told. 'You must do this,' he said. 'If you miss this moment everything will be lost.'[51]

'Should I sign a death sentence against myself?' asked Mikołajczyk.

'I wash my hands off,' said Churchill. 'As far as I am concerned we shall give the business up. Because of quarrels between Poles we are not going to wreck the peace of Europe. In your obstinacy you do not see what is at stake. It is not in friendship that we shall part. We shall tell the world how unreasonable you are. You will start another war in which 25 million lives will be lost. But you don't care.'

'I know that our fate was sealed in Tehran,' said Mikołajczyk.

'It was saved in Tehran,' said Churchill.

'I am not a person completely devoid of patriotic feeling, to give away half of Poland.'

'What do you mean by saying "you are not devoid of patriotic feeling"?' said Churchill. 'Twenty-five years ago we reconstituted Poland although in the last war more Poles fought against us than for us. Now again we are preserving you from disappearance, but you will not play ball. You are absolutely crazy.'

'But this solution [the Curzon Line] does not change anything.'

'Unless you accept the frontier you are out of business for ever. The Russians will sweep through your country and you people will be liquidated. You are on the verge of annihilation.'

Mikołajczyk still would not accept the loss of eastern Poland. Churchill told him that 'we will be sick and tired of you if you go on arguing'. The meeting ended with the Poles withdrawing in order to consider what they should do. But it was a foregone conclusion what decision they would eventually reach. How could it be otherwise? How could they 'play ball' as Churchill wanted? Mikołajczyk was being asked to sign an agreement that gave up eastern Poland to the Soviets at a time when Polish soldiers in the Allied army – many whom came from the very area of Poland that was to be relinquished – were fighting and dying for the Allied cause.

Churchill's outburst is significant partly because of his remark that unless the Poles signed the agreement 'the Russians will sweep through your country and you people will be liquidated'. This comment sits oddly – to say the least – with his view expressed at Tehran that Stalin should be allowed various territorial gains because the 'character' of the Soviet government had 'changed'.

The Poles returned to the British dacha and gave their verdict at three o'clock in the afternoon. Mikołajczyk, not surprisingly, said that he could not consent to the Curzon Line. Churchill, in an outburst full of invective, accused the Polish government in exile of being composed of 'callous people who want to wreck Europe'.[52] He said that if the Poles 'want to conquer Russia we shall leave you to do it. I feel as if I were in a lunatic asylum. I don't know whether the British government will continue to recognise you.'

Finally, he ended the meeting with the bitter – and, he must have known, untrue – remark: 'In this war what is your contribution to the Allied effort? What did you throw into the common pool? You may withdraw your divisions if you like. You are absolutely incapable of facing facts. Never in my life have I seen such people.'

Mikołajczyk was clearly shaken by his visit to Moscow – not just by the vehemence of Churchill's attack, but by the revelation that the Western Allies had agreed the future borders of his country behind his back at Tehran. Mikołajczyk was particularly distressed by the knowledge that Roosevelt had misled him. In June 1944, when he had visited Washington, Mikołajczyk had been told by the Americans that 'only Marshal Stalin and Prime Minister Churchill had agreed to the Curzon Line'. Roosevelt had been at his most skittish with Mikołajczyk during the meeting. 'I have studied sixteen maps of Poland this morning,'[53] he told him. 'In only three hundred years, parts of White Russia have been Polish, and parts of Germany and Czechoslovakia…. On the other hand, parts of Poland have at times been annexed to those countries.' As a result, said Roosevelt, 'it is difficult to untangle the map of Poland'. However, despite these 'difficulties', Roosevelt gave no hint that he had reached any kind of agreement about Polish borders – unofficial or official – with Stalin at Tehran.

Now, Mikołajczyk said in a letter delivered to the American ambassador in London, 'I learned with shocked surprise from Mr Molotov's statement at the meeting on October 13 that at the Tehran conference the representatives of all the three Great Powers had definitely agreed that the so-called Curzon line should be the frontier between Poland and the Soviet Union.'[54]

Once again, Roosevelt had been caught out. And his motive for concealing the truth from Mikołajczyk in June is obvious. The American President had expressed concern at Tehran that the several million American voters of Polish descent would be upset if the Soviets gained eastern Poland – and they could express their displeasure directly at the polls in the Presidential election in November 1944. But once Roosevelt was comfortably re-elected on 7 November, Mikołajczyk could no longer damage him. On the 22nd, Roosevelt replied blandly to Mikołajczyk's implied accusation of bad faith and said that 'if mutual agreement' was reached on the borders of Poland, then 'this Government would offer no objection'. (In private, that same month, Roosevelt expressed his views more frankly on the question of future European borders to Averell Harriman: '…he [Roosevelt] considered the European questions were so impossible that he wanted to stay out of them as far as practicable, except for the problems involving Germany'.[55]) As far as Mikołajczyk was concerned, he had heard and seen enough. He resigned on 24 November.

But despite his inability to force through an agreement on Poland, Churchill still ended his visit to Moscow in an optimistic mood. At a final dinner in the Kremlin, on 18 October, Churchill and Stalin chatted almost as old friends. But revealingly, when the conversation turned to the subject of Rudolf Hess, the Nazi who had flown to Britain just before the German invasion of the Soviet Union, Stalin demonstrated that his innate suspicion of the British remained. He congratulated the 'British Intelligence Service' for managing to convince Hess to make the journey to Britain. Churchill, who had just remarked that Hess was insane, denied British involvement in the affair. But Stalin added that members of the Soviet intelligence service also often did not reveal what they had been up to until after the event.[56]

Despite, by Churchill's own admission, Stalin leading a country that was capable in the immediate future of 'liquidating' Poland, the British Prime Minister remained convinced that the Soviet leader was someone whom he could – to use a more recent expression – 'do business with'. In November, just days after Mikołajczyk had resigned, Churchill told the Cabinet that: 'No immediate threat of war lay ahead of us once the present war was over and we should be careful of assuming commitments consequent on the formation of a Western bloc that might impose a very heavy military burden upon us.'[57]

Although his views about the stability of the post-war world were still capable of changing, it seemed to Churchill – on balance – that the Soviet Union would prove to be a genuinely cooperative member of the international community and he returned from Moscow in an upbeat mood. 'I have had very nice talks with the old Bear [Stalin],' he wrote to his wife Clementine. 'I like him the more I see him. Now they respect us and I am sure they wish to work with us.'[58]

Over the next few months, that hope would be shattered.

THE BATTLE FOR BUDAPEST

As the Big Three now prepared for what would become the most famous conference of the war, at Yalta in the Crimea in February 1945, one of the most momentous of all the battles of the Second

World War began in Hungary. The battle for Budapest is much less well known in popular history than other iconic events of the war like Stalingrad or the battle for Berlin; yet it was of real significance in terms of both scale and timing, since it illustrated how Soviet forces were capable of behaving as they advanced into central Europe.

Hungary had not been the most reliable ally of the Nazis. Initially the Hungarian government, under Admiral Horthy, had been reluctant to join forces with Germany. Not only was there a traditional Hungarian fear of German power, but the country's geographical position also made it vulnerable to conquest from the East. But after the Germans had conquered France in the early summer of 1940 the Hungarians reassessed their military and political priorities. Just as this one event changed Stalin's attitude to the Nazis, so it altered the Hungarians' position about the war. Now, they thought, they had a chance to ally themselves with the winning side and gain valuable new territory in Romania as a result. And so it proved when, in October 1940, the Hungarians joined the Axis and received Northern Transylvania from Romania as a consequence.

But by 1944 it was clear that the Hungarians had backed the wrong side. And after Hungarian forces had been crushed on the Eastern Front fighting alongside the Germans, Horthy had tried to manoeuvre a way out of the war. In March, however, once Hitler had learnt of Horthy's plans, he ordered German troops to occupy the country, and the Nazis proceeded to deport hundreds of thousands of Hungarian Jews to Auschwitz – helped, it must be said, by compliant members of the Hungarian gendarmerie. In October 1944 Horthy – kept on by the Nazis as head of state after their occupation – tried once again to broker a peace deal with the West, and once again the Nazis moved to prevent him. This time Szálasi Ferenc, the leader of the Hungarian fascist party, the Arrow Cross, replaced Horthy, and the Nazis strengthened their grip on the country.

That same month Stalin ordered an immediate attack on Budapest. In a heated phone call with the commander of the 2nd

Ukrainian Front, Rodion Malinovsky, Stalin insisted that the Hungarian capital must be taken 'in the next few days'. When Malinovsky replied that he needed five days for the task, Stalin said: 'There is no point in being so stubborn. You obviously don't understand the political necessity of an immediate strike against Budapest.'[59] The 'political necessity' was probably the forthcoming meeting of the 'Big Three' at which the post-war future of much of Europe would be discussed. But the Soviets did not take Budapest 'in the next few days' and, given the fierceness of German and Hungarian resistance, it was ludicrous of Stalin ever to expect them to. Indeed, it was not until Christmas that the Soviets managed to launch what they hoped would be the final assault on the city.

'On the outskirts of Budapest on certain lines there was very strong resistance,' says Boris Likhachev,[60] a Soviet tank commander who took part in the attack. 'And there were very powerful counter-attacks.' As head of the reconnaissance department of his tank corps, Likhachev was in the heat of the action. And he still vividly remembers the intensity of the battle for Budapest: 'The sound of the artillery fire! When a shell explodes you smell burning, and it irritates your eyes. And it affects your breathing. What is even worse is when a bomb explodes – your breathing system is affected. It's smothering you. There is no fresh air to breathe and all this smoke fills your lungs.... Several times I experienced this. To be inside the tank with the hatches closed – even though tanks have a ventilation system, it doesn't help. It's poor and ineffective. And a person cannot be inside a tank for long when there are explosions around.... With the tanks, especially tanks with heavy armour, on the one hand you feel safe, on the other hand you suffocate.'

Budapest is divided by the Danube. On one side is Pest, and the Red Army made good progress through its relatively flat terrain and wide streets. On the other side of the river is Buda. Here the hills made the attackers' task much harder, but on Christmas Eve the Soviets managed to capture the high ground overlooking Buda, and by Boxing Day the city was encircled. Just as he had with Stalingrad, Hitler ordered a fight to the last.

Budapest was declared a '*Festung*' – a fortified place that must not be surrendered. A total of seventy thousand soldiers – roughly equal numbers of Germans and Hungarians – prepared to defend the capital.

With the Red Army close, the citizens of Budapest were in a state of fear. Barna Andrasofszky,[61] who was a medical student at the time but had just been conscripted into a Hungarian military unit, remembers that 'there were very many bad signs, because we did hear what was happening with the Russians coming into the country'. Refugees who had fled from the northern area of Hungary already occupied by the Soviets 'were telling terrible things. Watches were taken away from everybody, and women – they did not care whether they were young or old – they [the Soviets] were taking them and they were raping them. So this was the news that was spreading around.'

On 17 January 1945, German and Hungarian troops withdrew from Pest into Buda, and the Germans blew up the five bridges across the Danube that linked the two halves of the city. Within Buda, particularly around the central fortress which was defended by SS troops, the fighting was intense. Eventually, worn out by the sheer force of the Red Army attack, the Germans attempted to break out – and all but a few thousand were killed or captured. On 13 February the city finally surrendered.

The soldiers of the Red Army, who had been told by Stalin to capture the Hungarian capital in 'a few days', had taken more than a hundred days to force a surrender. And in the immediate aftermath of their victory, some of the Soviets took their revenge.

Ivan Polcz was one of the first to witness what happened. He was thirteen on 11 February, just two days before the surrender, and was the only child of a respectable middle-class Hungarian family. During the siege he and his parents had hidden in the cellar of a relative's house in the suburbs. They had all heard rumours of how the Soviets 'did not respect women at all', but 'many people did not believe' that the Red Army soldiers would commit rape.

Two nights before Ivan's birthday, everyone in the cellar had heard heavy bombing. 'And then,' he says, 'all of a sudden two

Russian soldiers wearing white stormed into the cellar holding machine guns.' The Red Army soldiers shouted that they were looking for Germans. Finding none, they ran back out into the street. Horrified, Ivan watched as half an hour later German soldiers came into the cellar. But, not finding their enemy, they rushed away again.

Then, on the night of his birthday, 'an incredible number of Russian soldiers stormed into the cellar with guns. If it hadn't been so frightening we would have been laughing our heads off because they were dressed with other people's clothes. Men were even wearing women's boots.... They asked us if we had jewellery, but apart from taking our watches and some of the clothes which they liked they didn't do anything.' Subsequent groups of Red Army soldiers came first to plant cables to establish a telephone line and then to bring food: 'And so we were quite OK with them. And we thought to ourselves that the idea that they were aggressive with women, this is probably an invention of the Nazis to threaten us.'

But a few days later the atmosphere changed. At about ten o'clock at night two Red Army soldiers came into the cellar where, by now, about twenty-five people were sheltering – a mixture of elderly couples, younger couples and children. Ivan 'cannot remember' the faces of the Soviets, 'but they didn't look too nice'.

One of the young Hungarian husbands acted as interpreter and asked the soldiers what they wanted. When they told him, he 'started to tremble'. They had said that 'they needed a woman'. 'Of course, the interpreter got frightened because he was a young man with a wife who was there on one of those beds...so he said that here there are [only] mothers and elderly people, and they should leave us alone. But they did not want to go away. And then all the women who were there, they covered themselves with a blanket and they [the Soviets] started to take the blanket from them. I was terribly afraid because my mother was there and for her age – forty-eight – she was a good-looking woman. Next to her was her younger sister, and next to them was a councillor from the embassy with his wife and his sixteen-year-old daughter.'

When the soldiers reached the far end of the cellar they found a blonde young woman of seventeen, the maid of the couple who owned the villa. This was the woman they chose. They grabbed her and she started crying and pleading, shouting to the rest of the people in the cellar: 'Please help me! Help me!'

'Everybody was frozen – a stone,' says Ivan. 'This was a terrible moment. I will never forget about it. Everybody knew by then that the women were in real danger.... And then something happened which was at first sight quite strange.' The owner of the house, a retired military officer, started to talk to the maid. 'He said: "Please make this sacrifice for the sake of the country. And with this you will be able to save the other women here who will never forget this."'

'At the time,' says Ivan, 'I thought this a very mean statement – that he told her to "make this sacrifice on the altar of the Hungarian nation", but in a way she [the maid] did save my mother and all the other young women there. Then there was quite a lot of crying and the Russian grabbed her and took her upstairs...and after fifteen minutes this girl staggered back down the stairs. She was absolutely collapsing, and she said that she had been the victim of a very fierce atrocity and rape, and this animal even beat her up because she had been crying. And of course everybody else was crying...when they [the others in the cellar] saw this poor girl they didn't even dare to look at her.... It was a terrible case,' recalls Ivan. 'Even today I can still remember it quite vividly and I get goosebumps, even though I am seventy-five years of age.'

In the aftermath of the Red Army's victory in Budapest rape was almost ubiquitous. 'The worst suffering of the Hungarian population is due to the rape of women,' records a contemporary report from the Swiss embassy in Budapest. 'Rapes – affecting all age groups from ten to seventy – are so common that very few women in Hungary have been spared.... The misery is made worse by the sad fact that many Russian soldiers are diseased and there are absolutely no medicines in Hungary.'[62]

Fifteen-year-old Agnes Karlik[63] was one of the young Hungarian women who suffered personally at the hands of the Soviet forces.

Just like Ivan and his family, Agnes had been hiding in a cellar with her family during the siege. And, just like Ivan, she found the first Red Army soldiers she met 'not unpleasant. They were just making sure that there were no enemies in the building. They didn't stay long. They tried, actually, to be friendly.'

But the atmosphere soon changed: 'All of a sudden these rough type of soldiers entered the building and they were really unpleasant. They snatched watches and looted and pushed people around.... We tried to pacify them, but it was a very frightening time for all of us. The children were crying. And they started to pull women out with the excuse to come and help peel potatoes. And my sister and myself were dragged away.' Agnes' grandmother insisted on going with them: 'She tried to find out what they wanted and what they were doing. But they just pushed her around and we clung to her. And then they took us outside. There was snow everywhere and it was pretty cold.'

The soldiers dragged them into a tent nearby. 'They were screaming, and for myself I felt absolutely so frightened that I was just rigid. So they pushed us into this tent type of arrangement and they raped us [her and her sister]. We were just young. Very young. And we didn't know what they were doing because at that time children were brought up differently. Not so aware.... I was sixteen, almost sixteen. In November I was going to be sixteen. And my sister was fourteen. My grandmother tried to help us and they beat her up.... But she wouldn't leave us. And when it was all over she took us back. I still get nightmares about it.'

That night Agnes curled up and tried to fall asleep in a secluded section of the cellar where the clothes were kept: 'And I was woken up by another couple of hoodlums coming into that section. I don't know how they found me there. They must have been trying to loot. And there I was in the middle of it. And they raped me again. And again I just let myself go absolutely limp.'

Both of these Soviet men raped Agnes. And for her this terrible experience was even 'worse' than the rape she had endured earlier in the day. Without her grandmother present she felt 'such a lonely feeling of helplessness'. After the assaults were over she 'crawled out' and told her mother what had happened. 'I got hysterical actually when I got to my mother. And I remember I was in such a state that eventually they had to shake me to get me out of it.'

The effect on Agnes of these rapes was, understandably, profound: 'For a long time I felt really resentful against men, being able to do such a thing without any sort of good reason.... It makes you feel really resentful against mankind, more or less.' In hospital, immediately after the second attack, Agnes was given an internal examination to check that she was not seriously injured. This was not an uncommon occurrence, as a result of the severity of the attacks that many women endured.

Medical student Barna Andrasofszky[64] witnessed just such a case in a village outside Budapest in the spring of 1945. He was called into a house by an elderly woman and was told that there was a sick young girl inside. When he went in he saw that the living room was in 'disarray' and a young woman of about twenty-five was lying on a bed, covered in a blanket: 'I went up to her and took the blanket – it was covered in blood. And she was crying and she kept saying that she was going to die, and that she didn't want to live any more.' Barna was told that the young woman had been raped by 'maybe ten or fifteen' men. She was bleeding profusely from internal injuries sustained in the attack. Barna could not stem the flow of blood, and the woman was taken away to hospital. 'It was very difficult to come to terms that this was happening in the twentieth century,' he says. 'It was very difficult to see as a reality what the Nazi propaganda was spreading. But here we could see that in reality. And also we heard about many other terrible situations like this.'

Of course, there are cases in all armies of mistreatment of civilians on enemy territory. And there are many Red Army veterans who wish to contextualize these crimes as a common, if regrettable, historical occurence. This, for example, is the view of tank commander Boris Likhachev, who fought in the battle for Budapest: 'There might have been cases of maltreatment, but I don't know of them. But logically there could have been. Logically, because historically the winners always want to look for some benefits for compensation for the hardships. Recently I read about Alexander the Great's army. When Alexander took the southern states, women suffered the first for the army. Women cooked food and satisfied all the needs of the winners. This is history and this is very colourfully described. Take Napoleon and his victories. It was the same.'

But in the context of the Second World War in Europe this excuse is not sustainable – because as far as the crime of rape was concerned the Soviets were in a league of their own. The Western Allies committed no comparable crimes of this enormity – mass rape was not tolerated. And whilst there are no accurate figures for the overall number of women raped by Soviet men in Hungary, the crime was clearly committed on a massive scale – one estimate is that around fifty thousand were raped in Budapest alone. Witness this report from the Hungarian Communists in Kőbánya, which was presented to the Soviets in 1945. In January, so the report says, when the Red Army arrived, they committed a series of sexual crimes in an outbreak of 'mindless, savage hatred run riot. Mothers were raped by drunken soldiers in front of their children and husbands. Girls as young as 12 were dragged from their fathers and raped in succession by 10–15 soldiers and often infected with venereal disease…. We know that intelligent members of the Red Army are communists, but if we turn to them for help they have fits of rage and threaten to shoot us, saying: "And what did you do in the Soviet Union? You not only raped our wives before our eyes, but for good measure you killed them together with their children, set fire to our villages and razed our cities to the ground."'[65]

For the most part nothing was officially said about the crimes. Significantly, *Pravda*, the Soviet newspaper, never referred to them. And although there were – on occasion – attempts to enforce the official line that rape committed by Soviet soldiers was a crime, so few cases were prosecuted that it is impossible not to conclude that the offence was often tolerated by the Soviet authorities.

'No one paid attention to these things,' says Fiodor Khropatiy,[66] one of the few Red Army soldiers prepared to acknowledge that rapes took place at all in occupied eastern Europe. 'On the contrary, soldiers gossiped about it, and they were proud, they felt like heroes, that he slept with such and such a woman, one or two or three. This is what soldiers shared with each other...it was normal behaviour. Even if somebody was killed, such a thing wouldn't be reported, to say nothing of the fact of a soldier sleeping with a girl.... I feel hurt, because our army earned itself such a reputation, and I feel angry about the people who were acting that way. I am negative about such things, very negative.... To some extent, I can understand the soldiers. If you are at war for four years, and in the most horrible conditions, this [desire for] violent behaviour can be justified. I can justify the soldiers' desire to rape a woman, but not the execution of it, not the actual performance. Of course, it's natural to understand the desire to have a woman, because officers and soldiers, for four years, were deprived of any sex.' As to what proportion of the Red Army committed the crime of rape, Fiodor says: 'It's difficult for me to speak about percentages. Probably there were 30 per cent who did it.'

An insight into Stalin's views on the subject can be gained from his behaviour in the Kremlin in the winter of 1944 during a visit from Milovan Djilas, a leading Yugoslavian Communist. Djilas had previously criticized the behaviour of the Red Army in Yugoslavia. Just like the Communists of Köbánya, Djilas had been concerned by reports of rape and had complained to the Red Army authorities. Subsequently, at a banquet held at the Kremlin for the Yugoslavian delegation, Djilas' protest was clearly on Stalin's mind. He began by speaking about the horrors endured by the Red Army as they fought the Germans back out of the Soviet Union and then into eastern Europe. He then said: 'And such an army was insulted by no one else but Djilas! Djilas of whom I could least have expected such a thing, a man whom I receive so well! And an army which did not spare its blood for you!' Finally, Stalin said, 'Can't he [Djilas] understand it if a soldier who has crossed thousand of kilometres through blood and fire and death has fun with a woman or takes some trifle?'[67] The 'climax' of the evening, according to Djilas, was when 'Stalin exclaimed, kissing my wife, that he made his loving gesture at the risk of being charged with rape.' On another occasion, when Stalin was told that Red Army soldiers were sexually mistreating German refugees, he is reported to have said: 'We lecture our soldiers too much; let them have some initiative.'[68]

Stalin, at least, only condoned rape. But Beria, the head of the NKVD, was a rapist himself. In 1953, after Stalin's death, one of Beria's bodyguards revealed at the trial of the NKVD chief for 'treason' that he and a colleague would cruise the streets of Moscow in order to select potential victims for their boss, and then transport them to his house. And despite claims that these accusations were created only to help disgrace Beria after his fall from power, it is clear from other evidence – like that of an American diplomat who knew at the time about 'girls brought to Beria's house late at night in a limousine'[69] – that they have substance. Indeed, direct testimony from Tatiana Okunevskaya,[70] a Russian actress selected to be taken to Beria's house, confirms the method the NKVD chief used in order to commit rape: 'These are such awful memories. He undressed himself and rolled about in his luxurious bed, his eyes ogling me. He looked like...not quite like a jellyfish, but like an ugly, shapeless toad. He said: "Let's have supper. You are a long way from anywhere, so whether you scream or not doesn't matter. You are in my power now. So think about that and behave accordingly. Aren't you going to eat or talk to me?" I remained silent; I didn't know what to do. Even now that I am eighty I still wouldn't know what to do. All these years have passed but I am certain of one thing. I may be frightened, I may be robbed, my house may be burned, but already in the camp I was sure of one thing – if I was ever raped again, I would commit suicide.'

Khrushchev later revealed that Malenkov, who had once served as Beria's deputy, took him to one side at the time of Beria's arrest and said: '"Listen to what my chief bodyguard has to say." The man came over to me and said: "I have only just heard that Beria has been arrested. I want to inform you that he raped my step-daughter, a seventh-grader. A year or so ago her grandmother died and my wife had to go to the hospital, leaving the girl at home alone. One evening she went out to buy some bread near the building where Beria lives. There she came across as old man who watched her intently. She was frightened. Someone came and took her to Beria's home. Beria had her sit down with him for supper. She drank something, fell asleep, and he raped her."

'I told this man, "I want you to tell the prosecutor during the investigation everything you've told me." Later, we were given a list of more than a hundred girls and women who had been raped by Beria. He had used the same routine on all of them. He gave them some dinner and offered them wine with a sleeping potion in it.'[71]

All of which means, of course, that if reports of Red Army soldiers raping women in eastern Europe were sent to the NKVD in Moscow, they finally reached the desk of a rapist himself.

THE YALTA CONFERENCE

In preparation for the Big Three conference at Yalta, Stalin tried to drum up as much support as he could for his puppet government in Poland. It was a subject, for example, that dominated the visit of General de Gaulle to Moscow in December 1944.

De Gaulle, president of the provisional government of newly liberated France, was clear in his judgement of Stalin. The Soviet leader was 'a dictator secluded in his own craftiness, winning others over with an air of good nature which he applied to allay suspicion. But so raw was his passion that it sometimes showed through, though not without a kind of pernicious charm.'[72] And Stalin's passion – during his meetings with de Gaulle – was to ensure that Poland was subservient to Moscow.

Stalin put considerable pressure on de Gaulle to recognize the Lublin Poles as the legitimate government of Poland. Although de Gaulle had no practical power to determine events on the ground, it would obviously have been hugely to Stalin's advantage to have gained French recognition of his puppets before the Yalta Conference. But de Gaulle, despite the relative fragility of his position as leader of the new French regime (there had, as yet, been no elections), refused to comply with Stalin's wish. 'If I had determined not to commit France in the attempted subjection of the Polish nation,' wrote de Gaulle in typical portentous style, 'it was not that I had any illusions as to what this refusal might effect from a practical point of view. Obviously we had no means of keeping the Soviets from executing their plans. Further, I foresaw that America and Great Britain would let them proceed as they wished. But however little weight France's attitude might have at the moment, it could later be important that she had adopted it at that particular moment. The future lasts a long time. All things are possible, even the fact that an action in accord with honour and honesty ultimately appears to be a prudent political investment.'[73]

Revealingly, given that Churchill and Roosevelt were to form such a positive impression of Stalin at Yalta in a few weeks' time, the Soviet leader hid nothing of his bloodthirsty nature from de Gaulle. At one memorable banquet in the Kremlin that December, in front of both de Gaulle and Harriman, the American ambassador to Moscow, Stalin toasted the health of Chief Marshal Novikov, commander of the Red Army air force, in a distinctly sinister way. 'He has created a wonderful air force,'[74] said Stalin. 'But if he doesn't do his job properly then we'll kill him.' Stalin then spotted his Director of Supply, General Khruliov. 'There he is!' said Stalin. 'That is the supply director. It is his job to bring men and material to the front. He'd better do his best otherwise he'll be hanged for it. That's the custom in our country!'

De Gaulle gained a further insight into Stalin's character directly after the banquet when the French leader finally signed a treaty of friendship with the Soviet Union – though without recognizing the Lublin Poles. 'You have played well,' Stalin said to him. 'Well done! I like dealing with someone who knows what he wants even if he doesn't share my views!'[75] Stalin then remarked: 'After all, it is only death who wins.' Finally, he called over Boris Podzerov, his interpreter that night, and said: 'You know too much. I had better send you to Siberia.'

It was against the background of this meeting with De Gaulle, suffused with black humour, and in the happy knowledge that the war was progressing towards its end, that Stalin boarded a train from Moscow for Yalta in the Crimea in February 1945. He had just learnt that at the end of January Marshal Zhukov's Belorussian Front had crossed into Germany and were now encamped on the eastern bank of the river Oder, little more than 50 miles from Berlin. In the West he knew that the Allies had successfully repulsed Hitler's attack through the Ardennes, known as the Battle of the Bulge. And in the Far East General Douglas MacArthur was poised to recapture Manila in the Philippines, the British had forced the Japanese back across the Irrawaddy river in Burma, and American bombers were pounding the home islands of Japan. Victory now seemed certain – though, particularly in the war against Japan, it was uncertain just how soon and at what cost that victory would come.

The conference at Yalta has come to symbolize in the minds of many people the sense that somehow dirty deals were done as the war came to an end – dirty deals that brought dishonour on the otherwise noble enterprise of fighting the Nazis. But it wasn't quite like that. In the first place, of course, it was at the Tehran Conference in November 1943 that the fundamental issues about the course of the rest of the war and the challenges of the post-war world were initially discussed and in principle resolved. Little of new substance was raised at Yalta. Nonetheless, Yalta is important, not least because it marks the final high point of Churchill and Roosevelt's optimistic dealings with Stalin.

On 3 February Churchill and Roosevelt flew from Malta to Saki, on the flat planes of the Crimea, north of the mountain range that protects the coastal resort of Yalta. They, and their huge group of advisers and assistants – around seven hundred people in all – then made the tortuous drive down through the high mountain passes to the sea. Churchill, who had cherished the hope that the United Kingdom would be chosen as the site of the conference – one suggestion had even been Invergordon in Scotland – was not enthusiastic about the Crimea. He later described the place as 'the Riviera of Hades' and said that 'if we had spent ten years on research, we could not have found a worse place in the world'.[76] But once again Stalin's will had prevailed about the location of the conference.

There is no evidence that the bleak irony of the setting occurred to the Western Allies – that it was in the Crimea that they were about to discuss the future of millions of people, the very place where eight months earlier Stalin had demonstrated his own particular way of dealing with dissent, real or imagined, in deporting the entire nation of Tatars.

Much has been written about Roosevelt's physical state at the conference. Those who worked closely with him, like George Elsey, had noticed a profound deterioration of the President's health over the previous months, and Churchill had remarked on how sick Roosevelt looked at the time of the Quebec meeting in September. At Yalta, Lord Moran, Churchill's doctor, recorded: 'Everyone seemed to agree that the President has gone to bits physically.... I doubt, from what I have seen, whether he is fit for his job here.'[77]

Hugh Lunghi, who went to Yalta as part of the team from the British military mission in Moscow, remembers seeing the two leaders arrive by plane, and he too was surprised by the President's appearance: 'Churchill got out of his aircraft and came over to Roosevelt's. And Roosevelt was being decanted, as it were – it's the only word I can use, because of course he was disabled. And Churchill looked at him very solicitously. They'd met in Malta, of course, so Churchill, I suppose, had no surprise, as I had – and anyone else had who hadn't seen Roosevelt previously – to see this gaunt, very thin figure with his black cape over his shoulder, and tied at his neck with a knot, and his trilby hat turned up at the front. His face was waxen to a sort of yellow, waxen and very drawn, very thin, and a lot of the time he was sort of sitting, sitting there with his mouth open sort of staring ahead. So that was quite a shock.'

Roosevelt was a dying man at Yalta – there is no question about it. But whether or not Roosevelt's undoubted weakness affected his judgement is less easy to establish, with contemporary testimony supporting both sides of the argument. What is certain, though, is that Roosevelt's eventual accomplishments at Yalta were coherent and consistent with his previous policies as expressed at Tehran and elsewhere. His principal aims remained those of ensuring that the Soviet Union came into the war against Japan promptly once the war in Europe was over, and gaining Soviet agreement about the founding of the United Nations. The intricacies of the borders of eastern Europe mattered much less to him – illness or no illness.

Whilst Roosevelt's physical decline was clear to all at Yalta, just as obvious was Stalin's robust strength and power. As Hugh Lunghi saw it: 'Stalin was full of beans.... He was smiling, he was genial to everyone, and I mean really everybody, even to junior ranks like myself. He joked at the banquets more than he had before.' Ever since the Red Army victories of 1943 Stalin had taken to wearing military uniform, and he cut an imposing figure at Yalta. 'I must say I think Uncle Joe is the most impressive of the three men,' wrote the head of the British Foreign Office, Sir Alexander Cadogan, in his diary. 'He is very quiet and restrained.... He's obviously got a very good sense of humour and a rather quick temper!'[78] More than that, the Allied leaders felt that Stalin at Yalta was someone they could relate to on a personal level. Churchill had remarked the year before that 'if only I could dine with Stalin once a week, there would be no trouble at all. We get on like a house on fire.'[79]

Churchill and Roosevelt remained anxious to believe in Stalin the man. They clung to the hope that Stalin's statements of friendship, like his speech on 6 November 1944 in which he talked of the relationship with the Western Allies being based on 'vitally important and long standing interests',[80] meant that he was planning on future cooperation with the West. And by the time of Yalta Churchill, for example, could point to the fact that the Soviets had recently allowed the British a free hand in Greece – just as the 'percentages' discussions of October 1944 had suggested they would. In any case, the future peace of the world still depended on sustaining a productive relationship with Stalin. And so, with these thoughts careering around their minds, the two Western leaders remained predisposed to believe what evidence they could in order to bolster up the most convenient overall conviction: that Stalin was a man they could 'handle'.

At the first meeting of all three leaders, in the tsarist glory of the Livadia palace, the former holiday home of the imperial family, Roosevelt remarked that 'we understood each other much better now than we had in the past and that month by month that understanding was growing'.[81] The American President looked forward to some 'frank and free' speaking at the conference.

It was Poland, of course, that was to be the test case of the relationship with Stalin, and no subject was discussed more at Yalta. Despite the protests of the Polish government in exile, both Roosevelt and Churchill agreed that Stalin could keep eastern Poland. What mattered to Roosevelt and Churchill was that Poland – within its new borders – could be 'independent and free'. 'Great Britain,' said Churchill, 'had no material interest in Poland. Her interest is only one of honour because we drew the sword for Poland against Hitler's brutal attack. Never could I be content with any solution that would not leave Poland as a free and independent state.' Once again, one marvels at the ability of the Western leaders to mention only the convenient bits of recent history. They knew full well that only days after 'Hitler's brutal attack' on Poland from the West, the Soviet Union had made its own 'brutal attack' from the East. And it was the very gains the Soviet Union had made because of that attack that Churchill and Roosevelt had now agreed to accept.

Stalin remarked: 'The Prime Minister has said that for Great Britain the question of Poland is a question of honour. For Russia it is not only a question of honour but also of security', because the Germans had 'passed through' Poland twice in the last thirty years en route to the Soviet Union. But Stalin went on to say that 'it is necessary that Poland be free, independent and powerful'. He then said that as far as he was concerned, the Lublin Poles, who were now in the Polish capital as 'the Polish government', had 'as great a democratic base in Poland as de Gaulle has in France'. He also spoke once again, as he had to Churchill the previous October, of the need to 'maintain order behind the lines' and declared that 'there are agents of the London government connected with the so-called underground. They are called resistance forces. We have had nothing good from them but much evil.'

Stalin therefore kept to his position that elements of the Home Army (if not all of them) were 'bandits' and that the ex-Lublin Poles were the legitimate – if perhaps temporary – government of Poland. Unlike at Tehran, where he had stayed quiet in the face of Stalin's accusations about the Polish resistance, Churchill now made this gentle protest: 'I must put on record that the British and Soviet governments have different sources of information in Poland and get different facts. Perhaps we are mistaken but I do not feel that the Lublin government represents even one third of the Polish people. This is my honest opinion and I may be wrong. Still, I have felt that the underground might have collisions with the Lublin government. I have feared bloodshed, arrests, deportation and I fear the effect on the whole Polish question. Anyone who attacks the Red Army should be punished but I cannot feel the Lublin government has any right to represent the Polish nation.'

As Churchill and Roosevelt saw it, the challenge was to do what they could to ensure that the government of the newly constituted country was as representative as possible. And so Roosevelt sent Stalin a letter after the discussion that day in which he recorded his concern that 'people at home look with a critical eye on what they consider a disagreement between us at this vital stage of the war'.[82] He also stated categorically that 'we cannot register the Lublin Government as now composed'. Roosevelt proposed that representatives of both the Lublin Poles and the London Poles be immediately called to Yalta. Then the Big Three could assist them in jointly agreeing a provisional government in Poland. 'It goes without saying,' wrote Roosevelt at the end of the letter, 'that any interim government which could be formed as a result of our conference with the Poles here would be pledged to the holding of free elections in Poland at the earliest possible date. I know this is completely consistent with your desire to see a new free and democratic Poland emerge from the welter of this war.'

This put Stalin in something of an awkward spot. It was, of course, not in his interests to have the composition of any interim government of Poland worked out jointly with the other Allied leaders. It would make him merely one voice in three in the discussions, instead of the principal driver of events if matters were left until after the meeting disbanded. And how Stalin found his way out of this potentially uncomfortable situation tells us much about both his character and his acute sense of how real power operates.

He first practised the classic politician's ploy – delay. The day after receiving Roosevelt's letter, 7 February, he claimed that he had only received the communication 'an hour and a half ago'. He then said that he had been unable to reach the Lublin Poles because they were away in Kraków or somewhere else in Poland. However, Stalin said, Molotov had worked out some ideas based on Roosevelt's proposals – but 'these proposals were not yet typed out'.

Then Stalin made his cleverest move. He suggested that instead of discussing Poland – how could they, since he had just said he had not had time to respond to Roosevelt's suggestions in detail – the Big Three should turn their attention to the voting procedure for the new United Nations. This was the subject dearest to Roosevelt's heart, but one that had proved highly problematic at past meetings. The Soviets had been insisting that each of their republics should have one vote in the General Assembly, which would give them sixteen votes to America's one. They had argued that since Britain with its extensive Commonwealth and Empire effectively controlled a large number of potential votes, the Soviets deserved the same treatment. Now, in a clear concession, Molotov said that 'they would be satisfied with the admission of three or at least two of the Soviet Republics as original members'. This changed the atmosphere of the meeting in an instant. Roosevelt said he was 'very happy' to hear these proposals and 'felt that this was a great step forward which would be welcomed by all the peoples of the World'. Churchill agreed wholeheartedly with the American President, saying that he too 'would like to express his heartfelt thanks to Marshal Stalin and Mr Molotov for this great step forward.'

It was only then, after the happy discussion about the voting procedure in the new assembly of nations, that Molotov presented the Soviet response to Roosevelt's letter about Poland. He wrote that 'it would be desirable to add to the Provisional Polish Government some democratic leaders from Polish émigré circles', but added that they still hadn't been able to reach the Lublin Poles on the phone. As a result, 'time would not permit the carrying out of the President's suggestion to summon the Poles to Crimea'.

This was the most significant moment of the conference so far. Churchill and Roosevelt – it ought to go without saying, but it seems necessary to say it in this context – were sophisticated and experienced politicians; indeed, they were two of the most sophisticated and experienced politicians of the twentieth century. And yet they let Molotov and Stalin get away with what was obviously a crude ruse. Did anyone in the room really believe that the Soviets, having been given a day to do so, were unable to reach their own tame government of Poland on the telephone? Especially since it was so clearly in the interests of the Soviet Union not to have a deal brokered with the London Poles here at Yalta in the presence of the Western leaders? Yet neither Churchill nor Roosevelt raised the issue of the alleged inability of the Soviets to get hold of their own puppet government. Churchill responded to Molotov's proposal only with a comment about the exact borders of the new Poland. Molotov had finally revealed the details of the boundaries of the new Poland, as the Soviets saw them, with the western border along the rivers Oder and Neisse south of the city of Stettin. This would take a huge portion of Germany into the new Poland, and Churchill remarked that 'it would be a pity to stuff the Polish goose so full of German food that it got indigestion'.

The British were concerned lest so much territory was taken from the Germans that in the post-war world they would be permanently hostile to the new Poland, thus forcing the Poles closer to the Soviets. At the meeting, Churchill couched this concern as anxiety about the reaction of 'a considerable body of British public opinion' to the Soviet plan to 'move large numbers of Germans'. Stalin remarked in response that most Germans had 'already run away from the Red Army' in these regions. And in any case, as Churchill acknowledged, there would be plenty of space – since the Germans had already had 'six to seven million casualties in the war and would probably have a million more', and this would 'simplify' the problem.

Thus the request that Roosevelt had made the day before – that the Lublin and London Poles be brought to Yalta so that a deal for the provisional government of Poland could be thrashed out under the auspices of the Big Three – was successfully dodged by Stalin without a whimper from the Western leaders.

The next day the three leaders began their meeting by swiftly agreeing to Stalin's request that the Soviet Union receive territory in the East from Japan as the final price for the Red Army's partic- ipation in the Pacific war. Stalin claimed that the Soviets had historic claims on all this territory – something the Japanese still dispute, with justification, to this day.

The leaders then returned once more to the question of Poland. Churchill referred to this moment as 'the crucial point of this great conference'. In a lengthy speech he laid out the immen- sity of the problem the Western Allies faced. 'We have an army of 150,000 Poles who are fighting bravely. That army would not be reconciled to Lublin. It would regard our action in transferring recognition as a betrayal.' Churchill acknowledged that, if elec- tions were held 'with full secret ballot and free candidacies' this would remove British doubts. But until that happened, and with the current composition of the Lublin government, it was impos- sible for the British to transfer its allegiance from the London based Polish government in exile.

Stalin, in what must surely have been, for him, a speech laced through with irony, retorted: 'The Poles for many years have not liked Russia because Russia took part in three partitions of Poland. But the advance of the Soviet Army and the liberation of Poland from Hitler has completely changed that. The old resentment has completely disappeared...my impression is that the Polish people consider this a great historic holiday.' The idea that the former members of the Home Army, for example, were currently being treated to a 'great historic holiday' can only have been a black joke. Churchill, who, as we have seen, had admitted to Anders a few months before that he knew just how little current Soviet actions in Poland resembled a 'historic holiday', made no attempt to correct Stalin's calumny.

Stalin did, however, say that he agreed that the 'Polish government must be democratically elected. It is much better to have a government based on free elections.' But the final 'compromise' the three leaders came to on Poland so heavily weighted events in Soviet favour as to make this unlikely in the extreme. All that was agreed was that the 'ambassadors of the three powers in Warsaw' be charged with the 'responsibility of observing and reporting to their respective governments on the carrying out of the pledge in regard to free and unfettered elections'.

As regards the immediate composition of the Lublin government, again the Soviets won the day. The Western Allies now only requested that this group be 'reorganized' to include 'democratic' Polish leaders from abroad and within Poland. But it was the Soviets who would convene meetings with the foreign ministers of the three powers in Moscow to coordinate this.

Only the most inveterate optimist could have imagined that this weak formula could produce the desired result – a free and democratic Poland. 'Those of us who worked and lived in Moscow,' says Hugh Lunghi, 'were astounded that a stronger declaration shouldn't have been made, because we knew that there was not a chance in hell that Stalin would allow free elections in those countries when he didn't allow them in the Soviet Union.' Lunghi's depressing judgement was shared at the time by Lord Moran, who believed at Yalta that the Americans were 'profoundly ignorant' of 'the Polish problem'[83] and he couldn't understand why Roosevelt thought he could 'live at peace with them [the Soviets]'. Moran believed that 'it was plain at Moscow, last October, that Stalin means to make Poland a Cossack outpost of Russia, and I am sure he has not altered his intention here'.[84]

But Moran was mistaken. The American President was not 'profoundly ignorant' about Poland – he just didn't care as much about the Polish question as he did about some other key issues. Roosevelt, of course, paid lip service to the idea that the elections in Poland had to be be free and open. 'I want this election in Poland to be the first one beyond question,' he said to Stalin at Yalta. 'It should be like Caesar's wife. I did not know her but they say she was pure.'[85] Stalin, with characteristic caustic wit, replied: 'They said that about her, but in fact she had her sins.'

However, Roosevelt privately acknowledged that the deal reached on Poland was far from perfect. When Admiral Leahy told him that 'this is so elastic that the Russians can stretch it all the way from Yalta to Washington without even technically breaking it,' Roosevelt replied: 'I know, Bill, but it is the best I can do for Poland at this time.'[86] Which was a classic Roosevelt remark – true only so far as it went. The agreement was only 'the best' he 'could do' because of the low level of priority he gave to the issue.

What was important for Roosevelt was that a workable accommodation was reached with Stalin that augured well for the general post-war future of the world. And although his fellow American, the merchant marine officer Jim Risk, who had spent nearly nine months in the north of the Soviet Union, had formed the opinion that Stalin was as bad as Hitler, this was a view Roosevelt did not share. Indeed, just days before the Yalta Conference he even remarked to Richard Law, a British diplomat: 'There were many varieties of Communism, and not all of them were necessarily harmful.'[87] As Lord Moran put it, 'I don't think he [Roosevelt] has ever grasped that Russia is a Police State...'.[88]

For the hard-headed Admiral Leahy, however, the consequences of Yalta were clear the day the conference ended, 11 February 1945. The decisions taken there would 'make Russia the dominant power in Europe, which in itself carries a certainty of future international disagreements and the prospects of another war'.[89] But by the end of the conference, the leaders of the Western Allies and many of their key advisers were clearly putting their faith ever more in the individual character of Stalin. 'I have never known the Russians so easy and accomodating,' wrote Cadogan on 11 February, 'In particular, Joe has been extremely good. He *is*

[Cadogan's own emphasis] a great man, and shows up very impressively against the background of the other two ageing statesmen.'[90]

For the most part the Western Allies were pleased with what had been accomplished at the Yalta Conference. As well as agreement on Poland's new borders (albeit without the consent of the Polish people themselves or the Polish government in exile) and a promise from Stalin that there would be 'democratic' elections shortly in Poland, the demarcation zones for occupied Germany had been fixed – with the French being granted an area of occupation alongside the British, Americans and Soviets. In addition, Stalin had once again voiced his commitment to the United Nations and agreed to come into the war against Japan once Germany was defeated. And in the immediate aftermath of Yalta there was an increased belief amongst many in power in the West that Stalin could be relied upon to fulfil his promises. In large part, as we have seen, that was to do with his behaviour during the conference. Churchill remarked that what had impressed him was that Stalin listened carefully to counter-arguments and was then prepared to change his mind. And there was other evidence of a more practical nature that could be used to demonstrate Stalin's desire to reach an accommodation with the West – his obvious intention not to interfere in the British action in Greece, for example. But above all it was the impact of his personality that was crucial in the optimism that prevailed straight after Yalta.

There was, at least in public, a sense that the ideological gap between the West and the Soviet Union was closing, with new apparent respect on both sides. On the first day of the conference Churchill had said he felt that 'the three nations represented here were moving toward the same goal [democratic government] by different methods'. And just as Churchill, for example, in spirited form at the banquet on the first night of the talks, proposed a toast to the 'Proletarian masses of the world', so Stalin at the last feast of the conference remarked that Churchill was the 'bravest governmental figure in the world. Due in large measure to Mr Churchill's courage and staunchness, England, when she stood alone, had divided the might of Hitleritre Germany at a time when the rest of Europe was falling flat on its face before Hitler.' Stalin then added that 'he knew of few examples in history where the courage of one man had been so important to the future history of the world. He drank a toast to Mr Churchill, his fighting friend and a brave man.'

Could the Western powers have bargained differently – perhaps, as it turned out, more effectively – at Yalta? The answer, with hindsight, is yes, almost certainly.[91] It is notable, for example, that the Americans never used their considerable economic power to try to pressurize the Soviets to be more accommodating. The Soviets wanted a $6 billion line of credit in order to buy American equipment after the war, as well as an agreement on the amount of reparation they could take from Germany to pay for the conflict. Neither of these issues was discussed at Yalta, not least because most people involved thought that there would be a formal peace conference at the end of the war to resolve all the key issues once and for all. But such a conference would never take place. And a little over two months after Yalta, Roosevelt was dead.

IRON CURTAIN, 1948

NORWAY

FINLAND

SWEDEN

North Sea

DENMARK

Baltic Sea

SOVIET UNION

NETHERLANDS

EAST GERMANY

POLAND

BELGIUM

WEST GERMANY

LUXEMBOURG

CZECHOSLOVAKIA

SWITZERLAND

AUSTRIA

HUNGARY

ITALY

ROMANIA

YUGOSLAVIA

Adriatic Sea

BULGARIA

Black Sea

ALBANIA

GREECE

TURKEY

N

Territory gained by the Soviet Union in 1945

Countries under Soviet control

Other Communist countries

0   miles   200

0   km   200

6

THE IRON CURTAIN

THE COLLAPSE OF YALTA

The flawed agreement at Yalta was spun enthusiastically. In February, in the immediate aftermath of the conference, both the British and the Americans talked up what had been achieved in the Crimea.

Churchill informed the War Cabinet that he was quite sure Stalin 'meant well to the world and to Poland', and that 'Premier Stalin had been sincere'.[1] And on 23 February he told ministers that 'Poor Neville Chamberlain believed he could trust Hitler. He was wrong. But I don't think I'm wrong about Stalin.'[2] Hugh Dalton, present at the meeting, also recorded in his diary: 'The PM spoke very warmly of Stalin. He was sure – and Sir Charles Portal had said the same thing to me at the De La Rue dinner last Wednesday – that, as long as Stalin lasted, Anglo–Russian friend-ship could be maintained. Who would succeed him one didn't know. (Portal had said, "Perhaps Molotov. He's pretty wooden and he stammers and a stammer in Russian is not a pretty sound.")' In the House of Commons on 27 February Churchill continued to put the best gloss he could on the conference, and said he believed that 'Marshal Stalin and the Soviet leaders wish to live in honourable friendship and equality with the Western democracies. I feel also that their word is their bond.'[3]

Roosevelt's administration went further – much further. In Washington, the President was preceded home by James Byrnes, head of the war mobilization board, who announced not only that agreement had been reached at Yalta about the United Nations, but that as a result of the conference 'spheres of influence' had been eliminated in Europe, and 'the three great powers are going to preserve order [in Poland] until the provisional government is established and elections held'.[4]

Roosevelt, who explicitly congratulated Byrnes on this misleading press conference, clearly wanted the American public to focus on what he believed was the big achievement of Yalta – the agreement over the foundation and organization of the United Nations. The President, well aware that he was a sick man, wanted the UN to be central to his legacy. He would show the world that he had taken the internationalist ideals of Woodrow Wilson, as expressed in the failed League of Nations in the wake of the First World War, and – this time – had made them work.

The message, first proselytized by Byrnes, a close associate of Roosevelt, that the Big Three had effectively agreed on a new world order at Yalta was reinforced by Roosevelt himself when he talked to a joint session of Congress in Washington on 1 March. The decisions reached at Yalta about the United Nations, said Roosevelt, 'ought to spell the end of the system of unilateral action, the exclusive alliances, the spheres of influence, the balances of power, and all the other expedients that have been tried for centuries – and have always failed.'[5]

The American press enthusiastically embraced this selective version of Yalta. Their response was scarcely surprising, since Roosevelt had omitted to mention those bits of the Yalta agreement that didn't fit the romantic ideal he was selling (like the fact that he had agreed that the Soviet Union would have more than one vote in the General Assembly, and that the Soviets could hold the promised 'elections' in Poland unhindered by effective Western supervision). This was Roosevelt's final attempt to square the circle of his problematic relationship with Stalin with the principles of the Atlantic Charter. Yes, the Americans may have had to give way on the question of Poland's border in the East, but, he implied, freedom was on the way for the rest of Europe.

Of course, Roosevelt could point to the letter of the agreement in support of this conclusion. Had not Stalin, for example, signed up to 'free' elections in Poland? But Roosevelt must have known from the behaviour of Stalin and Molotov at Yalta – from their supposed inability to get hold of the Lublin Poles on the telephone to their refusal to let any future elections be properly monitored – that it was unlikely that Poland would be 'free'. Indeed, since Roosevelt had explicitly agreed that the post-war government of Poland would be 'friendly' to the Soviets, any future Polish administration was already circumscribed. Yet despite all this, Roosevelt hyped up an agreement that he himself had admitted privately was only 'the best he could get'.

Roosevelt's gloss on the Yalta agreement was bound to antagonize Stalin. The Soviet leader was the least 'Wilsonian' figure imaginable. He didn't believe in fine words; he believed in hard, practical reality. What mattered to him was where Soviet borders were and the extent to which neighbouring countries were amenable. A study of Soviet comment on Yalta confirms this analysis. Straight after the conference the front page of *Voina i rabochii klass* (War and the Working Class) carried an article asserting that 'the stern and emphatic language of the Crimean decision is as far from the pompous and diffuse language of Wilson's fourteen points... as heaven is from earth'.[6] And the response of *Pravda* to Byrnes's spin on Yalta was an article on 17 February that emphasized that the word 'democracy' meant different things to different people, and each country could now exercise 'choice' over which version it preferred.[7]

This was a long way from Roosevelt's vision. In fact, the Soviets were speaking the language of 'spheres of influence', the very concept that Byrnes and Roosevelt had just said was now defunct. Stalin had consistently favoured the idea of 'spheres of influence' for the major powers in Europe. It was because of his commitment to this idea that he had raised the question of postwar borders and a 'secret protocol' at his initial meeting with Eden in December 1941. This was also why the Soviets had reacted with such alacrity to Churchill's 'percentage' approach in October 1944. Stalin understood the meaning of such meetings and thought they had much more value than the 'pompous and diffuse language' not only of Wilson's Fourteen Points but also, by clear implication, of Roosevelt's United Nations.

Stalin was now receiving distinctly mixed messages about whether or not the West went along with his approach. He believed he had kept to his side of the bargain and showed that the concept of 'spheres of influence' was a two-way street – hadn't he allowed Churchill a free hand in Greece, where British troops had helped deny the Communist partisans power in December 1944? So where was the quid pro quo? Why was there this sudden talk of the end of 'spheres of influence' and 'balances of power' when the British action in Greece had clearly demonstrated Churchill's commitment to this practical reality?

Yes, Stalin had signed up to an agreement about 'free' elections in Poland, but, like the concept of 'democracy', there were, in his eyes, many ways of interpreting the word 'free'. As far as the Soviets were concerned, their 'elections' in occupied eastern Poland in the autumn of 1939 had been 'free'. Then there was the fact that Roosevelt – no matter what he said in public – had suggested privately at Tehran that he was not too concerned about the fate of Poland, apart from the practical matter of the reaction of Poles in the United States. In the light of all this it was perfectly possible – probably likely – that Stalin would not have predicted the extent to which both Roosevelt and Churchill emphasized Soviet commitment to a 'free' Poland on their return.

But it is a mistake to think that Stalin, at this stage, intended that all the eastern European states occupied by the Red Army should immediately somehow become mini-Soviet Unions. What he wanted was what he had wanted all along: 'friendly' countries along his border within an agreed Soviet 'sphere of influence'. Admittedly, he defined 'friendly' in a way that precluded what the Western Allies would have called 'democracy'. He wanted these states to guarantee that they would be close allies of the Soviet Union. He would carefully monitor their progress – and restrict political and other freedoms accordingly. These countries would most certainly not be 'free' in the way Churchill and Roosevelt wanted. But Stalin felt they need not become, in the immediate post-war years, Communist. In May 1946, Stalin expressed his views on all this in clear terms to Polish Communists. 'Your democracy is special,' he said. 'You have no class of big capitalists. You have nationalized industry in 100 days, whilst the English have been struggling to do that for the past 100 years. Don't copy western democracy. Let them copy you. The democracy that you have established in Poland, in Yugoslavia and partly in Czechoslovakia is a democracy that is drawing you closer to socialism without the necessity of establishing the dictatorship of the proletariat or the Soviet system. Lenin never said there was no path to socialism other than the dictatorship of the proletariat, he admitted that it was possible to arrive at the path to socialism using the foundations of the bourgeois democratic system such as Parliament.'[8]

However, Churchill, more than the other two members of the Big Three, faced a particular problem about selling the Yalta agreement on Poland. And that problem took physical form on 20 February, when the British Prime Minister came face to face with General Anders. The Polish commander had been outraged by the Yalta agreement, which he saw as a 'mockery of the Atlantic Charter', and wanted to confront the man who just six months earlier had made such emotional promises to him in the wake of Monte Cassino.

'You are not satisfied with the Yalta agreement,' said Churchill with what must have been an attempt at deliberate understatement.

'It is not enough to say that I am dissatisfied,' replied Anders. 'I consider that a great calamity has occurred.'

Anders made it clear to Churchill that his distress at the Yalta agreement was not merely idealistic – it had a deeply practical dimension too. 'Our soldiers fought for Poland,' he said, 'fought for the freedom of their country. What can we, their commanders, tell them now? Soviet Russia, until 1941 in close alliance with Germany, now takes half our territory, and in the rest of it she wants to establish her power.'

Churchill became annoyed with Anders, remarking: 'It is your own fault.' He said that, if the Poles had settled the eastern border earlier, 'the whole matter would now have been different'. He then added a remarkably hurtful remark, given the sacrifice made by the Poles in the British armed forces. 'We have enough troops today. We do not need your help. You can take away your divisions. We shall do without them.'⁹

It is possible to see in this brief exchange not only Churchill's continuing frustration with the Poles, but also the extent to which he felt politically vulnerable because of Yalta. His reputation now rested partly on the way Stalin chose to operate in Poland and the other eastern European countries. In order to preserve intact his own wartime record, he had to hope Stalin would keep to his 'promises'. Unfortunately for the British prime minister, this hope would shortly be destroyed by Soviet action in the territory they now occupied.

Field Marshal Sir Alan Brooke, Chief of the Imperial General Staff, met Anders and felt 'most awfully sorry for him, he is a grand fellow and takes this whole matter terribly hard'.¹⁰ Anders had told him that: 'After having been a prisoner, and seeing how Russians could treat Poles, he considered that he was in a better position to judge what Russians were like than the President or PM…. When in a Russian prison he was in the depth of gloom but he did then always have hope. Now he could see no hope anywhere. Personally his wife and children were in Poland and he could never see them again, that was bad enough. But what was infinitely worse was the fact that all the men under his orders relied on him to find a solution to this insoluble problem!… and he, Anders, saw no solution and this kept him awake at night.'

It soon became clear that Anders' judgement of Soviet intentions was an accurate one, as Stalin's definition of 'free' and 'election' soon became clear for all to see. Elections were held in Soviet-occupied Romania in March 1945, but when the majority of people voted for non-Communists the results were ignored and King Michael made to appoint a Communist-dominated administration. Romania had already been devastated by the arrest and deportation of nearly two hundred thousand 'fascists' – a term used loosely by the Soviets to include anyone who had served the previous regime or who they believed still opposed them. It was essentially the same method of occupation as had been practised in eastern Poland in the autumn of 1939. For the Soviets what mattered above all else, was the elimination of any opposition.

Churchill was never to make much of an issue of Soviet action in Romania – he felt constrained by the discussions around his 'naughty' document, which placed Romania firmly in the Soviet zone of influence. The month before, in January, when he had been told that the Soviets were forcibly deporting ethnic Germans (who formed a minority within Romania) he said in a note to the Foreign Office: 'Why are we making a fuss about the Russian deportations in Rumania of Saxons and others? It is understood that the Russians were to work their will in this sphere. Anyhow we cannot prevent them.'[11] And the following day, when the Foreign Office brought to the Prime Minister's attention the fact that other Romanians were being deported as forced labourers, he replied: 'I cannot see the Russians are wrong in making 100 or 150,000 of these people work their passage. Also we must bear in mind what we promised about leaving Romania's fate to a large extent in Russian hands.'[12] Churchill was clearly speaking the language of 'spheres of influence'.

But in February, and again in March, as regards Poland it was to be a different matter. In February 1945 the Soviet arrests of Poles continued, with trainloads of those judged recalcitrant sent east – including more than 240 truck loads of people from Białystok.[13] And in March, having tricked them into attending a meeting, the Soviets arrested and then imprisoned former members of the Polish underground council.

Both the American and British governments found it hard to reconcile the oppressive Soviet actions with the business-like leader they had seen at Yalta. So once more they fell back on what had by now become their standard excuse. Stalin was still trustworthy; it was other powerful but shadowy figures in the Kremlin who were preventing the agreement being honoured. Charles 'Chip' Bohlen, the prominent American diplomat and Soviet expert, recorded that by May 1945 the view of those in the State Department who had been at Yalta was that it was the 'opposition' that Stalin had encountered 'inside the Soviet Government' on his return from the conference that was responsible for the problems.[14] And, as Harry Hopkins put it, 'We felt sure we could count on him [Stalin] to be reasonable and sensible and understanding – but we never could be sure who or what might be in back of him there in the Kremlin.'[15] Meantime, Averell Harriman, in Moscow, deduced that it was 'Red Army Marshals' who were somehow now trying to pull the strings.[16]

But although these views were also broadly echoed in London, there were some British diplomats who had served in Moscow, such as Thomas Brimelow,[17] who questioned the evidence for sinister forces behind Stalin. And, of course, he was right. His more senior colleagues who represented the consensus in the Foreign Office, as well as the political leaders of America and Britain who subscribed to this theory themselves, were all wrong. There was no one behind Stalin pulling the strings. Moreover, from the first there had been an alternative explanation for the Soviet actions – one just as plausible if not more so. Stalin's occasional inconsistency of approach – like sending a conciliatory telegram almost at the same time as an accusatory one – could be read as a simple tactic to keep the West guessing. And now, at this crisis in the relationship, there was an even more likely explanation for Soviet behaviour: that Stalin was forcibly demonstrating that the American spin on Yalta was nonsense. He had always wanted the states that neighboured the Soviet Union to be 'friendly' by his definition – which meant eliminating anyone the Soviets considered a threat.

But it was not possible that either Churchill or Roosevelt would recognize that Stalin was simply being consistent. To begin with, each of them had too much political capital wrapped up in the idea that they could deal with the Soviet leader. As we have seen, long before he met Stalin, Roosevelt had expressed the view that he could 'handle' him. And Churchill had felt an emotional connection with the Soviet leader ever since his boozy late-night dinner in Stalin's apartments in the summer of 1942.

Each of the two Western leaders came to believe they could form a 'special' bond with Stalin. Both were wrong. Stalin had no 'special' bond with anyone. But in their attempt to charm him they had missed the fact that he had, in his own individual way, charmed them instead.

It was Churchill who felt most upset at the perceived Soviet breaches of Yalta – something that must have rather bemused Stalin. After all, Churchill had let the Soviets have a free hand in Romania without any problems, just as the Soviets had let the British use force to quash revolution in Greece. Didn't that therefore demonstrate the reality that Churchill supported the concept of 'spheres of influence'? Wasn't Churchill's protest on Poland – regardless of the precise wording of the Yalta agreement actually a case of double standards?

Churchill would have vehemently disagreed with this argument. For him Poland was special. He said in March, in a lengthy and emotional telegram to Roosevelt, that he saw Poland as the 'test case between us and the Russians of the meaning which is attached to such terms as Democracy, Sovereignty, Independence, Representative Government and free and unfettered elections'.[18] Moreover, 'He [Molotov] clearly wants to make a farce of consultations with the non-Lublin Poles – which means that the new government in Poland would be merely the present one dressed up to look more respectable to the ignorant, and also wants to prevent us from seeing the liquidations and deportations that are going on, and all the rest of the game of setting up a totalitarian regime before elections are held, and even before a new government is set up. As to the upshot of all this, if we do not get things right now it will soon be seen by the world that you and I, by putting our signatures to the Crimea settlement, have under-written a fraudulent prospectus.'

Roosevelt (whose ill health meant that his telegrams were now often drafted by his advisers, Byrnes or Leahy) replied to Churchill's message on 11 March, blandly saying that the 'only difference' between the British and Americans on this key issue was 'one of tactics'; and that Roosevelt's 'tactics' were not to escalate this business to Stalin before matters had been exhausted by their ambassadors in Moscow. But this attempt to calm Churchill down did not work. The Prime Minister wrote in even more emotional terms on 13 March: 'Poland has lost her frontier. Is she now to lose her freedom? That is the question which will undoubtedly have to be fought out in Parliament and in public here. I do not wish to reveal a divergence between the British and the United States governments, but it would certainly be necessary for me to make it clear that we are in the presence of a great failure and an utter breakdown of what was settled at Yalta, but that we British have not the necessary strength to carry the matter further and the limits of our capacity to act have been reached.'[19]

Roosevelt clearly thought Churchill was over-reacting. And it is not hard to see why. As the President subsequently pointed out, the agreement at Yalta could be read in such a way that Stalin could deflect many of the complaints. So why was Churchill so upset? He would claim it was because Stalin had broken his Yalta pledges. But it is likely there was more to it than that. Churchill knew he had an election coming up, and the British electorate would not take kindly to accusations that Poland, the country over which Britain had gone to war, had been betrayed. Moreover, Churchill's expansive rhetoric about Poland and Stalin (not least the comment that would come back to haunt him, about Chamberlain 'being wrong' to trust Hitler whilst he was sure he was 'right' to trust Stalin) meant that this was not an ordinary issue of foreign policy, but a principle that had come for him almost to define the latter part of his wartime premiership. Roosevelt, only just starting his new term in office and not burdened by these emotions, had no such worries.

But even at this most decisive time, Churchill's rhetoric was not all that it seemed to be. Although in public he could talk about the moral imperative behind the war, in private he revealed that he was a good deal less pure in his motives. On 13 February, on the way back from Yalta, he had argued with Field Marshal Alexander, who was 'pleading' with Churchill that the British should give more help with post-war reconstruction in Italy. Alexander said that this 'was more or less what we were fighting this war for – to secure liberty and a decent existence for the peoples of Europe'.

'Not a bit of it,' Churchill replied, 'we are fighting to secure the proper respect for the British people!'[20]

On 15 March Roosevelt sent a cold reply to Churchill's communication of the 13th: 'I cannot but be concerned at the views you expressed...we have been merely discussing the most effective tactics and I cannot agree that we are confronted with a breakdown of the Yalta agreement until we have made the effort to overcome the obstacles incurred in the negotiations at Moscow.'[21]

Churchill realized he had gone too far. And, as he usually did in moments of stress in the relationship with Roosevelt, he tried to charm his way out of the situation: 'I hope that the rather numerous telegrams,' he said on 17 March, 'I have to send you on so many of our difficult and intertwined affairs are not becoming a bore to you. Our friendship is the rock on which I build for the future of the world so long as I am one of the builders.'[22] Roosevelt did not reply, leading to the plaintive question from Churchill on 30 March: 'By the way, did you ever receive a telegram from me of a purely private character...?'[23] Roosevelt then merely acknowledged that he had received this 'very pleasing'[24] message.

But although during this period Roosevelt was less emotionally involved than Churchill over the question of Poland, he did get angry when Stalin accused the Americans of deception by holding a meeting with German officers in Berne in Switzerland about a possible surrender in Italy. Stalin saw this encounter as a reason for both the strengthening of German resistance against the Red Army in the East and the swift progress of the Western Allies through Germany. Roosevelt was furious that Stalin had effectively accused him of lying, writing on 4 April that 'I cannot avoid a feeling of bitter resentment toward your informers, whoever they are, for such vile misrepresentations....'[25]

In his reply, Stalin immediately moderated his attack. But even though he was prepared to back down on this issue, what he would not do was move an inch on his position on Poland. On 7 April he wrote to Roosevelt, who had finally sent a telegram of protest to the Soviet leader on 31 March, agreeing with the American President that: 'Matters on the Polish question have really reached a dead end.'[26] But Stalin was clear that the reason for this was that the Western Allies had 'departed from the principles of the Crimea Conference'.

The consequences of the ambiguous language, not just of the Polish agreement made at Yalta but of the whole debate about Poland between the Western Allies and Stalin for the last three years and more, were now plain for all to see. Stalin stated not just that the Lublin Poles should still make up the bulk of the new government (since the agreement at Yalta had called only for the existing provisional government to be broadened) but also that any other Poles who were invited to take part should be 'really striving to establish friendly relations between Poland and the Soviet Union'. The Soviets were, of course, the ones who would decide just who was 'really striving' to be their friend. It was the kind of indefinable test favoured by Stalin's regime – a positive version of the negative charge, which was virtually impossible to refute, that one was 'an enemy of the people'.

'The Soviet Government insists on this,' wrote Stalin, 'because of the blood of the Soviet troops abundantly shed for the liberation of Poland and the fact that in the course of the last 30 years the territory of Poland has been used by the enemy twice for attack upon Russia – all this obliges the Soviet Government to strive that the relations between the Soviet Union and Poland be friendly.'

Roosevelt, more than Churchill, recognized that, given the loose language of the Yalta agreement, there was little the Western Allies could do apart from protest – and there were limits even to that, given that Soviet cooperation was needed in other areas. One of the last telegrams Roosevelt sent to Churchill before his death read: 'I would minimize the general Soviet problem as much as possible because these problems in one form or another seem to arrive every day and most of them straighten out....'[27]

Roosevelt left the White House on 30 March 1945 to go on what would prove to be his final journey, to the health resort of Warm Springs in Georgia. Here his office was filled with documents about the forthcoming conference in San Francisco that would initiate the United Nations. Right to the end of his life,

Roosevelt never lost his focus on his vision of the UN. Alongside this grand ideal, the detailed question of Soviet infractions in Poland must have seemed to him relatively unimportant.

Perhaps appropriately, for a man who self-confessedly never 'let his right hand know what his left was doing', there was an element of deception around his death that April. Not just in the obvious sense – that he had deliberately concealed the extent of first his disability and then, more recently, his illness from the American people – but also in the demonstration of his most intimate feelings. Many years before, shortly after marrying his wife Eleanor, he had fallen in love with Lucy Mercer, then his wife's personal secretary. He had wanted to leave Eleanor for her, but had finally chosen to stay married and so preserve his political career. Now he wanted Lucy by his side. On 9 April he drove out to accompany her, and the painter Elizabeth Shoumatoff who was to paint his portrait, back to Warm Springs. On 12 April he finally fell victim to a cerebral haemorrhage. Unbeknownst to his wife Eleanor, it was Lucy who was with him the day he died.

Churchill, understandably, paid Roosevelt a tribute in the House of Commons, but, curiously, he did not choose to attend the President's funeral – something he later said he regretted. His excuse – pressure of work – was merely a convenient get-out. He was the most compulsive traveller of all the wartime leaders and could have made the journey if he had wished. Perhaps this was a final statement of disappointment – a small and ungenerous payback for the fact that Roosevelt had not supported him in the last weeks over the protests to be made to Stalin.

BATTLE FOR BERLIN

Meantime, the battle for Berlin raged. And both the planning and conduct of this final battle in the war in Europe demonstrate further signs of the disintegrating alliance with Stalin.

The planning for the operation had been conducted at the end of March and the beginning of April against the background of

Stalin's suspicion that the Western Allies were planning some kind of separate peace with Germany via the Berne talks – a suggestion that, as we have just seen, outraged President Roosevelt during his last days.

Stalin met Marshal Zhukov, the most prominent of the Soviet commanders, in the Kremlin late in the evening on 29 March, and handed him an intelligence document which suggested that the Western Allies were in discussion with Nazi agents. The Soviet leader remarked that 'Roosevelt wouldn't break the Yalta agreement [which placed Berlin well within the agreed Soviet zone of occupation of Germany] but Churchill was capable of anything.'[28]

Stalin had just received a telegram from General Eisenhower which, much to Churchill's subsequent annoyance, confirmed that the Western Allies were not pushing immediately forward to Berlin. In the double-think world that Stalin now inhabited, this was evidence of Allied deceit: if they had said they were not moving to take Berlin, then of course they were. It was all heavily reminiscent of the near-paranoid state Stalin had fallen into back in the spring of 1941 before the Nazi invasion. And so, in this spirit of saying the opposite of what one really intended, Stalin sent a telegram to Eisenhower on 1 April that stated that he agreed that the capture of Berlin should not be a priority since the city had 'lost its former strategic importance'.[29]

Then, in a move calculated both to speed the advance and deny Zhukov the glory of overall command, Stalin announced to his generals that he was splitting the task of capturing Berlin between two Soviet armies. It was a race between Zhukov's 1st Belorussian Front and Konev's 1st Ukrainian Front to see who could take the capital. 'Stalin encouraged an intrigue – scheming,' says Makmud Gareev,[30] then a major in the headquarters of Soviet 45 Infantry Corps and subsequently deputy chief of all Soviet forces. 'When they were drawing the demarcation line between the two fronts in Berlin, Stalin crossed this demarcation line out and said: "Whoever comes to Berlin first, well, let him take Berlin." This created friction.... You can only guess Stalin was doing it so that no one gets stuck up and thinks he was the particular general who took

Berlin.... At the same time he had already begun to think what would happen after the war if Zhukov's authority grew too big.'

On 16 April Zhukov's troops launched a massive attack on the Seelow Heights outside Berlin, and within four days had broken through this last major defensive position in front of the capital. By Hitler's birthday, the 20th, the Red Army was shelling the German leader's subterranean refuge – the Führerbunker.

For Vladen Anchishkin,[31] a captain in a mortar unit in Zhukov's Belorussian Front, this was the culmination of years of fighting: 'At last it was the end of the war, it was a triumph, and it was like a race, like a long-distance race, the end of the race. I felt really extreme – well, these words did not exist then – but I felt under psychological and emotional pressure. Naturally I didn't want to get killed. This is natural. I didn't want to be wounded. I wanted to live to the victory, but it was somewhere in the background, and in the foreground were the things I had to do, and this state of stress that was in me.'

And he was certain that the years of brutal warfare had changed him and his comrades: 'In the end, in the war itself, people go mad. They become like beasts. You shouldn't consider a soldier an intellectual. Even when an intellectual becomes a soldier, and he sees the blood and the intestines and the brains, then the instinct of self-preservation begins to work.... And he loses all the humanitarian features inside himself. A soldier turns into a beast.'

The battle for Berlin was one of the bloodiest and most desperate of the war. Although criticized since for his desire to leave the fight to the Soviets, Eisenhower was correct in the assumption that there would be heavy losses in the struggle. Around 80,000 Soviet soldiers died in the operation, 25,000 within the capital itself.

'So many of our people died – a great many, a mass,' says Vladen Anchishkin. 'It was a real non-stop assault, day and night. The Germans also decided to hold out to the end. The houses were high and with very thick foundations and basements and very well fortified.... And our regiment found itself in terrible confusion and chaos, and in such a chaos it's very easy to touch somebody else with your bayonet. Ground turns upside-down, shells and bombs explode.'

Within the chaos of the battle, the rivalry between Zhukov and Konev was intense. Anatoly Mereshko,[32] an officer with Zhukov's 1st Belorussian Front, was ordered to find out just which Soviet forces had captured a particular suburb of Berlin first: 'I got into my car with machine gunners. Rode up there and talked to the people in the tanks. One said: "I am from the Belorussian Front", another: "I am from the Ukrainian Front." "Who came here first?" I asked. "I don't know," they replied. I asked civilians: "Whose tanks got here first?" They just said: "Russian tanks." It was difficult enough for a military man to tell the difference between the tanks. So when I came back I reported that Zhukov's tanks got their first and Konev's tanks came later. So the celebration fireworks in Moscow were in his name.'

In the heat of the battle it was also clear that the race between Zhukov and Konev had not helped the soldiers to know just which forces were friendly and which were not: 'They [Zhukov and Konev] were rivals,' says Vladen Anchishkin. 'There was rivalry between two fronts. There was nothing criminal about it.... But this rivalry in Berlin did not always have a positive effect because sometimes soldiers didn't know who was where.... This was on the borders between the fronts, and a lot of people died only because of the rivalry between two fronts.'

Despite the difficulties, the Red Army fought with immense conviction in Berlin, fuelled by the sense that they were on a mission of retribution. 'We are proud to have made it to the beast's lair,' one soldier wrote home at the time. 'We will take revenge, revenge for all our sufferings.'[33] And one form which that 'revenge' should take was articulated by Ilya Ehrenburg, the Soviet propagandist, who wrote: 'Soldiers of the Red Army. German women are yours!'[34]

The rapes in Germany were on a massive scale – even more so than those in Hungary. Around 2 million women were attacked. In one of the worst examples of atrocity, a Berlin lawyer who had protected his Jewish wife through all the years of Nazi persecution tried to stop Red Army soldiers raping her, but was then shot. As he lay dying, he watched as his wife was gang raped.[35]

Potsdam, just outside Berlin, which was to be the site of the forthcoming final Allied conference, was devastated and much of it lay in ruins. Ingrid Schüler,[36] who lived in a block of flats within a mile of the site of the proposed conference, was seventeen years old when the Red Army arrived in April. 'My parents hid me,' she says. 'And we were extremely lucky because my mother was not raped...women were of huge importance to them [the Soviets]. That was the worst thing: the rapes.... I can tell you about a baker's family in our street. The Russians had gone into their house intending to rape the baker's wife. Her husband, who happened to be at home, stood in front of her trying to protect her and he was immediately shot dead. With the passage to the woman clear, she was raped.'

The scale of atrocities perpetrated by the Red Army in Germany in the first six months of 1945 was clearly immense. And the motivational factors were obvious as well. Vladen Anchishkin puts it this way: 'When you see this German beauty sitting and weeping about the savage Russians who were hurting her, why did she not cry when she was receiving parcels from [German soldiers on] the Eastern Front!' Only very occasionally, in their letters home, did the soldiers admit what was happening. 'They [the women] do not speak a word of Russian,' recorded one Red Army soldier in a letter he wrote in February 1945, 'but that makes it easier. You don't have to persuade them. You just point a Nagan [a type of revolver] and tell them to lie down. Then you do your stuff and go away.'[37]

Of course, as with the atrocities committed by the Red Army in Hungary, the rapes must be seen in the overall context of violent retribution. For years the Red Army had been fighting an enemy who had announced they were themselves conducting 'a war of annihilation'. This is something that Anchishkin can confirm because he himself committed the ultimate act of revenge in Czechoslovakia. When he and some of his comrades were fired on by a group of retreating SS soldiers, all his pent-up hatred burst through. Once they were captured, he had a number of these Germans brought in to see him – one by one.

'I was in such frenzy, I said: "Come on." There was this entrance into the apartment block. I said, "Bring them here for interrogation," and I had that knife, and I cut him.... I immediately killed that man with the knife,' he says. 'You can't imagine what a man is [like] – a man is as mellow and soft as a piece of butter, and the knife goes in very smoothly. Just one moment and the throat is cut. In films they show it not like the way I did it. [In real life] it's very quick and your victim no longer cries – you just see the bubble coming from his mouth and that's it. I was in such a state.... What could I feel? I can feel only one thing, revenge. You stab him here and you cut his throat. And then you only push him [over], and that's all. I felt, "You wanted to kill me? Now you have it. I waited for this – you were hunting me down for four years. You killed so many of my friends in the rear and on the front, and you were allowed to do that. But here I have the right." It's difficult to find decent words to express it. If you wanted [to know what I said], "You bitches! You asked for it."'

In Berlin the Germans could not hold out against the Red Army, and on the afternoon of 30 April 1945 Hitler took his own life. Typically, since the Führer could never accept that he had personally created the circumstances of this catastrophe, one of his last recorded statements was: 'If the German people lose the war, then they will have proved themselves unworthy of me.'[38]

A week later, early in the morning of 7 May, General Alfred Jodl, Chief of Staff of the German High Command, signed a document of unconditional surrender. The war in Europe was over.

THE NEW PRESIDENT

As the Red Army prepared to celebrate victory in eastern Europe, the deceased Roosevelt was replaced by his Vice President, Harry Truman, a sixty-year-old former senator from Missouri. Truman immediately brought a new energy to the presidency, as George

Elsey, working in the White House map room, discovered: 'Harry Truman was utterly unlike President Roosevelt in terms of a personal relationship. First of all, our impression of him – here's a guy who can walk. And he was vigorous, physically vigorous. He was only a few years younger than Franklin Roosevelt but in behaviour, attitude, speech and so on one would have thought he was twenty, twenty-five years younger. When he first came into the map room he walked briskly around, introduced himself to each of us – "I'm Harry Truman"…and he took an intense interest in what we had in the map room, wanted to read our files.… Truman was open and eager to learn, and was very willing to admit that he didn't know. Roosevelt would never have admitted that he didn't know everything himself.'

As for the Soviets, they knew little about this provincial politician – and what they did know, they disliked. After all, it had been Truman who had been quoted in the press as saying, in the immediate aftermath of the German invasion of the Soviet Union in 1941, that the Americans should assist whichever side was losing 'and that way let them kill as many as possible'.[39] Truman was unaware of the intricacies of American foreign policy; and so, in those early weeks of his presidency, in his dealings with the Soviet Union he relied on the old hands, Harriman and Hopkins. On 25 May, six weeks after Roosevelt's death, Harry Hopkins arrived in Moscow at Truman's request. He had spent much of the Yalta Conference in bed, sick with the cancer that was to kill him the following year, and although he was still unwell, he was anxious to help the new President.

Hopkins met Stalin on the evening of 26 May. It was an important meeting, not so much in terms of what was decided, but because Stalin's behaviour demonstrated that there was no doubt that he – rather than, allegedly, the 'people behind him' – controlled Soviet policy. In the initial moments of the meeting, Hopkins emphasized that 'public opinion' in America had been badly affected by the 'inability to carry into effect the Yalta agreement on Poland'.[40] Stalin replied by putting the blame for the failure squarely on the British, who, he said, wanted to build up a 'cordon sanitaire' on the border of the Soviet Union, presumably in order to keep the Soviets in check. Hopkins denied that the United States wanted any such thing, and added that the Americans were happy to see 'friendly countries' along the Soviet borders. The use of the trigger word 'friendly' seemed to cheer Stalin up, and he said that if that was the case, then 'we can easily come to terms' about Poland.

These two remarks by Hopkins – about the power of public opinion in America and his reiteration that the United States wanted a government that was 'friendly' to the Soviets – were used to his disadvantage by Stalin in the second meeting, on 27 May. The Soviet leader said that he 'would not attempt to use Soviet public opinion as a screen' but would, instead, speak about the feelings of his government. He then stated his position – which was just as Roosevelt had predicted it would be: the Yalta agreement meant that the existing Lublin government could simply be 'reconstructed'. 'Despite the fact they were simple people,' added Stalin, 'the Russians should not be regarded as fools, which was a mistake the West frequently made, nor were they blind and could quite well see what was going on before their eyes. It is true that the Russians are patient in the interests of a common cause but their patience had its limits.'[41] Stalin also remarked that if the Americans started to use the issue of Lend Lease as 'pressure' on the Russians, this was a 'funda-mental mistake'. (The Soviet leader clearly wanted to ensure that any post-war aid from America was not linked to political matters.) It was a bruising performance, and Hopkins was duly bruised. He denied both that he was 'hiding' behind American public opinion and that he was attempting to use the issue of Lend Lease as a 'pres-sure weapon'. Stalin replied that he had observed that his remark about public opinion had 'cut Mr Hopkins to the quick'.

It was classic Stalin – the use of calm, unemotional insults as a way of destabilizing an opponent. Stalin had the power to control his emotions, and to use offensive remarks as a way not of reliev-ing or expressing feeling but as a method of probing the strength of his opponent. He had recently insulted Roosevelt over the ques-tion of the alleged Berne negotiations, and then withdrawn the charge when the American President had shown his upset. Intriguingly, when Churchill had complained about Stalin's behaviour over the same issue, the Soviet leader had written back: 'My messages are personal and strictly confidential. This makes it possible to speak one's mind clearly and frankly. This is the advantage of confidential communications. If, however, you are going to regard every frank statement of mine as offensive, it will make this kind of communication very difficult. I can assure you that I had and have no intention of offending anyone.'[42]

Churchill, Roosevelt and Hopkins all appear to have been genuinely hurt by Stalin's insults, which implies that they believed they had a personal relationship with him. But Stalin knew that these negotiations had nothing to do with 'friendship' or 'personal relationships'. Stalin could not care whether anyone liked him or not. What mattered to him was power and credibility; the power to occupy countries on the border of the Soviet Union and impose 'friendly' governments on them, cloaked by the credibility of an interpretation – however stretched – of Yalta in order to defend Soviet actions. And in both respects, Stalin was winning. Little wonder that Eden, with all his experience of international negotiations, wrote that: 'If I had to pick a team for going into a conference room, Stalin would be my first choice.'[43]

At this meeting in May 1945, Stalin was almost toying with the new President's emissary. He told Hopkins that 'four or five' of the ministerial posts in the Polish provisional government could be given to Poles from the list 'submitted by Great Britain and America' – before allowing himself to be corrected by Molotov and saying it was just 'four' because 'he thought the Warsaw Poles [previously referred to as the 'Lublin' Poles] would not accept more than four ministries from other democratic groups'. This idea that he had to bow to the wishes of his own puppet government in Poland was a trick he had used before – but no one had yet dared say to his face that it was obvious nonsense.

Towards the end of the meeting, Hopkins made an impassioned appeal for the Soviets to allow the 'freedoms' so dear to the Atlantic Charter – freedom of speech, assembly and religion – to be allowed in the newly occupied territories. And in his response Stalin once again played with Hopkins, saying that 'in regard to the specific freedoms mentioned by Mr Hopkins, they could only be applied...with certain limitations'. Eventually, a 'compromise' of sorts was agreed – with five Poles from outside joining the new provisional government – something that was far from the ideal that Roosevelt and Churchill had hoped for in the immediate aftermath of Yalta.

The harsh reality was that Stalin and the Soviets were in possession of Poland and most of the other countries bordering the Soviet Union. And the Western powers could do little about it – a reality that was brought crushingly home to all concerned at the final conference of the three powers, held in the Soviet-occupied part of Germany.

THE POTSDAM CONFERENCE

In the wake of the destruction of Nazi Germany, the three Allied leaders agreed to meet in leafy Potsdam, just outside Berlin and the site of the grand palace of Frederick the Great. The location was symbolic not just of the subjugation of Germany but of the dominant role of the Soviets within eastern Europe. As at Yalta, it was the Soviet authorities who organized this conference. It is significant that at no point in the war or its aftermath did Stalin ever travel to a meeting that his own security forces did not oversee. As he knew, the more powerful the person, the more others travel to be in their presence.

At Yalta it had been agreed that Berlin would be divided into sectors, with each of the four powers (France was the fourth) controlling one area of the city. And it was clear to Ingrid Schüler, the teenager who in the early days of the Soviet occupation had hidden from potential Soviet rapists in the attic of the family flat, that 'there were two completely different worlds – [the world of] the Russians and [the world of] the Western Allies...because Wannsee [a nearby suburb of Berlin] was occupied by the Americans. We could see how wonderful it was. They got along

[with the locals], they chatted with one another. It was wonderful
– the streets were safe, people weren't afraid.' As far as Ingrid was
concerned, 'this alliance' between these 'two worlds' was 'incom-
prehensible'. 'In the East [there was] no democracy…it was well
known that they had no say, everything was imposed on them,
they were told what to do, they had no freedom at all. It was
common knowledge that many people were deported even at the
time…. And on the other side, that was freedom.'

One crucial matter had been finally settled before the Potsdam
Conference – Western recognition of the government of Poland.
In June the 'new' provisional government was established –
although to the uninitiated it looked very much like the 'old'
provisional government, with around 75 per cent of its members
supported by the Soviets. The previous inability of the Western
Allies to recognize the Soviet-backed Poles had, it was suspected,
been the cause of Stalin's refusal to allow Molotov to attend a
meeting in San Francisco to discuss the United Nations. This
problem had concerned Roosevelt deeply during his last days, and
although Stalin had finally relented and as a gesture to Truman
agreed that Molotov could go to the meeting after all, it was a sign
of just how ruthlessly the Soviets would play politics. There were
many other ways in which the Soviets could destabilize the relationship with the West if they wished. And now that a face-saving
formula had been found over the interim government of Poland,
both the British and Americans embraced it with alacrity. In the
process they confirmed once again their acceptance of the new
borders of Poland, which gave the Soviet Union almost all the
territory in the east of the country that they had taken in 1939
under the deal with the Nazis.

The Americans recognized the provisional government as the
legitimate rulers of Poland on 5 July, and the British followed one
day later. The bitterness of the remaining members of the Polish
government in exile and the other Poles who had fought alongside
the Western Allies was, understandably, immense. General Anders
wrote: 'Thus the Polish President, Mr Raczkiewicz, who in 1940
had been greeted at Paddington Station by King George VI, the

Polish Government in London, and the Polish forces, who had fought so long at the side of Great Britain and the United States, were discarded.... In 1940 Mr Churchill had assured General Sikorski that we were bound together in this war for life or death. But Soviet Russia was much stronger than these promises.'[44]

But unbeknown to Anders, by the time of Potsdam the British had already considered and rejected the possibility of imposing 'upon Russia the will of the United States and the British Empire'. In the wake of the Soviets' perceived failure to stick to the Yalta agreement, Churchill had ordered British military planners to consider a worst case, military option against the Soviet Union. Called, aptly enough, Operation Unthinkable, the final report was completed on 22 May 1945. It is in many ways a bizarre document, not least because it represents the contemplation of a sudden and immense change of course for British policy. The conclusion of the report was stark – and somewhat obvious: 'If our political object is to be achieved with certainty and with lasting results, the defeat of Russia in a total war will be necessary. The result of a total war with Russia is not possible to forecast, but the one thing that is certain is that to win it would take us a very long time.'[45] The Chief of the Imperial General Staff, Sir Alan Brooke, was less circumspect in his diary, writing on 24 May: 'This evening went carefully through the Planners' report on the possibility of taking on Russia should trouble arise on our future discussions with her. We were instructed to carry out this investigation. The idea is, of course, fantastic and the chance of success quite impossible.'[46] It was a long way from the initial military assessment of the capabilities of the Soviet Union back in the summer of 1941, when the Red Army had been expected to resist the Germans only for a matter of weeks. Now, the idea of 'conquering' the Soviet Union was something that few could contemplate seriously.

At the same time as Churchill was digesting this news, his relationship with Truman was getting off to a sticky start. Truman had recognized immediately that Britain was very much the minor partner in the triangular relationship with the Soviet Union. The new American President had not even bothered to discuss with

Churchill beforehand the Hopkins mission to Moscow. He had also declined Churchill's invitation to meet together to discuss tactics before the tripartite encounter with Stalin. And in a decision that added further tension to the already strained relationship, Truman sent Joseph Davies – the man who had memorably remarked to Stalin in May 1943 that after the war Britain would be 'financially through' – to Britain in order to explain American policy. The meeting between Davies and Churchill did not – to put it mildly – go well.

Truman had also received a number of passionate suggestions from Churchill about how the relationship with Stalin should be hardened because of the Soviets' failure to implement the Yalta agreement. In particular, Churchill suggested that the Western Allies should not withdraw from the area of Germany they currently occupied, which lay within the Yalta-agreed Soviet-controlled sphere. He even sent Truman a telegram warning that 'an iron curtain is being drawn down on their [the Soviet] front'.[47] But Truman wanted no dramatic confrontation with Stalin, especially one orchestrated by Churchill. The British Prime Minister got the impression that Truman was trying to edge him out of matters still more by asking the British to attend the Potsdam Conference only after the Americans had already spent time alone with Stalin. On this basis, said Churchill, he was simply 'not prepared to attend'.[48] As a result, the Americans agreed that he should be present from the beginning.

The Potsdam Conference began on 17 July 1945, with meetings held at the Cecilienhof, the former home of the German Crown Prince Wilhelm. The American President stayed near by in a grand house that had until recently belonged to a wealthy German publisher, Hans-Dietrich Müller Grote. But Truman did not know about the sinister history of the place until the 1950s, when the son of the former owner wrote to him. 'In the beginning of May the Russians arrived. Ten weeks before you entered this house, its tenants were living in constant fright and fear. By day and by night plundering Russian soldiers went in and out, raping my sisters before their own parents and children, beating up my old parents. All furniture, wardrobes and trunks etc. were smashed with bayonets and rifle butts, their contents spilled and destroyed in an indescribable manner....'[49]

But although at the time Truman did not know about these specific incidents, the general behaviour of the Red Army in Berlin was all too apparent. 'The Soviets were, of course, "liberating" everything in sight,' says George Elsey, who was part of the American delegation at Potsdam. 'Soviet trucks, mostly American-made, were hauling off anything that was haulable to be shipped back to the Soviet Union to help rebuild their economy. Even in the palace where the conference was being held, even when it was going on, the Soviets were stripping plumbing fixtures, stripping everything they could except from the small area where the conference itself was being held.'

Elsey and the other Americans were also aware of the attitude of the Soviets towards the Germans: 'We were hearing about the rapes – we were hearing them from the soldiers. British and American soldiers that were in the area had quite unbelievable stories about the behaviour of Soviets to the German populace. But finally when it was repeated over and over again I had to accept that this indeed was happening.... I don't think it made me feel differently about the Soviet Union as a whole – this was just the behaviour of men who'd been under enormous pressure for years, reacting in a human, brute manner.' American and British soldiers were not behaving in a similar way because, Elsey believed, 'their countries had not been subjected to all the problems that the Soviet Union had been for so many years. And we thought we had better discipline, better training, better behaviour, better education. They [British and American troops], after all, weren't peasants from God knows where – they were young, good British citizens, young, good American citizens. So we were proud of the fact that our troops were behaving well in contrast to the Soviets.'

At midday on 17 July, Harry Truman met Stalin for the first time. And Truman, like Roosevelt and Churchill before him, was impressed when he encountered the Soviet leader face to face. 'I can deal with Stalin,' he wrote in his journal.[50] 'He is honest – but smart as hell.' The new American President was quick to tell his Soviet counterpart how he liked to work: 'I told Stalin that I am no diplomat but usually said yes or no to questions after hearing all the argument. It pleased him.' They discussed Franco's role in Spain ('He wants to fire Franco,' recorded Truman, 'to which I wouldn't object'), Italy (Stalin, Truman wrote, wanted to 'divide up the Italian mandates') and the Chinese situation. Stalin also confirmed to Truman that he would be 'in the Jap war on August 15'.

But, as Truman well knew, there was a massive subject that was as yet unspoken between the United States and the Soviet Union – something the new American President called 'dynamite... which I'm not exploding now'. Truman himself had only learnt of the existence of this 'dynamite' less than three months earlier. On 25 April he had been briefed for the first time about the Manhattan Project – the attempt to develop a nuclear bomb. Despite the scale and cost of this work, Truman had not been told about it during Roosevelt's lifetime. Once he had been let in on the secret, however, he instantly grasped both the potential of the new weapon and its effect on the relationship with the Soviet Union. And just before the start of the Potsdam Conference a successful test of the weapon had taken place in the New Mexico desert – the bomb was exploded for the first time at the Almogordo test site on 16 July, the day before Truman met Stalin.

The existence of the bomb brought many new political questions to the fore: not least, whether or not to tell Stalin about it. Churchill and Roosevelt had both previously agreed not to inform Stalin about the development of the bomb – a sign that both of them still harboured suspicions about Stalin's ultimate trustworthiness; though some of their staff, such as George Elsey maintained that since the Soviet Union wasn't yet involved in the war against Japan, the conflict in which the bomb would be used, the existence of this new weapon was simply none of his business. The committee that Truman set up to advise him about the use of the bomb initially suggested a continuation of this policy and that the Soviets should learn about the new weapon only when it was used against the Japanese. But before Potsdam the advisers changed their minds and recommended that Stalin should be told. Truman discussed the question at a private lunch with Churchill on 18 July, and recorded that they now 'decided to tell Stalin about it'. Truman also said he believed the 'Japs will fold up before the Russians come in. I am sure they will when Manhattan appears over their homeland.'

Significantly, in that same journal entry Truman waxed lyrical about his chat with Stalin. He wrote that he had invited the Soviet leader to visit America, and was prepared to send the US battleship *Missouri* to collect him. Stalin had told him that 'he wanted to cooperate with US in peace as we had cooperated in war but it would be harder. Said he was grossly misunderstood in US and I was misunderstood in Russia. Told him that we could help to remedy that situation in our home countries and that I intended to try with all I had to do my part at home. He gave me a most cordial smile and said he would do as much in Russia.'

Churchill, despite his angry telegrams about Stalin's perceived breaches of the Yalta agreement, similarly softened once more when he met Stalin in the flesh. As Cadogan recorded in his diary: 'He is again under Stalin's spell. He kept repeating "I like that man".'[51] Cadogan, ever an intelligent if cynical apparatchik, added: 'I am full of admiration of Stalin's handling of him.'

Truman finally mentioned to Stalin, after the plenary meeting at Potsdam on 24 July, that the United States had 'recently tested a new weapon of unusual destructive force'.[52] Stalin asked no questions about the 'new weapon' and replied that he hoped the Americans would make good use of it against the Japanese.

The explanation for Stalin's lack of curiosity is simple: he already knew all about the Manhattan Project. The Soviets gained their information from spies who were scientists at Los Alamos, notably Klaus Fuchs and David Greenglass. At his trial in 1951, Greenglass revealed that he had been passing nuclear secrets to the Soviet Union since November 1944. The motive of many of these spies was not just straightforward Communist sympathies, but a desire that the Americans (and British, who shared in the research) should not have a monopoly on the physics behind the atomic weapon.

Zoya Zarubina was one of the Soviet officials trusted with the secret task of translating the American information about the nuclear bomb. 'We got these papers from somebody – well, let's call it "friends of the Soviet Union" – and from our own intelligence services, and we were very, very rapidly translating them for the Russians to understand.' Most of the material she worked with was of an extremely technical nature and so 'little by little we had engineers attached to us. We would do two pages and then the engineers would come and say: "No, no. This is foolish – can it be that?" We thought it a little like a mosaic, a puzzle…. Stalin knew more than I did – he knew from A to Z.'

Stalin had been so concerned to gain what advantage he could from Nazi atomic research that he had authorised Beria to send a specialised search team to comb Soviet-occupied Germany for information about German progress in this most crucial scientific area. The team, led by Colonel General Zavenyagin, arrived in Berlin even before the end of the war in Europe, and several prominent German scientists were traced, detained and transported to the Soviet Union.[53]

Truman had first mentioned the existence of this 'new weapon' to Stalin at the end of a fractious discussion among the three leaders about the Soviet attitude to the Yalta agreement. It was a meeting that crystallized the differences between them. The Western Allies complained that restrictions were being made on their representatives in the countries occupied by the Soviet Union. Stalin simply denied that this was so. Truman reiterated the demand that 'all satellite governments are reorganised on democratic lines as was agreed by all at the Yalta conference'. Churchill for his part said that 'With regard to Romania and in particular Bulgaria we know nothing. Our mission in Bucharest has been penned up with a closeness that approaches internment.'

'But,' said Stalin, 'you are citing these things as fact when they cannot be verified.'

'But we know this to be true,' replied Churchill, 'from our

representatives in these countries. Marshal Stalin would be very much astonished to read a long catalogue of difficulties encountered by their mission there. An iron fence has come down around them.'

'All fairy tales,' said Stalin.

'Of course,' said Churchill, 'we can call each others' statements fairy tales, but I have complete confidence in our representatives in these countries.'[54]

It was an exchange that symbolized the impotence of the Western powers – impotence with two seemingly untreatable causes. The first was the reality of the military situation – these eastern European countries were now occupied by Soviet forces, and it would take another war to get them out. The second cause had less of a practical nature, but was in a way more far-reaching. It was to do with language. The problems that the Americans and British created for themselves when they agreed that any future Polish government should be 'friendly' to the Soviets have already been seen. Now they were to experience similar problems over the word 'democratic'. Nearly six years earlier, for example, the Soviet authorities had decided to make occupied eastern Poland 'democratic'. This democracy had consisted of elections, true, but only specially selected 'friendly' candidates could stand for office. It was sham democracy – but still something that Soviet propaganda could trumpet as evidence of a commitment to 'freedom'. In just the same way, the 1936 Soviet constitution was promoted as one of the most liberal political documents in the world, promising as it did 'free' elections, the right to work and the right to leisure. Stalin, inaccurately portrayed as the author of the constitution (it was primarily conceived by Nikolai Bukharin) was praised at the time by *Pravda* as 'the wisest man of the epoch'.[55] All this enabled Stalin to maintain the propaganda position, as he did in the 24 July meeting with Truman and Churchill, that he was just as 'democratic' as they were – it was just that he practised a different kind of 'democracy'.

On 25 July, Churchill left Potsdam to return to Britain to learn the results of the general election that had been held earlier in the month – the result had not been available sooner because so many votes had been cast overseas. For Churchill the news was devastating. Labour had won by a landslide and now commanded a majority of 145 seats in the House of Commons. And although it is true that the Conservatives had run a lacklustre campaign, with Churchill committing the serious gaffe of saying that a socialist government would inevitably mean the imposition of some kind of secret police force, Labour's victory was the result not so much of a poor Conservative performance as a massive desire for change.

So the new Prime Minister, Clement Attlee, and Foreign Secretary, Ernest Bevin, took over leadership of the British delegation at Potsdam. Bevin, in particular, was a very different personality from his Conservative predecessor, Anthony Eden. Unlike Eden, who had been educated at Eton and Christ Church, Oxford, Bevin had worked as a labourer since the age of eleven. Pat Everett[56], who had been one of Anthony Eden's secretaries for nearly five years, found the change of boss particularly refreshing. Not least because in the entire time she had worked for Eden he had not bothered to learn her name: 'Well, he was a bit remote, you know, a bit remote. He always used to call me: "Miss ...er ...er...." I was really rather hurt. Once he was reading a memorandum, and there was a list of people who were going on the next flight, and my name was there. I was called Miss Gorn [her maiden name] then and his finger went down and he said: "Miss Gorn – who's that?" So I said: "That's me." And he says: "Oh, oh, is it?"'

With Bevin, the atmosphere was entirely different: 'He was very nice, you see. The first time I went to him, he says: "Come in, little missy, and sit down." So I went in and he said: "Now, what's your name?" So I said I was Miss Gorn, and he said: "And where are you from?" And I said: "Bristol." He said: "Well, now, so am I." I said: "Yes, I know." And he said: "What part of Bristol?" I said: "Well, my father had a house on the big main road out of Bristol", because being a doctor he had a big corner house. And he said: "Well, I'll be blowed! I used to drive my brewer's dray past your father's house to take my deliveries to the Blue Lion."'

It was Bevin, together with the new American Secretary of State James Byrnes (appointed by Truman on 3 July), who thrashed out with Stalin an agreement on reparations, and in the process prepared the way for the eventual division of Germany. Stalin had listened to their proposal and then suggested that 'with regards to shares and foreign investments, perhaps the demarcation line between the Soviet and western zones of occupation should be taken as the dividing line [between the Soviets and the Western Allies] and everything west of that line should go to the [Western] allies and everything east of that line to the Russians.'[57]

This agreement that, essentially, the Soviets could take whatever financial recompense they liked from Germany within their own agreed area of occupation, was one of the first moments when the division of the country between East and West became a real possibility. It symbolized the breakdown in trust and communication between the two sides – an acknowledgement that the mutual governance of Germany might never be achieved among the signatories of the Yalta agreement.

The Potsdam Conference finally ended on 2 August. Truman – who Stalin had privately remarked he found 'neither educated nor clever'[58] – left with the resolution that he would never return to Europe. He never did. And although he had found Stalin straightforward to deal with, he was under no illusions about the nature of the Soviet regime, which, he wrote to his mother, was 'a police government pure and simple: a few top hands just take clubs, pistols and concentration camps and rule the people on lower levels'.[59]

The day before the ship carrying President Truman back across the Atlantic landed at Norfolk, Virginia, a crucial message arrived from the Secretary of War. 'I decoded it,' says George Elsey, 'and took it to Truman. And the substance of it was very simply "Hiroshima bombed – greater effect than earlier tests", and that was all that needed to be said. Truman was elated when he announced to the crew that we had a powerful new weapon and that the war would almost certainly end – invasion [of Japan] would not be necessary.... The crew just erupted in an explosion of hilarity and joy and shouts and the pounding of the desks and tables and so on. That was the mood in which we returned to Washington.'

And though there was an attempt more than ten years[60] ago to portray Truman's decision to use the nuclear bomb against the Japanese as influenced to a large extent by a desire to demonstrate to Stalin the 'powerful new weapon' at the disposal of the Americans, other scholarship[61] has demonstrated this was not the case. The reason the bomb was dropped was – as common sense suggested all along – primarily because the Americans wanted to end the war as quickly as possible and, crucially, prevent the need to invade the Japanese home islands.

But the existence of the nuclear bomb did offer the possibility of a different way of dealing with Stalin – at least, Churchill thought so at Potsdam. According to Sir Alan Brooke, he was 'completely carried away!' Churchill said that 'we now had something in our hands which would redress the balance with the Russians!' Furthermore, 'now we could say if you insist on doing this or that, well we can just blot out Moscow, then Stalingrad, then Kiev, then Kuibyshev, Kharkov, Stalingrad, Sebastopol etc., etc.'[62] No doubt, after the sense of impotence Churchill had felt over the preceding months, this idea of blackmailing Stalin with the nuclear bomb was immensely attractive. But it was scarcely a practical way forward. Although it was one thing to threaten the leaders of a potentially belligerent country that, if they started a war, nuclear weapons would be used against them, it was quite another to say to the leader of a former ally that if he didn't regulate in an acceptable way the countries his forces currently occupied then his homeland would face annihilation. It was also clear that it would not be long before the Soviet Union possessed nuclear weapons of its own – and so it proved. The first Soviet nuclear test was carried out in 1949.

And the evidence is that even during the few post-war years before the Soviets acquired their own bomb, Stalin was not overly concerned by the apparent American advantage. He was well aware that the Americans didn't yet possess enough bombs to destroy the Soviet Union;[63] and he did not consider they would use the weapons they did have except under the severest provocation. Significantly, the existence of the nuclear bomb did not prevent Stalin challenging the West, a year before the Soviets tested their own nuclear weapon, at the time of the blockade of Berlin in 1948, when the Soviet leader tried, but failed, to remove the Western Allies from the city. 'I believe that Stalin,' said Andrei Gromyko, Soviet Deputy Foreign Minister, '[though] of course nobody actually asked him directly – embarked on that affair [i.e. the Berlin blockade] in the certain knowledge that the conflict would not lead to nuclear war. He reckoned that the American administration was not run by frivolous people who would start a nuclear war over such a situation.'[64]

THE SOVIET INVASION OF MANCHURIA

The dropping of the nuclear bomb on Hiroshima did not mark the end of the war. And three days after Hiroshima, the same day as the atomic bomb on Nagasaki, and almost three months to the day since the formal end of the war in Europe, the Soviets kept the promise they had made to Roosevelt and declared war on the Japanese. The Red Army moved into Manchukuo (as the Japanese had dubbed Manchuria) on 9 August. The timing of this action was not coordinated with the nuclear attacks – the Soviets had no knowledge of when or where the bombs would be dropped.

Operation August Storm, under the command of Marshal Vasilevsky, was a huge undertaking, involving more than one and a half million soldiers of the Red Army. The advance – on two fronts – made swift progress against an under-equipped and ill-prepared Japanese defence force. 'I was telling myself that I was going to fight for a noble cause,' says Ivan Kazantsev,[65] a battalion commander during August Storm. 'The Japanese had done a lot of harm to the Chinese and to ourselves as well.... Of course, the nuclear bomb [at Hiroshima] cooled off the samurais, cooled off their arrogance, but I don't think it put an end [to the war].'

Within his battalion fighting in Manchuria, one platoon was made up of soldiers from 'western Ukraine' who had been drafted into service. These 'western Ukrainians' maintained, says Ivan Kazantsev, that 'they were former Poles'. They came from part of eastern Poland, the territory that the Polish Prime Minister in exile had refused to relinquish in acrimonious discussions with Churchill and Stalin the previous year, but which was now occupied by the Soviets and recognized by the Allies as part of the Ukraine, a republic within the Soviet Union. These Poles – or 'Ukrainians' as Kazantsev saw them, using the politically correct Soviet terminology – were not happy to be fighting for the Red Army in Manchuria, thousands of miles from home: 'I came out the tent and saw that half of my soldiers, those western Ukrainians, were in tears. It was their "kulak" psychology, non-patriotic psychology. I was twenty-three years old but they were grown-up men in their later forties and older.... They were concerned about their families who they had left behind, about their plots of land.... We realized that ideologically they were different from us.... We knew that these people needed their morale boosting and they had to be enlightened politically, so we gave them classes of political education.'

It is a telling image of personal misery. Instead of basking in a liberated Poland – 'free and democratic' – as they had no doubt dreamt of since the start of the war, these previous citizens of Poland had now, against their will, been made citizens of the Soviet Union and drafted into the Red Army to fight the Japanese. No wonder they 'needed their morale boosting'.

On 15 August 1945, Emperor Hirohito announced that the Japanese would accept the terms of the Potsdam Declaration which had called for the Japanese to surrender or face 'prompt and utter destruction'. In his speech to the Japanese people, the first time they had heard the voice of their monarch, he said: 'Should we continue to fight, not only would it result in an ultimate collapse and obliteration of the Japanese nation, but also it would lead to the total extinction of human civilization. We have resolved to pave the way for a grand peace for all the generations to come by enduring the unendurable and suffering what is unsufferable.'

The Second World War was over. And Hirohito's instruction to 'endure the unendurable and suffer what is unsufferable' also encapsulated the task ahead for many of the unwilling subjects of the Soviet occupation of Eastern Europe.

LIFE BEHIND THE NEW 'IRON CURTAIN'

After the dictatorship of Adolf Hitler, the Allies had said that they wanted to bring 'democracy' to Germany. But in the German capital in the immediate aftermath of the war, it was clear that democracy would mean different things to different people. Berlin, as had been agreed by the Big Three, was divided into four sectors of occupation – British, American, French and Soviet – with the German capital as a whole sitting well within the Soviet zone of the country. In those early days it was relatively easy to travel between the different zones of the city – the Berlin Wall was not built until 1961. And Heinz Jörgen Schmidtchen[66] gives an idea of what the circumstances of occupation were like for someone whose home was in East Berlin, within the newly established Soviet Zone.

He was a teenager at the time, and had played little part in the conduct of the war. He had not fought in the German armed forces, but, like most young men, had joined the Hitler Youth. Now, the differences in style and substance between the occupying powers were very obvious to him: 'We saw Frenchmen who were not very well disposed towards us, we saw English who were friendly, but very distant, very reserved. We saw Americans who were the most accessible of all the Allied forces. We liked that best – we liked their style.' As for the Soviet forces, he was deeply wary of them. 'I knew that in the first days [of the occupation] my aunt had been raped. My other aunt, they just ripped the jewellery off her – didn't just take it off, they ripped it off her body. We never encountered individual soldiers – they were always in groups. What you saw was that vodka played a big role. They were very noisy. You'd see lorries with stuff they'd looted – furniture, even bits of wood, everything. That didn't seem normal to us. All of this was not something you could see in the Western sectors. They [the Soviet troops] took out of the houses what they could.'

In the months immediately after Potsdam, Schmidtchen and his friends wrestled with a new concept – 'democracy'. 'We tried to interpret the word "democracy" [but] we couldn't quite imagine how it would look in practical terms....' When he attended a

Communist Party meeting, he discovered that it was 'similar to what we knew before [under the Nazis]. Commands were issued. Other people had to listen.' It was only many months later, when he went to a meeting of the Socialist SPD in West Berlin, outside the Soviet sector, that he realized that 'democracy' could mean the freedom to voice your own opinions.

He and his friends started putting posters up for the SPD in East Berlin, but by the spring of 1946 his activities had come to the attention of the Soviet authorities. 'It was Saturday 9th May and I was about to leave the house when a German police officer approached me and asked my name, and then he told me on Monday I was to go to Russian headquarters. I asked him quite casually: "Why should I go there?" and he said: "Well, they want to question you." I asked him did I have to take anything with me, and he said: "No, you'll be back by lunch."'

As a result of this reassurance, he was 'fairly cheerful' when he walked over on Monday to the Soviet headquarters. But when he arrived and a guard took him upstairs 'suddenly I had the feeling that I had done something wrong. I felt sort of hot, although I didn't know what lay ahead.' He was questioned by a Soviet major, via an interpreter. 'He first asked me for my [identity] cards and then how things were – if I had enough to eat, that kind of thing. Until he suddenly said why were we against the Communists and the Russians? My question was, who were "we"? He ignored that and kept asking. He stayed quite calm. The interpreter became loud – she translated very loudly. I only listened to half of what she said, [and] the whole thing lasted about two hours.'

After this first interrogation he was taken downstairs to a cellar in the basement of the building. 'There was a bulb of maybe fifteen watts, and this terrible, terrible smell...my eyes got used to the bad light...there were people there and I squeezed myself between them...I felt like I was completely numb, I didn't know what to think.' There were seventeen people crammed into the cellar, and Schmidtchen realized that 'a few had already been in that cellar for three or four months and hadn't been able to wash themselves'. His life had been transformed in an instant. He had thought that he had only to answer a few questions and then be home in time for lunch. Now, 'I was so disappointed. I was seventeen years old. I really didn't know what was going to become of me. If I would ever come out.'

After fourteen days in the cellar, at three o'clock in the morning, Schmidtchen was called out for his second interrogation. This time both the interrogator and the interpreter were different. But the questions were essentially the same – 'why we were against the Red Army and the Communists'. He tried to explain his interest in politics, but the female interpreter grew angry and beat him first with her fists and then 'she took off her high heels and hit me in the neck with that. I've got a big scar there today.... After a while I was taken back to the cellar...the next morning my hair was cut off. That was the moment when I knew that I am in the same situation as the others. I'm nobody special here.... I didn't want to believe in evil – that you could be locked up when you're innocent. I really didn't want to believe in that. So that was a bit of hope. But every night when some people came back from their interrogations it did dawn on me that they were trying to break us. They were trying to destroy us. That maybe we might admit things that weren't true. I know that many did that. They were just so desperate. They were so afraid of being beaten [and of] the water cells [where prisoners were confined in small cells partly filled with water], and the pretend tribunals where they were sentenced to death [where prisoners were lied to, and told they were about to be shot].'

Schmidtchen was imprisoned in a variety of Soviet-run jails in East Germany. Conditions were appalling. In late 1946, for example, prisoners' rations were halved. 'They'd been insufficient before. But suddenly we just got a half litre of clear soup and a piece of bread. This was a death sentence. This was on 5 November 1946. From this time onwards to March the death rate was so large that even the Russians were shocked. In those months, I cannot remember a day when nobody died.... The only thought you have in the morning is will you get enough to eat today – to survive this day. We didn't believe we would ever be free again. We were vegetating. There were many moments when I would not have cared if I had died.'

Schmidtchen was finally released after more than eight years of captivity, having been brutally punished for the crime of wanting 'democracy'. Today he feels 'less rage now about those who had us taken there and locked us up. My rage is more with the people in present-day Germany who think about this time in contrast with that, and give people from that time high pensions and almost mock the victims. I've written not long ago to certain politicians, [saying] with the knowledge I now have I would not once try to do something for democracy and hang up posters. I would not do that.'

During their attempt to suppress any dissent and exercise control over their zone of occupation, the Soviets made use of what was left of the Nazi infrastructure – including concentration camps. John Noble,[67] who in 1945 was a twenty-two-year-old American citizen, was one of those who discovered this truth when he was imprisoned after the war in Buchenwald concentration camp just outside Weimar, within the Soviet Zone of Germany.

During the war he had lived with his family in Dresden, where his father owned a camera factory. They were all American citizens, and although not imprisoned by the Nazis, they were effectively interned: from 1939 their movement was restricted to the city of Dresden, and from 1941 they had to report regularly to the police.

In the spring of 1945, when the Red Army arrived in Dresden, the Soviets committed atrocities in direct view of the Nobles' family home: 'In the house next to ours, Soviet troops went in and pulled the women out on the street, had mattresses that they pulled out, and raped the woman. The men had to watch, and then the men were shot. Right at the end of our street a woman was tied on to a wagon wheel and was terribly misused.... Of course you had the feeling that you wanted to stop it, but there was no possibility to do that.' The open abuse of women and the general looting of the city continued for at least three weeks before a semblance of order returned. Even after this period, the Nobles regularly heard reports that women who worked in their camera factory had been assaulted on their journey to and from work.

To begin with, the Nobles believed that they themselves – and their factory – were relatively safe. They flew the Stars and Stripes over the factory roof and trusted in their American citizenship to protect them. But in the autumn of 1945 both John Noble and his father were arrested as they returned from West Germany, where they had been arranging a transport of camera lenses. The exact motive for their arrest is unclear, although John Noble believes that simple avarice is the most likely explanation – the Soviet authorities just wanted to control the camera factory themselves.

John and his father were sent first to Dresden prison, where they were incarcerated without charge. And because John served as a prison clerk he learnt first hand of the treatment meted out to his fellow inmates. In the first place, he was shocked to discover that children were imprisoned along with adults. 'Take, for example, a ten-year-old boy who was accused of blowing up a bridge,' he says. 'He said he didn't do it, and he was tortured. The doctor and I had to take him from the interrogation room back to his cell, and tried to patch him up as good as we could. He was called again. He again denied blowing up the bridge, was again tortured. The third time he couldn't take the torture any more and so he said: "Ok, I blew up the bridge." So they left him in peace for a while, but still in prison. And then they called him again and they said: "Look, we found out that bridge was never blown up. You lied to a Soviet officer. Because you lied to him we're going to give you ten years." He died in prison.'

Just as Heinz Jörgen Schmidtchen experienced starvation rations in Soviet captivity, so did John Noble. 'In Dresden prison I went through a starvation period – the whole prison went through a starvation period. During the night someone called from another cell. I could hear an echo in the prison hall: "If there was a God in heaven, he wouldn't let this happen".... And as I lay down on my bunk – it was the fifth or sixth day [of the starvation period] and I don't remember exactly – I prayed and I said: "Lord, close my eyes and keep them closed. I can't stand it any more, but if there is a life for me it's not mine – mine's over with. If there's a life, it's all yours." And that's when everything changed.'

It was this new spiritual strength, Noble believes, that helped sustain him through the weeks of near-total starvation. And when he was moved to Buchenwald in the autumn of 1948 he found conditions almost as bad as in Dresden prison. All around him people were dying. And the prisoners resorted to any method they could in order to gain a morsel more of food. 'In those barracks where people were literally dying, the guard would go through and touch the toe [of the prisoners lying in their bunks], and if it was still warm then he'd count [as someone to get the small daily ration of food].... So the prisoners tried to keep the toe [of a dead prisoner] warm... so that when the guard went through he thought: "He's still alive", so the food ration was there the next day.'

John Noble was fortunate to survive, because under the Soviet administration of Buchenwald more than seven thousand people died. And though many of those imprisoned at Buchenwald by the Soviets were former Nazi functionaries, there were also several prisoners who had been victims of Nazism. 'Two people in the barracks that Dad and I were in had been here during the Nazi period. Not as guards but as prisoners. And when you'd ask them: "What's the difference?" they'd say: "There is no difference between then and now." But I'd say: "How come? If you were a prisoner then, how come you're a prisoner now?" [And they replied] "Yeah, well, when you're against the regime you run into that danger of being arrested."'

When Buchenwald was finally closed by the Soviets in 1950 the inmates were transferred to a variety of other penal institutions. John Noble was sent to the labour camp complex at Vorkuta in the northern Urals. He was not released until 1955, by which time he had served more than nine years in prison. 'I can't say it any other way than you're numbed against the injustice,' he says, talking of his whole experience. 'Because everything around you was injustice. Not only in the camp – everywhere the Russians were there was injustice. It's just a matter of trying to survive to get this thing over with.'

By the time John Noble was in Buchenwald, in the late 1940s, the division of Europe was complete. Soviet-dominated regimes existed in East Germany, Poland, Czechoslovakia, Hungary, Romania and Bulgaria, and more 'independent' communist regimes (though still influenced by Stalin) had taken root in Yugoslavia and Albania.

In 1947 the Marshall Plan had been announced by the United States – a gigantic package of economic aid for Europe. It marked the death of the vindictive anti-German sentiments that had inspired the Morgenthau Plan. It was also the end of any pretence that Europe was not divided. Once it was clear that in order to benefit from the Marshall Plan any eligible country had to also subscribe to concepts alien to Stalin – like free trade and human rights – the Soviet leader demanded that all Eastern European countries reject the proposed American aid.[68] Instead, Stalin announced the Council for Mutual Economic Assistance (COMECON), which linked the Eastern bloc economically but provided no aid from the Soviet Union on the scale of the Marshall Plan. Within months, the Sovietization of much of eastern Europe had also taken place – the last steps on the path to Communism had, in the end, been travelled swiftly. With the creation of the military alliances of NATO (1949) for the West and the Warsaw Pact (1955) for the East, the battle lines of the Cold War were definitively drawn.

In parallel with this split in Europe went a gigantic shift in population unparalleled in European history – something that was largely a consequence of the wartime decisions taken by the Allied leaders. In the immediate aftermath of the war 2 million Poles left eastern Poland after it became part of the Soviet Union – a few went voluntarily, but most did not. Meantime, a total of more than 11 million Germans were thrown out of East Prussia, Czechoslovakia, Hungary and other eastern European countries. At least half a million of them died in the process. In addition, the Western Allies agreed to send back to the Soviet Union any Soviet citizens they came across – whether these people wished to be repatriated or not. Two million were returned; a number of them, particularly those who had fought on the German side, went unwillingly and were persecuted by the Soviet state on their return.

THE FARCE AND TRAGEDY OF KATYN AT NUREMBERG

Once Stalin had told a monumental lie, then he followed that lie through, wherever it took him. And so, in the wake of the defeat of Germany, Stalin resolved to frame the Nazis publicly for the murders at Katyn. At the Nuremberg war crimes trials the Soviets brought charges against German officers who, of course, had nothing to do with the killings.

From the beginning the Western legal experts were wary of the Soviet request to include Katyn on the list of war crimes to be tried. The American chief prosecutor advised his Soviet counterpart to drop the case, but the Soviets refused.

The Soviets used the Burdenko Commission report as a basis for the prosecution, and began coaching a variety of witnesses on the lies that they should tell in open court. But not everyone on the Soviet side went along with the deception. The assistant to the Soviet chief prosecutor, a lawyer called N. D. Zorya,[69] began to have doubts about the veracity of the material he was asked to present about Katyn. He had previously shown that he was uneasy about peddling untruths – in 1939 he had been demoted when he had announced that there were falsehoods in a case he had been told to prosecute. Zorya was thus precisely the wrong man, from the point of view of the Soviet authorities, to be involved with Katyn. So concerned did Zorya become about the Katyn 'evidence' that he asked if he could return to Moscow and discuss his doubts with Gorshensky, the General Prosecutor of the Soviet Union. He was refused permission and the very next day, 23 May 1946, was discovered dead in his room.

No one has ever established the exact cause of his death. But one of the Soviet translators at Nuremberg, T.S. Stupnikova, said she believed that his death was a 'warning to our lawyers' that 'it is unacceptable to stumble'. In that sense, the exact manner of his death was less important than the suspected reason for it – that he had complained about the task he was set. And his life could have been ended, she speculates, in a variety of ways: 'Did he commit suicide himself when he felt there was no way out? Or was it suggested to him to end it all and never see his wife and child again? Or maybe he was simply shot by Soviet specialist in such methods – Beria's boys working at Nuremberg.'[70]

In July 1946 the Nuremberg war crimes tribunal formally examined the murders at Katyn. Each side, Soviet and German, had been limited to calling three witnesses. Those on the Soviet side had all been carefully prepared over the preceding weeks. Professor Viktor Prozorovsky, a leading Soviet forensic scientist, told the court – as he had told the Burdenko Commission – that there was little doubt but that the Poles had been murdered in the autumn of 1941. Dr Markov, a Bulgarian medical expert who had originally been part of the German commission of investigation in 1943 that had blamed the Soviets for the crime, now reversed his testimony and said that it was the Germans who were really responsible.

The only witness the Soviets called who had lived and worked in the area at the time of the German occupation was Boris Bazilevsky, an academic who had been deputy mayor of Smolensk. Like many of the 'witnesses' called to the Burdenko Commission the year before, he was someone who had collaborated with the Germans, and it was obviously therefore massively in his interests to please his new Soviet masters. And he certainly did his best, creating a fantasy of lies for the benefit of the Soviet case. He said that 'in the spring of 1941, at the beginning of the summer, they [the Poles] were working on the restoration of the roads.'[71] He also claimed that in the autumn of that year he had asked his own boss, Menshagin, the mayor of Smolensk, to 'plead' for the release of one of the Soviet prisoners whom the Germans held, only to be told by Menshagin that he had learnt from a German officer that 'the Russians would be allowed to die in the camps while there were proposals to exterminate the Poles'. Bazilevsky also said that Menshagin added: 'You should understand this in the very literal sense of these words.' Two weeks later, he asked Menshagin: 'What was the fate of the Polish prisoners of war?' And Menshagin conveniently replied: 'They have already died. It is all over for them.' Bazilevsky then claimed he had overheard a German officer saying to Menshagin: 'The Poles are a useless people, and exterminated

THE IRON CURTAIN | 389

they may serve as fertilizer for the enlargement of living space for the German nation.'

The Soviet prosecutor told the court that Menshagin – obviously now the most crucial witness of all – could not be heard as a witness at Nuremberg because he had fled to the West with the Germans and had disappeared. This, like everything else in their Katyn presentation, was a lie. They knew exactly where Menshagin was – in a Soviet prison.

'Menshagin, at the time of the Nuremberg trials,' says Anatoly Yablokov,[72] a former Russian military prosecutor who investigated the Katyn massacre in the early 1990s, 'was in an NKVD internal prison from 1946 to 1951. And then for another nineteen years he was kept in Vladimir prison in a single cell...because his name was used as evidence – false evidence.' For twenty-five years Menshagin refused to confirm the lies that the Soviet authorities had told about him – and suffered accordingly: 'The fact that he was imprisoned for twenty-five years – for nineteen of them in solitary in a single cell, without any correspondence, letters, without meeting his relatives – this is a torture in itself.... His [Menshagin's] tough insistence [not to agree to the lies told at Nuremberg] inspired respect even from prison officials. They said that Menshagin was a man who wouldn't succumb to any pressure during interrogations. I feel deep respect for all people who refused to participate in these falsifications.'

Despite their best attempts to push through their fictional version of events at Katyn, the Soviets failed to frame the Germans for the crime. The inadequacies of the Soviet case were glaringly apparent. Bazilevsky, for example, appeared to have been coached in his responses when he was giving his evidence, and when the Soviet prosecutor tried to hurry him through his testimony he was admonished by the court. Also telling was the fact that, despite Bazilevsky admitting that he had collaborated with the Germans, he had not been punished by the Soviets.

But what finally caused the Soviet case to degenerate into legal farce was their inability to fix conclusively on just which German officer and which German unit they were blaming for the crime.

Although a 'Lieutenant Colonel Arnes' had been named in the Burdenko report as the man responsible for the murders, the Soviets could only find a German officer called Ahrens to put on trial – and even that allegation collapsed in the face of evidence from the defence. 'The Prosecution has up to now only alleged that Regiment Number 537,'[73] said Dr Stahmer, the defence counsel, on the second day of the hearing, 'was the one which had carried out these shootings and that [it was] under Colonel Ahrens' command. Today again, Colonel Ahrens has been named by the Prosecution as being the perpetrator. Apparently this allegation has been dropped and it has been said that if it was not Ahrens then it must have been his predecessor, Colonel Bedenck; and if Colonel Bedenck did not do it, then apparently, and this seems to be the third version, it was done by the SD [the intelligence section of the SS].'

As a result of this confusion, the crime of Katyn simply vanished from the list of offences tried at Nuremberg. No verdict was given, no judgement handed out. After the witnesses had been heard, there was only silence. It was not until Mikhail Gorbachev allowed the release of key archival material – including the infamous document signed by Stalin that led to the murder of the Poles – that the truth about Katyn was finally told to the world. An investigation into the crime was instigated by the Russian authorities in the 1990s, but no one was ever held to account for the murders.

THE FATE OF THE POLES

Once the war was over, the two hundred thousand and more Poles who had fought on the side of the Western Allies faced a difficult – almost impossible – choice. Should they return to Poland, a country now with changed national boundaries and under the domination of the Soviet Union? Or should they try to make a future for themselves elsewhere?

It was a choice made all the harder by the sense many of them felt that they had been discarded by the British. This belief that they were no longer wanted was symbolized by the omission of all the Polish army units from the Victory Parade held in London in the summer of 1946. Since the British government now formally recognized the Soviet-backed regime in Warsaw, these Polish servicemen in Britain were something of an embarrassment. Only the Poles who had fought in the Royal Air Force were asked to take part in the parade, and they refused out of loyalty to their comrades. 'We were like people who had done the hard work and whom nobody wanted any more,' says Wiesław Wolwowicz, who fought in the II Polish Corps at Monte Cassino. 'As a sign of gratitude they didn't even invite us to that parade – so it was some gratitude. I don't love the British side for that. I remember it – you can't forget about it. It was inhuman on their part.'

Winston Churchill, now leader of the opposition, said in the House of Commons on 5 June, just three days before the Victory Parade, that he 'deeply' regretted that 'none of the Polish troops, and I must say this, who fought with us on a score of battlefields, who poured out their blood in the common cause, are not to be allowed to march in the Victory Parade'. He also implicitly recognized the failure of the Western Allies to provide, as he had repeatedly promised they would, for a free and independent Poland. The Poles, he said, were now 'held in strict control by a Soviet-dominated government who do not dare to have a free election under the observation of representatives of the three or four Great Powers. The fate of Poland seems to be unending tragedy, and we, who went to war, all ill-prepared, on her behalf, watch with sorrow the strange outcome of our endeavours.'

Fewer than 15,000 of the men in the II Polish Corps who had fought under the command of General Anders decided to return to Poland at the end of the war. For the vast majority there seemed, as Anders himself put it, 'nothing ahead except a lifetime of roaming in exile'.[74]

Zbigniew Wolak[75] was one of the soldiers in Anders' army who faced the tough choice of whether to go home or not. He had fought in the Home Army in Warsaw and been captured by the Germans. When he was liberated from a prison camp by the advancing British forces he rushed to join the Polish units fighting in Italy. And thus, after the end of the war, and as a member of the British army, he found himself in England. It was here that the incident occurred that changed his life: 'I was out walking, in uniform, in a street in Chester with my English girlfriend. And a car comes along, a Morris Minor, and a British gentleman gets out in a Harris tweed jacket. He comes up to me and says: "Lieutenant, may I ask you a question?" I said: "Yes." He touches my Polish badge: "Just how long will you Poles want to continue eating English bread? Haven't you heard the war is over?" And my first impulse was to say: "Would you pose this question to the Poles who came in 1940, who came to help in the Battle of Britain?" That was quite a lesson for me – your friends don't want you when you are in trouble, and there is no friendship between nationalities.... The British were exhausted with the war. An average Englishman in Cheshire – he didn't understand.... They would tell us to go to hell.... At that time I did hold a grudge [against the British].... At the time we were full of romantic ideas and were sentimental – now I understand that we can't hold any grudge... [now] I see that people everywhere have similar problems and you can't count on anybody. Even your own countrymen. Human beings are always alone with their problems – that's the way it is.'

This encounter with the Morris Minor driver in Chester was the catalyst that made Zbigniew Wolak resolve to quit Britain. He was warned by friends not to return to Poland, but he ignored their advice. 'I said: "I'm alone. I have no family. I have no parents. I have nobody. And I don't accept this verdict of history that this is the end – that in spite of the rising we became a Soviet colony. And it should all be left [like that]. I want to be in Poland, and I want to share the fate of my generation."'

So Zbigniew returned to Poland, wearing his British army uniform – and was immediately imprisoned by the secret police for twenty-four hours. He was made to write his life story – a list of the most important events and dates – again and again so that the interrogator could pick up on any inconsistencies. 'And they told me directly: "Nobody wants you here in Poland. We don't need such people.'" When he was released, it was with the knowledge that he was condemned to do 'simple jobs and you can forget about studying'. Many years later, and after taking a series of menial jobs, Zbigniew did eventually manage to study at university. But he never felt secure and free in Communist Poland: 'This feeling of marginalization and being watched remained for my whole life.'

Although some of the returning Poles who had fought for the British were subjected to terms of imprisonment and persecution, the majority were able to get jobs, however menial, and survive. But – like all the other Poles – they were not living as free citizens in the free Poland of their dreams, the Poland they felt Churchill had promised.

STALIN'S REWARD

Once the war was won, Stalin faced a fundamental choice about how the Soviet Union should function as a state and how he should act as a leader. How should he reward those who had helped win the war? How should he deal with his returning servicemen who had seen first hand the capitalist world? Would he react in a way that was consistent with the hopes of the West, and somehow 'soften' his rule?

No, he would not. The immediate post-war years brought the return of a Stalin driven by suspicion to the point of paranoia. Anyone who had touched the West was at risk. The returning Soviet soldiers who had survived the appalling conditions of German captivity were some of the first to suffer. Stalin had voiced the view during the war that 'there are no Soviet prisoners of war – only traitors'; and, true to this philosophy, when those Red Army soldiers who had been captured by the Germans were released they were immediately imprisoned once again in an NKVD filtration camp, interrogated and then around half of them sent on to the Gulag.

Immediately after the war, even Soviet women who had married Allied servicemen were denied exit visas – and the consequent

personal suffering was, of course, enormous. Hugh Lunghi, an officer with the British military mission in Moscow had fallen in love
with a young Russian woman called Dina and wanted to marry her
and take her back to Britain. But when he put in a request to the
Soviet authorities he 'heard nothing more. It was the usual treatment one got – one just didn't hear anything more. We called it the
cotton wool treatment. You'd make a request and they'd say: "Yes,
we're dealing with it", and then you'd hear nothing more.'

Dina had already suffered as a result of her relationship with
Lunghi. She had admitted from the start of their friendship that
the NKVD had told her to spy on him – something that he was
relaxed about, given that he felt he had nothing to hide. But 'they
were disappointed, presumably, that she didn't supply them with
enough interesting material', and as a result she was briefly imprisoned twice during the war. But in the years immediately following
the end of the conflict, she was subjected to greater persecution,
and in 1947 was sent to a labour camp. Lunghi saw her when she
emerged, and was horrified to see her 'broken…terribly, terribly
depressed and appalled by it'.

Lunghi came to despise the Soviet regime with its 'double-
speak'. 'The Soviet media used language [like] "the freest, the
most democratic constitution in the world was the constitution
drawn up under Stalin in the 1930s".… And there was always the
catchphrase [that] these "bourgeois freedoms" [in the West] are
not the same as our freedoms – Soviet socialist freedoms – which
are the real freedoms'.

All this suffering and cynicism led him to believe that, although
'we received from ordinary people nothing but kindness and hospitality and friendship', the Soviet regime itself was at least as bad as
Nazism. But Lunghi recognized that the Soviets were 'the Ally we
could not do without. The war would have gone on far longer and
possibly Hitler would have invaded the United Kingdom if they
had not been our Allies', nonetheless, 'here we were fighting
[together] with someone who was actually worse – we really came
to think that Stalin was worse than Hitler, if that were possible. I
mean, it's like one devil being blacker than another.'

Stalin was not just suspicious of foreigners – he was jealous of his colleagues. In particular, he wanted to prevent his generals taking credit for the success of the Red Army during the war. Ever since the Tehran Conference, where he had arrived in military uniform, he had attempted to reposition himself as the military genius who had won the war for the Soviet Union. It was a performance that reached its zenith eighteen months later at Potsdam, when Stalin had been resplendent in the white outfit of Generalissimo of the Soviet Union. But he, and those closely around him, knew the truth. Not only had his military acumen not won the war, it was only after he had reduced his interference in the detailed tactical decisions of his generals that the Red Army had prospered.

At the Soviet Victory Parade, held in Red Square on 24 June 1945, the rumour was that Stalin had wanted to consolidate this false impression of military brilliance by taking the salute of the massed ranks of soldiers personally – on horseback. But after falling off his horse while practising for the parade, he had been forced to give up the idea. As a result, Marshal Zhukov took centre stage instead, and rode confidently in front of the assembled troops. 'The Victory Parade was a brilliant event in the life of the Soviet Union,' says Svetlana Kazakova,[76] then a communications officer in Zhukov's headquarters and someone who knew Zhukov personally. 'I can still see it in my mind's eye. It was a summer day – it was raining, but Red Square was decorated with red banners. People were wearing medals and orders, and they were shining so much that the light from them was reflecting on the whole of the Red Square. As the hands of the clock moved close to ten everyone stood at attention, and then there were chimes, Kremlin chimes, and at that moment Georgy Zhukov, three times Hero of the Soviet Union, rode into the square on a white horse. He sat on the horse as elegantly as if he was a junior lieutenant.' Forced merely to watch the glamorous figure of Zhukov trotting back and forth on his white horse, Stalin not surprisingly felt envy flowing through his veins. More than that, he watched Zhukov with an ever-growing sense of misgiving. Stalin, a keen student of history, was well aware of the immense popular power that a successful general could generate – had not Napoleon used his victories on the battlefield to usurp the French Revolution and snatch power from the politicians?

Zhukov would have to pay a price for his popularity. And payment began in the wake of the arrest in early 1946 of Alexander Novikov, the commander of the Soviet air force. He was pressured by the NKVD into 'confessing' that he had become 'embroiled in a web of crimes' relating to the acceptance of 'various goods from the front for my personal gain'.[77] This was a 'crime' that was ubiquitous and tolerated – unless, as in this case, Stalin wanted to find an excuse to punish someone who was, in his eyes, getting above himself. Novikov also confessed to 'politically dangerous' conversations with Zhukov. 'First and foremost,' he said, 'I would like to say that Zhukov is an exceptionally power-loving and narcissistic individual; he loves to be treated with honour, respect and servility and is intolerant of any opposition.' In addition, revealed Novikov: 'Zhukov is not afraid of inflating his own role in the war as a senior commander, going so far as to declare that all the fundamental plans for military operations were developed by him.'

Despite the ministrations of the NKVD, Novikov could not point to any concrete examples of Zhukov plotting against Stalin. But the picture of Zhukov that emerged from the forced confession was of a man who was hungry for military success and personal honour, vain, egotistical and intolerant of failure in others (a description that also fitted many of the most successful Western commanders). Couched in these terms, it ought to have been enough to send Zhukov to the Gulag – which is why what actually happened is so curious. At first, Zhukov's denunciation went according to the Stalinist norm. At a meeting in the Kremlin on 1 June 1946, after the substance of the accusations in Novikov's confession had been read, Molotov and Malenkov considered Zhukov 'guilty' of the charges, and Beria added that: 'Zhukov's problem is that he is not grateful – as he should be – to Comrade Stalin for all he has done. He respects neither the Politburo nor

Comrade Stalin and he should be put in his place.'[78] So far, so predictable. But then Marshal Konev, Zhukov's bitter rival, especially in the last months of the war, began to speak. He had a good deal to gain from the removal of Zhukov, but although he declared that Zhukov was 'a very difficult person' to work for, he 'categorically refused the accusation about political dishonesty and lack of respect of Central Committee. I consider Zhukov a person loyal to the party, to the government and personally to Stalin.' This was a view supported by Marshal Pavel Rybalko, the brilliant Soviet tank commander: 'It is not true that Zhukov is a conspirator. He has his faults, as everyone does, but he is a patriot, which he proved during the Great Patriotic War [Second World War].' Significantly, Rybalko also said that he believed 'the time has come to stop giving credence to testimony extracted by force in the prisons'.

The brave support of these two marshals – and one can only stand in awe at the courage necessary to speak out against the word of the NKVD – meant that Zhukov could form with his military colleagues a united front against Stalin. Zhukov told the Soviet leader that 'such accusations are without foundation. Ever since I joined the Party I have served it and the Motherland honourably. I have never been connected with any conspiracy.' Moreover, said Zhukov, he was certain that the evidence against him was 'lies' obtained 'under torture'.

Stalin's considered judgement at the end of the meeting was not that Zhukov be taken away to the cells of the Lubyanka, but merely that he needed 'to leave Moscow for a while'. He was removed from his post as military governor of the Soviet Zone of Germany and subsequently appointed commander of the Odessa military district on the Black Sea, far away from the Soviet capital. 'Stalin decided to remove him, to send him away, and long joyless days began,' says Svetlana Kazakova, who together with her husband kept in touch with Zhukov in his exile. 'Some people, toadies, immediately stopped making phone calls to him, but other people who were decent people were afraid to phone him because they knew the secret police were listening to the phone calls. You could only talk outside the house.... We were very hurt on behalf of Zhukov. In our hearts we were very upset, but we all kept silent. Our feelings could not change anything.... I think badly about this system because this cruel treatment was unfair, it wasn't justified, and the country did not benefit in any way. It lost a man who could have retained the army in a much better condition.'

But it could have been a great deal worse for Zhukov. Stalin had shown during the purges of the 1930s that he was prepared to have the most senior figures in the military tortured and killed. All of which leaves the intriguing question – why did Zhukov not suffer a similar fate? One answer that has been proposed is that Stalin felt a residual affection, even gratitude, to Zhukov for his part in winning the war, and so – when it came to the moment – he felt he could not destroy him. But this is surely a romantic idea.

One of the keys to Stalin's ability to function was his lack of genuine attachment to others. Unlike Hitler, for example, who always felt a sense of loyalty to those 'Old Fighters' like Hermann Göring who had been with him since the early days of the Nazi movement, Stalin saw all his comrades as potential rivals. For most of the time, their usefulness to him outweighed the threat he perceived. But this equation was always unstable, and could tip one way or another in an instant.

Thus the explanation for Stalin's relatively lenient treatment of Zhukov must almost certainly be that he judged that any immediate threat was not sufficient to justify torture and death. And since Zhukov had many loyal followers in the Red Army – as the solidarity of the Soviet marshals had demonstrated – Stalin thought it best to deal with Zhukov in stages. The first stage was his removal from his power base as military governor of Germany and banishment to the wilds of the Soviet Union. The next stage would depend on future circumstance. It could either be his trial and death, or his rehabilitation. After all, Zhukov might be needed in the future – suppose there was a sudden and unexpected war and his military talents were once again required? And so, having weighed the options available to him, and with an icy heart devoid of personal feelings of affection, Stalin resolved to send Zhukov not to the Lubyanka but to Odessa.

Having turned on the man who more than any other helped the Red Army win the war, Stalin then targeted his closest political comrade throughout the conflict, Molotov, by attacking his wife, Polina Zhemchuzhina. Stalin had long been suspicious of her – she was Jewish, and had family connections abroad, with a sister in Palestine and a brother in America. In December 1948 Stalin moved against her, in an action that he knew would shake her husband. Although the Soviet Foreign Minister had been given the nickname 'Old Boot Face' by British officials because of his intransigence and seeming lack of feelings, Molotov was very much in love with his wife, and any attack on her would also be an obvious and direct attack on him.

As a result of an NKVD 'investigation', a resolution was brought before the Politburo in December 1948 to expel Polina from the Communist Party. This was the traditional first step on the way to the Gulag. The Politburo decided that: 'It has been established, through verification by the Commission for Party Control, that P. S. Zhemchuzhina has, for a considerable period of time, maintained links and close relations with Jewish nationalists, suspected of espionage and unworthy of political trust.'[79] The less than convincing evidence quoted was that she had attended the funeral of one Jewish leader and been seen talking to another prominent Soviet Jew. In addition, she had 'on 14 March 1945' committed the offence of participating 'in a religious ceremony in a Moscow synagogue'. Thus the Politburo concluded, 'In spite of the warnings issued to P. S. Zhemchuzhina by the Central Committee of the All-Russian Communist Party regarding her unscrupulousness in interactions with individuals undeserving of political trust, she infringed this party ruling and continued to conduct herself in a manner which was politically inappropriate. In connection with the above mentioned, P. S. Zhemchuzhina is henceforth expelled from the membership of the All-Russian Communist Party.'[80]

The resolution was signed by every member of the Politburo present except one. Molotov could not bring himself to condemn his own wife, and so he abstained. But over the next few weeks he wrestled with the possible consequences of what he had done. After all these years of utter subservience to the will of Stalin, could he really make a stand against him – even on a point of principle related to the woman he loved? Ultimately, he decided he could not, and in January 1949 he wrote a letter to Stalin: 'I acknowledge I made a political mistake when I abstained from the vote about the expulsion of P. S. Zhemchuzhina from the party. I would like to inform you that I have thought about this question and I am now voting for the decision of the Central Committee. The decision reflects the interests of the party and the state and it is in line with the correct understanding of communist party ideology. I acknowledge my heavy sense of remorse for not having prevented Zhemchuzhina, a person very dear to me, from making her mistakes in connection with anti-Soviet Jewish nationalists.'[81]

One can only imagine Stalin's feelings as he read this grovelling apology from a man who now realized that, by standing up for his wife, he had placed himself in real danger. Most likely Stalin would have recognized the content and spirit of Molotov's apology as confirmation of his own view of the human condition. Faced with the threat of personal suffering, scarcely anyone would live and die for principle. And thus he proved once again, at least to his own satisfaction, that – when it came to the final test – almost all human beings were cynical and weak. Polina was arrested in January 1949 and sent into exile. She was released only after Stalin's death.

Stalin's desire to crush any potential opposition – and in particular anyone who showed true personal leadership and initiative during the war – was also demonstrated by his actions against the Soviet officials who had administered Leningrad during the war. The German siege of this city, which lasted from September 1941 to January 1944, was one of the most horrific and costly actions of the war. Over a million Soviets died, amidst scenes of starvation and cannibalism. The defence of Leningrad was led by Andrei Zhdanov, the local party secretary. And Stalin was extremely suspicious of the initiative that he and his colleagues had demonstrated during the siege. 'It is very strange that Comrade Zhdanov doesn't feel any necessity to contact us in

Moscow at this difficult time,' he wrote to Leningrad party officials during the war. 'We can suppose that Leningrad, together
with Comrade Zhdanov, is not in the USSR but on some little
island in the Pacific Ocean.'[82]

Despite Stalin's attacks on the Leningrad leadership, and in the
face of appalling losses, the city held out against the Germans and its
survival was subsequently lauded as an example of Soviet courage
and tenacity. But those who endured the siege had changed. 'I think
I was aware,' says Yulia Kaganovich,[83] a young woman at the time,
'that my life before the victory, during the siege, was in some sense
the life of a free person. I didn't feel that anyone was telling me what
to do. You were needed and we understood what had to be done.
A sense of having a fist pressing down on me and forcing me to do
what I felt was wrong, that wasn't there. There was a sense of freedom, which, by the way, I only appreciated afterwards.'

'In general,' says Valeri Kuznetsov,[84] son of the second-in-
command in Leningrad, Alexei Kuznetsov, 'the war cured very
many people of several illusions. To be more precise, it stopped
them believing in the infallibility of the central leadership.
Leningrad was unique. It was like a little island where people could
make their own decisions.'

This, of course, was anathema to Stalin. And his first move to
deal with this 'problem' was to move both leaders of wartime
Leningrad to the Kremlin, where they had little chance of acting
independently. Zhdanov, who during the siege had passed on
effective control to his deputy when he found he could not fully
cope, was sent in the spring of 1948 to a sanatorium. His drinking
problem, already bad, had recently become worse. And despite the
zeal with which Zhdanov had taken to his post-war task of perse-
cuting those writers and artists who did not conform to the
Communist 'ideal', Stalin was still suspicious of him. After a
month in the sanatorium, Zhdanov was dead.

But whilst Zhdanov's death remains merely 'mysterious', there
is no doubt about responsibility for the subsequent widespread
repression of several hundred people who had led Leningrad
during the siege, most notably Alexei Kuznetsov. Fabricated

charges were laid, claiming that the Leningrad Communist Party had siphoned off money in order to give themselves autonomy from Moscow – but in reality it was Stalin's own paranoia that was the cause of the arrests. 'I said to my wife: "This is madness," says Mikhail Tairov,[85] then a member of the Leningrad regional administration. "It makes no sense. Such good people that we survived the siege with – they are not guilty of anything." And the next day they arrested me as well.'

Valeri Kuznetsov remembers the day they came for his father. 'He got up and got dressed, and then I can remember him saying: "Wait for me. I'll be back soon for supper. Don't have supper without me...." He [his father] went on foot through the nearest gate of the Kremlin. He turned and waved to us one more time. We were all standing at the window. That was the last time we saw him.'

Kuznetsov and the other leading members of the Leningrad Party were tortured into making false confessions and then shot. At the same time, at least two thousand members of the Leningrad elite were removed from their positions of power. Stalin had never forgotten this 'island' of initiative in the wartime Soviet Union. And to Stalin, initiative meant independence. And independence meant treachery.

THE DEATH OF STALIN

On 1 March 1953 Stalin collapsed following a drunken evening at his dacha with his cronies. He died four days later. For many of his closest colleagues – like Khrushchev, Beria and Molotov – his death came only just in time. Stalin had been planning still more repressions, most likely targeting the remaining senior figures who had served alongside him in the war.

Stalin left an eastern Europe dominated by the Soviet Union. Poland, in particular, was certainly as 'friendly' to the Soviet Union as Stalin could ever have wished. The nature of that 'friendship' was epitomized by a visit paid by the Polish leader, Bolesław

Bierut, to Moscow in 1950. Bierut asked Stalin about the fate of a number of Polish Communist leaders who had travelled to the Soviet Union in the 1930s and had subsequently disappeared (presumed murdered). Stalin turned to Beria and asked: 'Where are they? I told you to look for them. Why haven't you found them?' Then, as Bierut left Stalin's office, Beria turned to the Polish president and said: 'Why are you fucking around with Iosif Vissarianovich [Stalin]? You fuck off and leave him alone – that's my advice to you – or you'll regret it.'[86] Crude as Beria's words were, they are a fitting reminder of the threat that always lay just beneath the surface of Stalinism.

After Stalin's death there was a loosening of persecution – but only in relative terms. Although many prisoners were released from the Gulag system, the fundamental freedoms of speech and religion were never respected within the Soviet Union. The victimization of those who had been deported or imprisoned under Stalin continued in many cases until the fall of Communism, whilst those who had tormented them continued to prosper. 'These people who were the guards, who participated in the deportations, who participated in all of those crimes, they all lived very well afterwards,' says Nina Andreyeva, who had been deported from eastern Poland to Kazakhstan in 1940. 'They all received ranks, posts, all kinds of privileges, absolutely everything. And that man [the guard on her transport to Kazakhstan], he doesn't live far from us at all [in former eastern Poland – now part of Ukraine]. And there is one shop that we would often meet him in. Then he remembered me very well. He would greet me and ask me: "Please tell me, where is your brother [who, she learnt only in 1990, had been murdered by the NKVD during the war]? Maybe he is somewhere abroad? Maybe he is somewhere that is opposed to the Soviet authorities?" That kind of thing…. We were divided up into black and white. They were white and we were always black. And there was nothing you could do about it because they had the power. They had the power and so they had the truth…. And [only] when the Soviet Union collapsed, he [the guard] started to treat me politely and with respect. And once he implored me:

"Nina, I beg you to forget what happened. How can I be guilty? I was simply obeying orders.'"

But whilst Nina may have withheld her forgiveness to the man who guarded her during her deportation, he – along with every-one else who took part in the crime – has been spared any official punishment.

Even today a visitor to Red Square can see by the Kremlin wall a monument to the man who most needed to be held to account for his actions, and yet never was – Joseph Stalin. Like many tyrants before him – and no doubt many tyrants to come – he escaped this life untouched by justice.

POSTSCRIPT

Could the Western leaders in the Alliance have prevented the Soviet dominance of eastern Europe by acting differently during their partnership with Stalin? Which is a polite way of asking whether we were partly to blame for what happened and all the resultant misery.

In practical terms, the only way of preventing the physical occupation of eastern Europe by the Red Army would have been for someone else to have occupied this territory first. That would have meant either bringing forward the date of the second front and D-Day by at least a year, to 1943, or to have entered into some kind of partnership with the Germans towards the end of the war – conditional, presumably, on Hitler and the rest of the Nazi leadership having first been removed.

The second of these two options is the easier to dismiss – even though at the time there were people on the Allied side who seriously thought the threat from the Soviet Union so great that we should have enlisted the German army against them. George Earle, the former Governor of Pennsylvania who appeared earlier in this book when he protested to Roosevelt about Katyn, even met Baron Kurt von Lersner, a close friend of Franz von Papen, the former Chancellor of Germany, to discuss this possibility.[1] Von Lersner visited Earle in secret in Istanbul in 1943 and proposed – on behalf of a group of well-connected conspirators – that the Western Allies accept only 'conditional' surrender from the Germans. The idea was that senior German officers – with prior knowledge of the Western Allies' support – would remove Hitler and the other leading Nazis, and then the Wehrmacht would join with Western forces to keep the Soviets out of central Europe and Germany. Earle actually sent this proposal to President Roosevelt.

It would have been a disastrous course of action. Perhaps the Red Army would have been forced back, but at a terrible cost in Allied lives. Even more importantly, the Europe that would have then existed after the war would have been a good deal less stable than the one we were actually left with. That is because, even after Stalingrad, the German army was still a fearsome fighting machine. If the Western Allies had fought alongside the Germans and then reached some kind of uneasy peace with the Soviets – who would, of course, have felt betrayed by the West, probably fuelling a future conflict – who would then have disarmed the German army? Germany would have been unoccupied by the Western Allies and still immensely powerful. So, thankfully, Roosevelt filed Earle's plan in the bin.

The idea of bringing forward the second front to 1943 is harder to reject so swiftly. Indeed, the issues are so complex that one historian has written a whole book about the subject.[2] It is clear that, had Churchill not pushed so hard for his 'soft underbelly' approach – and we have seen just how nonsensical a description that turned out to be of southern Italy – then it might have been possible to mount a cross-Channel invasion in 1943. Allied forces might then have reached much further into eastern Europe by the end of the war than they actually did. The Soviet influence over eastern Europe would thus have been lessened. The problem is that the cost in human terms for the Western Allies would have been enormous.

What is sometimes forgotten in the West is the massively disproportionate losses suffered by the Western Allies compared with the Soviets. The Americans and British each suffered around 400,000 dead, whilst the Soviet Union endured a death toll of 27 million. Stalin always believed that Britain and America were delaying the second front so that the Soviet Union would bear the brunt of the war – so that Soviet lives were lost instead of British, American or other Allied lives. At no point in the documents, or even anecdotally, do Churchill or Roosevelt ever say that this was the case. But this does not mean that it was not so – that at some visceral level these extremely smart Western politicians did not realize that it was to their advantage that the Red Army rather than their own boys died fighting the Germans in the hottest part of the action. It is obvious, but it is worth stating – both Churchill and Roosevelt relied on votes to stay in power. And no votes are gained by incurring massive casualties. Would Churchill and Roosevelt really have been prepared to sacrifice perhaps a million more dead each in order to ensure an independent eastern Europe after the war?

And although it is true that the Americans did openly favour a second front in 1943 (although we shall never know if this aspiration would actually have been carried through even if the British had agreed), Roosevelt was also keen to get the Soviets into the war against Japan in order to reduce the number of potential American deaths and to win the war more quickly. Roosevelt was a master at judging American public opinion – and he had an election to fight in 1944. So it's impossible to believe that keeping American casualties down wasn't also a priority for him on the Western, as well as the Pacific, Front.

As for Churchill, he was opposed to a second front almost up to the moment when D-Day was finally launched. He feared another Dunkirk and the consequent loss of British life. But his opposition was based on a straightforward analysis of political cost and benefit. If Britain's survival had in any part been linked to the launching of a second front in 1943, of course he would have pressed for one. As it was, with the Soviets battling it out with the Germans, there seemed to be little urgency.

But even given that the second front was delayed until 1944, there were still ways in which both Roosevelt and Churchill could have played their cards differently. The unpleasant recriminations following Yalta were to some extent the responsibility of the Western Allies. Yes, of course Stalin did not live up to his promises. But he almost certainly didn't think he was expected to. Both Roosevelt and Churchill in their different ways – the President with his secret 'chats' in Tehran, the Prime Minister with his 'percentages' discussion – had shown that they were not averse to hard talk about 'spheres of influence'. Stalin would most likely have perceived the content of those meetings as the reality, and aspects of Churchill and Roosevelt's public pronouncements as mere rhetoric to appease the voters.

And then there was the massive problem for Western political discourse caused by the huge, government-supported, pro-Soviet propaganda campaigns in both Britain and America. Describing the NKVD as a police force 'like the FBI', for example, only served to make it harder for people to understand what was going on at the end of the war when the relationship with the Soviet Union cracked apart. And the fact that George Orwell could not get his brilliant satire on the Soviet state, *Animal Farm*, published during the war shows how culturally dangerous the situation created by the false propaganda had become. One publisher, who had initially accepted the book, subsequently turned it down after an official at the British Ministry of Information warned him off. The publisher then wrote to Orwell, saying: 'If the fable were addressed generally to dictators and dictatorships at large then publication would be all right, but the fable does follow, as I see now, so completely the progress of the Russian Soviets and their two dictators [Lenin and Stalin], that it can apply only to Russia, to the exclusion of the other dictatorships. Another thing: it would be less offensive if the predominant caste in the fable were not pigs. I think the choice of pigs as the ruling caste will no doubt give offence to many people, and particularly to anyone who is a bit touchy, as undoubtedly the Russians are.'[3]

The twisting and manipulation of the facts during the war in order to portray Stalin as good old 'Uncle Joe' was not just damaging to the public psyche in the West, but also caused difficulties for those in power. Frank Roberts of the Foreign Office memorably remarked that it was 'a very awkward matter when we are fighting for a moral cause' that the Soviet Union was accused of the war crime at Katyn – especially, one might add, since by then the public perception of Stalin had been so airbrushed by Allied propaganda as to make this kind of action wholly inconsistent with his public persona. Sir Owen O'Malley, who was responsible for the Katyn report that Frank Roberts commented upon, wrote after the war of his own disillusionment: 'Between 1943 and the autumn of 1945...much more than the sacrifice of Poland was esteemed necessary to keep Stalin in a good temper; and to appease him an indifferent eye was turned upon his destruction and dismemberment of a number of smaller nations. One after another they were seized; Estonia, Latvia, Lithuania. Parts of Finland, a quarter Poland, all Poland, Czechoslovakia, Ruthenia, Yugoslavia, Hungary, Bulgaria, Rumania, Albania, a quarter of Austria and a third of Germany. Oh it was grievous to see so many pleasant and diverse communities being herded in a spiritual and cultural gas chamber! What a falling off was here from the bright morning of the Atlantic Charter and the sun-capped waves of the USS *Augusta*'s quarterdeck! All this also was trying for the Poles. It was also trying for me too, for I had numerous friends in the countries named. The lucky ones – if they were women – were just raped, of the unlucky ones, one had water poured into his lungs through a rubber tube; another had all his fingertips sawn through with a hacksaw half way up his nails.'[4]

It was impossible, of course, to reconcile the noble Stalin of 'Mission to Moscow' with the crime of Katyn or the tortures that O'Malley describes. But still, there was a middle way which might have been pursued politically during the war – even given the rosy pro-Soviet propaganda that was being churned out – one which recognized the value of the Soviet Union as a fighting ally, but which reaffirmed the policy that, as Churchill put it in January 1942, the Western Allies adhered to 'those principles of freedom and democracy set forth in the Atlantic Charter and that these principles must become especially active whenevere any question of transferring territory is raised'.[5]

Ultimately, this course of action might have accomplished little in practical terms. Perhaps Stalin would still have exercised control over much of eastern Europe. But for sure, the Western Allies would at least have lived up to the principles that they said they were fighting the war to protect. And it is worth reiterating that to propose that the political leaders of Britain and America should have behaved in this more straightforward way is not to put forward something radical or naive – it is only to suggest that

Roosevelt and Churchill should have stuck to the policy that they themselves followed in 1942. Only later in the war did the controversial deals with Stalin truly begin.

There would have been risks in this approach, of course. But the idea that Stalin would, over this issue, seriously have tried to exit the war after the victories of 1943 in some kind of peace deal with Hitler is verging on the fanciful. As a result of the invasion of the Soviet Union, there was no basis of trust left between Stalin and the Nazis, and in any event Hitler – as he told Ribbentrop at the time – would never have countenanced the idea of peace with Stalin.

All of which leaves us with the important question; to what extent was this a 'moral' war? Well, obviously Nazism was immoral – one of the most immoral ideologies that has ever existed – so any war conducted by the Western democracies committed to the elimination of that scourge must surely have been fundamentally moral. Equally, the ideals of the Atlantic Charter, with their commitment to free elections and the rule of law, all exude moral content. The problem comes when we add the Soviet Union to the mix. That regime committed any number of horrendous crimes, many perpetrated when it was allied to the West. And particularly in relation to Poland, the immorality of the Soviet Union tainted the actions of the Western leaders. The Western Allies' treatment of the Poles was unworthy: from the cover-up over Katyn to the secret deal at Tehran that eventually shifted Polish borders without the consent of the Poles; from the meeting in Moscow when Churchill accused members of the Polish government in exile of being 'callous people who want to wreck Europe', to the exclusion of Polish troops from the Victory Parade in London in 1946. It is a sad catalogue – and one I certainly wasn't taught in school when I was told that we should all only 'feel good' about the conduct of the Western Allies in the Second World War.

Ultimately, it is better to consider this conflict not just as a 'moral' war, but as a more conventional one as well. Because if we see this war as being about power politics and the attempt to prevent the Nazis controlling Europe, and the Japanese controlling China and Southeast Asia, then it makes a lot of sense. The Western powers wanted to win the war at the least cost possible, and in pursuit of that goal they – to paraphrase Churchill – made an alliance with the Devil.

The central popular myth that surrounds the war, a kind of Hollywood version of the history, is that this is a simple story of an alliance of good people who fought an alliance of bad people. It's an immensely consoling way of looking at the past, and it's sad to let it go. But let it go we must.

NOTES

INTRODUCTION

1. The 'Soviet Union' is the accurate term to describe the country at the time of the Second World War. However, many people used the word 'Russian' when they meant 'Soviet' (and indeed many still do so today). Stalin would often describe the country he ruled as 'Russia', and Churchill, Roosevelt and the Nazis did the same. But it is inaccurate, because during the war the Soviet Union consisted of sixteen republics, of which only one was Russia. Stalin himself was not Russian, but Georgian. Not to use the terms 'Soviet' and 'Soviet Union' is – not least – to diminish the massive contribution to the war made by citizens from the other fifteen republics.
2. David Dilks (ed.), *The Diaries of Sir Alexander Cadogan OM 1938–1945*, Cassell, 1971, pp. 708–9, entry for 11 February 1945.
3. Alex Danchev and Daniel Todman (ed.), Field Marshal Lord Alanbrooke, *War Diaries 1939–1945*, Phoenix, 2002, p. 483, entry for 28 November 1943.
4. Alanbrooke, *War Diaries*, p. 608, entry for 15 October, 1944.
5. Alanbrooke, *War Diaries*, pp. 299–300, entry for 13 August 1942.
6. John Lewis Gaddis, 'Presidential Address: The Tragedy of the Cold War', p. 4, quoted in Amos Perlmuter, *FDR and Stalin 'A Not So Grand Alliance'*, University of Missouri Press, 1993, p. 17.
7. Quoted in Ben Pimlott (ed.), *The Second World War Diaries of Hugh Dalton 1940–1945*, Jonathan Cape, 1986, entry for 13 January, 1942, p. 348.
8. PRO FO 371/34577, O'Malley's report on Katyn, 24 May 1943.

CHAPTER ONE: An Alliance in All but Name

1. See General Ernst Köstring, *Erinnerungen aus meinem Leben* (*Memoirs of My Life*) *1876–1939*, Verlag E. S. Mittler und Sohn, Frankfurt am Main, Vol. 1, p. 142.
2. Lord Alanbrooke, BBC TV interview.
3. Though Stalin claimed he was born on 21 December 1879, new research has shown he was actually born on 6 December 1878. See Robert Service, *Stalin*, Pan Macmillan, 2004, p. 14.
4. Gustav Hilger, *The Incompatible Allies*, New York, 1953, p. 301.
5. Laurence Rees, *Nazis: A Warning from History*, BBC Books, 1997, p. 93.
6. From BBC interview with Reinhard Spitzy.
7. Rees, *Nazis: A Warning from History*, p. 93.
8. Talbott, Strobe (ed.), *Khrushchev Remembers*, Deutsch, 1971, p. 307.
9. BBC interview.
10. V. N. Pavlov (the Soviet interpreter), '*Avtobiographicheskii Zametki*' (Autobiographical Notes), in the journal *Novaya I Noveyshaya Istoria*, 2000, pp. 98–99.
11. From BBC interview with Herbert Döring, SS manager of the Berghof.
12. Max Domarus, *Hitler: Speeches and Proclamations*, Vol. 2, 1935–8, I. B. Tauris, 1992, Nuremberg Party rally, 13 September 1937.
13. J. Noakes and G. Pridham, *Nazism: A Documentary Reader 1919–1945*, University of Exeter Press, 2001, Vol. 2, p. 278.
14. Geoffrey Roberts, *The Unholy Alliance – Stalin's Pact with Hitler*, I. B. Tauris, 1989, p. 149.
15. G. Roberts, *The Unholy Alliance*, p. 152.
16. From notes written by Gustav Hilger of the 27–29 September talks between the Soviets and the Germans in Moscow. Quoted in Ingeborg Fleischhauer's article 'Molotov und

Ribbentrop in Moskau' in *Vierteljahrshefte für Zeitgeschichte*, 3/1991.
17. *Izvestiya*, quoted in Roberts, *The Unholy Alliance*, p. 109.
18. Stalin's speech to the 18th Party Congress, 10 March 1939. Full speech in English in J. V. Stalin, *Problems of Leninism*, Foreign Languages Press, Peking, 1976, pp. 874–942.
19. Quoted in Roberts, *The Unholy Alliance*, pp. 140–1.
20. Andrew Roberts, *The Holy Fox: The Life of Lord Halifax*, Phoenix Press, 1997, p. 166.
21. Andor Hencke, under-secretary in the German Foreign Office, testimony under American interrogation 12–15 October in Wiesbaden: Institut für Zeitgeschichte München, PL (GPA) [1–12–50].
22. BBC interview for Rees, *Nazis: A Warning from History*.
23. Hencke interrogation and his memorandum of the conversation of 23 August in Politisches Archiv, Berlin, ADAP DVII DOK 213.
24. Hilger, *The Incompatible Allies*, p. 304.
25. Hencke interrogation DOK 213.
26. Hencke, DOK 213.
27. Johnnie von Herwarth, *Memoirs*, Collins, 1981, p. 167.
28. Heinrich Hoffmann, *Hitler Was My Friend*, Burke, 1955, p. 110.
29. Hoffmann, *Hitler Was My Friend*, p. 112.
30. Feliks Chuev, *Molotov Remembers* [7-9-71], Ivan Dee Inc., 1993.
31. Hencke, ADAP DVIII DOK 213.
32. Laurence Rees, *The Nazis: A Warning from History*, BBC DVD, episode 3.
33. BBC interview.
34. BBC interview.
35. Roberts, *The Holy Fox*, p. 157.
36. Roberts, *The Unholy Alliance*, p. 159.
37. Speech by Molotov before the Supreme Soviet of the USSR, 31 October 1939.
38. Dmitri Volkogonov, *Stalin: Triumph and Tragedy*, Weidenfeld and Nicolson, 1991, p. 361.
39. Jan Gross, *Revolution from Abroad*, Princeton University Press, 1988, p. 11.
40. BBC interview.
41. BBC interview.
42. This city, with its many name changes during the twentieth century, from Lemberg under the Austro-Hungarian Empire and then Nazi rule, to Lwów under Polish control, to Lvov under Soviet domination and now Lviv as part of Ukraine, is an exemplar of the boundary fluctuations in central Europe at the time.
43. BBC interview.
44. BBC interview.
45. Testimony from Gross, *Revolution from Abroad*, p. 44.
46. Köstring, *Erinnerungen aus meinem Leben*, pp. 144–6.
47. Erich Kordt, *Wahn und Wirklichkeit* (Delusion and Reality), Stuttgart, 1948, pp. 220–8.
48. Hilger's notes in *Vierteljahreshefte für Zeitgeschichte*, 3/1991. See Fleischhauer, *Dokumentation. Der deutsch-sowjetische Grenz und Freundschaftsvertrag vom 28 September, 1939. Die deutschen Aufzeichnungen über die Verhandlungen zwischen Stalin, Molotov and Ribbentrop in Moskau*, pp. 457–64.
49. Ibid.
50. Hencke interrogation, p. 25, and Karl Schnurre, *Aus einem bewegten Leben, Heiteres und Ernstes*, Bad Godesberg, 1986, pp. 90–5.
51. Hencke interrogation, p. 25.
52. Ibid.
53. Hilger, *The Incompatible Allies*, New York, 1951, p. 314.
54. Hilger in *Vierteljahreshefte*, p. 466.
55. Simon Sebag Montefiore, *Stalin and the Court of the Red Tsar*, Weidenfeld and Nicolson, p. 321.
56. Andor Hencke, in letter of 28 January 1941 to photographer Helmut Laux, Politisches Archiv, Berlin, ADAP DVIII-161, Appendix 1.
57. Hilger, *The Incompatible Allies*, p. 314.
58. Constantine Pleshakov, *Stalin's Folly*, Weidenfeld and Nicolson, 2005, pp. 43–4.
59. Władysław Anders, *An Army in Exile*, Macmillan, 1981, pp. 14–15.
60. William L. Langer and S. Everett Gleason, *The Challenge to Isolation, 1937–1940*, New York, 1952, pp. 160–1.

61. *Hansard*, 20 September 1939, Prime Minister's statement.
62. Seeds despatch, 18 September 1939, FO 371/23101.
63. Ibid.
64. Seeds despatch, 30 September 1939, FO 371/23103.
65. Kirkpatrick report, 1 October 1939, FO 371/23097 F207–8.
66. Perth to Cadogan, 5 October 1939, FO 371/23104 F38, 65, 68–9.
67. Cadogan to Perth, 3 November 1939, FO 371/23104 F38, 65, 68–9.
68. Written answer by R. A. Butler MP, 19 October 1939.
69. BBC interview.
70. Gross, *Revolution from Abroad*, p. 89.
71. Anders, *An Army in Exile*, p. 16.
72. Hencke, notes written immediately after the American interrogation 12/15/1945 in Wiesbaden.
73. Wolfgang Praeg and Werner Jacobmeyer, *Das Diensttagebuch des Deutschen Generalgouverneurs in Polen 1939–1945*, Stuttgart, 1975.
74. Diary of the Soviet delegation of the German–Soviet border commission, in Archive of the Russian Federation, Moscow, p.27 d66 (entry of 27/10/1939) F O11 Op 4.
75. For the latest figures see Stanislaw Ciesielski, Wojciech Materski and Andrzej Packowski, *Represje Sowieckie wobec Polakow I Obywateli Polskich*, Warsaw: KARTA 2000, p. 12.
76. 6 October 1939, CAB 65-2, 39-7.
77. Snow to FO, 21 October 1939, CAB 84–8.
78. Chiefs of Staff report, 27 October 1939, CAB 104.
79. BBC interview.
80. Alan Bullock, *Hitler and Stalin: Parallel Lives*, HarperCollins, 1991, p. 731.
81. 18 December 1939, CAB 65–2, 118-3.
82. Archive of the Russian President, RF.F3 Op 30 D 199 P3–5.
83. Archive of the Russian President, RGAASPI F 17 Op 162 D 26 L 119.
84. BBC interview.
85. Russian prosecutors in the early 1990s categorized the murder of the Poles as a 'crime'–which makes Stalin a criminal even by Russian law. This fact has not received widespread publicity.
86. George Sanford, *Katyn and the Soviet Massacre of 1940*, BASEES/Routledge series on Russian and East European Studies, 2005, p. 297.
87. See the work of Wojciech Materski on Katyn published in Zbrodnia Katynska po 60 latach, Warsaw: NKHBZK, 2000, p. 27.
88. See the work of Natalia Lebedeva and Wojciech Materski (p. 30 in Sanford, *Katyn*).
89. The BBC has obtained a video copy of this interrogation from which these quotes are taken.
90. BBC interview.
91. BBC interview with Anatoly Yablokov.
92. See German investigation into Katyn: 'Amtliches Material zum Massenmord von Katyn; Berlin: F. Eher Nachf, pp. 114–35.
93. Quoted in Gross, *Revolution from Abroad*, p. 211.
94. BBC interview.
95. Reproduced in *Katyn 1940–2000: Documents*, Vyes Mir, Moscow, 2001, Document No. 93, p. 674.
96. Sanford, *Katyn*, p. 27.
97. *New York Times*, 15 April 1940, L4, p. 5.
98. Kennard to Halifax, 18 May 1940, C5744/116/55.
99. Kennard to Strang, 30 April 1940, FO 371/24472.
100. Strang to Kennard, 14 May 1940, FO 371/24472.
101. BBC interview.
102. Gustav Hilger's Notes (published by Dr Ingeborg Fleishhauer), p.464.
103. Bundesarchiv Freiburg, RM 11–35, Kriegsmarine M. Att. Russland von 05 Oktober 1939 bis 20 April 1940, Band 1, p. 7, Scan 09.
104. Bundesarchiv Freiburg, RM 11–35, Kriegsmarine M. Att. Russland von 05 Oktober 1939 bis 20 April 1940, Band 1, p. 103, Scan 118.
105. Bundesarchiv Freiburg, RM 11–39, Oberkommando der Kriegsmarine, M. Att.

Russland-BN (Basis Nord) vom 29 August 1940 bis 11 März 1941, p. 37, Scan 42, out of the Action report of VM Murmansk, Moscow, 10 October 1940.

106. Letter from the Naval Attaché von Baumbach to the Naval High Command, in copy to the High Command of the Wehrmacht, Moscow, 08 November 1939, Bundesarchiv Freiburg, RM11-35, Kriegsmarine M. Att. Russland vom 05 Oktober 1939 bis 20 April 1940, Band 1, p. 43, Scan 53.

107. Doctor's report about the health situation on board the *Phoenicia* from February until September 1940, p. 1, Scan 03. This is the report which was attached to his private diary. Bundesarchiv Freiburg, RM12II–161.

108. Ibid., Scan 04.

109. Bundesarchiv Freiburg, RM12II–161, 4 May, p. 7, Scan 13.

110. Bundesarchiv Freiburg, RM12II–161, 4 May, p. 9, Scan 15.

111. Clive Ponting, *Winston Churchill*, Sinclair Stevenson, 1994, p. 442.

112. For a full discussion of these crucial Cabinet meetings see PRO Cab 65/13 and PRO Cab 66/7, plus John Lukacs, *Five Days in London*, Yale University Press, 2001, and Ian Kershaw, *Fateful Choices*, Penguin, 2007, pp. 11–54.

113. *Dalton Diaries*, pp.26–8, and *The Churchill War Papers*, Vol. 2, pp. 182–84, Sinclair Stevenson, 1997.

114. Winston S. Churchill, *The Second World War*, Penguin Classics, 2005, Vol.2, p. 88.

115. Churchill, *The Second World War*, Vol. 2, pp. 23 and 51.

116. Edward Crankshaw, *Khrushchev Remembers*, Deutsch, 1974, pp. 156–7.

117. BBC interview.

118. Kershaw, *Fateful Choices*, p. 69.

119. Tobias R. Philbin III, *The Lure of Neptune*, University of South Carolina Press, 1994, pp. 137–42.

120. BBC interview.

121. War diary of the Komet, Bundesarchiv, RM100-49, pp. 55–6.

122. Robert Eyssen, HSK Komet, Kapernfahrt auf allen Meeren, 2nd edition, Koehlers Verlagsges, 2002, pp. 42–3.

123. Letter of the German Naval Attaché in Berlin, Baumbach, to the Naval High Command in Berlin, 30 September 1940, in Bundesarchiv Freiburg, RM 11–39, p. 33.

124. Albert Speer, *Inside the Third Reich*, Phoenix, 1996, p. 172.

125. Pavlov, 'Autobiographical Notes', pp. 104–5. This is also the source for the preceding summary of the talks.

126. Hilger's notes, Nazi–Soviet relations 1939–1941, University Press of the Pacific, 2003, p. 253.

127. Ibid., p. 254.

128. Pavlov, 'Autobiographical Notes'.

129. Testimony before the Select Committee of the Senate into the Katyn Massacre, 2nd Session, US government publications, 1952, part 4, p. 555.

130. Churchill to Roosevelt 31 July 1940, C20x., in Warren F. Kimball, (ed.), *Churchill and Roosevelt, the Complete Correspondence*: Vol. 1, Alliance Emerging, Collins, 1984, pp. 56–7.

131. See Robert Dallek, *Franklin D. Roosevelt and American Foreign Policy 1932–1945*, Oxford University Press, 1981, p. 51.

132. Ibid., p. 59.

133. From 17 December 1940 press conference, documents held in Franklin D. Roosevelt Library, Hyde Park, New York.

134. Dallek, *Franklin D. Roosevelt*, p. 218.

135. FDR speech, 10 February 1940, to American Youth Congress in Washington DC.

136. Gabriel Gorodetsky, *Grand Delusion, Stalin and the German Invasion of Russia*, Yale University Press, 1999, p. 56, Intelligence report of 29 September 1940.

137. BBC interview.

138. Krebs letter to Oberquartiermeister IV in the General Staff in Berlin, 15 April 1941. Bundesarchiv/Militararchiv Vol.1 (July 1937 to June 1941).

139. Evan Mawdsley, 'Crossing the Rubicon – Soviet plans for Offensive War in 1940–1941', *International History Review*, 25 (2003), p. 853. Also Kershaw, *Fateful Choices*, p. 280.

140. Chris Bellamy, *Absolute War: Soviet Russia in the Second World War*, Macmillan, 2007, p. 97.

141. Gorodetsky, *Grand Delusion*, p. 174.
142. Presidential Archive, Moscow, F3. Op 50 D 415Ll, 50–52.
143. Winston Churchill, *The Second World War: The Grand Alliance*, Houghton Mifflin Books, 1986, p. 316.
144. Quoted in Gorodetsky, *Grand Delusion*, p.244.
145. Mawdsley, 'Crossing the Rubicon – Soviet Plans for Offensive War', p. 864.
146. Hilger, *Incompatible Allies*, p. 312–13.

CHAPTER TWO: Decisive Moments

1. BBC interview.
2. BBC interview.
3. This is the Russian version of Lwów.
4. Bellamy, *Absolute War*, p. 187.
5. O. Romaniv and I. Fedushchak, *Western Ukranian Tragedy 1941*, Shevchenko Society, Ukranian Free University Foundation in USA, Library of Ukranian Studies, N18, Lviv – New York, p. 155.
6. BBC interview.
7. Serge Krushchev (ed.), *Memoirs of Nikita Krushchev: Commissar, Vol. 1*, Penn State University Press, 2005.
8. Anastas Mikoyan, *Tak Bylo (It Was Like This)* Vagrus, Moscow, pp. 390–2.
9. Ibid, p. 390.
10. Ibid.
11. Francoise Thorn, (ed.), Sergio Beria, *Beria, My Father*, Duckworth, 2003, p. 71.
12. Dimitri Volkogonov, *Stalin: Triumph and Tragedy*, Weidenfeld and Nicolson, 1991, p. 413.
13. Churchill BBC Radio Broadcast, 22 June 1941 (BBK/C/87).
14. John Colville, *The Fringes of Power. Downing Street Diaries 1939–1955*, Weidenfeld and Nicolson, p. 350.
15. Bullock, *Hitler and Stalin, Parallel Lives*, p. 768.
16. Joan Beaumont, *Comrades in Arms: British Aid to Russia, 1941–1945*, Davis-Poynter, 1980, p. 26.
17. Quoted in *New York Times*, 24 June, 1941, p. 7.
18. Ross Munro, *Gauntlet to Overlord: The Story of the Canadian Army*, Mulberry Books Toronto, 1946, p. 284.
19. Ibid.
20. Ibid., p. 286.
21. Major Blake's report, 28/8/41 FO/371/29492.
22. Memo, 11 September 1941, FO 371/29490.
23. Warner memo, 17 September 1941, FO 371/29490.
24. Text of 7.15 bulletin, 9 September 1941, BBC Empire News, FO 371/29490.
25. Telegram from Cripps to Foreign Office, 9 September 1941, FO 371/29490.
26. Churchill, *The Grand Alliance*, p. 406.
27. Dallek, *Franklin D. Roosevelt*, p. 278.
28. Herbert Feis, *Churchill–Roosevelt–Stalin: The War They Waged and the Peace They Sought*, Princeton University Press, 1957, p. 10.
29. David M. Kennedy, *Freedom from Fear*, Oxford University Press, 1999, p. 406.
30. James MacGregor Burns, *Roosevelt: The Soldier of Freedom*, Harvest Books, 2002, p. 114.
31. Dilks (ed.), *Cadogan Diaries*, p.423, entry for 6 August, 1941.
32. Harold Ickes, *The Secret Diary of Harold L. Ickes*, Da Capo, 1974, 12 May 1940.
33. *Daily Mail*, 24 April, 1935.
34. Bullock, *Parallel Lives*, p. 811.
35. BBC interview.
36. BBC interview.
37. BBC interview.
38. BBC interview.
39. BBC interview.
40. Georgii Kumanev, *Ryadom So Stalinym: Otkrovennye Svidetelstva* (Next to Stalin), Bilina, Moscow, 1999, pp. 272–73.

41. BBC interview.
42. BBC interview.
43. *Hitler's Table Talk*, translated by Norman Cameron and R. H. Stevens, entry for 17 October 1941, Phoenix Press, 2000, p. 68.
44. BBC interview.
45. Dallek, *Franklin D. Roosevelt*, p. 285.
46. BBC interview.
47. *The Crime of Katyn, Facts and Documents*, Polish Cultural Foundation, London, 1989, p. 87.
48. Interview with Sir Frank Roberts for *The Cold War*, a BBC/Turner Broadcasting co-production.
49. Eden's 17 December 1941 telegram to Churchill via Foreign Office, FO 371/29655.
50. Dilks (ed.), *Cadogan Diaries*, p. 422, entry for 17 December 1941.
51. Anthony Eden (Rt Hon the Earl of Avon, KG, PC, MC), *The Eden Memoirs: The Reckoning*, Cassell, 1965, p. 302.
52. Sir Frank Roberts, *Dealing with Dictators*, Weidenfeld and Nicolson, 1991, p. 59.
53. *Eden Memoirs*, p. 302.
54. Eden telegram to Churchill, 5 January 1942, PREM 3/399/7.
55. Churchill note to Eden, 7 January 1942, FO 371/32864.
56. BBC interview.
57. BBC interview.
58. Quoted in William Taubman, *Khrushchev: The Man and His Era*, Free Press, 2003, p.167.
59. Ibid., p. 168.
60. Laurence Rees, *Horror in the East*, BBC Books, 2001, p. 72.
61. Churchill to Roosevelt, 7 March 1942, FO 954/25.
62. Roy Douglas, *From War to Cold War, 1942–1948*, London, 1981, p. 7.
63. BBC interview.
64. John M Carroll, George C Herring, *Modern American Diplomacy*, Rowan and Littlefield, 1995, p. 83.
65. Warren F. Kimball (ed.), *Churchill and Roosevelt: The Complete Correspondence*, Vol. I, Princeton University Press, 1984, p. 421, FDR to Churchill, 18 March, 1942.
66. Eleanor Roosevelt, *This I Remember*, Greenwood Press, 1975, p. 199.
67. O. A. Rzheshevskii, *Voina I Diplomatica*, Nauka, Moscow, 1997, p. 170.
68. Hopkins memorandum, 29 May 1942, in Hopkins papers, in FDR Presidential Library, Hyde Park, New York.
69. Alanbrooke, *War Diaries*, p. 269, entry for 21 June 1942.
70. See Professor S. H. Cross (the American interpreter), notes from 11a.m. conference on Saturday, 30 May 1942, Molotov Visit, Book 5, in FDR Library, Hyde Park, New York.
71. O. Rzheshevski, *Vojna I diplomatia*, Moscow, 1997, p. 176.
72. Hopkins memorandum, 3 June 1942, in FDR Library, Hyde Park, New York.
73. Bellamy, *Absolute War*, p. 421.
74. Ibid., p. 424.
75. See annexe to the minutes of the Chiefs of Staff committee, 16 May 1942, PRO CAB 79/21.
76. Prime Minister's minute to General Ismay, 17 May 1942, PRO D 100/2.
77. Minutes of War Cabinet meeting, 18 May 1942, CAB 65/26.
78. BBC interview.
79. BBC interview.
80. BBC interview.
81. BBC interview.
82. BBC interview.
83. BBC interview.
84. Quoted in Burns, *Roosevelt: The Soldier of Freedom*, p. 182.
85. REF AND 237/168 PRO.
86. BBC interview.

CHAPTER THREE: Crisis of Faith
1. BBC interview.
2. Nikolai Baibakov, *Ot Stalina do Yel'tsina* (From Stalin to Yeltsin), GazOil Press, Moscow, 1998, pp. 64–5.
3. Stalin to Churchill, 23 July 1942, T 1031/2 FCO.
4. Clark Kerr to Foreign Office, 25 July 1942, FO 371/32911.
5. Lord Moran, *Winston Churchill, the Struggle for Survival 1940–1965*, Heron Books, 1966, entry for 1 August 1942.
6. Winston S. Churchill, *The Second World War: The Hinge of Fate*, London, 2005, p. 428.
7. Lord Alanbrooke, remark in BBC interview.
8. CAB 66/28/3, p. 19 PRO.
9. CAB 120/65, PRO.
10. Churchill, *The Hinge of Fate*, p. 440.
11. Martin Kitchen, *British Policy Towards the Soviet Union During the Second World War*, Macmillan, 1986, p. 136.
12. See Charles Richardson, *From Churchill's Secret Circle to the BBC*, Brassey's, 1991, p. 139.
13. Alanbrooke, *War Diaries*, p. 301.
14. Ibid.
15. Arthur Bryant, *The Turn of the Tide*, London, 1957, pp. 461–4.
16. Lord Moran diary, entry for 14 August 1942, pp. 60–1.
17. Ibid., entry for August 15, p. 62.
18. FO 800/300 PRO.
19. Pavlov, 'Autobiographical Notes', pp. 98–9.
20. This account of the meeting is compiled from: Churchill, *The Hinge of Fate*, pp. 446–7, Vladimir Nikolaevich Pavlov, 'Autobiographical Notes', pp. 98–9; A. H. Birse, *Memoirs of an Interpreter*, London, 1967, p. 102.
21. FO 800/300 PRO.
22. Cadogan to Eden, FO 800/404.
23. Churchill, *Hinge of Fate*, p. 448.
24. Alanbrooke, *War Diaries*, entry for 13 August, 1942, pp. 299–300.
25. BBC interview.
26. BBC interview.
27. BBC interview.
28. BBC interview.
29. English translation available at www.ibiblio.org.
30. Information Bulletin, Embassy of the USSR, 10 November 1942.
31. BBC interview.
32. Burns, *Roosevelt: The Soldier of Freedom*, p. 310.
33. BBC interview.
34. BBC interview.
35. BBC interview.
36. Burns, p. 315.
37. Ibid.
38. BBC interview.
39. PRO CAB 66/36.
40. Ibid.
41. John H. Lauck, *Katyn Killings: In the Record*, Kingston Press, 1988, p. 55.
42. FO 371/34571 PRO Churchill to Eden 28 April 1943.
43. Kimball (ed.), *Churchill and Roosevelt: The Complete Correspondence*, Vol. I, pp. 400–402.
44. O'Malley was appointed ambassador to the Poles in February, 1943.
45. Sir Owen O'Malley, *The Phantom Caravan*, John Murray, 1954, p. 234.
46. FO 371/34577.
47. FO 371/34577.
48. PRO PREM 3/353, p. 101.
49. See Kimball, *Churchill and Roosevelet*, Vol. III, C-4 12/2, Churchill to FDR, 13 August, 1943, p. 389.
50. Charles Bohlen, *Witness to History*, Norton, 1973.

51. William H. Standley, *Admiral Ambassador to Russia*, Chicago, 1955, p. 368.
52. Ibid., p. 369.
53. Joseph E. Davies papers, Manuscript Division, Library of Congress, Washington DC, entry for 20 May 1943.
54. FRUS, Conferences at Cairo and Tehran 1943, Washington 1961, pp. 3–4.
55. Reynolds, *In Command of History*, Penguin Books, 2005, p. 381.
56. Memo, 21 July 1942, CAB 66/26, WP (42) 311 (TNA).
57. Churchill to Attlee, 29 July 1942, PREM 3/499/9 (TNA).
58. Susan Butler (ed.), Arthur Schlesinger (fwd), *My Dear Mr Stalin, the Complete Correspondence of Franklin D. Roosevelt and Joseph V. Stalin*, Yale University Press, 2005, pp. 136–8.
59. W. Averell Harriman and Elie Abel, *Special Envoy to Churchill and Stalin, 1941–1946*, Random House, 1975, pp. 216–7.
60. Churchill to Roosevelt, 25 June 1943, no. 328, Kimball, *Complete Correspondence*, Vol. II.
61. Roosevelt to Churchill, 28 June 1943, no. 297, Kimball, *Complete Correspondence*, Vol. II.
62. Harold Nicolson, *Diaries and Letters, 1939–1945*, Collins, 1967, p. 277.
63. See OSS report no. A-5094, 11 May 1943, and OSS report no. A-9469, 9 August 1943; also George Wiseman to Christopher Warner, British Foreign Office, 11 August, 23 1943, N 4898/66/38, FO 371/36956. Quoted in Vojtech Mastny, *Russia's Road to the Cold War*, New York, 1979.
64. Mastny, *Russia's Road to the Cold War*, pp. 73–85.
65. BBC interview.
66. Quoted in Dallek, *Franklin D. Roosevelt*, p. 543.
67. The original of this diary is kept by Memorial in Moscow.
68. BBC interview.
69. BBC interview.
70. BBC interview.
71. Figures from Bellamy, *Absolute War*, p. 583.
72. This section of Roes's recollections is taken from his interview for Mother of All Battles, *BBC Timewatch*, 1993, Dai Richards (producer), Laurence Rees (executive producer).

CHAPTER FOUR: The Changing Wind

1. Speech by President Bush in Riga, Latvia, on 7 May 2005.
2. Keith Sainsbury, *The Turning Point*, Oxford University Press, 1986, p. 11.
3. Dallek, *Franklin D. Roosevelt*, p.423 (for the full minutes of Cairo, see FRUS, *The Conferences at Cairo and Tehran*, 1943, pp. 291–455).
4. Ibid., p. 426.
5. *Sovetsko-Angliiskie Otnosheniya vo vremya velikoi otechestvennoi voiny, 1941–1945*, Izdatel'stvo politicheskoi literatury, Moscow, 1983, Vol. 1, document 301.
6. Moran, *Winston Churchill, the Struggle for Survival*, entry for 28 November 1943.
7. Ibid.
8. BBC interview.
9. See FRUS, *The Conferences at Cairo and Tehran*, 1943, Bohlen minutes, pp. 482–6.
10. Quoted in William Roger Louis, *Imperialism at Bay*, Oxford University Press, 1986, p. 181.
11. John Morton Blum (ed.), *Morgenthau Diaries 1941–1945*, Houghton Mifflin, 1967, entry for 15 September 1944.
12. PRO CAB 99/25.
13. Moran, *Winston Churchill, the Struggle for Survival*, entry for 28 November 1943.
14. PRO PREM 3/136/8 pp.2–3 (also recorded in FRUS Bohlen minutes, p. 512).
15. Churchill to Eden, 16 January 1944, PRO PREM 3/399/6.
16. Remark reported by Sumner Welles, quoted in Gaddis, *The United States and the Origins of the Cold War*, Columbia University Press, 1972, p.41. For a full discussion of these issues see 'Churchill, Roosevelt and the Stalin Enigma 1941–1945', in Reynolds, *From World War to Cold War*, Oxford University Press, 2007.
17. FRUS Cairo and Tehran, 30 November 1943, p. 584.
18. For a detailed discussion of these issues see Martin H. Folly, *Churchill, Whitehall and the Soviet Union 1940–1945*, Macmillan Press, 2000.

19. Tehran Conference: minutes of Meetings of Military Experts held at the Soviet Embassy Tehran on Monday 29 November at 10.30 a.m., CAB 99/25, p. 128 PRO.
20. FRUS, pp. 482–6.
21. Second Plenary Meeting, see FRUS The Conference at Cairo and Tehran, p.533–540.
22. FRUS minutes, pp. 552–5.
23. Churchill, *The Second World War*, Vol. 5, pp. 329–30.
24. Elliot Roosevelt, *As He Saw It*, Greenwood Press, 1974, pp. 186–91.
25. Moran, *Winston Churchill, the Struggle for Survival*, entry for 28 November 1943.
26. Alanbrooke, *War Diaries*, p. 485, entry for 29 November 1943.
27. Quoted in Ralph Levering, *American Opinion and the Russian Alliance 1939–1945*, University of North Carolina Press, 1976, p. 74.
28. Alanbrooke, *War Diaries*, pp. 486–7, entry for 30 November 1943.
29. As told to Frances Perkins, subsequently recorded in *The Roosevelt I Knew*, Harper and Row, 1965, pp. 83–5.
30. Roosevelt, *As He Saw It*, pp. 174–6.
31. FRUS Conferences at Tehran, pp. 594–6.
32. Katyn Massacre testimony to Senate, p. 2109.
33. Ibid, p. 2102.
34. PRO PREM 3/136/9, pp. 12–13.
35. Clayton Koppes and Gregory Black, *Hollywood Goes to War: How Politics, Profits and Propaganda Shaped WWII Movies*, Free Press, 1987, p. 191.
36. Dallek, *Franklin D. Roosevelt*, p. 439.
37. Samuel I. Rosenman (ed.), *The Public Papers and Addresses of Franklin D. Roosevelt*, Harper, 1938–1950, 13 Vols, 1943, pp. 553–62.
38. The Russian military prosecutor. A. Yabolov has written about Kiselev's case in an article 'Katinskoe prestuplenie: Barometr sostoyania prava v chelevecheskom izmerenii (The Katyn Crime: a measurement of the state of human rights)', Yablokov and Yazhborovskaya, *In Mezhdu Proshlim I Budushchim (Between the Past and the Future)*, pub. Nezavisimoe izdatelstvo 'Peak', Moscow, 1999, pp. 272–74.
39. Burdenko to Molotov, 2 September 1943, and Molotov's comments on the letter. GARF F 7021, Op 114 D 8 L 18-24.
40. Moscow embassy to Foreign Office, 25 January 1944, PRO PREM 3/353.
41. Moscow embassy to Foreign Office, 23 January 1944, PRO PREM 3/353.
42. Quoted in full in Katyn Massacre testimony to Senate, testimony of John Melby, p.2150.
43. Ibid, p. 2147.
44. Report of 25 January 1944, PRO PREM 3/353.
45. Churchill to Eden, 30 January 1944, PRO PREM 3/353.
46. O'Malley despatch, 11 February 1944, PRO FO371/39390 C2099.
47. Katyn Massacre testimony to Senate, p. 2111.
48. BBC interview.
49. See Earle's testimony at the Katyn Massacre hearings, p. 2197.
50. Ibid, p. 2204–7.
51. Letter from FDR to Earle, 24 March 1945. Facsimile copy printed in *Confidential* magazine, August 1958 (Vol. 6, no. 3), as part of article by George Earle, 'FDR's tragic mistake'.
52. Letter Beria to Stalin, 10 May, 1944. Published in Stalin's deportations 1928–1953, Mezhdunarodnuy Fond Demokratia Rosiya 20 vek, Moscow, 2005, p. 496.
53. J. Otto Pohl, 'The Deportation and Fate of the Crimean Tatars', paper presented at the 5th Annual World Convention of the Association for the Study of Nationalities ('Identity and the State: Nationalism and Sovereignty in a Changing World'), Columbia University, 13–15 April 2000.
54. BBC Interview.
55. BBC interview.
56. BBC interview.
57. Pohl, 'The Deportation and Fate of the Crimean Tatars'.
58. Ibid.
59. BBC interview.

60. BBC interview.
61. M. Blumenson, *Salerno to Cassino*, US Government Printing Office, 1969, p. 286.
62. Quoted in Matthew Parker, *Monte Cassino*, Headline, 2003, p. xvii.
63. Ibid, see plate section.
64. Quoted in Martin Gilbert, *The Road to Victory*, Heinemann, 1989, p. 667.
65. BBC interview.
66. Quoted in Parker, *Monte Cassino*, p. 182.
67. Fred Majdalany, *Cassino: Portrait of a Battle*, Longmans, 1957, p. 91.
68. Quoted in ibid, p. 215.
69. Anders, *An Army in Exile*, p. 163.
70. BBC interview.
71. BBC interview.
72. Anders, *An Army in Exile*, p. 176.
73. BBC interview from episode 1 of *D-Day to Berlin*, Andrew Williams (producer), Laurence Rees (executive producer), transmission on BBC1, 20 April 2005.
74. Ibid.
75. BBC interview.
76. Earl Ziemke, *Stalingrad to Berlin: The German Defeat in the East*, US Army Historical Series, Office of the Chief of Military History, Washington DC 1987, p. 316.
77. BBC interview.
78. BBC interview.
79. Brian Glyn Williams, *A Homeland Lost. Migration, the Diaspora Experience and the Forging of Crimean Tatar National Identity*, PhD dissertation, University of Wisconsin, 1999, p. 56.
80. BBC interview.
81. Aleksandr Nekrich, *The Punished Peoples: The Deportation and Fate of the Soviet Minorities at the End of the Second World War*, Norton, 1979, pp. 113–14.
82. BBC interview.
83. Keith Sword, *Deportation and Exile: Poles in the Soviet Union 1939–1948*, Macmillan Press, 1994, p. 149.
84. Anders, *An Army in Exile*, p. 191.

CHAPTER FIVE: Dividing Europe
1. Norman Davies, *Rising '44*, Pan Books, 2004, p. 226.
2. Quoted in ibid., p. 164–5.
3. Quoted in Jan Ciechanowski, *The Warsaw Rising of 1944*, Cambridge, 1974, p. 285.
4. BBC interview.
5. Quoted in *Documents on Polish–Soviet Relations 1939–1945, Vol. 2, 1943–1945*, General Sikorski Historical Institute, p. 309, doc.179.
6. Quoted in ibid, p. 309–22, doc.180.
7. *Stalin's Correspondence with Churchill, Attlee, Roosevelt and Truman, 1941–1945*, E. P. Dutton, 1958, doc. 311.
8. BBC interview.
9. Neil Orpen, *Airlift to Warsaw. The Rising of 1944*, University of Oklahoma, 1984.
10. Quoted in *Documents on Polish–Soviet Relations 1939–1945*, p. 334, doc.189.
11. Davies, *Rising*, p. 321.
12. Winston S. Churchill, *The Second World War*, Vol. 4, p. 118.
13. R-606 in Kimball, *The Complete Correspondence*, Vol. 3, p. 296.
14. BBC interview.
15. Quoted in Davies, *Rising '44*, p. 249.
16. *Trials of War Criminals Before the Nuremberg Military Tribunals*, US Government Printing Office, Washington, 1949–53, Vol. XIII, p. 323, and P. Padfield, *Himmler, Reichsfuehrer-SS*, Henry Holt and Co., New York, 1990, p. 469.
17. BBC interview.
18. Translated from the Polish minutes of the meeting of Anders and Churchill on 26 August 1944, taken by Lieutenant Lubomirski and now held in the Polish Institute and Sikorski Museum, London, ref. KOA.4b.

19. Churchill to Eden, 7 January 1942, FO 371, 32864.
20. BBC interview.
21. Davies, *Rising '44*, p. 302.
22. Ibid., p. 348.
23. BBC interview.
24. General Curtis E. Lemay, MacKinlay Kantor, *Mission with LeMay: My Story*, Doubleday, 1965, p. 565.
25. Henry Morgenthau Jnr, 'Our Policy Toward Germany', *New York Post*, 28 November 1947, p. 18.
26. See Foreign Relations of the United States (FRUS): Quebec 1944, pp. 325–6.
27. Moran, *Winston Churchill, the Struggle for Survival*, entry for 13 September 1944.
28. FRUS, Quebec, p. 361.
29. The view expressed by John Dietrich in his *The Morgenthau Plan: Soviet Influence on American Postwar Policy*, New York, 2002, p. 54–6.
30. *Eden Memoirs*, p. 476.
31. FRUS, p. 362, Morgenthau's recollections.
32. Morgenthau Diary, vol. 783, p. 35–9, Franklin D. Roosevelt Library, Hyde Park, New York.
33. John Morton Blum (ed.), *Morgenthau Diaries 1941–1945*, Houghton Mifflin, 1967, p. 342.
34. *Documents on Polish–Soviet Relations 1939–1945*, p.339, doc.191.
35. Quoted in Moran, *Winston Churchill, the Struggle for Survival*, entry for 13 September 1944, and in FRUS, p. 325.
36. David Rees, *Harry Dexter White: A Study in Paradox*, 1974, University of Michigan, p. 270.
37. See Venona document at www.nsa.gov/venona/document, 18 October 1944.
38. Quoted in broadcast form in *D-Day to Berlin*, episode 3 at 8 minutes, Andrew Williams (producer), Laurence Rees (executive producer), transmission BBC1, 4 April, 2005.
39. Quoted in Dallek, *Franklin D. Roosevelt*, p. 477.
40. Ibid.
41. Frederick Gareau, 'Morgenthau's Plan for Industrial Disarmament in Germany', *Western Political Quaterly*, Vol. 14, no. 2, June 1961, pp. 520.
42. PRO PREM 3/434/2, pp. 4–5.
43. Meeting 21 May 1944, FO 371, 39402.
44. Stalin's order 31 October 1944 to the 6th air force army. Historia Sovetko-Polskix Ostnashenii Moskva 1944, p. 43.
45. PRO PREM 3/66/7 and Clark Kerr's record of the meeting PRO FO 800/30.
46. PRO PREM 3/434/2, pp. 10–14.
47. FRUS, The Conferences at Cairo and Tehran, 1943, p. 256 and p. 531.
48. PM to War Cabinet, 17 October 1944, CHAR 20/181 (CAC).
49. Geoffrey Roberts, *Stalin's Wars*, Yale, 2006, p. 220.
50. Russian minutes from the meeting with the London Poles, 13 October 1944, published in O. Rzheshevski, Stalin and Churchill, Moscow Navka 2004, pp. 444–8.
    Translation of Polish transcript, 'Documents on Polish–Soviet Relations Volume III, London, pp. 405–415, Sikorski Institute.
51. Note on a conversation concerning the Curzon Line between M. Mikołajczyk and Mr Churchill, held in the presence of members of the Polish delegation; GSHI A.11.49/Sow/4-b. (Translation from Polish) Documents on Polish–Soviet Relations 1939–1945, Vol. II 1939–1945, Sikorski Institute.
52. Ibid.
53. Quoted in Yohanan Cohen, *Small Nations in Times of Crisis and Confrontation*, State University of New York Press, 1989.
54. Quoted in Anders, *An Army in Exile*, p. 239.
55. Quoted in Dallek, p. 503.
56. Kitchen, *British Policy towards the Soviet Union*, p. 237.
57. CAB 65-48, 157, 27 November 1944.
58. Quoted in Mary Soames, *Clementine Churchill*, Houghton Mifflin, 1979, p. 361.

59. Quoted in Krisztian Ungvary, *Battle for Budapest*, I. B. Tauris, 2006, p. 4.
60. BBC interview.
61. BBC interview.
62. Quote in Ungvary, p. 286.
63. BBC interview.
64. BBC interview.
65. BFL XXV 4a 002645/1953 Budapest Capital Archive and Ungvary, p. 287.
66. BBC interview.
67. Milovan Djilas, *Conversations with Stalin*, Penguin, 1962, p. 76.
68. Quoted in Richard Overy, *Russia's War*, Allen Lane, 1998, p. 261.
69. Amy Night, *Beria, Stalin's First Lieutenant*, Princeton University Press, 1993, p. 97.
70. Interview in BBC *Reputations* on Lavrenti Beria, first transmitted BBC2 1994, Helen Bettison (producer), Laurence Rees (executive producer).
71. Crankshaw, *Khrushchev Remembers*, p. 338.
72. Quoted in Gregor Dallas, *Poisoned Peace 1945 – the War that Never Ended*, John Murray, 2005, p. 327.
73. Charles de Gaulle, *The Complete War Memoirs*, Richard Howard (translator), Carroll and Grad, 1998, p. 750.
74. Jean Laloy (unofficial Russian–French interpreter), *'A Moscou: Entre Staline et De Gaulle, Decembre 1944', Revue des Etudes Slaves*, Paris, 1982, p. 147.
75. de Gaulle, *The Complete War Memoirs*, p. 756–7.
76. Robin Edmonds, *Big Three*, Penguin, 1992, p. 409.
77. Moran, *Winston Churchill, the Struggle for Survival*, entry for 4 February 1945.
78. *Cadogan Diaries*, entry for 8 February 1945, p. 706.
79. Quoted in Martin Gilbert, *Road to Victory: Winston S. Churchill 1941–1945*, Houghton Mifflin, 1984, p. 664.
80. Stalin's speech quoted in *On the Great Patriotic War of the Soviet Union*, Moscow, 1944.
81. FRUS, Conferences at Malta and Yalta. Yalta discussions are from pp. 547–996.
82. FRUS, p. 726.
83. Moran, *Winston Churchill, the Struggle for Survival*, diary entry for 3 February 1945.
84. Ibid., entry for 10 February 1945.
85. Burns, *Roosevelt: The Soldier of Freedom*, p. 573.
86. Quoted in ibid, p. 572.
87. Meeting with Roosevelt, 22 December 1944, FO 371/44595.
88. Moran, *Winston Churchill, the Struggle for Survival*, entry for 9 February 1945.
89. Admiral Leahy, Yalta diary, p.33, entry for 11 February 1945, in William Leahy, *I Was There*, Whittlesey House, 1950.
90. *Cadogan Diaries* entry 11 February 1945, pp. 708–9..
91. See the analysis in David Reynolds, *Summits*, Penguin: Allen Lane, 2007, p. 131.

CHAPTER SIX: The Iron Curtain
1. British War Cabinet minutes, 19 February 1945, WM (43) 22.1 CA.
2. Pimlott (ed.), *Dalton Diaries*, entry for 23 February, 1945, p. 836.
3. House of Commons debates, 5th series, Vol. 408, 27 February 1945.
4. Fraser Harbutt, *Churchill, America and the Origins of the Cold War*, Oxford University Press US, 1986, p. 92.
5. McJimsey (ed.), *Documentary History of the Franklin Roosevelt Presidency: Vol 14 Yalta*, University Publications of America 2001–3, doc.144.
6. Quoted in Harbutt, *Churchill, America*, p. 93 .
7. Ibid.
8. Vostochnaya Evropa v Dokumentakh Rossiiskikh Arkhivov, 1944–1953, doc. 151. Quoted in Geoffrey Roberts, *Stalin's Wars*, Yale University Press, 2006, pp. 247–8. See pp.228–253 of *Stalin's Wars* for a detailed discussion of these issues.
9. Anders, *An Army in Exile*, p. 256.
10. Alanbrooke diary entry for 22 February, 1945, p. 665.
11. FO 954/23, 18/1/45.
12. FO 954/23, 19/1/45.

13. Figures quoted in Dallas, *Poisoned Peace*, p. 422.

14. Bohlen, *Witness to History*, p. 217.

15. Quoted in Robert E. Sherwood, *Roosevelt and Hopkins, an Intimate History*, Enigma Books, 2008, p. 832.

16. Balfour to Warner, 30 May 1945, FO371/47862/N6417. Quoted in Martin Folly, *Churchill, Whitehall and the Soviet Union 1940–45*, Hutchinson, 2000, p. 144.

17. Martin Folly, *Churchill, Whitehall and the Soviet Union 1940–1945*, Hutchinson, 2000, p. 146.

18. Warren F. Kimball (ed.), *Churchill and Roosevelt, the Complete Correspondence*, Vol. 3, *The Alliance Declining*, Princeton University Press, 1984, Kimball C-905, 8 March 1945, p. 547–9.

19. Churchill to Roosevelt, 13 March 1945, Kimball C-910, p. 565.

20. *Cadogan Diaries*, 13 February 1945.

21. Roosevelt to Churchill, 15 March 1945, Kimball R-718, p. 568.

22. Churchill to Roosevelt, 17 March 1945, Kimball C-914, p. 574.

23. Churchill to Roosevelt, 30 March 1945, Kimball C-927, p. 597.

24. Roosevelt to Churchill, 31 March 1945, Kimball R-731, p. 601.

25. Susan Butler (ed.), *My Dear Mr Stalin: the Complete Correspondence*, Yale University Press, 2005, Roosevelt to Stalin 301, 5 April 1945, p. 315.

26. Ibid., Stalin 303, 7 April 1945, p. 318.

27. Ibid., Roosevelt's note of 11 April 1945 to Churchill, p. 321.

28. Stalin, quoted by Zhukov in John Erickson, *Road to Stalingrad*, Weidenfeld & Nicolson, 1985, p. 721.

29. John Lamberton Harper, *American Visions of Europe*, Cambridge University Press, p. 128.

30. BBC interview.

31. BBC interview.

32. BBC interview.

33. Letter from a soldier named Bezuglov to his collective farm. Quoted in Catherine Merridale, *Ivan's War*, Faber and Faber, 2005, p. 260.

34. Quoted in Dallas, *Poisoned Peace*, p. 7.

35. Anonymous, *A Woman in Berlin*, Virago, 2005, p. 17.

36. BBC interview.

37. Captured letter. In Bundesarchiv, RH2-2688, 13; also quoted in Merridale, *Ivan's War*, p. 267.

38. Milan Hauner, *Hitler – A Chronology of His Life and Time*, Macmillan Press, 1983, entry for 30 April, 1945.

39. Quoted in *New York Times*, 24 June, 1941.

40. Sherwood, *Roosevelt and Hopkins, an Intimate History*, p. 851.

41. Ibid., p. 855.

42. Churchill to Roosevelt, 11 April 1945, Kimball, Vol. 3, C-941, p. 624.

43. Anthony Eden (Lord Avon), *The Reckoning* p.504, entry for 4 January 1945, p. 514.

44. Anders, *An Army in Exile*, p. 275.

45. Report by joint planning staff, 22 May 1945, CAB 120/691 109040.

46. Alanbrooke, *War Diaries*, p.693, 24 May 1945.

47. Churchill to Truman, 10 May 1945, FRUS, 1945, *Foreign Relations of the United States The Conference of Berlin*, 1945, Washington, 1960, Vol. 1, pp. 8–9.

48. Churchill to Truman 31 May 1945, FRUS, 1945, *The Conference of Berlin*, Vol. 1, p .53.

49. Robert S. Mackay: "This Mr. President is the Story of the Little White House." The Truman House in Potsdam 1892–2002/ "Sie werden verstehen, es bewegt micht sehr." Ein Haus und seine ergreifende Geschichte von 1892 bis zur Gegenwart, Friedrich Naumann Stiftung, Potsdam, 2002, pp. 24–5.

50. Facsimile copies of this journal can be seen at www.trumanlibrary.org.

51. *Cadogan Diaries*, 17 July 1945, p. 764.

52. FRUS *The Conference of Berlin, 1945*, Vol. 2, pp. 378–9.

53. Norman M. Naimark, *The Russians in Germany: A History of the Soviet Zone of Occupation, 1945–49*, Belknap, 1995, pp. 205–30.

54. FRUS, *The Conference of Berlin, 1945*, Vol.2, pp. 359–62.

55. *Pravda*, 25 November 1936.
56. BBC interview.
57. FRUS, pp. 566–9.
58. Quoted in Sebag Montefiore, *Stalin and the Court of the Red Tsar*, p. 508.
59. Quoted in Dallas, *Poisoned Peace*, p. 567.
60. Gar Alperovitz, *The Decision to Use the Nuclear Bomb*, Vintage Books, 1996.
61. See, for example, Robert H. Ferrell (ed.), *Harry S. Truman and the Bomb: a Documentary History*, Worland, 1996; and in particular David Holloway, *Stalin and the Bomb*, Yale University Press, 1996.
62. Alanbrooke, *War Diaries*, entry for 23 July 1945, p. 709.
63. Holloway, *Stalin and the Bomb*, pp. 42–87.
64. Andrei Gromyko, *Memoirs*, New York, Doubleday, 1989, pp. 391–2.
65. BBC interview.
66. BBC interview.
67. BBC interview.
68. Robert Service, '*Comrades*': *World History of Communism*, Pan Macmillan, 2007, pp. 239–50.
69. I. S. Yazhborovskaya, A. Y. Yablokov and V. S. Parsadanova, *The Katyn Poison in Soviet–Polish relations*, Rosspen, 2001, pp. 185–92. Published in Russian as *Katinskii Sindrom v Sovetsko–Polskikh Otnosheniakh*.
70. Ibid, and Stupinkova's memoirs, *Nothing but the Truth – from Nuremberg to Moscow*, Moscow, 1998.
71. Testimony from Nuremberg trials day 168, 1 July, 1946. Morning session/Vol.XVII Nuremberg IMT.
72. BBC interview.
73. Testimony from Nuremberg trials, day 168, Monday, 1 July 1946. Afternoon session.
74. Anders, *An Army in Exile*, p. 288.
75. BBC interview.
76. BBC interview.
77. A. N. Yakovlev and V. Naumov (eds), *Georgi Zhukov, Minutes from the October 1957 Plenum of the CCCP USSR and Other Documents*, Rossiya XX Vek, Moscow, 2001.
78. Yakovlev and Naumov (eds), *Georgi Zhukov*, p. 681. Prilozhenia. Footnote 1.
79. Quotes gathered Yakovlev and Naumov (eds), *Georgi Zhukov*, pp. 586–91. Appendix. Memorandum from S. V. Abakumov. Also from Konev's memoirs as published in B. Sokolov, *Neizvestny Zhukov (Unknown Zhukov)* Rodiola-Plius, Minsk, 2000, p. 519. See also P. G. Pikhoya, *Soviet Union: History of Soviet Power, 1945–1991*, Novosibirsk, 2000, p. 37.
80. Y. Gorlizki and O. Khlevniuk, *Cold Peace. Stalin and the Soviet Ruling Circle, 1945–1953*, Oxford University Press, New York, 2004, p. 198. Note 28 – Resolution of the Central Committee of the Communist Party; Report by T. T. Shkiratov and Abakumov regarding P. S. Zhemchuzhina.
81. Letter from Molotov to Stalin, 20 January 1949, in Russian State Archive of Social and Political History, F. 17, Op. 163, D. 1518, L. 164.
82. Quoted in BBC *Timewatch: Stalin and the Betrayal of Leningrad*, Martin Balazova (producer), Laurence Rees (executive producer) transmission BBC2, 9 August 2002.
83. BBC interview.
84. Ibid.
85. Ibid.
86. Teresa Toranska, *Stalin's Polish Puppets*, Collins Harvill, London, 1987, p. 146.

POSTSCRIPT

1. See article by George Earle in *Confidential* magazine, August 1958, Vol. 6, no. 3, p. 15.
2. John Grigg, *1943: The Victory That Never Was*, Methuen, 1980.
3. George Orwell, 'The Freedom of the Press', first published in *The Times Literary Supplement*, 15 September, 1972.
4. O'Malley, *The Phantom Caravan*, p. 232.
5. See page 122 of this book.

INDEX

ACKNOWLEDGEMENTS

I first need to thank Roly Keating, Glenwyn Benson and Emma Swain for commissioning the television series, *WW2: Behind Closed Doors*, which I wrote and produced alongside this book. At the BBC I also want to acknowledge the help I received from Keith Scholey. He was my boss from the beginning of the series to very nearly the end (he left the BBC in June 2008) and was a tower of support and good advice throughout. I owe him a very great deal.

Many other people helped me make the TV series, notably Andrew Williams, who directed the drama sequences; Michaela Liechtenstein, Martina Carr and Simon Baker, the associate producers; Elena Yakovleva, our Russian researcher; Sally Chick, the series researcher; and Giselle Corbett, Patricia Fearnley, Kriszta Fenyö, Cara Goold, Alexei Haigh, John Kennedy, Ivan Kytka, Adam Levy, Anna Mishcon, Julia Pluwak, Basia Pietluch, Kate Rea, Anna Taborska, Rosie Taylor, Frank Stucke and Christine Whittaker. Alan Lygo brilliantly cut the programmes – he is a film editor of genius – and Martin Patmore, the cameraman, and Brian Biffen, the sound recordist, were once again my cheerful companions across the wilds of Eastern Europe and the former Soviet Union as I sought to direct the documentary elements of the series. In addition I want to mention how grateful I am to Samuel West for his work not just on this series but on my four previous projects on the Second World War and the Nazis. Sam has read every word of commentary I have written for television for more than ten years and has done so brilliantly.

I also received a wealth of advice from our academic consultants: Professor Robert Dallek, Dr Natalia Lebedeva, Professor David Reynolds, Professor Robert Service and Dr Sergej Slutsch.

Professor Sir Ian Kershaw, Professor Robert Service and a number of other friends and colleagues read this book in manuscript form, and I thank them all for their comments. I am particularly grateful to Sir Ian (to whom this book is dedicated) for his reflections on the Postscript.

At BBC Books Martin Redfern and Jake Lingwood were a great help, as was my literary agent, Andrew Nurnberg. I have also much benefited from talking to Dan Frank at Pantheon, my American publisher. At KCET in Los Angeles, Megan Calloway, Mare Mazur and Karen Hunt were a joy to work with. At PBS, Sandy Heberer, in particular, made a number of valuable and insightful criticisms of the films.

I also thank all the first-hand witnesses to history who agreed to be interviewed for this project. There are so many of them that I hope they will forgive me for thanking them collectively here – their names, and their immensely valuable testimony, pervade the pages of this book.

I also thank my family, as ever, for their continued loving support. But I end by mentioning my parents. For some reason their memory was very much in my mind over the last three years as I worked on this book and the TV series – which is strange, because both of them have been dead for more than thirty years. Maybe it was because it was their stories of the war that first excited my interest in this subject when I was child. But in remembrance of them, I feel I need to record here that they both died in great suffering and they both died much too young.

BBC Worldwide would like to thank the following individuals and organizations for providing photographs and for permission to reproduce copyright material. While every effort has been made to trace and acknowledge copyright holders, we would like to apologize should there be any errors or omissions.

Abbreviations : t: top, b: bottom, l: left, r: right, c: centre, tl: top left, tr: top right.

Plate Section 1:
1c and 1b: Getty Images; 2t: Roger Viollet/Getty Images; 2b: Popperfoto/ Getty Images; 3t: ullsteinbild/TopFoto; 3bl: ullsteinbild/TopFoto; 4t: ullsteinbild/TopFoto; 4b: Hugh Lunghi; 5t: Imperial War Museum (A12022); 5c (overlay): Bettmann/Corbis; 5b: Topfoto; 6: Mary Evans Picture Library/Alexander Meledin; 7tl: Valentina Ievleva; 7tr: National Portrait Gallery, London; 7b: RIA Novosti; 8t: akg-images/ullstein bild; 8b: Topfoto.

Plate Section 2:
1t: George Elsey; 1b: Popperfoto/Getty Images; 2: Reuters/Corbis; 2b (overlay): Popperfoto/ Getty Images; 3t: : Nikanor Perevalov; 3b: Topfoto; 4t: Tadeusz Ruman; 4b: Zbigniew Wolak; 5t: Yevgeny Khaldei/Corbis; 5bl: Halina Stopi´nska; 5br: John Nobel; 6t: Yevgeny Khaldei/Corbis; 6b: Bettmann/Corbis; 7: Imperial War Museum/EPA/Corbis; 8: Topfoto.